JOURNAL FOR THE STUDY OF THE OLD TESTAMENT
SUPPLEMENT SERIES
31

Department of Biblical Studies
The University of Sheffield
Sheffield S10 2TN
England

IN THE SHELTER OF ELYON

Essays on Ancient Palestinian
Life and Literature

in Honor of

G.W. AHLSTRÖM

Edited by
W. Boyd Barrick and John R. Spencer

Journal for the Study of the Old Testament
Supplement Series 31

Published by
JSOT Press
Department of Biblical Studies
The University of Sheffield
Sheffield S10 2TN
England

Printed in Great Britain
by Redwood Burn Ltd.,
Trowbridge, Wiltshire.

British Library Cataloguing in Publication Data

In the shelter of Elyon.—(Journal for the study of the Old Testament
supplement series,
ISSN 0309-0787; 31)
1. Bible. O.T.—Criticism, interpretation,
etc.
I. Barrick, W. Boyd II. Spencer, John R.
III. Ahlström, G.W. IV. Series
221.6 BS1171.2

ISBN 0-905774-65-5

CONTENTS

PART III
Faith and Cult

PART IV
History and Historiography

PREFACE

We were students of G.W. Ahlström at the University of Chicago, the first of a growing number to receive a doctorate degree in Old Testament studies under his direction. We arrived at Chicago knowing little about the man or his work; he had published comparatively little that was readily accessible to the American undergraduate in the mid-1960s. Once at Chicago we heard rumors of a frosty Swedish presence in the corner office on the third floor of Swift Hall, someone who 'did his own thing' (in the patois of the time), remote, aloof, and slightly out-of-place, and with an accent more difficult to penetrate than Eliade's. Conventional wisdom advised studying with someone else in the field. Fortunately for us, we did not heed that advice. As our interests germinated and our familiarity with his work grew, we gravitated more and more toward his courses. They were rigorous—we quickly learned why he had prefaced an autobiographical essay in *Criterion* (6.2 [1967], 37-38) with the text of Proverbs 12.1!—but they were even more stimulating. The prevailing consensus on issue after issue began to appear less than certain as alternative lines of inquiry were pursued and provocative new interpretations were introduced for consideration. We were challenged to follow through on these ideas to see where they might lead. It was an invigorating experience and one of lasting value. The institutional reward for our labors was the doctorate. But the reward which truly mattered was at last to *lägga bort titlarna* with our teacher—at his initiative, to be sure—a sign that the fine line between student and younger colleague had been crossed.

This *Festschrift*, occasioned by Gösta's sixty-fifth birthday, is offered as an expression of respect and affection for our teacher, and as a small repayment for what we have learned and continue to learn from him. Several other former students from Chicago and from Uppsala are among the contributors. The volume, however, does not reflect the outlook of a single 'school' any more than does the

honoree. Instead, each contributor responds to an aspect of Gösta's scholarly work from his own particular vantage-point. The result, we believe, is a distinctive collection honoring both the man and his distinctive contribution to the study of ancient Palestine. We wish to thank all who participated in this project. We are especially grateful to David J.A. Clines of JSOT Press for his encouragement, and his care in seeing these pages through the press. To Gösta we extend the sentiments of all:

Nå, ödmjukaste tjänare, gunstig herr värd,
den skålen blir dig tillkänd, tömd och förärd.

(C.M. Bellman)

W. Boyd Barrick
John R. Spencer

ABBREVIATIONS

AB	Anchor Bible (Garden City, New York)
AGJU	Arbeiten zur Geschichte des antiken Judentums und des Urchristentums (Leiden)
AHW	*Akkadisches Handwörterbuch*, 2 vols (Wiesbaden: Otto Harrassowitz, 1965)
AJSLL	*American Journal of Semitic Languages and Literature*
AnBib	Analecta Biblica (Rome)
ANEP	*The Ancient Near East in Pictures*, ed. J.B. Pritchard (Princeton: Princeton University Press, 1954)
ANET	*Ancient Near Eastern Texts*, ed. J.B. Pritchard (Princeton: Princeton University Press, 1969)
AOAT	Alter Orient und Altes Testament (Neukirchen-Vluyn)
APOT	*Apocrypha and Pseudepigrapha of the Old Testament*, ed. R.H. Charles (Oxford: Clarendon Press, 1913)
AS	Assyriological Studies (Chicago)
ASTI	*Annual of the Swedish Theological Institute in Jerusalem*
ATD	Das Alte Testament Deutsch (Göttingen)
BASOR	*Bulletin of the American Schools of Oriental Research*
BHS	*Biblia Hebraica Stuttgartensia* (Stuttgart: Deutsche Bibelstiftung, 1977)
BKAT	Biblischer Kommentar. Altes Testament (Neukirchen)
BWANT	Beiträge zur Wissenschaft von Alten und Neuen Testament (Stuttgart)
BWAT	Beiträge zur Wissenschaft von Alten Testament (Leipzig)
BZAW	Beihefte zur *Zeitschrift für die alttestamentliche Wissenschaft* (Berlin)
CAD	*Chicago Assyrian Dictionary* (Chicago: Oriental Institute, University of Chicago Press, 1956—)
CBQ	*Catholic Biblical Quarterly*
CBOTS	Coniectanea Biblica, Old Testament Series (Lund)
ETR	*Etudes Théologiques et Religieuses*
FRLANT	Forschungen zur Religion und Literatur des Alten und Neuen Testaments (Göttingen)
HAT	Handbuch zum Alten Testament (Tübingen)
HKAT	Handkommentar zum Alten Testament (Göttingen)
HR	*History of Religions*
HTR	*Harvard Theological Review*

HUCA	*Hebrew Union College Annual*
ICC	International Critical Commentary (Edinburgh)
IEJ	*Israel Exploration Journal*
IDB	*Interpreter's Dictionary of the Bible*, ed. G.A. Buttrick (Nashville: Abingdon Press, 1962)
IDBSup	*Interpreter's Dictionary of the Bible, Supplement*, ed. K. Crim (Nashville: Abingdon Press, 1976)
Interp	*Interpretation*
JAAR	*Journal of the American Academy of Religion*
JAOS	*Journal of the American Oriental Society*
JBL	*Journal of Biblical Literature*
JCS	*Journal of Cuneiform Studies*
JR	*Journal of Religion*
JSOT	*Journal for the Study of the Old Testament*
JSOTSS	*Journal for the Study of the Old Testament*, Supplement Series (Sheffield)
JSS	*Journal of Semitic Studies*
JTS	*Journal of Theological Studies*
KAT	Kommentar zum Alten Testament (Gütersloh)
KHC	Kurzer Hand-Commentar zum Alten Testament (Tübingen)
MEE	Materiali epigrafici di Ebla (Napoli)
OTL	Old Testament Library (London/Philadelphia)
PEQ	*Palestine Exploration Quarterly*
RB	*Revue biblique*
RGG	*Die Religion in Geschichte und Gegenwart*, 3rd edn, ed. K. Galling (Tübingen: J.C.B. Mohr, 1959)
SBLDS	Society of Biblical Literature, Dissertation Series (Chico, California)
SBLMS	Society of Biblical Literature, Monograph Series (Chico, California)
SBT	Studies in Biblical Theology (London/Naperville, Illinois)
SEÅ	*Svensk Exegetisk Årsbok*
SHANE	Studies in the History of the Ancient Near East (Leiden)
SJTh	*Scottish Journal of Theology*
StTh	*Studia Theologica*
SVT	Supplements to *Vetus Testamentum* (Leiden)
TDOT	*Theological Dictionary of the Old Testament*, ed. G. Botterweck and H. Ringgren (Grand Rapids, Michigan: Eerdmans, 1977–)

ThZ	*Theologische Zeitschrift*
TR	*Theologische Rundschau*
TWAT	*Theologisches Wörterbuch zum Alten Testament*, ed. G. Botterweck and H. Ringgren (Stuttgart: Kohlhammer, 1970—)
UF	*Ugarit-Forschungen*
UUÅ	*Uppsala Universitets Årsskrift* (Uppsala)
VaB	*Vorderasiatische Bibliothek* (Leipzig)
VT	*Vetus Testamentum*
WMANT	Wissenschaftliche Monographien zum Alten und Neuen Testament (Neukirchen-Vluyn)
WUNT	Wissenschaftliche Untersuchungen zum Neuen Testament (Tübingen)
ZAW	*Zeitschrift für die alttestamentliche Wissenschaft*
ZDPV	*Zeitschrift des Deutschen Palästina-Vereins*
ZTK	*Zeitschrift für Theologie und Kirche*

THE 'UPPSALA SCHOOL' OF BIBLICAL STUDIES

Arthur L. Merrill and John R. Spencer

It has been noted that the expression 'Uppsala School', while commonly used to designate the form of biblical study at the University of Uppsala, is a somewhat misleading way of characterizing the work done in biblical studies at Uppsala.[1] Of course, the expression was largely formulated in response to the seminal studies of one person, Ivan Engnell, Professor of Old Testament at the University of Uppsala from 1947 to 1964. It has been, however, almost 20 years since the death of Professor Engnell, and it is appropriate, especially in the context of this volume dedicated to Gösta W. Ahlström, a student of Engnell, to look at the phenomenon that gave rise to the expression and at the development of the 'Uppsala School' in the intervening years.

This examination of the 'Uppsala School' will consist of four sections. It begins with a consideration of the University of Uppsala itself and the environment for study which exists there. The subsequent three sections deal with several areas of research on which members of the school have focused their scholarly attention. One area of consistent interest has been oral tradition and the related study of the Masoretic Text. Another concern centers on understanding the religion of ancient Israel. This involves not only the religion of Israel, but the way in which non-Israelite religions have influenced the religious practices in Israel. A final focus is on the 'traditio-historical' or 'history of tradition' approach to the study of the Old Testament. This approach, at least for some members of the School, provides the umbrella under which all aspects of Old Testament study, including those discussed here, should be gathered. This approach, in turn, leads to the argument that the application of 'history of tradition' methodology is the best process for obtaining good exegetical understandings of the biblical text.

The University of Uppsala

The University of Uppsala provides a unique context for biblical studies. As the oldest university in Sweden, founded in 1477, it takes pride in its long and rich history, and it has produced outstanding scholars in many fields of academic study.[2] Located near Gamla Uppsala, the site of the mounds of the ancient Viking kings, its traditions are tied to the ancient past, as exemplified in the on-going celebration of *Vapurgisafton*. With the presence of the Cathedral and the residence of the Archbishop of Sweden, there are also ties to the long history of Christianity in the country. More than one of the graduates of the theological faculty have gone on to become bishops of the Church of Sweden.[3]

The University system itself has contributed to the character and shape of Old Testament study at Uppsala. The theological faculty does not stand in isolation but is integrated into the scientific study that is carried on throughout the university. The student who seeks to pursue doctoral candidacy must encounter not only the theological disciplines but also the humanistic studies of the rest of the university. When the dissertation has been successfully defended the candidate is not only awarded the degree but also receives a docent position and stipend, permitting the person to remain for some years as a teacher in the university. When that position is terminated the person, if a professorship is not vacant, then usually becomes a Lektor or pastor in a church. It has been observed that this kind of university structure provides a 'hotbed' for the development of outstanding scholarship.[4] In addition, there has increasingly been emigration abroad, and the world has been enriched by such movements.

The library of the university has also been invaluable resource to Old Testament study. As the depository for all books published in Sweden and with generous budgets that have allowed for virtually unlimited purchasing, the resources of the library are probably unexcelled. Within that context has evolved the 'exegetical room', a unique non-circulating library containing the basic texts which the researcher might need. It is thus the natural meeting place for scholars at all levels of study where the ongoing research of each is made known and discussed by all. One's breaks at the local *conditorri* are likewise enriched by the discussion of issues that are of current interest.

It is therefore appropriate to talk about an 'Uppsala School' in that there is indeed an institution which helps to shape the character of

study as well as a group of scholars with similar emphases and identifiable types of solutions. In particular one should note that not only was Ivan Engnell a catalyst, especially for Old Testament study, but that his contemporaries were Geo Widengren in History of Religions (1940-1974), H.S. Nyberg in Semitic Languages (1931–1959) and Harold Riesenfeld in New Testament (1953–present). Surely all were strong individuals with their own emphases and particular idiosyncracies. Yet together they helped to form a distinctive approach to the ancient world and the particular texts of their disciplines.

It is in this interrelationship and its dynamic that we might truly find a distinctiveness, for it was particularly these four fields of scientific study which helped to develop the commonalities which can be designated by the expression 'Uppsala School'. One has only to read H.S. Nyberg's personal account of Old Testament research in Sweden to see how the development of these fields led to the shape and structure of approach at Uppsala.[5]

Nor can one talk about an 'Uppsala School' without observing that its work needs to be seen in the larger context not only of Swedish research, especially at Lund, but also in the other Scandinavian countries. Here Norway and Denmark play a particularly significant role. In Finland the University of Helsinki and the Academy at Åbo are dependent upon Swedish influence though the work done there has had its own significant import; and in Iceland Old Testament studies are carried on by Professor Thor Thordarson who was trained not in Scandinavia but at the University of Chicago.

In Norway it is particularly the work of Sigmund Mowinckel, a student of Hermann Gunkel, in his *Psalmenstudien* which has been of seminal importance.[6] Though in many ways Mowinckel was the heir of German form and literary criticism, his contributions to the cult-functional understanding of the Psalms were of great impact on the scholars of Uppsala. His successor, Arvid S. Kapelrud, not only received his doctoral degree from Uppsala, but has also carried on many of the characteristic emphases which have been noted for the 'Uppsala School'.[7] Kapelrud's successor at Oslo is Magnus Ottosson, also from Uppsala.

From Denmark the influence of two other scholars should be noted. One is Vilhelm Grønbech, the historian of religion whose work in Teutonic religion emphasized the 'cult as creative drama'. The other is Johannes Pedersen whose groundbreaking *Israel: Its*

Life and Culture not only raised the basic issue of how the literature was to be understood but also argued for the examination of Israel as an entity among and like the nations, rather than as a theological concept or a comparative phenomenon.[8]

No understanding of the 'Uppsala School' can be complete without the recognition of two other factors. One is the problem of language. Swedish is not an international language, and the Swedish scholars are keenly aware that their work needs to be translated if they wish to communicate with the rest of the world. The best scholarship of the land must also produce works in Swedish for the church, the university and the schools, for the work of Old Testament scholarship is never totally divorced from the needs of the rest of society. The other factor that should be noted is that during World War II Sweden, like the rest of Scandinavia, was cut off from the rest of the world of scholarship. Their relative isolation during this period caused the scholars of Uppsala to develop their own distinctive perspectives.

One can see from this discussion of the University of Uppsala and the 'Uppsala School' of biblical studies that many geographical, linguistic, environmental, and cultural factors have contributed to the development of the 'Uppsala School'. It is not merely a particular teacher or indeed even a particular university, but a milieu which has given impetus and opportunity to many who have come in contact with it. It is a great university which has spawned an important 'School' of biblical studies.

Text and Oral Tradition

It is a self-evident truism that any study of the Old Testament is the study of the text; all else is interpretation and reconstruction on the basis of the text. So it is surprising that most interpreters of the 'Uppsala School' appear to ignore the critical importance of textual studies in the work of the 'School'. When one looks at the dissertations produced at Uppsala one can see that the examination of the Masoretic Text and of the versions has been an integral part of the study.[9] And one should note that the initial research of the 'Uppsala School' that dealt with the scriptures was based on text-critical studies.

Here H.S. Nyberg's seminal studies were of critical import. In his initial study on the text-critical problem of the Old Testament,[10] he set up the argument over against the critical orthodoxy of his day.

Whereas the Old Testament was seen as a written phenomenon, Nyberg argued that tradition in the West was seldom written but predominantly oral. Furthermore, the written Old Testament was a creation of the Jewish community after the Exile, and therefore one could not seek the *ipsissima verba* of the Old Testament personalities and writers; one could deal only with the tradition of the words. That was the primary task of the interpreter of Scripture. The age of a manuscript is not the clue to its significance, though judgments need to be made on many bases and in different manners. For Nyberg the consonantal text of the Hebrew did have primary importance, with the vocalization of the text representing a later interpretation. In his retrospective article[11] he notes that Professor H. Almkvist always insisted that his students use two modern scientific commentaries and an unvocalized text of the Hebrew to shake any residual dogmatism about the verbal inspiration of the text.

For this reason one can note that the exegetical methods that developed sought to preserve the consonantal Hebrew text. The emphasis was not only on grammar, as influenced by Pedersen, but also on Near Eastern patterns of thought and on cultic realities. All of these methodologies were used to argue for understanding the *recensio* of the text rather than to make emendations. Engnell in particular felt that the Dead Sea Scrolls supported this contention[12], though others have argued that they also show that a separate and equally early tradition underlies the LXX at times.

Nyberg's thesis that the tradition of the Old Testament was primarily oral until the exilic and post-exilic periods became axiomatic in Engnell's research. He followed Nyberg's arguments quite closely, maintaining that 1. the tradition of the text in its final form is the most important, 2. the text is the form shaped by the Jewish community, and 3. we can no longer ascertain what is original and what is secondary. Therefore, according to Engnell, 'what we have before us are living oral traditions, committed indeed to writing, but firmly formed and fixed already in the oral stage so that even the written form signifies in itself nothing absolutely new and revolutionary'.[13] It is in the light of such a statement that C.R. North could suggest that 'if, as he [Engnell] maintained, oral transmission had all the fixity of written, it was quite in order to apply source-analytical methods to the study of it.'[14]

Geo Widengren entered into the argument on the nature of the transmission of tradition with several studies. His arguments against

Engnell again raise the question of whether one can indeed speak of an 'Uppsala School'. For Widengren, the question of oral tradition is not a presupposition but an area of interpretation. One cannot assume the priority of oral or written transmission; this must be ascertained in every instance. Thus he could state, 'it is wrong to contrast oral and written tradition too much'.[15] From his history of religions perspective he seeks to distinguish not only between Indo-European and Semitic religions but also between 'nomadic' and urban cultures. For Widengren this was particularly crucial when it came to evaluating prophetic literature. The reference to written sources and to the act of writing in the Old Testament led him to assume that written transmission was characteristic of most of those materials that are now extant. It appears to have been partly under the influence of Widengren that Engnell later made the distinction in the prophetic literature between the '*diwan* type' and the 'liturgy type'; the former is definitely oral in its original character, whereas the latter has to be distinguished as to being oral or written.[16]

Helmer Ringgren, Engnell's successor in the chair of Old Testament (1965–present), picked up Widengren's notion that oral and written transmission should not be played off against each other, and also argued that each case must be examined for itself. The latter he did in a comparison of specific passages which are found in parallel in the Old Testament.[17] He concluded that while there are a significant number of variants which are graphic in nature and therefore due to written tradition, there are even more which are the consequence of oral transmission. He was hesitant to draw any far-reaching conclusions from this analysis and, in his usual irenic and mediating position, asked that others refrain from doing so. As a final note, Ringgren also observed that it is difficult to say at what point the oral tradition was fixed in writing, though he posited the possibility that an oral tradition existed alongside the written tradition up to the time of Masoretes.

The Religious Context

The study of religion in ancient Israel, for the 'Uppsala School', is focused around the term 'cult'. Indeed, for the school this is virtually a 'buzz word' for the religious aspects of society.[18] Study of cult, then, is seen as of paramount importance and necessity in understanding ancient Israel. This means not only study of cult in general in ancient Israel, but also studying such major relationships as king and cult, and prophet and cult. It necessarily follows, for the school,

that one looks at cult in the larger ancient Near Eastern world in order to see the manner in which Israelite cult coheres with or diverges from the context which spawned Israelite religion. A fundamental assumption here is that Israelite religion is not a pure type which emerged unscathed, unique, and *ex nihilo*. Rather, the school advocates that it is essential that one be cognizant of the dynamic contextual quality of Israelite religion. This is not to suggest, however, that Israelite religion was a product of an evolutionary development (as per Wellhausen). On the contrary, one must be aware of the syncretistic nature of Israelite religion.

The study of Israelite cult and the external influences upon the cult can be traced to some of the faculty at Uppsala at the turn of the century. Perhaps most prominent was Erik Stave who was a professor of Biblical Exegesis from 1899 to 1922. In 1900 he published *Über den Einfluss des Parsismus auf das Judentum*.[19] This early study of Persian influences on Judaism paved the way for many more comparative religion studies. Two early scholars at Uppsala who worked in this area were Nathan Soderblom and Tor Andrae.[20] However, it was not just the faculty and their studies which influenced the students at Uppsala.[21] Prime examples of that are the works by the Danish scholars Vilhelm Grønbech, in comparative religion, and Johannes Pedersen, in the psychological analysis of Israelite religion, and the Norwegian scholar Sigmund Mowinckel, on the cultic basis of the Psalms. The work of these scholars fed into the formation and development of the 'Uppsala School'.

One of the areas in which this concern for cult is evident is in the study of the prophets of the Old Testament. A. Haldar's dissertation, *Associations of Cult Prophets Among the Ancient Semites*, examines the prophetic groups in Israel and the ancient Near East and their association with the sanctuary and cult.[22] This perspective is continued in Haldar's *Studies in the Book of Nahum*, in Widengren's *Literary and Psychological Aspects of the Hebrew Prophets*, in Kapelrud's *Joel Studies*, in Engnell's *Call of Isaiah*, and in J. Lindblom's *Prophecy in Ancient Israel*.[23] Each of these works places a special emphasis on the relationship between the prophet and the cult. Contrary to analyses by other 'scholars', the prophet is not seen as anti-cult or ignorant of cultic practices and participation. Rather, the prophet lashes out at unacceptable (i.e. non-Yahwistic) cultic practices. He is not opposed to cult, just the inappropriate cult. Furthermore, the prophet is not seen as an individual called from an

isolated existence into the prophetic role. On the contrary, it is argued that the prophet often comes from a circle of prophets and produces a circle of followers who are knowledgeable of and participants in the cultic practices of the society.[24] Finally (and this in part presupposes the discussion of 'history of tradition' methodology), the 'Uppsala School' is most reluctant to view a prophet as incapable of issuing prophecies of weal as well as woe. The quickness with which others remove such 'messages of hope' from the prophetic material provokes sharp criticism from scholars such as Engnell. Using literary, psychological, linguistic, textual, and traditio-historical arguments, Engnell contends that prophecies of hope are inherently intertwined with the prophecies of doom. In addition, the combination of doom and hope in the Old Testament is consistent with such patterns found in other ancient Near Eastern prophetic traditions.[25]

Mention of the ancient Near East brings to the fore again the importance the 'Uppsala School' sees in looking outside of Israel in the hope of better understanding the Old Testament. In relation to prophets, the prime example of this is J. Lindblom's *Prophecy in Ancient Israel*, where emphasis is placed on examples of prophecy not only in the ancient Near East, but outside of that context, in order to understand better the prophets in Israel.

A second area which manifests this concern for cult is that of kingship. The origin of this focus can perhaps be assigned to Mowinckel in his *Psalmstudien*, whose work gave rise to numerous subsequent studies. However, it was Engnell's *Studies in Divine Kingship* which firmly tied kingship to the 'Uppsala School'.[26] Prior to Engnell's book, there existed numerous studies on kingship. Most notably there were A.M. Hocart's book *Kingship* (1929) and the collection of essays in *Myth and Ritual*, edited by S.H. Hooke.[27] These books became instrumental in what has been called 'patternism', the argument that certain cultural patterns were common to different cultures. The difficulty with this approach, as Engnell and others from the 'Uppsala School' pointed out, was that the 'elements of the Near Eastern pattern should not be presupposed in Israel simply because they existed elsewhere'.[28] Nevertheless, unfortunately and incorrectly, the 'Uppsala School' was associated with 'patternism.'

The contributions of Engnell to the study of kingship were followed by a number of other works on the topic, especially Widengren's *Sakrales Königtum im Alten Testament und im Judentum*, H. Ringgren's *Messiah in the Old Testament*, and G.W. Ahlström's

Psalm 89.[29] In all of these works the fundamental argument is that there was a clear connection between the God and his chosen servant, the king. The king thus had a sacral quality (e.g. son of God, Ps. 2.7; 89.19-28; 2 Sam. 7.14) which was akin to, but not identical with, understandings of kingship found elsewhere in the ancient Near East.

The keys to understanding these various studies in cult, prophecy, and kingship by the 'Uppsala School' are two. First, the religion of ancient Israel must be studied as it is, without the imposition of later or modern presuppositions on the text of the Old Testament. Secondly, the religion of Israel must be studied within its larger ancient Near Eastern context, apart from which no clear understanding of the religion of the Old Testament can be attained.

The 'Traditio-Historical' Method

As previously indicated, the 'traditio-historical' or 'history of tradition' approach to biblical studies has played a prominent role in the 'Uppsala School'. This is especially true of Engnell, who argued that this 'history of tradition' approach is the culmination of all previous methodologies and that all the critical tools of biblical scholarship should be seen as contained within the scope of this approach.

The origin and general definition of the phrase 'traditio-historical' is somewhat clouded. Indeed, Knight lists some seventeen different understandings of what is meant by it.[30] Part of the confusion arises from the question of what to include within the scope of 'history of tradition'; and the answer varies depending on the scholar who is asked. For the purpose of understanding this methodology within the 'Uppsala School', it is easiest, and best, to look at the discussions of Ivan Engnell, the prime proponent of the 'history of tradition' method at Uppsala.

In one sense, Engnell saw 'history of tradition' as the 'final' development in the methodological approaches to the Old Testament. The first step was that of source or literary criticism as practiced by Wellhausen. However, the evolutionary nature of Wellhausen's arguments and his reliance on the assumption of early written materials caused Engnell to regard this methodology as inadequate. The second stage was that of form criticism. For Engnell, Gunkel's work in this area was extremely important as it opened up the discussions of oral tradition and literary types, but also as it acted as a corrective on Wellhausen. However, Engnell saw 'history of tradition'

as the ultimate development in the approach to the Old Testament, drawing upon the positive aspects of these two previous stages, and going a step further by correctly combining 'analysis' and 'synthesis'.[31]

First of all, then, the 'traditio-historical' approach is an analytical method 'which demands a thoroughly unprejudiced reconsideration of all aspects of the entire material'.[32] Within this analytic approach are two major considerations. Part of the first consideration is what would normally be called form criticism, the identification of the different literary types, their original *Sitz im Leben*, and their function. However, Engnell adds the factor of oral tradition as it influenced the tradition units and collections. The second consideration of 'analysis' entails a study of 'contemporary views' (i.e. at the time of composition). What is really implied is an examination of the larger cultural and religious context to see if there are any syncretistic influences.

The second aspect of the method is that of 'synthesis', which is 'the interpretation of smaller units in relationship to their context'.[33] This involves a study of the function of the individual units in relation to the position and context they presently occupy in the text. 'Analysis' alone, according to Engnell, is a one-sided approach which yields a distorted 'understanding and interpretation of the text'.[34] Thus, one must examine the unit within the 'final form' of the text.

In some senses, Engnell's 'traditio-historical' method is not *a* method but the drawing upon several methods to produce an exegesis. This is well summarized by Ringgren:

> It must be admitted that Engnell's 'history of tradition' is not one coherent method but rather a complex of methods . . . it includes confidence in the Masoretic text, a correct understanding of the Hebrew language in the light of comparative linguistics and of Pedersen's psychological viewpoints, the rejection of literary criticism on the assumption that most of the texts were transmitted orally, analytical and synthetical investigation of the final literary product, i.e. of the Biblical Books in their present form, and a correct understanding of the impact of Near Eastern, especially Canaanite religious traditions on the religion of Israel.[35]

Engnell's understanding and application of the 'traditio-historical' method has not gone without challenge from those affiliated with 'Uppsala School'. One of the main critics is S. Mowinckel, whose position is expressed in *Prophecy and Tradition*. Mowinckel's comments focus on two issues. The first involves Engnell's rejection

of literary criticism. Mowinckel sees literary criticism as a necessary and useful tool and cites the attempts to define the extent of Baruch's work in Jeremiah as an example to support his contention. A second issue for Mowinckel is the use of oral tradition. One should not, as Engnell seems to do, use oral tradition as a way of explaining the present written form and then ignore the developments which took place in the oral stage, as units were constructed and shaped into larger collections. Mowinckel asserts that in addition to the 'final form' of the text, the development in the oral stage can and should be studied. This position leads Mowinckel to claim that 'in Engnell's terminology the term "traditio-historical" seems to have lost much of its original relation to history, i.e. the study and explanation of the origin, growth and development of different traditions and the tradition mass'.[36]

Engnell's response to Mowinckel came in an article entitled 'Profetia och Tradition'.[37] First of all, Engnell asserts that oral tradition and literary criticism are not necessarily mutually exclusive, which suggests that literary criticism is not totally rejected by Engnell as his critics have often claimed. Secondly, Engnell does allow that different literary types are not transmitted in the same manner. Specifically, he says that the 'liturgical' type of prophetic literature was probably written down from the beginning and the *diwan* type was transmitted by circles of followers or disciples in a oral form before it was committed to writing.[38]

This discussion of the 'traditio-historical' method has shown some of its origins, debates, and developments within the 'Uppsala School'. It is clear that the methodology has assumed a place of prominence within the school, although differences of application do remain. And while Engnell maintained that it was the method which supplanted all others, most members of the school would adhere to its value as an additional, and necessary, method for the exegete.

It is apparent from this presentation of the methods and foci of the members of the 'Uppsala School' that it is by no means a unified school. Debates and differences of opinion have often filled the ranks. The dialogue has not only helped to maintain the dynamic, lively quality of the school, but it has also shown the difficulty of simply talking about a 'school'. This difficulty is further compounded by the realization that not all members of the 'Uppsala School' are or have been at Uppsala. One might just as easily talk of a 'Scandinavian School', with its major center at Uppsala.

However, putting aside the real differences that do exist, it is clear that a certain perspective is shared by those of the 'Uppsala School'. This perspective considers oral tradition a fundamental cornerstone of Old Testament study. It holds the received text with extreme seriousness if not sanctity. It sees the necessity of analyzing the larger historical, cultural, and religious context within which the Old Testament was produced. It argues for the study of the development or history of tradition. And it insists that the Old Testament, as the manifestation of Israelite religion, be studied without the overlay or coloring of any later religious tradition.

NOTES

1. G.W. Anderson, 'Some Aspects of the Uppsala School for OT Study,' *HTR* 43 (1950), 239; H.H. Schrey, 'Die alttestamentliche Forschung der sogenannten Uppsala-Schule', *ThZ* 7 (1951), 321; H. Ringgren, 'Les recherches d'Ancien Testament en Scandinavie', *ETR* 46 (1971), 419.

2. H. Ringgren, 'Old Testament Exegesis', in *Faculty of Theology at Uppsala University*, ed. by H. Ringgren (Stockholm: Almqvist and Wiksell, 1976).

3. A. Bentzen, 'Skandinavische Literatur zum Alten Testament, 1939–1948', *TR* NF 17 (1948–1949), 309.

4. Bentzen, 'Skandinavische Literatur', 309.

5. H.S. Nyberg, 'Die schwedischen Beiträge zur alttestamentlichen Forschung in diesem Jahrhundert', *SVT* 22 (1972), 1-10.

6. S. Mowinckel, *Psalmstudien*, vols. I-VI (Kristiana: J. Dybwad, 1921–1924) = *The Psalms in Israel's Worship*, trans. by D.R. Ap-Thomas (Nashville: Abingdon Press, 1962).

7. A.S Kapelrud, *Joel Studies* (UUÅ 1948:4; Uppsala: Lundequist, 1948).

8. J. Pedersen, *Israel: Its Life and Culture*, 4 vols. in 2 (Copenhagen: Banner og Korch, 1926).

9. As an example see G.W. Ahlström, *Psalm 89* (Lund: C.W.K. Gleerup, 1959).

10. H.S. Nyberg, 'Das textkritische Problem des Alten Testaments am Hoseabuche demonstriert,' *ZAW* 52 (1934), 341-54.

11. Nyberg, 'Die schwedischen Beiträge', 4.

12. I. Engnell, *A Rigid Scrutiny: Critical Essays on the Old Testament*, trans. by J.T. Willis (Nashville: Vanderbilt University Press, 1969), 9-10.

13. I. Engnell, *Gamla Testament I* (Stockholm: Diakonstyrelses, 1945), 29.

14. C.R. North, 'Ivan Engnell: An Appreciation', in I. Engnell, *Studies in Divine Kingship in the Ancient Near East*, 2nd edn (Oxford: Basil Blackwell, 1967), xx.

15. G. Widengren, *Literary and Psychological Aspects of the Hebrew Prophets* (Uppsala: Lundquist, 1948), 56.

16. Engnell, *Rigid Scrutiny*, 166f.

17. H. Ringgren, 'Oral and Written Transmission in the Old Testament', *StTh* 3 (1950), 34-59.

18. 'The attitude of the religious individual towards the power (or powers) governing fate, manifests itself in some definitive action, normally regulated by the communal organization in some way or other. The collective term for these actions is *cult* (Lat. *cultus* from *colere* "till", "cultivate").

'Earlier phases of the history of religion regarded the cult as a symptom of degeneration. We now know that all religion finds expression in the cult as its principal means of expression' [Helmer Ringgren and Åke V. Strom, *Religions of Mankind* (Philadelphia: Fortress Press, 1967), xxxvi].

Included within the idea of cult are actions such as prayer, sacrifice, and ritual. In addition, there are sacred spots (e.g. temples), officials (e.g. priests, prophets, and in some cases the king), and institutions (e.g. national religion, church, sect) which fall under the rubric of cult (Ringgren and Strom, xxxiv-xxxix). See also Engnell, *Rigid Scrutiny*, 21ff.

19. Erik Stave, *Über den Einfluss des Parsismus auf das Judentum* (Haalven: Erven F. Bohn, 1900).

20. Ringgren, 'Old Testament Exegesis', p. 42.

21. This is in part why calling this whole movement the 'Uppsala School' is a bit misleading. Not all of the contributors to the ideas and development of this perspective on OT studies were Swedish, let alone studied at Uppsala. Thus, it might be more appropriately called the 'Scandinavian School' of OT studies. One must still acknowledge, however, the centrality of Uppsala in this movement. See discussions of G.W. Anderson, 'Some Aspects of the Uppsala School', 239-56, esp. p. 239; and Douglas A. Knight, *Traditions of Israel* (SBLDS 9; Missoula, Montana: Society of Biblical Literature, 1973), 292-95, 303.

22. A. Haldar, *Associations of Cult Prophets* (Uppsala: Almqvist and Wiksell, 1945).

23. A. Haldar, *Studies in the Book of Nahum* (UUÅ 1946:7; Uppsala: A.B. Lundequist, 1947); G. Widengren, *Literary and Psychological Aspects*; A.S. Kapelrud, *Joel Studies*; Ivan Engnell, *The Call of Isaiah* (UUÅ 1949:4; Uppsala: Lundequist, 1949); Johannes Lindblom, *Prophecy in Ancient Israel* (Oxford: Basil Blackwell, 1962); and Erling Hammershaimb, *Amos*, trans. by John Sturdy (Oxford: Blackwell, 1970).

24. An interesting development of this idea comes from Robert Wilson, who is not a product of the 'Uppsala School'. In his *Prophecy and Society in Ancient Israel*, (Philadelphia: Fortress Press, 1980), he draws upon anthropological and sociological analyses to argue that the prophets, whether 'central' or 'peripheral' intermediaries, must come out of a support group.

25. Ivan Engnell, *Rigid Scrutiny*, 123-79; idem, 'Profetia och Tradition', *SEÅ* 12 (1947), 110-39; and idem, 'Profetismens ursprung och uppkomst', *Religion och Bibel* 8 (1949), 1-18.

26. Ivan Engnell, *Studies in Divine Kingship* (Uppsala: Almqvist and Wiksell, 1943), 2nd edn (Oxford: Basil Blackwell, 1967).

27. A.M. Hocart, *Kingship* (London: Oxford University Press, 1927); and S.H. Hooke, *Myth and Ritual* (London: Oxford University Press, 1933).

28. Ringgren, 'Old Testament Exegesis', 45.

29. Geo Widengren, *Sakrales Königtum im Alten Testament und im Judentum* (Stuttgart: Kohlhammer, 1955); Helmer Ringgren, *Messiah in the Old Testament* (SBT I, 18; London: SCM Press, 1956); and G.W. Ahlström, *Psalm 89*.

30. Knight, *Traditions of Israel*, 21-25.

31. Knight, *Traditions of Israel*, 263.

32. Engnell, *Rigid Scrutiny*, 4.

33. Engnell, *Rigid Scrutiny*, 5.

34. Ringgren, 'Old Testament Exegesis', 44.

35. Engnell, *Rigid Scrutiny*, 5.

36. S. Mowinckel, *Prophecy and Tradition* (Oslo: J. Dybwad, 1946), 18.

37. Engnell, 'Profetia och Tradition', 110-39.

38. This debate over 'tradition history' raises again the discussion of the 'final form' of the text and one's attitude toward the received Masoretic text. What has developed in the 'Uppsala School' is a tendency to resist emendations of the text, almost to the point of sanctifying the received form of the text. One of the earliest proponents of this perspective was Nyberg in his 1935 book, *Studien zum Hoseabuche* (UUÅ 6; Uppsala: Lindequist, 1935). In that volume, Nyberg staunchly defended the correctness of the Masoretic text and rejected the various emendations suggested at that time. This perspective was adopted by Engnell and clearly shaped his understanding of 'traditio-historical' methodology when he focuses on the present or received form of the text. For Engnell, it is not necessary or possible to recover the *ipsissima verba* or to reconstruct an 'Ur-Text' (Engnell, *Rigid Scrutiny*, 9-10). This, of course, is the crux of the argument between Engnell and Mowinckel just discussed. However, whether one sides with Engnell or Mowinckel, the 'Uppsala School' has maintained a reluctance, even abhorrence, to emending the text. An excellent example of that is R.A. Carlson, a student of Engnell, in his book *David the Chosen One* (Uppsala: Almqvist and Wiksell, 1964), where the 'final form' of the text is taken with utmost seriousness.

G.W. AHLSTRÖM IN PROFILE

W. Boyd Barrick

Gösta W. Ahlström was born on August 27, 1918, in the steel town of Sandviken in east-central Sweden. His father, Tage K.J. Ahlström, was a Methodist minister. At the age of 15, his natural parents having died, he and a brother were forced to assume support of the family. Gösta took a job with a wholesale firm dealing in shoes and other leather goods, and in active competition with the firm that had hired his brother. Thus was cultivated a certain independence of mind and of spirit that would later characterize his scholarly career. He kept that job for eight years, during which time he pursued his education through correspondence courses, culminating in a gymnasium diploma in 1943. The following year he entered the University of Göteborg (Gothenburg) where he studied Greek, Hebrew, and philosophy. In 1945 he moved on to the University of Uppsala. There he studied in the Faculty of Theology (teol. kan., 1950; teol. lic., 1955; teol. dr., 1959) and simultaneously from 1951 in the Faculty of Humanities (fil. kan. in History of Religions, Semitic languages, and Assyriology, 1961). During 1957 he studied at Basel and Heidelberg through an international fellowship from the Olaus Petri Foundation. At Uppsala he served as Instructor in Old Testament from 1954 to 1959, as Docent of Old Testament from 1959 to 1964, and as Professor *pro tempore* of Old Testament in 1961.

The intimate connection between the Church of Sweden and Swedish history and culture has stimulated Ahlström's interest in history and religion at an early age. Reading Tor Andrae's biography of Nathan Söderblom (Professor of the History of Religions at Uppsala, 1901–1914, and Archbishop of Uppsala, 1914–1931) proved especially influential, expanding the horizon of this interest and sharpening his academic goals. At Uppsala he came under the spell of Ivan Engnell and Geo Widengren, the central pillars of the so-called 'Uppsala School' of Old Testament studies. Through them the entire

cultural and political world of the ancient Near East became the necessary context for Old Testament exegesis, an approach congenial to someone whose 'historical' mind was unwilling from the start to take the Old Testament as a theological treatise speaking first and foremost to the concerns of latter-day Judaism or Christianity. A concern for *Wissenschaft* alone remains the central motivation of Ahlström's scholarship.

The scholar's task, for Ahlström, is to ascertain as fully as possible what the ancient text says of its own time and place—be the text by Mesha or by Malachi. What that text might also be saying to modern man is the goal of theological, not historical, study, and Ahlström is deeply skeptical of the probity of seeking to accommodate the two. It is, of course, impossible to view the past except from the perspective of one's own time and place in the present. This is true not least of all in matters of religion. The discipline of biblical studies, like the academic study of religion generally, is often thought by outsiders to be a professional extension of the ministry. Many practitioners, motivated at least in part by a faith rooted in the Bible, would not entirely disagree with this opinion. And yet a biblical faith, even loosely held, can inadvertently color the scholar's view of the biblical past, conditioning the questions he asks of the texts and the answers he is prepared to hear from them. Ahlström's defense against this danger has been to view the biblical past with the respectful but dispassionate eye of an antiquarian, as a subject worthy of study for no greater reason than that it is interesting in its own right. This is an attitude more typical of Assyriologists and Egyptologists than of biblicists. Ahlström would agree that to place one small corpus of surviving ancient Near Eastern literature into a category of special meta-historical 'relevance' is to play favorites among these extinct peoples. For the historian, the poetry of Enheduanna is no more 'relevant' (or 'irrelevant') than the poetry of David (or whomever). The historian may personally prefer one over the other for aesthetic or theological reasons, but this cannot be allowed to intrude upon his professional judgment of them as evidence of the history, life, and culture of their respective segments of the ancient past.

In 1962, with the encouragement of J. Coert Rylaarsdam, then chairman of the Bible field in the Divinity School, Ahlström accepted an invitation to come to the University of Chicago as a visiting professor of Old Testament. He became a full member of the Divinity School faculty the following year. The decision to stay at

Chicago was not an easy one—Jimmy's is a very long way indeed from Offendahl's! As a unique international center for Near Eastern studies generally, the University has been an ideal setting for Ahlström's teaching and research. Within the Divinity School faculty he has straddled both the Bible and History of Religions fields, adding a distinctively Scandinavian perspective—and, one should add, accent—to each. Through his emphasis on history and philology in biblical study, the bonds between the Divinity School and the Department of Near Eastern Languages and Civilizations were renewed, at first informally and since 1974 through a joint appointment. Some of his most satisfying teaching has been done under the Department's aegis. On July 1, 1976, he became Professor of Old Testament and Ancient Palestinian Studies in the Divinity School and in the Department of Near Eastern Languages and Civilizations of the University of Chicago. The growing number of students in the Divinity School and in the Department who have completed doctoral studies under his direction and the range of topics addressed in the dissertations are witness to the quality of the scholar, the teacher, and the man.

Ahlström has been actively associated with the American Schools of Oriental Research since coming to Chicago. This association reflects the growing importance of archaeology in his scholarly work. Archaeology had long been a professional interest, but Palestinian archaeology as a discipline did not exist in Scandinavia and no actual experience had been possible. During 1969–1970, as the Annual Professor at the Albright Institute of Archaeological Research in Jerusalem, he was able to learn the discipline 'in the field' at excavations at Gezer, Isawiya, and the southern wall of the temple area in Jerusalem, and in the ASOR survey around Ta'annek. He subsequently served as a staff member at the ASOR excavations at Caesarea Maritima (1972), Idalion, Cyprus (1974), and Carthage (1977), and the Smithsonian excavation at Tell Jemme (1973). The season at Idalion was cut short by the Turkish invasion of the island, a remarkable experience Ahlström recounted with characteristically wry good humor in the ASOR *Newsletter* (January, 1975, pp. 1-4). He is a past president of the ASOR Alumni Association (1972) and has served as a trustee of the Albright Institute (1970–1974) and on the steering committee of the ASOR Institute at Carthage (1976–1978). He is also a member of the Archaeological Institute of America, Der Deutsche Verein zur Erforschung Palästinas, the

American Oriental Society, and the Society of Biblical Literature (president of the Midwest Section, 1976–1978).

In 1952 Ahlström married Rie Brorson Fich, originally from Aalborg, Denmark. They have two children, Pernille, an art historian in Uppsala, and Hans, currently a college student in Michigan.

G.W. AHLSTRÖM: A BIBLIOGRAPHY

Beth Glazier-McDonald

1. Review: A Theology of Salvation: A Commentary on Isaiah 40–55, by U.E. Simon. *Svensk Teologisk Kvartalskrift* (1954), 196-97.
2. Review: Interpretationes ad Vetus Testamentum pertinentes Sigmundo Mowinckel Septuagenario Missae. *Svensk Exegetisk Årsbok* 20 (1955), 58-66.
3. Review: Recent Discoveries in Bible Lands, by W.F. Albright. *Svensk Exegetisk Årsbok* 21 (1956), 152-53.
4. Gammaltestamentlig Litteratur. *Kristendomslärarnas Förenings Årsbok* 2 (1958), 51-55.
5. *Psalm 89: Eine Liturgie aus dem Ritual des leidenden Königs*. Lund: C.W.K. Gleerup, 1959.

    Verse by verse commentary largely composed of word studies; begins with a discussion of *maśkil* by which the superscription characterizes the psalm, concluding that a *maśkil* is a 'Jahresfestpsalm zu den Riten der Lebenserneuerung' (p. 26); claims a northern provenance for the psalm (v. 13); emphasizes 'den solaren Zug des Charakters Jahwehs' (v. 16); discusses 'DWD-David', positing the existence of a Jerusalem DWD cult and relating it to the *ldwd* superscription.

6. Profeten Natan och Tempelbygget. *Svensk Exegetisk Årsbok* 25 (1960), 5-22. (See #12.)
7. Review: Gamla Testamentet, by T. Andersson. *Svensk Pastoraltidskrift* 2 (1960), 20.
8. Review: Det Gamle Testamente IV: Skriftene I, del oversatt av S. Mowinckel. *Svensk Exegetisk Årsbok* 25 (1960), 148-52.
9. Review: Die politischen Voraussagen der Propheten, by E. Jenni. *Svensk Exegetisk Årsbok* 25 (1960), 168-69.

10. Review: The Rise of the Prophets, by N.J. Bull. *Svensk Exegetisk Årsbok* 25 (1960), 170-71.
11. Review: Zur Frage des Kanaanäischen Ursprungs des alttestamentlichen Prophetismus, by J. Lindblom. *Svensk Exegetisk Årsbok* 25 (1960), 171-72.
12. Der Prophet Nathan und der Tempelbau. *Vetus Testamentum* 11 (1961), 113-27.

    Concludes that Nathan was a Jebusite (he is not mentioned in OT texts prior to David's conquest of Jerusalem), that he, with Zadok, represented the Jebusite position in David's court, and that 'er führt offenbar das Wort der alten jebusitischen Tradition Jerusalems, deren Widerstand gegen den beabsichtigten Tempelbau so stark war, dass David von seinem Plan zurücktreten musste. Die Zeit war für ein solches Unternehmen noch nicht reif' (cf. 2 Sam. 7 [p. 127]).

13. Review: Das Problem der altorientalischen Königsideologie im Alten Testament, by K.-H. Bernhardt. *Svensk Exegetisk Årsbok* 26 (1961), 135-43 (in English).

    Expansive critique of Bernhardt's views of royal ideology and related matters, showing that on methodological and substantive grounds 'the author has not by any means succeeded in issuing a death certificate' for the notion of sacral kingship in Israel (p. 143).

14. Die Königsideologie in Israel: Ein Diskussionsbeitrag. *Theologische Zeitschrift* 18 (1962), 205-10.

    Continuation of the *Diskussion* with K.-H. Bernhardt begun in #13.

15. Uppsala och Prästutbildning. *Kvällsposten*, March 21, 1962, p. 2.
16. Articles appearing in *Svenskt Bibliskt Uppslagsverk*, 2nd edn, ed. by I Engnell. Stockholm: Nordiska Uppslagsböcker, 1962-1963.

    Vol. 1: Ahab, Ahas, Amalek, Ammon, Bilean, Blodsman, Brasa, Bägare, Bördeman, Dan, Domare, Envigeskämpe, Fårklippningsfesten, Grotta, Hundpenning, Hår, Ir-Hammela, Käpp.

Vol. 2: Mackeda, Papyrus Nash, Paran, Parbar, Pibeset, Pitom, Pul, Raamses, Ribla, Rost, Sjöfolken, Skrud, Smink, Spottning, Söderlandet, Tadmor, Timnat-Heres, Trakonitis, Tryfon, Upphöjelse, Åsnan.

17. *Aspects of Syncretism in Israelite Religion*. Horae Soederblomianae V. Lund: C.W.K. Gleerup, 1963.

    Discusses the problem of Canaanite elements in the religion of Israel, with special attention paid to phenomena illustrative of the areas of agreement between Canaanite and Israelite religion; concludes that 'phenomena connected with the Canaanite cultus had such a powerful hold on the religious consciousness of the Israelites that they proved virtually impossible to abolish' (p. 88).

18. Messias i Gamla Testamentet. *Kristendomslärarnas Förenings Årsbok* 7 (1963), 95-109.

    General survey of the 'Swedish' way of looking at the question; no longer fully representative of the author's opinions.

19. Review: Creation Legends of the Ancient Near East, by S.G.F. Brandon. *Journal of Religion* 44 (1964), 341-42.
20. Ivan Engnell (1906-1964). *History of Religions* 4 (1965), 337-38.
21. Oral and Written Transmission: Some Considerations. *Harvard Theological Review* 59 (1966), 69-81.

    Discusses techniques used in handing down oral and written traditions (e.g., parallelismus membrorum); agrees with I. Engnell that the length of time before the fixation of traditions varied a great deal; criticizes Engnell's thesis that most OT literature was not written down before the exilic and post-exilic time; maintains that laws (cf. Hos. 8.12; Jer. 2.8; 1 Sam. 10.25) and even some prophetical utterances (cf. Is. 8.1; 30.8; Jer. 36.6, 8) were written down earlier.

22. Review: Ancient Mesopotamia: Portrait of a Dead Civilization, by A.L. Oppenheim. *Journal of Religion* 46 (1966), 72-74.
23. Review: The Praise of God in the Psalms, by C. Westermann. *Journal of Religion* 46 (1966), 336-37.
24. Review: The Psalms Scroll of Qumran Cave 11 (11QPs^{a}), by J.A. Sanders. *Journal of Religion* 47 (1967), 72-74.

25. *'eder. Vetus Testamentum* 17 (1967), 1-7.
26. A self-presentation. *Criterion* 6.2 (1967), 37-38.
27. Some Remarks on Prophets and Cult. *Essays in Divinity VI: Transitions in Biblical Scholarship*, ed. by J.C. Rylaarsdam. Chicago: University of Chicago Press, 1968, pp. 113-29.

    Points out that the existence of widespread syncretism in Israelite religion, based on the identification of El and Yahweh, 'is the background against which one has to see the difficult task of the prophets in their struggle against the "wrong" cult' (p. 129); shows that we must deal with two competing official forms of Yahwism, the northern Israelite one and the southern or Jerusalemite one.

28. Solomon the Chosen One. *History of Religions* 8 (1968), 93-110.

    Stresses that Israelite kingship 'must not only be explained historically but also accounted for on ideological or theological grounds' (p. 103); points out, using the example of Solomon, that although he was appointed by his father David, he was also chosen by his God (1 Kgs 1.48), that he came to the throne in accordance with the will of Yahweh (1 Chron. 29.1; 2 Sam. 12.25), and that, as a result of his being divinely chosen, he possessed the *ruaḥ* of Yahweh, making his kingship charismatic (2 Sam. 7.12ff.).

29. Notes to Isaiah 53.8f. *Biblische Zeitschrift* 13 (1969), 95-98.
30. *hammōreh liṣdāqāh* in Joel II 23. *Supplements to Vetus Testamentum* 17 (1969), 25-36. (Reprinted with minor changes in #34.)

    Concludes that *hammōreh* is a title designating the 'leader' of the Jerusalem temple cultus who will establish 'right order' (*ṣᵉdāqāh*) which will result in fertility; suggests that the book of Joel reflects the time of Zerubbabel's disappearance and that the phrase under discussion refers to the promise of a new teacher and leader.

31. Problems in Formgeschichte (review of Was ist Formgeschichte?, by K. Koch). *Journal of Religion* 50 (1970), 186-89.
32. *'addîr, 'adderet. Theologisches Wörterbuch zum Alten Testament* I, ed. by G.J. Botterweck and H. Ringgren. Stuttgart: W. Kohlhammer, 1970, cols. 78-81.

33. Review: Internationale Zeitschriftenschau für Bibelwissenschaft und Grenzgebiete. *Church History* 39 (1970), 278.
34. *Joel and the Temple Cult of Jerusalem*. Supplements to Vetus Testamentum 21. Leiden: E.J. Brill, 1971.

    See especially: Ch. 2, Covenant Phraseology; Ch. 4, The Day of Yahweh (a cultic day in origin in which the deity manifests himself in the temple where he lives); Ch. 6, The Time of the Book (between 515 and 500 B.C., based on historical and linguistic criteria).

35. An Israelite God Figurine from Hazor. *Orientalia Suecana* 19-20 (1970-1971), 54-62.

    Discusses the seated deity figurine from the shrine at Hazor B, Str. XI; considers it to be a foundation deposit since the jar containing the figurine was found under an undisturbed cobbled floor; proposes that it could depict either Yahweh, the main god of the Israelites, or Baal, a Canaanite god widely worshipped by the Israelites.

36. A Poem. *American Schools of Oriental Research Newsletter* 9 (April, 1972), 4.
37. A Nabatean Inscription from Wadi Mukatteb, Sinai. *Ex Orbe Religionum: Studia Geo Widengren* I. Studies in the History of Religions 21. Leiden: E.J. Brill, 1972, pp. 323-31.
38. Syncretism and Religious Parties in Ancient Israel (review of Palestinian Parties and Politics that Shaped the Old Testament, by M. Smith). *History of Religions* 12 (1973), 372-77.

    Praises the author's major theses and general presentation; responds to numerous specific points with supplementary and occasionally critical notes.

39. Review: Untersuchungen zur sogennante Baruchschrift, by G. Wanke. *Biblica* 54 (1973), 125-27.
40. Review: Sacrifice in the Old Testament, by G.B. Gray (1971 reprint). *Journal of the American Oriental Society* 93 (1973), 397.
41. *'addîr, 'adderet. Diccionario teologico del Antiguo Testamento* I, ed. by G.J. Botterweck and H. Ringgren. Madrid: Ediciones Cristianidad, 1973, pp. 78-79. (Translation of #32.)
42. Review: The Covenant Formulary in the Old Testament, Jewish and Early Christian Writings, by K. Baltzer. *Journal of Religion* 54 (1974), 94-95.

43. Review: Gezer I: Preliminary Report of the 1964-1966 Seasons, by W.G. Dever, H.D. Lance, and G.E. Wright. *Journal of the American Oriental Society* 94 (1974), 277-78.
44. Review: Die Geschichte vom Aufstieg Davids (1 Sam. 15–2 Sam. 5), by J.H. Grønbaek. *Journal of Near Eastern Studies* 33 (1974), 360-61.
45. Prophecy. *Encyclopedia Britannica*, 15th edition, Macropedia 15. Chicago: Encyclopedia Britannica Inc., 1974, pp. 62-68.

    Following a discussion of the word 'prophet' and some general characteristics, gives a typology of prophecy and an overview of prophecy in the ancient Near East, including Mesopotamia, Israel and Judah, Judaism, Christianity, Islam, etc.

46. Review: Mourning Cry and Woe Oracle, by W. Janzen. *Theologische Literaturzeitung* 99 (1974), cols. 418-419.
47. *'addîr*, *'adderet*. *Theological Dictionary of the Old Testament* I, ed. by G.J. Botterweck and H. Ringgren. Grand Rapids: William B. Eerdmans, 1974 (revised edition, 1977), pp. 73-74. (Translation of #32.)
48. Isaiah VI 13. *Journal of Semitic Studies* 19 (1974), 169-72.

    Discusses the agricultural and military motifs in the passage, translating: 'But if now a tenth of it be left then it will turn and become burnt-over land; as the terebinth and the oak (after their) breaking down a wooden stump of them (remains). A pure seed is that stump.'

49. An Israelite God Figurine, Once More. *Vetus Testamentum* 25 (1975), 106-109.

    Responds to criticisms by O. Keel (in *VT* 23 [1973], 336) against his interpretation of the seated deity figurine from Hazor B (see #35).

50. Exodus from Cyprus. *American Schools of Oriental Research Newsletter* 7 (January, 1975), 1-4.
51. Review: Scrolls from Qumran Cave I, ed. by F.M. Cross, D.N. Freedman, and J.A. Sanders. *Journal of the American Oriental Society* 95 (1975), 111.
52. Some Comments on John Bright's 'History of Israel' (review of A History of Israel, by J. Bright, 2nd edition). *Journal of the American Oriental Society* 95 (1975), 236-41.

Critically discusses problems of method and interpretation which are seldom recognized by the theological interpreters of Israel's history; argues for the need for a reconstruction of the history of Israel according to the principles of modern historiography.

53. Heaven on Earth—at Hazor and Arad. *Religious Syncretism in Antiquity*, ed. by B.A. Pearson. Missoula, Mont.: Scholars Press, 1975, pp. 67-83.

Based on the idea of the temple as heaven on earth, suggests that the seated figurine and the ten stelae found in the holy-of-holies of the LB Canaanite temple at Hazor C are deity symbols (the seated figure represents the moon god, the ten stelae other deities of the Canaanite pantheon); maintains that the three stelae found in the holy-of-holies of the Israelite temple at Arad, constructed during Solomon's reign, parallel those at Hazor and thus confirm that the Israelites worshipped more than one deity.

54. *zayit*. *Theologisches Wörterbuch zum Alten Testament* II, ed. by G.J. Botterweck and H. Ringgren. Stuttgart: W. Kohlhammer, 1975, cols. 564-69.
55. Review: Das Buch Nahum, by H. Schulz. *Journal of Semitic Studies* 21 (1976), 184-85.
56. Judges 5:20f. and History. *Journal of Near Eastern Studies* 36 (1977), 287-88.

Concludes that the Song of Deborah (Judg. 5) was composed some time after all the tribes mentioned in it became Israelite, but before Judah did so (c. 1000 B.C.) because Judah is not mentioned in the poem; contends that the poem's distance from the event it celebrates and the poet's use of mythological motifs render its historical reliability suspect.

57. King Jehu—A Prophet's Mistake. *Scripture in History and Theology: Essays in Honor of J.C. Rylaarsdam*, ed. by A.L. Merrill and T.W. Overholt. Pittsburgh Theological Monographs 17. Pittsburgh: Pickwick Press, 1977, pp. 46-69.

Analyzes the nature of Jehu's revolt; concludes that it was a politically motivated *coup d'état*, most likely supported by a pro-Assyrian party of army officers, court officials, and other conservative groups discontented with

Joram's unsuccessful military efforts against Aram-Damascus, and legitimated by the prophet Elisha who furnished 'the usurper with the oracle of divine election' (p. 58).

58. Review: The Published Works of William Foxwell Albright, by D.N. Freedman. *Journal of the American Oriental Society* 97 (1977), 336.
59. Historia och Myt i Dom. 5:18ff. *Svensk Exegetisk Årsbok* 41-42 (1976-1977), 5-9. (Somewhat extended translation of #56.)
60. Review: Digging up Jerusalem, by K.M. Kenyon. *Journal of Near Eastern Studies* 37 (1978), 62-67.
61. KRKR and T̲PD. *Vetus Testamentum* 28 (1978), 100-102.

    Analyzes the use of the roots KRKR and T̲PD in Ugaritic (UT 51.IV. 28ff.; 2 Aqht II.10ff.; UT 49.III.15f.); concludes that they specify actions within the emotional range of ṢḤQ, 'to laugh', with which they are parallel; translates KRKR as 'to snap the fingers', T̲PD as 'to stamp the feet'; relates his findings to *mpzz wmkrkr* in 2 Sam. 6.14.

62. Winepresses and Cup-Marks of the Jenin-Megiddo Survey. *Bulletin of the American Schools of Oriental Research* 231 (1978), 19-49.

    Gives a systematization of the different types of winepresses found in the survey (in all 117); discusses dates, the wine-making process, and the problem of cup-marks found in and close to vats and presses.

63. Review: Imperialism and Religion: Assyria, Judah and Israel in the Eighth and Seventh Centuries BCE, by M. Cogan. *Journal of the American Oriental Society* 98 (1978), 509-11.
64. I Samuel 1,15. *Biblica* 60 (1979), 254.
65. The House of Wisdom. *Svensk Exegetisk Årsbok* 44 (1979), 74-76.

    Discusses the origin and function of the seven pillars in the house of Wisdom (Prov. 9.1); points out that such a construction technique is part of the Phoenician-Punic architectural tradition and not south Palestinian. In the EB II settlement at Byblos a house was found in which were six pillars along opposite walls and a seventh placed between the two rows as a ridge pole support, all resting

on stone bases; concludes that such an architectural custom explains why the verb ḤṢB, 'to cut', is used in the OT text (seven stone pillar foundations had to be cut out).

66. Review: Von Sinuhe bis Nebukadnezar, ed. by A. Jepsen. *Theologische Literaturzeitung* 104 (1979), cols. 726-28.
67. Kung Manasse: ein religiös traditionalist. *Religion och Bibel* 38 (1979), 9-11. (An expanded English version appears in #78.)
68. A Note on a Textual Problem in I Kings 4:16. *Bulletin of the American Schools of Oriental Research* 235 (1979), 79-80.
69. Another Moses Tradition. *Journal of Near Eastern Studies* 39 (1980), 65-69.

In addition to archaeological remains, support for the thesis that the conquest tradition in the book of Joshua is 'a literary product and not a reflection of actual history' is found in the existence of a tradition in 1 Sam. 12.8 which 'clearly states that Moses and Aaron led the people out of Egypt and let them settle "in this place" (i.e., the central hill country) on Yahweh's behalf' (p. 67).

70. Is Tell ed-Duweir Ancient Lachish? *Palestine Exploration Quarterly* 112 (1980), 7-9.

No: on the basis of Eusebius' *Onomasticon* (120.20f.) and strategic considerations contends that 'the only site which one might consider to be the biblical Lachish is Tell 'Eṭūn . . . c. 3 km. south of Beth 'Auwa' (p. 7).

71. Review: The Tribes of Israel, by C.H.J. de Geus. *Journal of Near Eastern Studies* 39 (1980), 322-25.

Generally lauds the work, but criticizes the author's acceptance of Gunneweg's thesis that the Levites were foreigners who became the particular priests of the Yahweh cult; maintains that 'it is more likely that the Levites were priests appointed by the crown for duty in the national sanctuaries of the kingdom. As such, the biblical writers compared them to the *gerim* because they were not landowners. In reality, they did not need to own property since they lived off the land of the state temples' (p. 323).

72. Review: The Royal Dynasties of Israel, by T. Ishida. *Journal of the American Oriental Society* 100 (1980), 70-74.

Is impressed with the wealth of information in the book, but criticizes, e.g., the author's unsubstantiated position that the Israelites 'designed the structure of the monarchy as a political institution' prior to Saul's appearance on the historical scene (p. 52); his contention that 'divine designation and popular acclamation played no part in determining the characteristic feature of the Israelite monarchy' (p. 52: Ahlström maintains that the basis for kingship is the will of the deity which the prophet announced); and his assertion that the biblical texts are 'strikingly free of mythological character' concerning the origin of kingship (p. 26: Ahlström points out that there are texts stating that Yahweh himself either willed the kingship, chose the king, or gave birth to him, and that whenever a god is said to speak or act we are in the mythological realm).

73. *zayit*. *Theological Dictionary of the Old Testament* IV, ed. by G.J. Botterweck and H. Ringgren. Grand Rapids: W.B. Eerdmans, 1980, pp. 58-62. (Translation of #54.)

74. Was David a Jebusite Subject? *Zeitschrift für die alttestamentliche Wissenschaft* 92 (1980), 285-87.

Yes: Points out that during the reign of King Saul Bethlehem was part of the Jerusalemite kingdom, and on this basis argues that David the Bethlehemite originally was 'a Jebusite subject who chose a career in the army of the new Canaanite kingdom of Saul' (p. 287); contends that this explains the ease with which he was able to take the Jebusite city of Jerusalem and the fact that he did not slaughter its population.

75. Amos Nya Språkdräkt. *Svensk Tidskrift* (1980.7), 290-95.

A critique of the Swedish Bible Commission's new translation of the book of Amos.

76. King Josiah and the DWD of Amos 6:10. *Journal of Semitic Studies* 26 (1981), 7-9.

Suggests that the ten men mentioned in Amos 6.9 are the ten 'tribes' of Israel, the dead nation; the DWD (v. 10) is a reference to King Josiah, the Davidite, whose actions

against the 'brother people' of the north were justified through a prophecy.

77. Review: The Early History of Israel, by R. de Vaux. *Journal of Religion* 61 (1981), 337-38.
78. *Royal Administration and National Religion in Ancient Palestine.* Studies in the History of the Ancient Near East 1. Leiden: E.J. Brill, 1982.

    Investigates the intimate relationship between state and religion, observing that 'religion was an expression of the life of the community, and therefore constituted a part of the political system'; that the god was the ruler of the nation with the king, as his viceroy, as the administrator of his god's territory, building and organizing both state and cult (Ch. 1); that fortress cities, fortresses, store cities, royal sanctuaries (Ch. 2) and their priests (Ch. 4) were the visible arms of the central government in its administration of the different areas of the nation, all of which comprised the territory of the nation's god. See especially the discussion of the 'acropolis phenomenon' (pp. 15-25) and the 'Levitical cities' (pp. 51-65) and his assessment of the reign of King Manasseh (pp. 75-81; cf. #67).

79. Where Did the Israelites Live? *Journal of Near Eastern Studies* 41 (1982), 133-38.

    Points out that in the early IA population increase in the Palestinian hill country did not lead to the building of new cities; that urban areas were constructed only when the hill country areas were incorporated into the territorial states of Israel and Judah; and that these cities served mainly governmental purposes (fortress cities, store cities, and administrative centers). The majority of the population lived in unwalled villages around and in between the urban centers.

80. Was Gad the God of Tell ed-Duweir? *Palestine Exploration Quarterly* 115 (1983), 47-48.

    Perhaps: Examines an inscribed pottery fragment found in the LB temple (Str. VI) at Tell ed-Duweir.

81. Tell ed-Duweir: Lachish or Libnah? *Palestine Exploration Quarterly* 115 (1983), 103-104.

Responds to criticisms by G.I. Davies (in *PEQ* 114 [1982], 25-28) concerning the identity of Tell ed-Duweir (see #70) and proposes that it may be Libnah.

Forthcoming:

82. Review: The Discoveries of Dura-Europos, by C. Hopkins, ed. by B. Goldman. *Journal of Religion*.
83. Review: Prophecy and Society in Ancient Israel, by R.R. Wilson. *Journal of Near Eastern Studies*.
84. Review: The Encounter with the Divine in Mesopotamia and Israel, by H.W.F. Saggs. *Journal of Religion*.
85. The Tell Siran Bottle Inscription. *Palestine Exploration Quarterly*.
86. The Early Iron Age Settlers at Tel Masos (Khirbet el-Meshâsh). *Zeitschrift des Deutschen Palästina-Vereins*.
87. Review: The World History of the Jewish People IV:1: The Age of the Monarchies: Political History, and IV:2: The Age of the Monarchies: Culture and Society, ed. by A. Malamat and I. Eph'al. *Journal of Near Eastern Studies*.
88. Giloh: A Judahite or Canaanite Settlement? *Israel Exploration Journal*.
89. An Archaeological Picture of Iron Age Religions in Ancient Palestine. *Studia Orientalia*.
90. Review: The Art of Biblical Narrative, by R. Alter. *Journal of Religion*.
91. Review: La Déesse TNT: une étude sur la religion canaanéo-punique, by F.O. Hvidberg-Hansen. *Journal of Near Eastern Studies*.
92. The Cultroom at 'En Gev.

PARENTHESES IN A SNOWSTORM:
G.W. Ahlström and the Study of Ancient Palestine

W. Boyd Barrick and John R. Spencer

It is not surprising that G.W. Ahlström is identified with the 'Uppsala School' of Old Testament scholarship. Such an identification is unavoidable given his association with the University of Uppsala in the formative stages of his scholarly career. Not uncommonly, however, members of the second and third generations of such 'schools' will move beyond the classic parameters, reconsidering, modifying, expanding, or even rejecting the views of the founders; and this is the case with Ahlström and his relationship with the 'Uppsala School'. Thus, in acknowledging Ahlström's work as teacher and scholar, it is appropriate to consider the extent to which Ahlström has remained 'within the fold' and the extent to which he has gone his own way.[1] That is the purpose of this essay.

Ahlström's work reflects three broad areas of concern: questions of literature; questions of religion; and questions of history. His contributions in each of these areas will be examined, calling special attention to how his work relates to the scholarly tradition out of which he came. Finally, the remaining essays in this volume will be surveyed as they relate to these major themes of Ahlström's work.

Questions of Literature

Ahlström's published work on the literature of the Hebrew Bible focuses on two issues. The first is the reliability of the received Hebrew Text (MT). The second issue concerns oral tradition and tradition history. Both issues are central features of the distinctive perspective of the 'Uppsala School'.

Like others of the 'Uppsala School', Ahlström seeks to understand the biblical writings as they exist rather than as reconstructed through emendation. His goal always is to make sense out of the MT as it stands, and in so doing he will often move beyond a linguistic

study of the passage. Three recent examples (all in 1979) will illustrate the point. In a discussion of the problematic phrase קשת רוח in 1 Samuel 1.15, rather than alter the MT Ahlström draws on the usage of the root קשה in Ezekiel 3.7 to yield 'obstinate or stubborn of spirit' and an interpretation appropriate to the context of the passage.[2] His treatment of the text of 1 Kings 4.16 draws on paleography, *defective* versus *plene scriptum*, and Samarian papyri to conclude that 'we must accept the Hebrew text tradition as it stands'. Once the emendations are rejected, he proceeds to offer an effective interpretation of the text.[3] In his study of the seven pillars of the 'House of Wisdom' in Proverbs 9.1, Ahlström employs archaeology and architecture to show that the MT's reference to 'cutting' the pillars is preferable to the usual emendation ('set up'), and, in turn, he argues for the Phoenician origin of the proverb.[4]

Ahlström's attitude toward the MT is clearly a product of his training at Uppsala. One must be cautious in emending the MT. It is not acceptable to change a text simply because it seems incomprehensible. The change must be supported by hard evidence, and for Ahlström this primarily means evidence from other Hebrew manuscripts. However, this conservative attitude toward the *textus receptus* tends to overlook the potential value of other textual traditions. Hence, the LXX is rarely used in textual analysis, even though it exists in a much older form than the MT (as represented by Codex Leningradensis). It sometimes appears as if there is an innate prejudice against the LXX within the 'Uppsala School', and to the extent that this blindness is perpetuated, the approach to textual criticism taken by Ahlström will be limited.

Ahlström's contributions to the discussion of oral tradition and tradition history come from the earlier portion of his career. His first major work in this area was his dissertation, *Psalm 89* (1959), a fruit of the 'inspired research directing' of Engnell.[5] The close association with Engnell is reflected in Ahlström's setting of the psalm within the context of an annual festival, probably a kind of renewal festival for a vegetation deity ('Dwd').[6] His study of the tradition of the psalms, of their role in the religious life of the people, and of the oral preservation of the psalm by circles of priests likewise places Ahlström solidly within the 'Uppsala School'.

Ahlström addresses the issue of oral tradition more directly in 'Oral and Written Transmission: Some Considerations' (1966).[7] He focuses on the process by which material is preserved and handed on

('transmission'), rather than on the initial creation of the material. This process of preservation, Ahlström argues, is not necessarily fixed. Indeed, both fixed and unfixed texts could be transmitted in the same period. The 'fixity' of the material is dependent on the particular 'circle of tradents' who preserve the text, a priestly circle being much more likely to have a 'fixed' text than a wandering 'popular minstrel'.[8] As to when the oral texts became written texts, Ahlström strongly—and rightly—disagrees with Engnell's untenable position that most of the OT materials were not in a written form until after the Exile. Citing such passages as Jeremiah 2.8, 1 Samuel 10.25, Joshua 24.25f., and Deuteronomy 31.19ff., Ahlström argues that many of the sacred traditions or 'holy words' would have been preserved and written down within the temple community.[9] In addition, Ahlström sees many of the 'prophetic utterances' as likely to have been put in writing early, before the Exile, and perhaps without any significant oral stage. This responsibility for moving the material into a written form belongs to the disciples of the prophets (like Baruch for Jeremiah—Jer. 36). The impetus for their early appearance in a written form is the realization that the prophets' words are the 'words of Yahweh'.[10]

The issues of transmission history and oral tradition figure prominently in Ahlström's study of *Joel and the Temple Cult of Jerusalem* (1971), in which he traces the use of earlier motifs and traditions by the tradents of Joel. While not subscribing to Engnell's view of tradition history as the methodological capstone of biblical studies, like Engnell he sees the importance of the 'final form' of the text and the need for an objective analysis of the text and its background. The word studies in Chapter One (e.g., רקד, אני and שרת) and Chapter Five (devoted to המורה לצדקה) demonstrate this concern for understanding the final form as well as his disinclination to alter the MT.[11] Ahlström is also concerned with the context and history of the traditions which appear in Joel. This means identifying the *Sitz im Leben* of the materials within the Israelite context and considering the earlier, often non-Israelite, origins of the contents. For example, of Joel 1.19-20 he concludes:

> The prophet seems to be picking and choosing phrases and motifs from his vast knowledge of cultic material, in the present case, material associated with lamentations. For this reason his composition mirrors many old features from rites of weeping and lamentation, of death and devastation, as well as from hymns of joy and restoration.[12]

Similarly, in discussing the 'Day of Yahweh' in Joel, Ahlström argues one must look at the way 'foreign' motifs have influenced the theophanic description of Yahweh. Ahlström cautions against seeing these motifs as entirely 'foreign' but at the same time urges recognition of the ways in which ideas from the cults of Baal Hadad and El have penetrated the traditions of Yahweh.[13]

While Ahlström's studies clearly grow out of the 'Uppsala School's' approach to oral tradition and tradition history, he has left some of the questionable aspects by the wayside. In regard to oral tradition, D.A. Knight has observed, 'Ahlström holds it to be necessary to take the factor of oral transmission into consideration, but he tones down markedly the importance which was invested in it in the early publications of other Uppsala scholars'.[14] Concerning tradition history, Ahlström sees it not as the 'final' development in the methodological approaches to the Old Testament, but as one of the many critical tools to be employed by the investigator. One must clearly trace the history of biblical traditions to earlier Israelite and even non-Israelite origins. However, historical, form critical, cultural/social, and redactional studies must also be taken into consideration when analyzing a text.

Ahlström has been criticized for his application of 'tradition history' methodology. However, that criticism has been a bit misplaced; for it is a criticism not of his use of the methodology *per se*, but of the ultimate origins to which he attributes particular traditions. For example, Knight states that Ahlström's 'postulated mythical background' (specifically of Ps. 89) creates some problems.[15] Ahlström often postulates a religious/cultic/mythical context which initially gave rise to many of the traditions which appear in the Israelite religion. This reflects his training at Uppsala as well as the history of religions influence of the University of Chicago. While many such as Knight find this approach 'problematic', little has been suggested by way of alternative possibilities. This in itself may speak for the soundness of the approach.

The essays in Part II of the present volume deal with questions of literature and tradition. Consistent with Ahlström's aversion to emendation, P.A.H. de Boer seeks to understand the *textus receptus* of Psalm 81.6a; he finds a new but quite plausible understanding of the verse which leaves the text intact. These same concerns arise on a larger scale in Norman Habel's discussion of the Elihu section of Job. He examines the literary as well as textual basis for the integrity of

the material in order to allow the 'objective' literary concerns to be the primary informant rather than presupposed theological criteria or needs. Conrad L'Heureux grapples with the 'redactional history' of Isaiah 5.1–10.4, giving a meticulous analysis (something not unknown to Ahlström and the 'Uppsala School') of the meter, alliteration, and strophic pattern, to unpack the process by which the 'author' composed the present form of the passage. Dennis Pardee breaks new ground with his innovative analysis of Psalm 89, using a detailed 'experimental' method to study the metrical form of the psalm. Taking Ahlström's article on 'Oral and Written Transmission' as a starting point, John Van Seters shows how Joshua 24 is inclusive of older traditions and investigates the process by which Joshua 24 came to occupy its present place within the Hexateuch. Each of these essays, in its own way, pays apt tribute to Ahlström by taking seriously the methodologies he has employed in the analysis of the MT and by applying them creatively in new and imaginative ways.

Questions of Religion

The clear center of gravity of Ahlström's scholarly career has been the ideas and practices that constituted 'religion' for the ancient Israelites and their neighbours. He is perhaps best described as an historian of the religions of ancient Palestine, with a special interest in the religion—or better, religions—of the Iron Age inhabitants of that particular region of the Near East. Ahlström's understanding of Israelite religion, of its origins, and of the proper approach to the study of it, took shape at Uppsala especially under the tutelage of Ivan Engnell. While virtually all of Engnell's publications deal with Israelite religion either directly or indirectly, he presented his view *in extenso* only in Swedish, most notably in a chapter of *Gamla Testamentet*[16] and later in several articles in *Svenskt Bibliskt Uppslagsverk*.[17] These presentations remained inaccessible to most scholars outside Scandinavia until an English digest appeared in 1969.[18] They provide a convenient frame of reference for assessing the main lines of Ahlström's work in this area.

Engnell identified three distinct phases in the pre-exilic history of Israelite religion. The first is the desert or nomadic phrase, the so-called 'religion of the Patriarchs' (although not exactly as depicted in the 'greatly idealized snapshots of the Pentateuch'[19]) characterized by the worship of the West Semitic high-god El in various guises. In

the second phase this 'El of the fathers' was rejuvenated as Yahweh (-El) through the experience of Moses and a federation of tribes under his leadership. The third and best documented phase is the 'period of syncretism' arising from the encounter between the Mosaic religion and the religious life of the land of Canaan. The result was 'peaceful assimilation, a fusion of Israelite and Canaanite elements, although now and then, and in different places, this encounter [took] the form of violent conflicts'.[20] As in time the Israelites came to be part of the native population of Canaan—and therefore 'Canaanites'—the Mosaic Yahweh(-El) came to be completely identified with the local manifestations of the Canaanite El. Of these mergers, the most important was with El Elyon of Jerusalem, achieved through the enterprise of David and especially Solomon, so that 'Yahweh–El Elyon became *the* Israelite god from then on'.[21] Thus, for Engnell, this third phase saw the transformation of Yahweh into a national god of Israelite Canaan, and the concomitant 'Canaanization' of Israelite religion at the official and popular levels alike. Opposition to this syncretism existed from the beginning, but these were unrepresentative minority voices such as the Rechabites and the reactionary (or literary) prophets. The latter were themselves not untouched by this 'Canaanization' despite their criticisms and supposed wilderness idealism. They did not perpetuate unadulterated Mosaic Yahwism, but advocated a 'correct' form of Canaanized Yahwism.[22]

Ahlström views the history of Israelite religion in much the same way. His teaching and writings on the subject have concentrated on the 'period of syncretism'. His major treatise is *Aspects of Syncretism in Israelite Religion* (1963), an extended commentary on 'a number of phenomena illustrative of the areas of agreement between Canaanite and Israelite religion'.[23] His opening sketch of the syncretization process[24] stresses the central features of Engnell's position outlined above; it is a succinct statement of the 'givens' undergirding all of Ahlström's work. He proceeds to document this thesis by examining several interwoven strands of evidence: the general Canaanite-Israelite religious symbiosis at such old cult centers as Ophrah and Gibeon; the specific Jebusite-Israelite symbiosis at Jerusalem under David and Solomon; the importance of Canaanite cult objects and of the worship of gods other than Yahweh, especially Asherah, in normal Israelite religious life; and the office of the 'queen-mother' (גבירה) as indicative of the place of the mother-goddess in the official pantheon (*sic*!) of Israelite Jerusalem. The discussions are wide-

ranging and suggestive, often very original, occasionally idiosyncratic, and provocative throughout. The aggregate is a forceful and generally persuasive defense of the proposition that 'the cultus, in common with the culture, was "canaanized": not merely tolerated but accepted as being a necessity in the Canaanite milieu'.[25]

Like Engnell, Ahlström can speak of Israelite religion as a type of Canaanite religion.[26] But his position is more nuanced than this. The phrase 'Israelite religion' is, for Ahlström, a generic designation embracing 'a number of different forms of religion, clearly having one thing in common—that all are nominally expressions of the worship of Yahweh'—but diverging to a greater or lesser degree in emphasis and detail.[27] One must think in terms of different blends of Canaanite and Israelite ingredients which together constitute the religions of Iron Age Palestine.[28] This diversity of expression is due, first of all, to the fact that 'Canaanite religion' was not identical throughout Canaan; considerable local and regional diversity existed, which the Israelites inherited. It is due also to the heterogeneous origin of the Israelites themselves; each of the tribes and non-tribal elements (such as Jerusalem) 'which was to play its part in the history of the Israelite nation had its own tradition, its own area and its own [religious as well as socio-political] history'.[29] Thirdly, we must reckon with a changing spectrum of attitudes and special interests such as naturally exists in any society. This includes those small groups that, with a more profound understanding of what Yahweh and his worship ought to be, 'set themselves up in opposition to the situation as they found it, and laid down their own views as to how their religion should have been shaped'.[30] The ultimate triumph of these groups 'produced the new form of religion that is called Judaism'.[31] Molded by their notions of authentic Yahwism, the biblical picture of Israelite religion all but obliterated the true texture of religious life in Iron Age Palestine. The surface contours of the texts are misleading. In *Aspects of Syncretism* Ahlström mines some of what lies buried beneath.

A great part of Ahlström's research has been devoted to the Jebusite-Israelite symbiosis. This instance of syncretism is of special historical significance because of the great influence it exerted, through the temple of Solomon and the royal and priestly establishments surrounding it, on the course of Israelite life and thought before and after the Exile. It also serves as a relatively well-documented test case illustrative of the syncretizing process itself.

Like Engnell, Ahlström considers the hallmark of this symbosis to have been the merger of the Israelite Yahweh(-El) with the Jebusite El Elyon, a form of the Canaanite high-god with marked solar characteristics.[32] At Bethel, by contrast, Yahweh came to be identified more with the local form of the fertility-god Baal and thus was unrecognizable as Yahweh to those like Amos whose conceptions of the deity were refractions of the Jerusalem norm.[33] The Jebusite-Israelite symbiosis did incorporate the fertility-god but as a separate cult figure, 'Dwd', and included the mother-goddess Asherah as well. Most direct evidence for these two deities has been suppressed in the received tradition, but a number of allusions remain, chiefly in materials relating to kingship and the royal cult in Jerusalem. Mention has been made of Ahlström's discussion of the 'queen-mother'. He concludes that her position was 'an ideological replica of that of the mother of the gods', and that her influence at court rested on a cultic basis, specifically her role as consort of the king in the *hieros gamos* ritual.[34] As for 'Dwd', Engnell had postulated that it was a Jebusite 'appellative or a proper name of the "vegetation deity" corporalized in the king'.[35] Ahlström develops this thesis in the course of an exposition of the cultic role of the king, in *Psalm 89*.[36]

The relationship between king and cult is one of the hallmarks of the 'Uppsala School' and especially the work of Engnell. In his major work on the subject, *Studies in Divine Kingship in the Ancient Near East* (1934), Engnell studied the relationship of king and cult in ancient Egypt, Mesopotamia, Anatolia, and in the West-Semitic region. He was very aware of the debt due to James Frazer and *The Golden Bough*, but he also knew the limitations of the 'patternism' found in Frazer's work.[37] Engnell moved in his own direction, drawing heavily on the original sources and texts to establish the way the ancient peoples understood their king and his ideological or cultic relationship with the god. Engnell sought to elucidate the specific nature of that relationship: the king as divine in Egyptian culture, the king's 'identity' with the god in Sumero-Accadian kingship, the 'deification' of the king at his coronation in the West-Semitic materials.[38] Although some Old Testament texts are mentioned, Engnell did not treat Israelite kingship directly; he had intended this volume to be 'background to my subsequent treatment of the O.T. material'.[39] However, that promised treatment never appeared. As C.R. North indicates, Engnell was beaten to the punch by H. Frankfort's *Kingship and the Gods* and A.R. Johnson's *Sacral Kingship*

in Ancient Israel, 'less brilliant but more cautious scholars [who] set out to disprove his conclusions in advance'.[40]

In *Psalm 89* Ahlström builds upon the 'background' presented by Engnell. As indicated by the subtitle of the book, Ahlström sees the psalm as 'Eine Liturgie aus dem Ritual des leidendes Königs'. In discussing the ideological relationship between the king and the god he stresses that the king is chosen by god and is god's servant, messiah, and son. Concerning verse 4 Ahlström states, 'dass Jahwe selbst einen Bund mit dem König, seinem Auserwählten, schliesst', and he shows how this is consonant with many ancient Near Eastern cults.[41] In regard to verse 21, Ahlström states, 'Die Wahl des Königs und der Dynastie hat mit anderen Worter göttlichen Ursprung. So ist es auch Jahwe selbst, der mit seinem heiligen Öl seinen König salbt'.[42] And in discussing verses 26-27, Ahlström writes, 'Jahwe selbst erklärt hier durch das Orakel, dass der König sein Sohn and Erstgeborener ist . . . Diese Geburt des Gottessohnes geschieht nun in dem Augenblick, in dem der Auserwählte, der König, mit Jahwes heiligen Öl gesalbt wird, wodurch er den Geist des Gottes, רוח יהוה, erhält, 1.Sam 16:13'.[43] These examples illustrate Ahlström's adherence to the 'sacral' kingship expression of the intimate relationship between the king and the cult in ancient Israel.

This perspective is refined and vigorously defended in a number of typically lengthy review articles. Ahlström criticizes Karl-Heinz Bernhardt on several fronts, including his neglecting of the subtle but significant distinction between 'sacral' and 'divine' kingship and his failure to grasp the cultic dimension of 'sacral' kingship, which led him to see Psalm 2.7 as a literal statement about 'physiche Zeugung' and to miss the cultic aspect of 'Neugeburt'.[44] Ahlström's most focused statement on the subject to date is his study of 'Solomon, the Chosen One' (1968). Rejecting the popular distinction drawn by Alt between charismatic and dynastic kingship, he argues that Solomon was enthroned because Yahweh had selected him to be king—he is God's (as well as David's) 'Chosen One'.[45] Ahlström also takes John Bright and others to task for their 'theological interpretation' of history and for seeing kingship as 'essentially pagan' and incompatible with the worship of Yahweh. These positions reflect a prejudicial attitude out of keeping with objective scholarship.[46] In addition, that kingship took a unique form in Israel 'cannot be established as historical fact—indeed, like elsewhere in the ancient Near East, it is a divine institution demonstrating god's selection of the king'.[47]

Ahlström's position on king and cult remains consistent throughout. He continues to maintain that kings in Israel were divinely selected and ritually enthroned. They may not have been gods (Egypt) or equated with gods (Mesopotamia), but through ritual enthronement ceremonies they were Yahweh's chosen (Ps. 89.3), Yahweh's messiahs (Ps. 89.20), and Yahweh's sons (Ps. 2.7; 89.26f.; 2 Sam. 7.14).

Engnell spoke of a 'Canaanite cult pattern . . . completely dominated by sacral kingship, which was taken over in Israel, and especially in Jerusalem, by David'.[48] This 'cult pattern' included 'sham fights, the "passion" and "death" of the divine king, his "resurrection" and victory over the powers of chaos, his enthronement and sacred marriage and "fixing of destiny"—that is, the "creating" of fruitfulness for the time to come and its necessary prerequisite, rain'.[49] Read against this background, *Psalm 89* is the most 'patternistic' of Ahlström's published work. He argues, *inter alia*, that the psalm reflects ritual ceremonies associated with the fertility-god which featured the resurrection of the king and his reinstallation on the throne.[50] These ceremonies, as in this and other psalms, and the royal ideology which they express are part of the Jebusite legacy inherited by David and melded into the official religion of the state through Jerusalem.[51] The extent of the legacy is the theme of Ahlström's study, *Joel and the Temple Cult of Jerusalem* (1971). He examines a wide range of 'Canaanitisms' in the book of Joel which, he maintains, are for the most part 'old theological and cultic ideas as they were at home in the performances of the temple cult at Jerusalem' and officially sanctioned by its priesthood.[52] In sum, Ahlström leaves no doubt that in the Jebusite-Israelite symbiosis the Jebusite elements predominate.

The religio-political circumstances which gave rise to this onesidedness are outlined in 'Der Prophet Nathan und der Tempelbau' (1961) and amplified in later works. The assimilation process began with David the Bethlehemite who, Ahlström argues, probably was himself a Jebusite subject, Bethlehem being within the political and religious orbit of Jerusalem in the time of Saul, and not an 'Israelite' at all.[53] At the very least, following acquisition of the city he 'was concerned, as far as possible, to adapt himself to the Jerusalem situation'.[54] With the city, David inherited its traditions of rule and of religion, together with institutions (such as king Araunah's *goren*-sanctuary) and personnel (such as Nathan and Zadok) through which they could be perpetuated.[55] David pursued a deliberate syncretizing policy (e.g.

the transfer of the Ark) in order to legitimate himself as an Israelite king and Jerusalem as the religious and political capital of his Israelite nation. In political terms, this policy required holding in balance the Jebusite and Israelite factions at court. This is the background of Nathan's oracle concerning the building of a new temple (which the later tradents have reshaped for their own purposes) and of the power struggle over the succession. The accession of Solomon and the removal of Abiathar from court marked the final victory of the Jebusite faction, manifested in the purely Canaanite temple erected on Mt Zion and the installation of the Zadokite priesthood as the religious leaders of the kingdom.

At this juncture it would be in order to call attention to the methodological stance that informs the findings which have just been discussed. Ahlström has described his research as 'an approach to the Israelite religion that considers the factual happenings and meanings as well as the interpretative tendencies that sometimes are to be found in the textual material'.[56] He would characterize his approach as scientific or descriptive: 'Our task is thus to ask what the Old Testament phenomena meant for the Israelites and in addition to trace their origin and development'; consequently, 'scholarly research in the fields of the Old Testament cannot use any methods other than those used in dealing with the other Near Eastern extinct religions'.[57] The theological relevance of this material, whether it be Genesis or Enuma Elish, he cheerfully leaves for others to determine on the basis of the groundwork he has laid.[58] His work has tended to concentrate more on the facts behind the tradition ('what the Old Testament phenomena meant for the Israelites') than on the tradition itself.

Consistent with the Scandinavian perspective generally, Ahlström is especially concerned to place the religious life of ancient Israel within its historical and cultural environment before speaking of the unique or distinctive features it might have. Ancient Near Eastern material is freely drawn upon to help explain a biblical text. However, it would misrepresent Ahlström to label him a 'patternist', at least as that term is commonly used with reference to the 'Uppsala School'.[59] 'Comparativist' would be closer to the mark.[60] This distinction arises from Ahlström's recognition that the usefulness of comparisons is contingent on demonstrable historical or cultural connections between the peoples in question. Even then, a comparison only suggests a possible context for interpretaion but does not in

itself prove that interpretation to be correct or the connection to be established. Engnell also acknowledged these limitations in principle,[61] although they were not always evident in practice. In his use of comparative data Ahlström has been somewhat more circumspect than Engnell and somewhat more daring than Helmer Ringgren, Engnell's successor at Uppsala.

Talk of religious 'symbioses', however, goes beyond suggestive comparisons to the active interaction between different contiguous religions and the direct influence of one upon the other. 'Borrowing', the dynamic of religious and cultural syncretism, is a subject in need of much careful study. A 'patternist' does not allow for change in the material being borrowed, suggesting that the Israelites in Canaan adopted completely and indiscriminately the 'way of Canaan'. Ahlström does not go that far, except perhaps hyperbolically against the other extreme which holds that the Israelites in Canaan only *looked* like Canaanites, having borrowed forms but not content. One must assume that when such borrowings take place the environment of the receiving culture will affect changes in the borrowed material as it is integrated into that culture. A convenient example is Genesis 1.1–2.4a, clearly a 'borrowing' from Enuma Elish but adapted to an Israelite setting. This qualification must be applied as well to such basic institutions as kingship and temple ideology. It is not enough to say that the Israelites, through David and Solomon, inherited the Jebusite patterns and simply changed the name of the deity in question. Ideas too accompanied the Ark into Jerusalem, and it is doubtful that they would have vanished entirely with Abiathar's expulsion. In what manner did they alter the Jebusite patterns to create a Jebusite-Israelite 'symbiosis'? While Ahlström has correctly stressed the 'Canaanization' of Israel, more attention must be paid to the 'Israelization' of Canaan if the idea of 'symbiosis' is to be more than a theoretical construct.[62]

Aspects of the religious life of ancient Palestine are considered in Part III below. That five of the six contributors to this section are Scandinavian scholars testifies to the priority that this area of research continues to have on the agenda of the 'Uppsala School'. In his study of Joel, Ahlström offers numerous keen observations about the covenantal relationship between Yahweh and his people. The importance of the covenant in pre-exilic Israel's theological self-understanding is underscored in the essay by Arvid S. Kapelrud in the present volume. Ahlström's investigations of temple ideology in

Israel[63] are the point of departure for Benedikt Otzen; the heavenly vision motif in Jewish apocalyptic literature, Otzen argues, perpetuates the Old Testament theophanic tradition as expressed in sanctuary legends and prophetic call narratives, marking a further development or application of the ideological intersection of heaven and earth that undergirds the entire temple cultus. Menahem Haran lifts the veil of mystery from Exodus 34.29-35; in both Israelite and Mesopotamian thought the radiance of the gods is transferred to their earthly representatives, most conspicuously the king and here the person of Moses. Haran's essay goes well beyond Ahlström's treatment of this topic in *Psalm 89*.[64] Geo Widengren, in his masterful study of the prophetic theme of 'the gathering of the scattered', finds the theme to date from at least the time of Jehu and to have originated in Mesopotamia. It is an excellent illustration of the creative use of Mesopotamian data to illuminate Israelite concepts and customs that is characteristic of the 'Uppsala School'. Pursuing this same issue in a series of Assyriological notes, Åke W. Sjöberg raises serious questions about the assumed Mesopotamian influence on certain OT passages. The cultural influence of Phoenicia during the ninth century has figured in a number of Ahlström's recent writings,[65] and this is the general topic considered by Magnus Ottosson in his investigation of the political and religious dimensions of Elijah's activity at Zarephath.

Questions of History

Questions of history, as distinct from questions of religion, have emerged as a major focus of Ahlström's research. This significant shift in emphasis is his most dramatic departure from the classic agenda of the 'Uppsala School'. It is particularly evident in his teaching at the University of Chicago, facilitated by a formal affiliation since 1974 with the Department of Near Eastern Languages and Civilizations (where, coincidentally, the study of Syro-Palestinian languages and archaeology is a growing strength), and is realized especially in his year-long course on Syro-Palestinian history. It is reflected too in his published work.

The broad outlines of Ahlström's view of the history of ancient Israel emerge in a series of lengthy review articles published between 1973 and 1981.[66] Through these critical dialogues with Bright, de Vaux, de Geus, and others, he defines his own position on the central

issues facing the historian. Not least among these is the basic question of historical method, and on this score he finds the recent syntheses generally defective: 'there is still a need for an ordinary history book on the subject of ancient Israel . . . which eschews theology in favor of the sound methodology of modern secular historiography'.[67] This is a timely challenge and Ahlström, for one, intends to respond to it. The manuscript for just such a book is 'in progress'.

A major concern of Ahlström's published historical inquiries is the interrelation of the religious and secular dimensions of Israelite life during the monarchy. Contributing to the 'sacral kingship' debate in 'Solomon, the Chosen One' (1968), Ahlström points out the necessary correlation between royal ideology and the political realities of being or aspiring to be a king in ancient Israel.[68] Two later studies further develop this theme. In search of the historical David behind the biblical portrayals, Ahlström asks 'Was David a Jebusite Subject?' (1980); several diverse strands of evidence lead to the conclusion that David was, in fact, a non-Israelite Jebusite usurper who constantly needed to justify his kingship.[69] The interplay of religious, political, and socio-economic factors which brought another royal usurper to power are examined in 'King Jehu—A Prophet's Mistake' (1977), Ahlström's most comprehensive historical reconstruction and analysis to date.[70] The larger question of the function of religion in the operation of the Israelite state during the monarchy is addressed in *Royal Administration and National Religion in Ancient Palestine* (1982).[71] Ahlström first establishes the role of the king as 'administrator of the god's territory' and then examines the governmental consequences of that role in terms of city building, administration, priesthood, and cult. It is an excellent example of Ahlström's approach to the study of Israelite history, trying to show, on the one hand, how 'intimately interwoven religion and the state were', and, on the other hand, employing the tools of scholarship and historiography to their fullest.

A second concern of these historical inquiries has been the premonarchical stage of Israel's history. In 'Another Moses Tradition' (1980) Ahlström grapples with the vexing problem of the 'Conquest'. From the terse note in 1 Samuel 12.8 and archaeological data which conflict with the dominant biblical picture of the invasion, he concludes that 'the conquest theme is a literary product and not a reflection of actual history'.[72] His consideration of 'Judges 5:20f. and

History' (1977) gives cause to doubt the historical reliability of the Song of Deborah.[73] Asking 'Where did the Israelites Live?' (1982), he draws upon literary and archaeological evidence to attempt a reconstruction of the settlement pattern during the early Iron Age. He concludes that the new cities built at this time served mainly governmental rather than residential purposes; the majority of the Israelite people lived in unwalled villages in the vicinity.[74]

In discussing Ahlström's reconstruction of the history of Israelite religion, it was noted that he, like Engnell, speaks in general terms of a Canaanite-Israelite religious symbiosis and a specific Jebusite-Israelite religious symbiosis. It is argued that the 'Israelites' drew heavily from 'Canaanite' and 'Jebusite' religious and cultural traditions. 'Nathan und der Tempelbau' (1961) examines the historical background of the Jebusite-Israelite symbiosis. Ahlström's more recent historical studies dealing with this period have complicated this theoretical construction. For Ahlström there was no Israelite unity before the monarchy. He rejects—rightly—the notion that 'all Israel' participated in the Exodus and the existence of a tribal league as advocated by Noth, Bright and others. *Who*, then, were the parties in these religious symbioses? If the Jebusites can be identified by location (Jerusalem and its environs, including Bethlehem), how are we to identify—and distinguish between—'Israelites' and 'Canaanites' resident in Palestine? Perhaps it is time to stop talking about pre-monarchic 'Israelites' entirely, and speak instead about diverse groups of Palestinians who, in forming the monarchy, became Israelites. Ahlström seems clearly to be moving in this direction.

A dominant methodological characteristic of Scandinavian scholarship in the fields of Old Testament and the history of religions is its primary reliance upon textual evidence and philological argumentation.[75] Ahlström's training at Uppsala stressed the Semitic languages in classical fashion; it is not surprising that detailed word studies make up a large portion of the arguments in *Psalm 89* and *Joel*. Increasingly, however, artifactual evidence has come to play a major role in Ahlström's research. Engnell acknowledged the value of archaeology,[76] but in this respect Ahlström has moved well beyond his teacher. This is especially apparent in his work since 1969–1970 when he served as Annual Professor at the Americal Schools of Oriental Research (now the Albright Institute of Archaeological Research) in Jerusalem. From a survey done at that time he produced an exhaustive study of wine presses (1978), by far the most technical

of his writings on archaeological subjects and having little direct bearing on or reference to biblical materials.[77] It testifies to the fact that, for Ahlström, archaeology is not merely a source of 'background' information for the biblicist.

Site identification is an archaeological problem of special importance to the historian, and few excavated sites have greater historical significance than Tell ed-Duweir, usually identified as ancient Lachish. Ahlström, never content to accept uncritically the 'assured results' of earlier research, has taken up the question of this identification. From the writings of early travelers, geographical considerations, ostraca, and the archaeological record, he finds reason to believe that the site may be ancient Libnah, not Lachish.[78] This effort reflects Ahlström's control of the varied source materials necessary for historical reconstruction, and exemplifies his zest for scholarly debate whenever the evidence leads him away from the prevailing consensus.

Ahlström's integrative use of archaeological and literary data in the study of the history and religious life of ancient Palestine is well illustrated in his analysis of 'An Israelite God Figurine from Hazor' (1970–1971). In what is essentially an archaeological argument he shows that the early Israelite residents at Hazor did, in fact, possess cultic statuary in good 'Canaanite' style. If the figurine represents Baal, Ahlström argues, it is evidence that the syncretization process at Hazor began almost as soon as the Israelites arrived on the scene (assuming, of course, that the 'Israelite' newcomers were not themselves also 'Canaanites'). If it is not Baal, and if the archaeological record has been read correctly, the only other candidate is Yahweh.[79] In either case, the find adds weight to Ahlström's contention that 'the prohibition of images originated in Canaan as a reaction against the idol-worship so prevalent among the ethnic groups of the Israelites'.[80] His recent study of an inscribed rim fragment from Tell ed-Duweir (1983) finds it a reference to the deity Gad ('Fortune'), suggesting that the site had been a cult center for this deity in pre-Israelite times.[81] His views, noted above, regarding the worship of the goddess Asherah among the Israelites have been enhanced by the recent finds at Kuntilet Ajrud.[82] A broader synthesis giving 'An Archaeological Picture of Iron Age Religions in Ancient Palestine' will soon appear.[83]

Mention already has been made of several studies of literary and historical issues in which archaeology figures preeminently in

Ahlström's argument.[84] This tendency will most certainly continue, especially as work on his planned 'History of Israel' progresses. Ahlström would be quick to admit that he is not an academically trained archaeological professional, what some would term a 'Palestinian archaeologist'. But neither is he a 'biblical archaeologist' in the narrow (and often pejorative) sense of the term. For Ahlström, an historian of ancient Palestine self-consciously non-theological in his approach to the subject, the task is to learn from artifacts and texts alike and then move beyond both to reach the extinct life of the past.

The essays in Part IV of the present volume respond to the historical focus of Ahlström's work. Peter R. Ackroyd and Siegfried Herrmann probe the historian's task as interpreter. The biblical historians have left us with interpretations of Israel's past colored by pronounced theological or ideological biases. Ahlström's sharpest polemics have been directed against the tendency of many latter-day interpreters to adopt many of those same biases without critically examining 'the historicity of the OT texts and the art of "theological history" they present' from the neutral stance of a disinterested spectator.[85] Ackroyd provides just such an examination of biblical presentations of Ahaz and Hezekiah; his discussion appropriately complements Ahlström's recent treatments of Manasseh about whom few historians since the Chronicler have had anything kind to say.[86] On the other hand, the modern interpreter in seeking to penetrate the *Tendenz* of his sources may fall victim to the biases of his own critical methodology. This has been a frequent criticism of the 'Uppsala School', and some of Ahlström's work is open to it as well. Herrmann finds this to be a serious flaw in several of the latest studies of the books of Samuel; in particular, he cautions against letting societal factors eclipse individual personalities in explaining the rise and character of the kingdom of David. This interest in individuals as expressed in the artistry of biblical historiography is the subject of an exploratory essay by Jack M. Sasson. The interplay of individual and society is taken up again by Thomas W. Overholt who expands upon Ahlström's understanding of royal charisma by placing it in the context of current sociological and anthropological research. His remarks also address some of the reservations expressed by Herrmann regarding the use of social-scientific analytical categories to clarify Israel's past. Finally, Stephen A. Kaufman touches upon these methodological concerns in a suggestive outline of the history of four

social welfare institutions documented chiefly in Pentateuchal legislation and paralleled elsewhere in the ancient Near East.

Conclusion

This review of Ahlström's scholarly career has found him to have remained aligned with the 'Uppsala School' but to have moved beyond its classical boundaries. His work on biblical literature reveals a sustained concern for the integrity of the MT and for the process of transmission of oral and written texts. On the subject of oral transmission in particular, his views have moved away from the extreme position taken by Engnell and others. In the study of Israelite religion Ahlström's agenda is that set by Engnell. The religious life and institutions of ancient Israel cannot be divorced from their ancient Near Eastern context if they are to be understood correctly. But Ahlström is more cautious in comparing Israelite phenomena with that larger context. In addition, he has sought new ways to understand the process of syncretization from which the religions of Israel emerged. His most dramatic development, however, has been in the area of historical inquiry and the importance of archaeological data in his research.

Ahlström clearly retains the fundamental orientation and predispositions of the 'Uppsala School'. Taking many of Engnell's basic teachings and intuitive suggestions, he has expanded and confirmed some, modified and corrected others. In this respect he stands on the giant's shoulders. But from this vantage point his perspective is different and his vision sharper.

The history and culture of ancient Palestine is a landscape bewildering in its complexity, with numerous conflicting evidential cross-currents and few certain landmarks to guide even the seasoned explorer—not unlike a Swedish blizzard. Nonetheless, a few areas of relative clarity do exist. Ahlström's research has sought to identify and demarcate these areas of clarity to produce, as it were, 'parentheses in a snowstorm'. This phrase originated as a passing remark dropped by Ahlström in a classroom lecture on Old Testament history at Chicago. It reveals the sly humor which enlivens his teaching and conversations but appears all too rarely in his publications.[87] It also aptly describes the somewhat episodic, parenthetical nature of much of his scholarly work. His great synthesis awaits. Meanwhile, the essays which follow are offered as further enlargements of Ahlström's 'parentheses' for the benefit of future explorers.

NOTES

1. The characteristic features of the 'Uppsala School' have been described elsewhere in this volume. See 'The "Uppsala School" of Biblical Studies' by Merrill and Spencer.
2. G.W. Ahlström, '1 Samuel 1,15', *Biblica* 60 (1979), 254.
3. G.W. Ahlström, 'A Note on a Textual Problem in 1 Kgs 4.16,' *BASOR* 235 (1979), 79-80.
4. G.W. Ahlström, 'The House of Wisdom,' *SEÅ* 44 (1979), 74-76.
5. G.W. Ahlström, *Psalm 89: Eine Liturgie aus dem Ritual des leidenden Königs* (Lund: Gleerup, 1959), 7.
6. Ahlström, *Psalm 89*, 26, 172-73. On 'Dwd' see below.
7. G.W. Ahlström, 'Oral and Written Transmission: Some Considerations,' *HTR* 59 (1966), 69-81. See also his 'Problems in Formgeschichte,' *JR* 50 (1970), 186-89 (a review of *The Growth of the Biblical Tradition: The Form Critical Method* by Klaus Koch [New York: Charles Scribner's Sons, 1969].
8. Ahlström, 'Oral', 70.
9. Ahlström, 'Oral', 72-75.
10. Ahlström, 'Oral', 81.
11. See specifically, G.W. Ahlström, *Joel and the Temple Cult of Jerusalem* (SVT 21; Leiden: E.J. Brill, 1971), 1-22, 98-110. Throughout the book one sees the attempt to clarify not change the text. For a similar approach, see G.W. Ahlström, 'אדר', *VT* 17 (1967), 1-7.
12. Ahlström, *Joel*, 52. See also p. 59 for a discussion of Joel's usage of the earlier tradition of שוב שבות.
13. Ahlström, *Joel*, 81-83. See also below.
14. Douglas A. Knight, *The Traditions of Israel* (SBLDS 9; Missoula: Society of Biblical Literature, 1973), 326.
15. Knight, *Traditions*, 326.
16. I. Engnell, *Gamla Testament I* (Stockholm: Svenska Kyrkans Diakonistyrelses Bokförlag, 1945), 109-67.
17. I. Engnell, *Svenskt Bibliskt Uppslagsverk*, 2nd edn (Stockholm: P.A. Noestedt & Söner, 1962). See especially cols. 762-73.
18. Ivan Engnell, 'Old Testament Religion', in *A Rigid Scrutiny: Critical Essays on the Old Testament*, trans. and ed. J.T. Willis (Nashville: Vanderbilt University Press, 1969), 35-39. An overview of Engnell's views can be found in G.W. Anderson, 'Some Aspects of the Uppsala School of Old Testament Study', *HTR* 43 (1950), esp. 249-53, and in the course of a survey of research trends at mid-century in G.W. Anderson, 'Hebrew Religion', in *The Old Testament and Modern Study*, ed. H.H. Rowley (London: Oxford University Press, 1951), 283-310, esp. 287f. Cf. also J.T. Willis, 'I. Engnell's Contributions to Old Testament Scholarship', *ThZ* 26 (1970), 392f.; and the article on the 'Uppsala School' by Merrill and Spencer earlier in this volume.
19. Engnell, 'Old Testament Religion', 37.

20. Engnell, 'Old Testament Religion', 39.

21. Engnell, 'Old Testament Religion', 40; cf. 36.

22. Engnell, 'Old Testament Religion', 45f. Cf. Engnell, 'Prophets and Prophetism', in *A Rigid Scrutiny*, 123-79.

23. G.W. Ahlström, *Aspects of Syncretism in Israelite Religion* (Lund: Gleerup, 1963), from the Foreword.

24. Ahlström, *Aspects*, 9-14.

25. Ahlström, *Aspects*, 88. The point recurs elsewhere in Ahlström's writings; e.g. 'Some Remarks on Prophets and Cult', *Essays in Divinity VI: Transitions in Biblical Scholarship*, ed. J.C. Rylaarsdam (Chicago: University of Chicago Press, 1968), 128.

26. Cf., e.g., Ahlström, *Aspects*, 32, 49f.

27. Ahlström, *Aspects*, 33. Cf. Engnell, 'Old Testament Religion', 48.

28. In this connection note Ahlström's remark that 'a discussion about the syncretism in the history of the Israelite religion must take into account not only that the Israelites have adopted and become assimilated to Canaanite religious phenomena but also that Israelite cult phenomena and ideas may have been adopted by Canaanites and Jebusites living together with the Israelites' ('Some Remarks on Prophets and Cult', 123 n. 40).

29. Ahlström, *Aspects*, 22.

30. G.W. Ahlström, 'Gösta W. Ahlström', *Criterion* 6:2 (1967), 38. This was a short autobiographical and methodological sketch done for *Criterion* to celebrate the One Hundredth Anniversary of The Divinity School of The University of Chicago.

31. G.W. Ahlström, 'Syncretism and Religious Parties in Ancient Israel', *HR* 12 (1973), 376 (a review of *Palestinian Parties and Politics that Shaped the Old Testament* by M. Smith [New York: Columbia University Press, 1971]).

32. Ahlström, *Aspects*, 13. On the solar character of El Elyon see p. 28; and especially idem, *Psalm 89*, 85ff., 95. See also Engnell, 'Old Testament Religion', 40.

33. See, e.g., Ahlström, 'Some Remarks on Prophets and Cult', 117f.; and idem, *Joel*, 45.

34. Ahlström, *Aspects*, 76, 78f.

35. Ivan Engnell, *Studies in Divine Kingship in the Ancient Near East* (Oxford: Basil Blackwell, 1943), 176. See his further remarks in *Rigid Scrutiny*, 82ff.; and in *Svenskt Bibliskt Uppslagsverk*, cols. 618-56.

36. On 'Dwd' see especially Ahlström, *Psalm 89*, 163-73.

37. Engnell, *Studies*, 1-2.

38. Engnell, *Studies*, 15, 38, 78.

39. Engnell, *Studies*, 174.

40. From C.R. North's introduction to the reprint of Engnell's *Studies in Divine Kingship*, xxi.

41. Ahlström, *Psalm 89*, 50.

42. Ahlström, *Psalm 89*, 103.
43. Ahlström, *Psalm 89*, 111-12.
44. G.W. Ahlström, review of *Das Problem der altorientalischen Königsideologie im Alten Testament unter besonderer Berücksichtigung der Geschichte der Psalmexegese dargestellt und kritisch gewürdigt*' by Karl-Heinz Bernhardt, in *SEÅ* 26 (1961), 135-43. See also idem, 'Die Königsideologie in Israel', *ThZ* 18 (1962), 205-10.
45. G.W. Ahlström, 'Solomon, the Chosen One', *HR* 8 (1968), 93-110.
46. 'Pagan' is a term which has always rankled Ahlström. We have never known an occasion in public, class, or print where he has not objected to the term. This objection is in part because it is anachronistic to use the term in the ancient Israelite context; it is a Latin term for 'country dweller' whose first known usage was by Valentinian I in 370 CE in reference to the people who lived in the country and had not yet converted to Christianity. More seriously, the term implies a superiority over, rejection, and condemnation of those who do not accept your belief; for Ahlström, this prejudicial attitude has no place in scholarship.
47. G.W. Ahlström, 'Some Comments on John Bright's "History of Israel"', *JAOS* 95 (1975), 239. See also his review of *The Royal Dynasties in Ancient Israel: A Study on the Formation and Development of Royal-Dynastic Ideology* by Tomoo Ishida, in *JAOS* 100 (1980), 70-74.
48. Engnell, 'Old Testament Religion', 36.
49. Engnell, 'Old Testament Religion', 26. See further his 'New Year Festivals' in *A Rigid Scrutiny*, 180-84. Cf. idem, *Studies in Divine Kingship*, passim, and idem, 'The Ebed-Yahweh Songs and the Suffering Messiah in "Deutero-Isaiah"', *BJRL* 31 (1948), 54-93.
50. Ahlström has not addressed these matters directly in print since these early statements. It is clear from his teaching, however, that he would now modify many of these positions.
51. Cf. Ahlström, *Psalm 89*, 182.
52. Ahlström, *Joel*, 59 and passim.
53. Ahlström, 'Was David a Jebusite Subject?', *ZAW* 92 (1980), 285-87.
54. Ahlström, *Aspects*, 37.
55. Cf. Ahlström, 'Der Prophet Nathan und der Tempelbau', *VT* 11 (1961), 113-27.
56. Ahlström, 'Gösta W. Ahlström', 38. See note 30.
57. Ahlström, 'Gösta W. Ahlström', 37. See note 30.
58. See the observations by J.C. Rylaarsdam in *Essays in Divinity VI: Transitions in Biblical Scholarship*, (Chicago: University of Chicago Press, 1968), 14.
59. So H. Ringgren, *Israelite Religion*, trans. D.E. Green (Philadelphia: Fortress Press, 1966), 4 and n. 6. Cf. Ahlström's observations in *SEÅ* 26 (1961), 135-43; and 'Die Königsideologie', 205-10.

60. According to Engnell, 'a correct patternism is *the* correct comparative method' ('The Science of Religion', in *A Rigid Scrutiny*, 25).

61. Engnell, 'The Science of Religion', esp. 24f.

62. Cf. note 28 above. This may be easier said than done, however; see below.

63. G.W. Ahlström, 'Heaven on Earth—At Hazor and Arad', in *Religious Syncretism in Antiquity*, ed. B.A. Pearson (Missoula: Scholars Press, 1975), 67-83.

64. Ahlström, *Psalm 89*, 85-89.

65. Cf. G.W. Ahlström, 'King Jehu—A Prophet's Mistake', in *Scripture in History and Theology*, ed. A.L. Merrill and T.W. Overholt (Pittsburgh: Pickwick Press, 1977), 46-69; and idem, 'House of Wisdom', 74-76.

66. Ahlström, 'Syncretism and Religious Parties' (1973), 372-77; idem, 'Some Comments on Bright's "History of Israel"' (1975), 236-41; idem, review of *Imperialism and Religion: Assyria, Judah, and Israel in the Eighth and Seventh Centuries B.C.E.* by M. Cogan, in *JAOS* 98 (1978), 509-11; idem, review of *Von Sinuhe bis Nebukadnezar* by A. Jepsen, in *Theologische Literaturzeitung* 104 (1979), cols. 726-28; idem, review of *Royal Dynasties in Ancient Israel* by T. Ishida (1980), 70-74; idem, review of *The Tribes of Israel* by C.H.J. de Geus, in *JNES* 39 (1980), 322-25; and idem, review of *The Early History of Israel* by R. de Vaux, in *JR* 61 (1981), 337-38.

67. Ahlström, 'Some Comments on Bright's "History of Israel"', 241.

68. G.W. Ahlström, 'Solomon, the Chosen One', 93-110.

69. G.W. Ahlström, 'Was Daviḍ a Jebusite Subject?', 285-87.

70. G.W. Ahlström, 'King Jehu—A Prophet's Mistake', 46-69.

71. G.W. Ahlström, *Royal Administration and National Religion in Ancient Palestine* (SHANE 1; Leiden: E.J. Brill, 1982). This volume is an outgrowth of a doctoral seminar on 'Sanctuaries and Priesthoods' at Chicago in 1975, and was further developed in a Presidential address to the Mid-West Section of the Society of Biblical Literature and the Middle West Branch of the American Oriental Society in 1978. This is also the inaugural volume of a new series by E.J. Brill, Studies in the History of the Ancient Near East (SHANE).

72. G.W. Ahlström, 'Another Moses Tradition', *JNES* 39 (1980), 65-69, esp. 67.

73. G.W. Ahlström, 'Judges 5:20f. and History', *JNES* 36 (1977), 287-88. Cf. also the version in *SEÅ* 41-42 (1976–1977), 5-9.

74. G.W. Ahlström, 'Where did the Israelites Live?', *JNES* 41 (1982), 133-38.

75. Cf. G. Widengren, 'Early Hebrew Myths and Their Interpretation', in *Myth, Ritual, and Kingship*, ed. S.H. Hooke (Oxford: Clarendon Press, 1958), 155.

76. Cf. Engnell, 'Traditio-Historical Method in Old Testament Research', in *A Rigid Scrutiny*, 5.

77. G.W. Ahlström, 'Wine Presses and Cup-Marks of the Jenin-Megiddo

Survey', *BASOR* 231 (1978), 19-49.

78. G.W. Ahlström, 'Is Tell ed-Duweir Ancient Lachish?', *PEQ* 112 (1980), 7-9; and idem, 'Tell ed-Duweir: Lachish or Libnah?', *PEQ* 115 (1983), 103-104. The latter is a rebuttal to G.I. Davies, 'Tell ed-Duweir = Ancient Lachish: A Response to G.W. Ahlström', *PEQ* 114 (1982), 25-28.

79. G.W. Ahlström, 'An Israelite God Figurine from Hazor', *Orientalia Suecana* 19-20 (1970–1971), 54-62; and idem, 'An Israelite God Figurine, Once More', *VT* 25 (1975), 106-109. The latter is a rebuttal to O. Keel, 'Genesis XXXV 4b', *VT* 23 (1973), 336.

80. Ahlström, *Aspects*, 17.

81. G.W. Ahlström, 'Was God the God of Tell ed-Duweir?', *PEQ* 115 (1983), 47-48.

82. Cf. Ahlström's, observations in *JAOS* 98 (1978), 509 n.1.

83. G.W. Ahlström, 'An Archaeological Picture of Iron Age Religions in Ancient Palestine', *Studia Orientalia* (forthcoming). In the meantime, cf. W.C. Dever, 'Material Remains and the Cult in Ancient Israel: An Essay in Archaeological Systematics', in *The Word of the Lord Shall Go Forth: Essays in Honor of David Noel Freedman*, ed. C.L. Meyers and M. O'Connor (Winona Lake, Ind.: Eisenbrauns, 1983), 572-87.

84. E.g., Ahlström, 'House of Wisdom', 74-76; idem, 'Another Moses Tradition', 65-69; and idem, 'Where did the Israelites Live?', 133-38.

85. Ahlström, in *JAOS* 98 (1978), 511. See also, Ahlström, 'Some Comments on John Bright's "History of Israel"', 236-41.

86. G.W. Ahlström, 'Kung Manasse, en religiös traditionalist', *Religion och Bibel* 38 (1979), 9-11; idem, *Royal Administration*, 75-81. Cf. also his observations in *JAOS* (1978), 509-11.

87. Cf. G.W. Ahlström, 'Exodus from Cyprus', *ASOR Newsletter* 7 (January, 1975), 1-4.

PSALM 81.6a
Observations on Translation and Meaning of One Hebrew Line

P.A.H. de Boer

Introduction

Although the meaning of the separate words in Psalm 81.6a is more or less certain, there exists much uncertainty about the sentence as a whole, which is apparent in the diversity of translations and explanations. The ancient versions, the expositions in midrashim, commentaries of former and recent centuries, and translations and explanations of the last century all reflect learning and ingenious imagination. They affirm at the same time how difficult it is to reach a reasonable understanding of the sentence. Any new study of the line bears out this statement, and my attempt, a re-evaluation of some old ideas together with some new ideas, will be no exception.

Psalm 81.6a has two parts, עדות ביהוסף שמו and בצאתו על ארץ מצרים, which belong together. I will begin with the second part.

Psalm 81.6aβ

The verb יצא connected with Egypt (מצרים) recalls the post-biblical phrase for the exodus from Egypt, the deliverance from bondage, יציאת מצרים. The usual construction is the verbal form followed by the preposition מן. However, Psalm 81.6 reads על. Driver assumes that the Hebrew preposition also means 'from', on the ground of Keret II vi 9, where he translates '(the plague) from (*'al*) (his head)'.[1] This assumption is shared by M. Dahood and used in several places, including our Psalm verse.[2] The Greek and Latin versions read ἐκ and *de*, but it seems improbable that their *Vorlage* read מארץ. Rather, it seems probable, I think, that they took ἐκ and *de* in agreement with the standard connection which also occurs in the Book of Psalms (e.g., Ps. 114.1, בצאת ישראל ממצרים). Their explanation of the whole line leads to the equating of Joseph with Israel, the people that went forth from Egypt. The Syriac version considers the preposition על

similar to אל and ל, as is the case in a late phase of the Hebrew language. The Aramaic paraphrase seems to suggest a reading of 'to go from (gaol)' as well as the meaning 'to rule over', probably hinting at Genesis 42.6 (שליט על). This version does not equate Joseph with the people but considers Joseph to be a personal name, the hero of the Joseph story in the book of Genesis.

Besides Psalm 81.6, the phrase יצא על occurs in Genesis 19.23; Zechariah 5.3; Genesis 41.45; Esther 1.17; and 2 Kings 24.12. Genesis 19.23 causes no problems to the translators. The Greek rendering is ἐξέρχομαι ἐπί, the Syriac and Aramaic is *npq ʿl*, and the Latin is *egressus est super*. Modern translations present the same picture, 'to rise on' or 'upon', 'se lever sur', and 'aufgehen über'.

In Zechariah 5.3 the prophet Zechariah likens the sallying forth of the curse over the country to the rising of the sun on the land. It is translated as ἐκπορεύομαι ἐπί, *npq ʿl*, *egredior super* in the ancient versions, and also, without any essential difference, in the modern translations as 'to go out over', 'se répandre sur', and 'ausgehen über'. The curse goes out over the face of the whole land and is a power executing judgment.

In Genesis 41.45b the phrase is ויצא יוסף על ארץ מצרים. The Syriac and Aramaic version both maintain the preposition, rendering *npq ʿl*. The Targum adds explicatively, *šālîṭ* (cf. Gen. 42.6), which can be compared with the addition in the Aramaic rendering of Psalm 81.6. The Greek version, with the exception of the Mss O $^{-58\ 72}$ and Syh, where ἐξέρχομαι ἐπί is the rendering of יצא על, does not translate the phrase. The Vulgate reads *egressus ad*.

Those who omit Genesis 41.45b, in agreement with the Septuagint, consider the phrase a miserable variant of v. 46b ('and Joseph went out from the presence of Pharaoh, and went through all the land of Egypt') or think that the phrase found its place in the text by accident. Some scholars emend the text, reading ויסב את[3] or ויצו.[4] Ibn Ezra's explanation, 'Joseph's name went out, i.e. he became famous', may have influenced Vatablus and his school in Paris, where we find *egressus est fama Ioseph* explained with *notus fuit in tota illa regione*.[5] Related ideas are found in Ehrlich's *Randglossen*, 'die Verbreitung von dessen (Joseph's) Kunde' and in Speiser's Genesis commentary, 'And Joseph became known through the land of Egypt', with the note that the precise meaning is uncertain.[6] Both of these interpreters draw upon Esther 1.17, where the term יצא על in their opinion means 'to spread, become familiar'. Soferno's explanation (sixteenth century),

'to go out as ruler', is related to Paulus Fagius' paraphrase *suâ pompâ procedebat, cum magnificentia quadam et majestate declarabatur esse princeps*. A similar explanation can often be found in modern translations and commentaries. Ed. König translates, 'und Joseph zog aus über das ganze Land Ägypten dahin',[7] and explains the sentence with, 'Dasz er "auszog" (45b) bedeutet soviel wie: als seinen Herrschaftsbezirk einnehmen (vgl. das *yāṣā'* in Ps. 19.5 und 81.6)'.[8] The Dutch Bible Society Translation (1951) adds between brackets 'als heer', as ruler ('en Jozef ging uit, [als heer] over het land Egypte'). L. Köhler translates, with a question mark, Genesis 41.45 and Psalm 81.6 with 'Verfügung haben über', W. Baumgartner tranlates יצא as '(z. Inspektion) bereisen', and L. Segond's translation has 'partir pour visiter'.[9] The New Jewish Translation (1967) reads, 'Thus Joseph emerged in charge of', the NEB (1970) has 'And Joseph's authority extended over', and the Roman Catholic Dutch Translation (1975) reads 'Zo kreeg Josef volmacht over'. The meaning of על as 'over' can be found in the renderings of the Revised Version (1884), the Revised Standard Version (1951) ('went out over') and in de Fraine's commentary (1963) ('trok uit over').

In this discussion of ways of translating Genesis 41.45b, B. Jacob's major work on the book of Genesis must be mentioned separately.[10] Jacob's commentary appeared in 1934 and is often neglected in the discussion. He translates literally, referring to Genesis 19.23, 'und Joseph ging auf über das Land Ägypten'. His explanation starts from Joseph's elevation, and, in his opinion, Pharaoh's gift, the daughter of the priest of the sun-god to be Joseph's wife, confirms the supposition that Joseph received the title of king, 'sun of the country'. To support this, Jacob refers to Amarna letter 107, ln. 9. Jacob may have overestimated the influence of the idea of the rising of the sun in his explanation of the pericope. However, his emphasis on the royal position, Joseph awarded with royal power, seems right. Recently, Jacob found an enthusiastic supporter in E.I. Lowenthal, who renders Psalm 81.6a as 'And Joseph shone forth over the land of Egypt'.[11]

Other scholars translate the phrase יצא על with 'partir pour'[12] or 'put circuler au'.[13] The meaning of the preposition (על) is then considered to be equal to אל and ל, as is true of a later phase of the language.

The phrase under discussion should be considered, in my opinion, in relation to the decrees of the Pharaoh concerning Joseph. Joseph

becomes the second in command in the country. He is to be in charge of the food rationing and is to be the ruler of the whole country. The symbols of his authority are a signet ring of the Pharaoh, royal garments, a golden chain, a chariot (second to the king's chariot), and a special salutation to be used by the population; moreover, he has the absolute right of say concerning the people, a new name, and the daughter of a priest as his wife. V. 45b now summarizes this inauguration by the statement, 'Thus Joseph rose over the land of Egypt', i.e. became Egypt's highest authority next to the Pharaoh. Furthermore, the passage is part of a story. The narrator put words in Pharaoh's mouth in order to explain the reason for Joseph's unbelievable elevation. Joseph is a man with the spirit of the Gods, and with that quality he is the most discreet and most wise man in his empire (vv. 38, 39). Redford, in his thorough study of the Joseph story, speaks rightly of an investiture with a 'superlative tenor'.[14]

As was noted above, both Ehrlich and Speiser support their explanation of the phrase in Genesis 41.45b by referring to Esther 1.17. Esther 1.17 in the Septuagint reads διηγεῖσθαι, ('to describe, set out in detail'). The Syriac and Targumic renderings of the text maintain the sense of the Hebrew phrase with *npq ʿl*. The Vulgate, however, reads *egredior ad*. Vatablus' *divulgabitur* and Drusius' *fama facti* are paraphrases which are commonly found in modern translations and explanations as 'become known to', 'sera connue de', and 'bekannt werden'. Nevertheless, some translators keep to the original sense of יצא.[15] It is evident, however, that all consider the preposition על equal to אל or ל, an opinion more easily accepted because of the late date of the book of Esther.

There are, I think, some arguments for an explanation of the scene in the story of Esther in accordance with the literal meaning of the phrase יצא על, as I have tried to demonstrate in the texts treated previously. Queen Vashti's refusal to come to the party of her husband, the king, became not only *known* to all women but became *authoritative* in the world of the women. Therefore, it seems possible to paraphrase the Hebrew text as follows: 'her word will rise over them', i.e. will take the lead and set the fashion in the world of women. Hence, as a translation of the passage (v. 17) I venture to present, 'For the queen's word will exercise an influence over all women, causing them to look with contempt upon their husbands, since they will say, "King Ahasuerus commanded Queen Vashti to be brought before him, but she did not come"'.

The ancient versions of 2 Kings 24.12 render יצא על with 'to go to', ἐξέρχομαι ἐπί, *npq l*, and *egredior ad*. The Targum maintains the preposition על but considers it to be equal to אל or ל. Nicolaus of Lyra (fourteenth century) and a Lapide (seventeenth century) explain *dedidit se in potestatem victoris* by referring to the prophet Jeremiah's advice to leave the city and to go out to the Chaldeans (Jer. 38.2; *ex concilio Jeremiae*). The rendering of 'to go unto' is widely used in our translations and commentaries.[16] Other scholars go one step further and translate 'to give oneself up to'.[17] Josephus' tendentious use of the pericope in *The Jewish War* (VI.103ff.) furnishes proof of the antiquity of this application of the text. He speaks of

> a splendid example before you in Jeconiah, king of the Jews. He, when the king of Babylon made war on him through his own fault, of his own accord left the City before its capture, and with his family submitted to voluntary imprisonment rather than surrender these holy places to the enemy and see the House of God go up in flames. For that he is celebrated by all Jews in the sacred record, and memory, flowing through the ages eternally new, passes him on to future generations immortal.

Josephus mentions this as a splendid example, even if it were dangerous. He adds, 'But I can guarantee your pardon from the Romans'.[18]

It is certain that in Josephus' time the preposition על had been used interchangeably with the prepositions אל and ל. Josephus' usage of 2 Kings 24.12 was based on his personal attitude in the turmoil of his days. *The Jewish War* is doubtless the apology of a man who has placed himself on the Roman side. Therefore, I doubt whether we can use his rendering of Jehoiachin's conduct as an argument for an emendation of the Hebrew text (אל instead of על) or for a late date of the text, thus ascribing it to the period in which the language did not distinguish על from אל.[19] One need only note that in 2 Kings 18.18, 31, יצא אל has been used for 'to go forth to'.

It is beyond the purpose of this article to discuss text and meaning of the passage 2 Kings 24.8ff. It suffices here to recall that there are differences between the traditions preserved in Kings, Jeremiah, and the Babylonian texts about the conquest of Judah and Jerusalem by the Babylonians. Moreover, the text in 2 Kings 24 is evidently a composite from different sources. V. 10 speaks about the servants of Nebuchadnezzar, and v. 12 speaks about the king himself. In addition, Klostermann has already called attention to the disparity in time

between vv. 12a and 12b.[20] It seems possible to assume that 'the king of Babel', mentioned without the name of the king, originally meant 'the servants of Nebuchadnezzar', corresponding with v. 10. The confusion in the passage gives occasion, I think, for supposing more than one attack on the city.

If we stick to the meaning of יצא על, as demonstrated above, it is possible to translate and explain 2 Kings 24.12a as follows: 'And Jehoiachin, Judah's king, had a stronger position than Babel's king' (i.e. the Babylonian attacker). Judah's king rose over, or had the power to oppose, the unit of the Babylonian army. Accordingly, this first line of the verse would then be a reminiscence of an unavailing attack. A later attack, however, led to the downfall of the town and the deportation of the king, his family, his servants, and his officials.

We return to the phrase בצאתו על in Psalm 81.6. The Greek and Latin versions understood Israel to be the subject of the infinitive construct of the verb יצא. The name Israel could indicate the Northern tribes, or perhaps only Ephraim and Manasseh, the 'sons of Joseph', or all the twelve tribes. The Syriac and Aramaic versions, however, consider Joseph, the hero of the story in the book of Genesis, as the subject of the phrase. This interpretation is based on Genesis 41.45 and appears already in Midrash Rabbah on Numbers 7.49. The Midrash explains the particular spelling of Joseph's name (see discussion below) as an indication of Joseph's divine power. Through this power Joseph knew the seventy languages, which is the midrashic explanation of Psalm 81.6b. Simeon de Muis, whose commentary on the book of Psalms appeared in Paris in the first part of the seventeenth century, observes about the argument that Joseph is the subject of the phrase, 'Non omnino rejicienda est haec opinio'. Muis himself, however, considers God to be the subject, an opinion borrowed from David Kimḥi. This explanation occurs also in other commentaries and may date back to the Midrash Rabbah on Qoheleth. There, the Joseph of the story in Genesis belongs to the string of persons who have been pursued and therefore are chosen by God, 'And God seeks what has been driven away [= pursued]' (Eccl. 3.15). Joseph was pursued by his brothers, and the Holy One, blessed be He, chose Joseph, and, as it is said, 'He appointed it in Joseph for a testimony, when He went forth against the land of Egypt' (Ps. 81.6).[21] A similar line of thinking frequently occurs in recent times.[22]

From an early date until the present, references to God's punishments of the Egyptians (Ex. 7–12) have been used to explain Psalm 81 as the establishment of a feast in remembrance of the deliverance of the people of Israel from bondage in Egypt. Exodus 11.4 is often the basis for the main argument, but the Hebrew phrase used in it is יוצא בתוך מצרים, not יצא על. Also, Isaiah 19, which describes the coming of Israel's God to disturb Egypt, does not use our term but the verb בוא. And Exodus 15.25, which concerns the establishment of rites (חק ומשפט) connected with the miracle of sweetening the bitter water of Marah, does not contain a remembrance of God's sallying forth against Egypt or any word akin to Psalm 81.6.

In the Hebrew Bible we do not have the idea of God sallying, or going forth against Egypt, or going to Egypt; and Joseph, the hero of the story in Genesis, did not go to Egypt of his own free will but was taken down to that country (Gen. 39.1; cf. 37.28). He never sallied forth against Egypt. If we respect the Hebrew text, it is inevitable, in my opinion, to translate the phrase of Psalm 81.6 (בצאתו על ארץ מצרים) with 'his rising over the land of Egypt'. The sentence is directly alluding to the story of Joseph, to Joseph's power, and to the authority awarded him by the Pharaoh (Gen. 41.45).[23]

A further consideration in Psalm 81.6 is the preposition ב in בצאתו. It has generally been rendered as an adjunct of time (*cum, when, quand, da/als*); however an exception is A.R. Johnson's rendering. Johnson thinks that the preposition in this context has a causal force. He translates, 'Because of His sallying forth against the land of Egypt'. The rendering *because* is to express the great divine act of salvation—according to him the theme of the whole poem—'in freeing the Hebrews from the tyranny of their Egyptian taskmasters and their recognition of the fact that as a result He and He alone should be the God of Israel'.[24] Apart from this argument derived from the context, demonstrated in a masterly fashion but in my opinion not wholly convincing, there are other reasons to prefer the causal meaning of the preposition in the phrase under consideration. In syntactical studies little or no attention is given to a causal meaning of ב. Gesenius-Kautzsch has one line in a paragraph on *beth instrumenti*, 'cf *bĕ propter*, Gen 18.28, 19.16'.[25] Joüon observes that the preposition rarely has 'une nuance proprement causale'. In this context he mentions the cases of Genesis 19.16, Exodus 16.7, and 2 Chronicles 28.6.[26] However, more places such as Genesis 29.20 and Exodus 16.8 can be added. The construction of these phrases is

similar to Psalm 81.6, which is, in my opinion, another case of the same syntactical feature. I base my supposition that Joseph, the hero of the story in Genesis, is the subject of the phrase צאתו על ארץ מצרים on the fact that Joseph was elevated to and entrusted with a position of ultimate authority over Egypt by the Pharaoh who saw that the future of his throne and his country depended on the man who possessed divine power, and whose shrewdness and wisdom were beyond everyone else's. The election of Joseph by God in Psalm 81 goes hand in hand with the purport of the story-teller. This brings us to the first part of v. 6a.

Psalm 81.6a

Joseph's adventurous career in Egypt from prisoner to acting king, from eliminated member of the clan of Jacob to rescuer and indisputable head of the family, is in my opinion the source of the second part of the Hebrew line under discussion. The names of Joseph's Egyptian sons are Palestinian names, and outside the story there is not the slightest trace of an Egyptian origin or Egyptian sojourn for the tribes of Ephraim and Manasseh. The silence of the rest of the Hebrew Bible on the subject of the Joseph story has but some late exceptions.[27] One of the exceptions is Psalm 81.6 of which Redford cautiously observes that the text is 'obscure'. He states, 'the antiquity of a "statute" (an allusion to the covenant relationship?) is somewhat connected with Joseph's "going forth over Egypt" (cf. Gen. 41.46—read v. 45)'.[28]

The first part of v. 6a is עדות ביהוסף שמו. The phrase שים ב has been rendered in the ancient versions with 'to place in'. However, the Targum reads 'to place upon'. The midrashic explanation, 'because he did not draw near to the wife of his master', is an allusion to the Joseph story, in agreement with the Aramaic rendering of the second part of the line. The idea of commitment, a precept laid on and considered obligatory, is implied in עדות, μαρτύριον, *testimonium*, and *sāhădûtā'*. The term is used in different contexts and hence we find a variety of renderings such as testimony, decree, law, solemn charge, and, recently, covenant, pact. Covenant or pact is proposed by J.C. Greenfield in a study on 'Stylistic Aspects of the Sefire Treaty Inscriptions'. Greenfield reads the Sefire inscription I A line 7 as *śmw 'dy' 'lhn*, and observes, 'This idiom is the equivalent of Akkadian *ādē šākānū* and Hebr. *śym 'dwt*. An interesting example is *'edut biyhōsēp*

śāmō, "He (God) made a covenant (or pact) with Joseph (= Israel)" (Ps. 81.6)'.[29] Neither Greenfield nor Fitzmyer, who adopted the meaning of Greenfield, give arguments for their translations of שים עדות ב with 'conclude a treaty (or pact) with'.[30]

Psalm 78.5 (ויקם עדות ביעקב ותורה שם בישראל) seems to be close to Psalm 81.6. The two verbs in Psalm 78.5 used in parallelism mean 'to erect, establish', probably originally to erect stelae, stones, tablets, commemorative columns, with texts recalling names or precepts. Remembrance does not mean only sentiments about the past, bygone events, deceased persons. Memorials also serve to speak of everlasting authority.[31] עדות and תורה are also synonyms in Psalm 78.5. תורה in this poem has been used in parallel with 'the words of the deity' (v. 1), the story of God's wonderful acts (vv. 4, 7 and cf. vv. 12ff.), and ברית, covenant (v. 10). If vv. 5 and 6 of Psalm 81 belong together, עדות is parallel to חק and משפט (v. 5). Among the acts of God to be commemorated, Psalm 78 mentions the wonders of the splitting the sea (Ex. 15.8) in v. 12 and the signs, the plagues 'set in Egypt' (שם במצרים) in v. 43. Here, the plagues are given in an order different from the tales in Exodus. The Joseph story, however, is not quoted in the long poem. The exclusive Judean character of the poem is evident in the lines, 'He rejected the tent of Joseph; he did not choose the tribe of Ephraim; but he chose the tribe of Judah, Mount Zion which he loves' (vv. 67f.).

The phrase שים ב occurs nearly a hundred times in the Hebrew Bible. Almost everywhere the preposition in this phrase is a *beth locale*.[32] In a number of places *beth locale* is followed by a geographic name, the name of a town, a country, or a land.[33] In Psalm 78.5 the names Jacob and Israel are used in connection with the phrase שים ב. So, names of a tribe or a land wherein a decree is promulgated, or a law enacted, can be rendered with 'the territory of . . .'

The reading ביוסף (ביהוסף) is unique in the Hebrew Bible. Greenfield's position would lead to an emendation (שָׂם instead of שָׂמוֹ or to a reading of שָׂמוּ, which makes the subject a plural form, the Gods. His explanation of the name Joseph as synonymous with Israel may be right but leaves open whether Israel indicates the northern kingdom, or all the tribes of Israel, the dream of some post-exilic circles (see Jer. 31 and Ezek. 27) and post-biblical literature.[34] In addition, there are cases where the name Jacob is similar to Judah. As an example, the wording of Psalm 77.16, the redemption of 'the sons of Jacob and Joseph', suggests a reference to the southern and northern kingdoms.

Furthermore, in Psalm 80.2 the phrase 'O shepherd of Israel' is paralleled by 'thou who leadest Joseph like a flock', and both terms indicate the same God. Finally, according to style and purport, both poems belong to post-exilic times.

Given this post-exilic setting, one must also remember that the idea of Joseph's right of primogeniture (1 Chron. 5.1, 2) has been handed down in history with a Judean revision. However, this passage in Chronicles still preserves evident traces of an existing hope of restoration of the independence of the people with the House of Joseph as its centre. The Joseph story itself can be characterized as an encouragement during hard times. The story might have had its origin and setting in circles which nourished hopes of a restoration with the name Joseph as the focus and with aspirations entertained through pictures of an imaginary past. Most of the Hebrew texts, collected and revised, enlarged and rewritten, in order to encourage the remnants of the people in Palestine and elsewhere, have a Judean tendency, but there are scattered fragments wherein non-Judean, sometimes even anti-Judean, ideas are preserved. It seems certain, I think, that the Joseph story of the book of Genesis belongs to these texts, albeit that the composition we have also has a Judean recension.[35]

The word order of the phrase in Psalm 81.6, Joseph before the verb, must indicate the emphasis on the name. Combining this with the frequently used phrase שים ב, leads to a rendering, 'It was in (the territory of) Joseph that he instituted it as a testimony'. Moreover, instead of 'the territory of', 'the house of' or 'the flock of' or 'the tent of' can be substituted by those who do not like the supremacy of the Judean leaders and reject an equation of Joseph with Judah.

The object of the verb שים, described in v. 5 as a statute for Israel, as an ordinance of Jacob's God, will be חג. Eventually it will become יום חג (v. 4), the cultic feast, a day of loud singing, shouting, and music produced by several instruments (vv. 2-4). It is probable, therefore, that v. 6a belongs to the preceding verses (2-5).

Conclusion

The translation and explanation presented here, partly reconstructed out of the history of our discipline and partly the outcome of some new research and some imagination, also solves, I think, the riddle of the unique spelling of the name Joseph. The attempts to read in the

spelling of the name *yhwsp* the divine name *yāh* or *yāhû*, in order to express God's reward for Joseph's piety and moral firmness (midrash on Lev. 17.3), or Joseph's divine wisdom made public in his ability to understand foreign languages (midrash on Num. 7.49), do not convince modern interpreters.[36] The assumption of text corruption by pure accident may not be out of the question, but an explanation on the ground of a reasonable hypothesis is preferable. I venture to suppose that the spelling is intentionally manufactured to suggest an alternative reading, namely Jehudah instead of Joseph.

The unique spelling would then be an indication of Judean opposition to those believers who nourished hope of a restoration of the House of Joseph. It would be at the same time an example of the narrow horizons of the scribes and those who recited the sacred songs in later times. A real radical change was no longer allowed. Moreover, a confusion about the meaning of the second part of the line, a remembrance of the Exodus story instead of the Joseph story, might have been of some influence.

Finally, it is worth remembering that a part of the people expected that the Messiah would come forth out of the House of Joseph. Psalm 81.6 could have been a witness of their faith.

NOTES

1. G.R. Driver, 'Hebrew Roots and Words', *Die Welt des Orients* I, 5 (1950) 406-415; idem, *Canaanite Myths and Legends* (Edinburgh: T. & T. Clark, 1956); and idem, 'Review of A.L. Oppenheim, editor-in-chief, *Assyrian Dictionary*, vol. 16, 1962, pp. xv, 262, Oriental Institute, University of Chicago', *JSS* 9 (1964) 346-50.

2. M. Dahood, *Psalms*, 3 vols (AB 16, 17, 17A; Garden City, New York: Doubleday, 1966-1970). In vol. 3, p. 396, Dahood gives a summary of all the cases.

3. J. Olshausen, *Die Psalmen* (Leipzig: S. Hirzel, 1853), 340.

4. See E. Kautzsch, *Die Heilige Schrift* (Tübingen: J.C.B. Mohr, 1910); *Die Heilige Schrift* (Zürich: Zwingli-Verlag, 1907-1931), known as the 'Zürcher Bible'; and recently, A. van Selms, *Genesis* (Nijkerk: G.F. Callenbach, 1967), vol. 2, p. 215.

5. Quotations from biblical commentaries prior to 1700 are taken from M. Polus (Matthew Poole), *Synopsis Criticorum* (Frankfurt: B.C. Wustii, 1694).

6. A.B. Ehrlich, *Randglossen zur hebräischen Bibel*, vol. I (Leipzig: J.C. Hinrichs, 1908); E.A. Speiser, *Genesis* (AB 1; Garden City, New York: Doubleday, 1964), 311, 314.

7. Why König and other scholars (see J. de Fraine, *Genesis* [Roermond en Maaseik: J.J. Romen, 1963]; the New English Bible [1970]; and Dutch Roman Catholic Translation [1975]) add 'ganze' ('whole') remains unexplained.

8. Ed. König, *Genesis* (Gütersloh: C. Bertelsmann, 1925), 697.

9. Ludwig Koehler and Walter Baumgartner, *Lexicon in Veteris Testamenti Libros* (Leiden: E.J. Brill, 1953); W. Baumgartner, *Hebräisches Lexikon zum Alten Testament* (Leiden: E.J. Brill, 1974); and L. Segond, *La Sainte Bible* (Paris: La Société Biblique, 1953).

10. B. Jacob, *Das erste Buch der Tora, Genesis* (Berlin: Schocken Verlag, 1934).

11. E.I. Lowenthal, *The Joseph Narrative in Genesis* (New York: Ktav Publishing, 1973).

12. Roland de Vaux, *La Sainte Bible* (Paris: Editions du Cerf, 1956) (= La Bible de Jérusalem); and E. Osty, *La Bible, Genèse* (Paris: Editions Rencontre, 1970).

13. E. Dhorme, *La Bible* (Paris: Bibliothèque de la Pléiade, 1956).

14. D.B. Redford, *A Study of the Biblical Story of Joseph* (SVT 20; Leiden: E.J. Brill, 1970), 87.

15. A. Barucq in *La Bible de Jérusalem* (1956), has 'ne manquera pas de venir à la connaissance de'; and W. Dommershausen, *Die Estherrolle* (Stuttgart: Katholisches Bibelwerk, 1968), 31, has 'wird zu (aller Frauen) hinausgehen'.

16. The following are a more or less representative sample: O. Thenius, *Die Bücher der Könige* (Leipzig: Weidmann, 1849), 449; A. Klostermann, *Die Bücher Samuelis und der Könige* (Nördlingen: C.H. Beck, 1887), 486; I. Benzinger, *Die Bücher der Könige* (Freiburg: J.C.B. Mohr, 1899), 197; The Leiden Translation (1899); O. Eissfeldt, 'Die Bücher der Könige', in *Die Heilige Schrift des Alten Testaments*, ed. E. Kautzsch and A. Bertholet, 4th edn (Tübingen: J.C.B. Mohr, 1932); and The Dutch Bible Society Translation (1951).

17. Revised Standard Version (1951); de Vaux, *La Bible de Jérusalem* (1956); John Gray, *I and II Kings*, 2nd edn (London: SCM, 1970), 759f.; and E. Osty, *Premier et Deuxième Livre des Rois* (Paris: Rencontre, 1970).

18. Quotations from Josephus are from G.A. Williamson (trans.), *Josephus, The Jewish War* (rev. edn, Harmondsworth, Middlesex: Penguin Books, 1970), 333.

19. Josephus' examples, which he borrows from the Bible, are wholly determined by the author's aim in writing his *The Jewish War*, which was certainly not a historical, and still less a textual, piece of work.

20. Klostermann, *Die Bücher Samuelis*.

21. This translation is that of A. Cohen, *Ecclesiastes* (London: Soncino Press, 1939; 3rd edn, 1961).

22. See the marginal readings in Revised Version and the Revised Standard Version. See also F.M.Th. Böhl, *De Psalmen* (Groningen: J.B. Wolters, 1947); the Dutch Bible Society Translation (1951); R. Tournay and R. Schwab in *La Bible de Jérusalem* (1956); J.P.M. van der Ploeg, *Psalmen* (Roermond en Maaseik: J.J. Romen, 1973); E. Osty, *Le Livre des Psaumes*, 2nd edn (Paris: Rencontre, 1971); the Dutch Roman Catholic Translation (1975); and A.R. Johnson, *The Cultic Prophet and Israel's Psalmody* (Cardiff: University of Wales Press, 1979), 6ff.

23. The Latin texts of this verse (Ps. 81.6) are often literal renderings of the Hebrew. See Johannes Calvin's commentary of 1557, where he has *quum egressus est super terram Aegypti* (A. Tholuck [ed.], *Ioannis Calvini in Librum Psalmorum Commentarius* [Berlin: Apud Gustavum Eichler, 1836]); and Benedictus Arias Montano's commentary (1573) where he has *cum exiret ipse super terram Aegypti*. However, these literal renderings do not mean their explanation is acceptable. Ed. König in his explanation of Genesis (1925) mentions 'more or less taking as his dominion, compare Ps. 19.5 and 81.6', but he forgot this observation in his later (1927) commentary on Psalms. See König, *Genesis*, and idem, *Die Psalmen* (Gütersloh: C. Bertelsmann, 1927), 332f.

24. Johnson, *Cultic Prophet and Israel's Psalmody*, 6ff.

25. E. Kautzsch (ed.), *Wilhelm Gesenius' Hebräische Grammatik*, 24th edn (Leipzig: F.C.W. Vogel, 1885), 366ff. In a more recent edition it reads under *beth pretii*, a variety of *beth instrumenti*, 'also, in a wider sense, Gn 18.26, *bĕ* for the sake of; 1 S 3.13' (E. Kautzsch [ed.], *Gesenius' Hebrew Grammar*, trans. A.E. Cowley, 28th edn [Oxford: Clarendon Press, 1910; 16th repr., 1982], 380).

26. P. Joüon, *Grammaire de l'hébreu biblique*, 2nd edn (Rome: Pontifical Biblical Institute, 1947), §170j, p. 524.

27. As an example one can observe Ecclus 49.15 where it says, 'and no man like Joseph has been born'. For studies of such post-biblical material, see Redford, *Study of the Biblical Story of Joseph*, p. 249, n. 2. In addition, add H.W. Hollander, 'Joseph as Ethical Model in the Testaments of the Twelve Patriarchs' (Ph.D. dissertation, University of Leiden, 1981).

28. Redford, *Study of the Biblical Story of Joseph*, 248-49.

29. J.C. Greenfield, 'I. Stylistic Aspects of the Sefire Inscriptions', *Acta Orientalia* 26/27 (1965f.), 9.

30. J.A. Fitzmyer, *The Aramaic Inscriptions of Sefire* (Rome: Pontifical Biblical Institute, 1967), 12f., 16f., 32, 60.

31. See P.A.H. de Boer, *Gedenken und Gedächtnis in der Welt des Alten Testaments* (Stuttgart: W. Kohlhammer, 1962).

32. Once it is a *beth temporale*, 1 Kings 2.5, 'to shed blood in time of peace'.

33. Aram-Damascus (2 Sam. 8.6; 1 Chron. 18.6); Edom (2 Sam. 8.14);

Shechem (Josh. 24.25); Bethel and Dan (1 Kings 12.29); Samaria and Damascus (1 Kings 20.34); Jerusalem (2 Kings 21.4); and Egypt (Ex. 15.26; Jer. 32.20; Ezek. 15.26; Ps. 78.43).

34. Note that the Sefire inscriptions translated with 'to conclude a treaty' (I A line 7, I B line 6) are not constructed with the preposition *beth*. Thus, they cannot be taken as a similar phrase to the Psalm text.

35. See Redford, *Study of the Biblical Story of Joseph*, 244ff.

36. Elision of the *he* from an original form *yĕhōsēp* is not a plausible theory. H. Bauer and P. Leander, *Historische Grammatik der hebräischen Sprache des Alten Testaments* (Halle: M. Niemeyer, 1918-22), 229, explain *yĕhûkal* (Jer. 39.3) as a 'Neubildung' of an original form ('Ursemitisch') *yûkal* (Jer. 38.1), being the usual form in biblical times. Both forms of the same name are *hapax legomenon*. *yōsēp*, however, is a regularly used form, even outside the Joseph story. For obvious reasons Bauer and Leander do not adduce the spelling *yĕhōsēp* as an example of an original, vanished form of the name Joseph.

THE ROLE OF ELIHU IN THE DESIGN OF THE BOOK OF JOB

Norman C. Habel

I. *Introduction*

Elihu is an enigma. He is regularly viewed as an annoying anticlimax, a lame intruder or a pious appendix. His speeches are considered redundant, his language prosaic and his theological contribution minimal. Attempts to redeem him as the spokesman for a mature poet are problematic.[1] Efforts to find him a locus within the literary design of the book remain tentative.[2] The approach of most interpreters has been to focus on the content rather than the context of Elihu's arguments, his thought rather than his function in the structure of the Joban narrative. They have tended to ask the question, 'What is Elihu saying that is new or profound?', rather than, 'What is Elihu doing that is significant in the design of the book?' Theological rather than literary considerations have usually prevailed.

It is my contention that Elihu plays an important role in the design of the book of Job. His role deserves attention, even if he were to utter nothing new or profound—though this is not the case. An exploration of Elihu's role in the literary design of Job demands that we hear three voices, (a) that of Elihu himself as a character and speaker, (b) that of the narrative designer of the book of Job, and (c) that of the poet as critic. The first voice provides us with Elihu's self-understanding as portrayed by the poet of the Elihu passages; the third voice is the poet's verdict on Elihu's role, a voice heard through the innuendos, subtleties and tone of the Elihu speeches; and the second voice is that of the overall designer of the structure of Job as a text, the one who integrated Elihu into the narrative plan of the book. The voice of the poet and the voice of the designer may belong to the same person, but that is a matter for later consideration.

I count it a privilege to include this study in a volume honoring Gösta Ahlström whose writings and lectures have been a model of

meticulous scholarship for me and others over the years. My study takes into account two major concerns of Gösta: methodology in interpreting ancient texts and the role played by figures such as the גבירה in Israelite society. This analysis of the Elihu speeches explores the significance of discerning the function of such roles in the literary design of a text.

II. *What Role Does Elihu See Himself Playing in the Joban Story?*

For Elihu the dispute between Job and his friends has reached an impasse. In his opening apology (ch. 32) he maintains that he has patiently analyzed the arguments of the friends and found them wanting (32.11-14). More specifically he alleges,

> To you I paid close attention,
> but behold there is no arbiter for Job,
> no one among you to answer his charges. (32.12)

The terms מוכיח 'arbiter', and עונה 'answerer', are technical juridical terms.[3] Recent research into the legal terminology of Job has exposed the significance of the forensic metaphor as one dominant feature of the book.[4]

The arbiter (מוכיח) is an official of the city gate who presides over civil cases and recommends a resolution for disputes[5] (cf. Is. 9.21; Amos 5.10). In Job the hiphil of the verb יכח can mean 'plead or defend a case' (13.3, 6, 15; cf. 23.7), or 'arbitrate between conflicting parties' (16.21). Job longed for such an arbiter who could mediate between himself and God:

> If only there were an arbiter between us,
> one who could lay his hand on both of us. (9.33)

Is Elihu suggesting that since no arbiter has arisen to resolve Job's case and pronounce a verdict, he will assume that role? Apparently so!

The עונה, which literally means 'one who answers', is apparently used here as a synonym of מוכיח. In a forensic context the verb ענה can mean 'to testify' (Ex. 23.2; Num. 35.30; Deut. 19.16, 18; Job 15.6), 'to respond to a summons' (Jer. 7.13; Job 9.16; 13.22) or 'to answer charges' (Job 9.14-15). Elihu is clearly not responding to a summons or answering charges against himself. He is a third party whose 'answer' is an attempt to resolve a dispute between others. Nor is he testifying on behalf of Job or the friends in their dispute. The

parallelism between עונה and מוכיח, in the tight chiastic construction of this verse, indicates that these terms are probably used here as synonyms or complementary legal terms.[6] In this context, therefore, ענה apparently means to adjudicate, resolve or decide a dispute. Elihu, it seems, is the self-designated 'adjudicator' of Job's case.

As the potential arbiter Elihu castigates the friends for abdicating their responsibility in the dispute and leaving the resolution of Job's case to God.

> How can you say,
> 'We have found wisdom!
> Let El, not a mortal, refute him.' (32.13)

He chides the friends for their inept attempts to refute Job (32.14), and laments the crisis created by the absence of anyone capable of 'answering' and thereby resolving the case (32.15-16). In the face of this critical situation Elihu asserts his intention to 'answer' the dispute with his own arguments and verdict (32.17, 20). Elihu justifies his role as arbiter by appealing to his inner wisdom (32.8), his meticulous scrutiny of the arguments (32.11) and, above all, his impartiality (32.21-22). Job 32 is thus the apology of Elihu for assuming the role of arbiter. In the speeches which follow, however, Eilhu is far from impartial. He clearly sides with El and his answer becomes a case for the defense of his God.

Elihu begins his work as arbiter by summoning Job to appear before him. Using the traditional juridical summons formula he cries,

> Now hear my arguments, Job,
> and give ear to my every word. (33.1)

The 'words' which Elihu pronounces are here the decisions (cf. Deut. 17.9) and arguments he presents rather than the 'charges' of the plaintiff or defendant (as elsewhere, 9.14; 33.13). Elihu orders Job to appear before his 'judge' and prepare a defense.

> Refute me if you can.
> Prepare your case before me. Take your stand. (33.5)

The hithpael of the verb יצב is often used in the sense of appearing publicly before an authority figure such as a king (cf. 1.6; Ex. 9.13). Thus Elihu assumes the posture of the ranking official who has the right to call Job before him for a civil trial.

After citing the plea of Job as defendant (33.8-11), Elihu declares that Job is clearly wrong and that he, Elihu, is ready to prove it (33.12a). Central to Job's case is the claim that God is inaccessible in a civil court of law and thus never 'answers' the counter-charges of those he has falsely accused. Elihu's answer is a brilliant but unsympathetic legal manoeuvre. God speaks eloquently, argues Elihu, but in ways that Job does not hear; he provides a trial, but not in the city gate where Job would prefer it. Litigation for Job is a 'trial' (ריב) in his bones, an indictment by pain (33.19). His body is itself the court for his case with God. Elihu closes his opening court speech by summoning Job to defend himself before a decision is pronounced and he is instructed in the truth (33.31-33).

Elihu's first speech as arbiter is addressed to Job (ch. 33). His second speech, however, is directed to the assembled court (ch. 34). Three times this assembly is summoned in forensic terms (vv. 2, 10, 16). Its members are to serve as judges who test arguments just as the palate 'tastes' food (v. 3). 'Taste' is that special ability of discernment expected of elders in authority (cf. 12.20). Elihu invites this legal assembly to assist him in the process of determining justice in Job's case.

> Let us determine ourselves what is justice.
> Let us judge between us what is defensible. (34.4)

The court is expected to confer with Elihu as its spokesman and concur with him in the pronouncement of a verdict (vv. 34-37). The wise man of the court is here designated 'one who hears' (שמע, v. 34), a term which may mean 'judge', or in this case 'one who concurs in judgment'.[7] Elihu is the arbiter who presents the decisive arguments before the court and appeals to the assembled elders to support his decision.

Job 34 is clearly a trial speech before a public assembly. The claim of Job as defendant is announced at the outset of the trial. El, contends Job, has deprived Job of litigation and therefore of justice (vv. 5-6). Elihu's 'answer' to Job is that El could not possibly be guilty of perverting justice (vv. 10, 12, 17) and that Job's demand for civil litigation is quite improper:

> Indeed, it is not for a mortal to set a time,
> to come before El in litigation (משפט). (v. 23)

Job cannot expect a civil suit with the God of heaven as the plaintiff.

Elihu, however, is willing to oblige and judge Job's case in the absence of God. Elihu, quite evidently, rules in favor of God and against Job. Job is then given the opportunity to admit his mistakes and ask for instruction from his enlightened arbiter (vv. 31-33).

In his final speech Elihu turns from addressing the claims of Job and his friends directly, to a public defense of God (chs 36-37).

> Bear with me a little and I will convince you.
> For there are still the arguments on Eloah's side.
> I will glean my knowledge from far afield;
> I will prove my Creator innocent. (36.2-3)

This defense includes a series of appeals to Job to move beyond the confession of his mistakes to a forthright response of praise (36.24) and wonder (37.14). Job is reminded that thunder is yet another mode of divine communication which he ought to heed as an answer (37.2-5). Elihu concludes his speeches with a challenge to Job to defend himself by doing the impossible, that is, by supplying the human words needed to conduct a public legal suit against God. Elihu has performed his role as arbiter in the accepted human mode of his society. If Job can indicate another way, let him demonstrate his method or capitulate to Elihu's verdict.

> Educate us in what we should say to him!
> We cannot prepare a case in the dark.
> Can he be informed when I would press charges?
> Does a mortal testify when confused? (37.19-20)

As the spokesman of the court he announces the futility of pressing a civil suit against the invisible God. The only acceptable response of humans is to fear him, since he does not fear them—no matter how wise they may be (37.23-24). Job ought therefore to accept Elihu's trial as a surrogate for a civil suit with God himself present to press charges.

III. *What Role Does Elihu Play in the Design of the Book?*

It needs to be recognized, from the outset, that two distinct disputes develop and interact in the main cycle of Joban discourses. The first is between Job and his friends, the second between Job and his God. These disputes, in turn, are set against the prose background of the celestial dispute between Yahweh and Satan at an assembly of the divine council.[8]

The dispute between Job and his companions arises when they fail to fulfill their roles as friends. Their designated role as 'friends' was to console and sustain Job in his tragedy (2.11-13),[9] but, according to Job, they fail miserably (6.14-30). Their proper task was to support and defend Job against the accusation of Shaddai. Job, however, stands alone without a friend or advocate (19.13-27). He appeals for compassion from his former friends, but none is forthcoming (19.21). The three companions gradually abandon their role as friends and become biased disputants with Job about the meaning of his condition. Their dialogue is transformed into a dispute with each party defending a personal or traditional interpretation of Job's situation and his accusations against God. The three companions thus assume a role similar to that played by the 'friends' in the Babylonian Theodicy; their betrayal of the role of a 'friend' proper, however, is exposed by Job himself.

As disputants in a wisdom debate, the friends assume that Job's plight is itself the evidence of divine charges against Job for specific wrongdoings. His afflictions are his indictment; there is no need for a trial. The traditional nexus between suffering and sin governs their argumentation. Progressively they accuse him of blatant transgressions which he has refused to confess (11.6; 15.5-6; 22.4-7), and confront him with elaborate portrayals of the ways and fate of the wicked man.

Job, in his role, moves first from being a pious and submissive patriarch in the prose frame, to a cursing, despairing sufferer at odds with his God and his friends (chs 3-8). With chapters 9 and 10, Job contemplates more than laments; he explores the possibility of having an actual civil suit with God where the charges of God are formally laid and Job has an opportunity to prove his innocence publicly (9.2-4, 14-21; 10.2; 13.3-23). A central theme in Job's dispute with God is the absence of litigation whereby justice can be achieved for falsely accused mortals like Job. Job longs for a formal trial where he has an arbiter, advocate or mediator to guarantee justice in court (9.32-35; 16.18-22; 19.23-27). But a trial with God present as the opponent seems a virtual impossibility (9.2-4). Job, moreover, does not trust his God to play fair in any civil suit that might be arranged (9.14-16).

> If I summoned him to court and he responded
> I do not believe he would listen to my plea. (9.16)

Nevertheless, Job pursues the idea of litigation (13.3) and castigates

his friends for arguing God's case for him (13.7-8). Job demands that God emerge from hiding, summon Job to appear formally in court and present him with a suit of particulars (13.22-23).[10] Job claims that he has been cast in the role of an indicted defendant before God without any formal charges having been laid or litigation permitted. Job is ready to persist in his demand for a civil suit, even if he dies in the attempt (13.15).

The key to the legal metaphor in Job is, as Dick has demonstrated, Job's final oath (ch. 31).[11] Job abandons his dispute with his friends and concentrates on a direct confrontation with God as his legal opponent (איש ריב). These closing verses are no pious plea for help, but a formal demand for a public trial before an appropriate judge or arbiter. Job's official plea reads,

> Oh that someone would conduct my hearing.
> Here is my signature. Let Shaddai answer me.
> Let my adversary at law draft a document. (31.35)

Job's oath formalizes his trial request and terminates any pre-trial discussions with his friends. Nothing short of an actual public trial, with a writ from the adversary, an arbiter designated and an appropriate court assembled, would now suffice.

At this point Elihu enters to hold a public hearing on Job's case. The narrator makes it quite clear that all of Job's claims (דברים) have been presented (31.40c), and that the pre-trial dispute with his friends has proved fruitless (32.1). Elihu now appears as the arbiter for the trial. He justifies his role, summons Job to a hearing, specifies the charges, appeals to the assembly of local judges, pronounces a verdict and defends the justice of God. Elihu's speeches are therefore both logical and significant in the sequence of the Joban story. Elihu provides the civil trial which Job had demanded; none of the friends were willing to pursue the case after Job had pronounced his oath (32.3-5). Elihu does not believe it necessary or proper for God to appear in person at a trial set by humans (34.23-24). God has provided ample testimony to his position through various modes of indirect communication including dreams, visions, illnesses, the cult and natural phenomena.

Elihu, it seems, represents the position of a younger generation who believes that God no longer appears or speaks directly as in the heroic past. Nor does Job, in Elihu's opinion, have the heroic capacity to force the *deus absconditus* to manifest himself in all his

visible or audible splendor. Job is found guilty by Elihu's court of local sages. The advent of Yahweh in the tempest, therefore, comes as a shock finale. His 'answer' from the whirlwind is the unexpected response of the hidden God, the audible word of the hitherto silent opponent (40.6-14). Significantly, Yahweh does not appear at this point as the judge, but as Job's opponent. He interrupts the human trial with a challenge to his human accuser. The defence of a human arbiter like Elihu pales into insignificance before the speeches of the Almighty himself. The heroic era is not past; the Creator does intervene when no human spokesman can do justice to his majesty. Heroes like Job can still force him to leave the clouds.

The speeches of Elihu are thus a logical conclusion to the legal metaphor which climaxes in the oath of Job (ch. 31). First, the trial conducted by Elihu corresponds to the earthly dispute of the friends with Job; these discourses represent the appropriate, orderly and humanistic patterns of wisdom tradition. Second, the response of Yahweh from the tempest corresponds to Job's dispute with his hidden God and his formal appeal for a civil trial. Third, the ironic verdict in the prose epilogue (42.7) draws both disputes together and pronounces a final decision. God finally speaks as judge. His celestial verdict declaring Job in the right has its counterpart in the earthly verdict of Elihu finding Job in the wrong.

IV. *What is the Poet's Verdict on the Role of Elihu?*

Is it only the narrative designer's creative talent that makes the Elihu speeches seem relatively insignificant by strategically locating them between Job's formal demand for litigation and Yahweh's overwhelming 'answer' from the whirlwind? Or is there also within the text of the Elihu's speeches themselves evidence of the poet's judgment about the role and position of Elihu? It is my contention that in his portrait of Elihu's role as arbiter, the poet also suggests indirectly that Elihu is a fool, albeit a brilliant young fool, but nevertheless a fool. In so doing he renders an implicit verdict on what Elihu is doing and saying. The three friends are judged publicly by Yahweh after the speeches are concluded (42.7). Elihu, however, is permitted to condemn himself from his own mouth.

The subtle characterization of Elihu as a fool demands that we clarify the various categories of fool relevant to the wisdom context of Job.[12] Of these, four deserve special consideration.

a. *The simple fool* (פתי) is naive, uninitiated in the world of knowledge. Wisdom and folly appeal for his allegiance (Prov. 9.4, 16). The simple fool, who is the target of wisdom instruction (Prov. 1.4) and the concern of wisdom herself (Prov. 1.22), is easily led astray (Prov. 1.32). He is gullible and lacking in prudence (Prov. 1.4; 7.7). As a youth Elihu could be excused for being untutored or simple. Elihu, however, claims to have intuitive knowledge of the truth. He is no ignoramus; he possesses understanding within himself (32.7-8, 17-18). He is a self-taught man.

b. *The churlish fool* (נבל) tends to be associated with the lower classes of society (Prov. 30.22), outcasts who scorn the ways of the righteous (Ps. 39.9; 74.22). Job considered it the height of disgrace that he should be mocked by such scum (30.8-9). He insulted his own wife by calling her a member of this class (2.10). Elihu obviously does not belong in this category; he is identified as a reputable youth whose family pedigree is known to those present (32.2).

c. *The stupid fool* (כסיל) is characterized in some detail in Prov. 26.1-11. This figure is a social failure; public honor and status are quite inappropriate for him to bear (Prov. 26.1, 8; 19.10). This type of fool is incorrigible and unteachable; the only language he understands is the rod (Prov. 20.3; 26.3). To entrust him with a responsible task is to court disaster (Prov. 26.6). He is a tragedy in the eyes of his parents and a frustration to any wisdom teacher (Prov. 10.1; 17.24). He is a social reject, whose opinions are not worthy of public attention (Prov. 14.7-8).[13]

The friends never accuse Job of being a *stupid fool* nor would they identify Elihu as one, even though all parties seem to ignore his speech. Elihu, for all his pomposity, is not a recalcitrant ignoramus; he may be presumptuous but he is not a social disgrace (cf. Prov. 3.35).

d. *The brash fool* (אויל) seems to be distinguished from the *stupid fool* (כסיל), though in some contexts the terms are used almost interchangeably. In Prov. 26.12 the *stupid fool* is clearly differentiated from the 'man who is wise in his own eyes'. This latter figure, in several passages, seems to be synonymous with the *brash fool* (אויל). He has intelligence but lacks wisdom.

> The way of the *brash fool* is right in his own eyes,
> but the wise man heeds advice. (Prov. 12.15)

The vexation of this fool is immediately apparent; he blurts out his

feelings (Prov. 12.16). Unlike the wise who store their knowledge, brash fools are garrulous (Prov. 10.8, 14). They are untactful babblers characterized by unfruitful speech.[14] According to Eliphaz, these fools let their passions get the better of them (Job 5.2). Only when the brash fool keeps silent may he be counted wise (Prov. 17.28). Because he is wise in his own eyes, the fool rejects the approved path of wisdom and the instruction of his father (Prov. 1.7; 15.5).

This opinionated fool is also portrayed as impulsive and hotheaded (Prov. 12.15; 14.17, 29). He is cast in the same mold as the hot-tempered speaker in the Egyptian Instruction of Amenemope.[15] The hot head and the cool mind are ideal types outlined in this wisdom text; the former is impulsive and outspoken, the latter composed and patient. These Egyptian types are described by McKane,

> There is strength in silence and weakness in garrulity or inept speech. The man who talks and talks will not be taken seriously by anyone, but the silent man inspires respect and fear. Wrangling and loss of temper in debate are flaws, and the instinctive hot rejoinder should be avoided. The tranquil man will not speak if he suspects that his judgement has been impaired by the high temperature of the debate.[16]

The portrait of the brash, overconfident, self-educated, articulate fool (אויל) is quite distinct from that of the *stupid fool* who would be incapable of participating in such dialogue and who only understands the rod. By contrast it is the talk of the *brash fool* that is his rod (Prov. 14.3); he suffers from the verbal spasms of his own tongue. Wisdom is not merely a matter of intellect, but also of instruction in prudence, composure and restraint.

Elihu fits the image of the brash but intelligent young fool, even though he does not formally bear the epithet אויל. He is passionate, prone to anger, self-opinionated, assertive and loquacious. He claims no instruction in wisdom, no knowledge from tradition, no guidance from esteemed teachers. He contends that as a human being he possesses wisdom within himself and is therefore capable of discerning the truth without instruction from others. Because he has breath from Shaddai, he intuitively knows the correct word to speak. Elihu can instruct himself from the resources of the spirit within; he is wise in his own eyes (33.33). Ironically Elihu advises his friends to be silent while he teaches them wisdom, when it is characteristic of the wise that they are silent (33.33; cf. Prov. 17.27-28).

It is not necessarily a new idea to consider Elihu a fool of some kind. As Davidson and Toy write,

> The ancients for the most part passed a very severe judgment on Elihu: he is a buffoon, a boastful youth whose shallow intermeddling is only to be explained by the fewness of his years, the incarnation of folly, or even Satan himself gone a-mumming.[17]

Whedbee interprets Elihu as the *alazon* (Gk., 'buffoon') in the book of Job as in a comedy.[18] Our concern here is not to employ the classical model of Greek comedy to locate Elihu, though this may be a valid literary approach, but to discern evidence from the text itself as to some of the ways in which Elihu is portrayed as a fool within his role as arbiter.

A comparative study of the language used in Elihu's apology and the opening banter employed in the previous discourses, discloses that Elihu has appropriated much of the terminology used in a derogatory way by the previous speakers. Yet Elihu takes these terms in a positive sense; he does not seem to appreciate the nuances and niceties of the earlier debating style. The most striking example of his clumsiness appears in 32.17-18. The poet, with wry humor, has Elihu spout the sarcastic language of Eliphaz as if it were inspired truth. Eliphaz has said, in a snide remark to Job,

> Should a wise man *answer* with a 'mind of *wind*',
> and *fill* his *belly* with an east wind? (15.2)

That is precisely what Elihu plans to do (32.17-18). He intends to *answer* according to the dictates of his own *mind* or knowledge, because he is *filled* with personal discourses and has a *belly* bursting with *wind*. Unwittingly Elihu characterizes himself as a windbag and a fool in the very terms Eliphaz has used to taunt Job. Elihu is thus identified as a brash fool—intelligent, respectable, and articulate, maybe, but nevertheless a fool.

The fact that this opening apology so depicts Elihu does not render his speeches irrelevant. They reflect the position of a typical self-taught member of the community, the individual who claims to know wisdom intuitively and to discern truth by interior contemplation.

Thus, the characterization of Elihu as a brash fool is evident not only in the explicit statements about his hot temper in the prose introduction (32.1-5), but also in the rhetoric of the apology (ch. 32) and the arrogant assertions made at various points in his subsequent speeches (e.g. 33.5-7, 31-33; 34.2-4, 31-33; 36.2-4; 37.19-20). Among

the various examples of Elihu's arrogant folly, two are singled out for comment. In 33.4-7 Elihu summons Job to appear before him as judge. By this manoeuvre, Elihu has taken up the challenge Job extended to his God (in 13.17-23). There Job had established two conditions for his trial with God: that his 'terror' not overwhelm him in an earthly court, and that his 'hand' not oppress him as a human being (13.21). Elihu, with the sarcastic arrogance of a man playing the role of God, asserts,

> My terror need not dismay you;
> My hand need not oppress you. (33.7)

Then, when Elihu marshalls his arguments for the defense of El, he claims,

> Truly, my arguments are flawless;
> Before you stands a master of reasoning. (36.4)

The idiom rendered 'master of reasoning' (תמים דעות) could be translated 'master mind', a presumptuous claim to say the least. For later, when Elihu describes God, he speaks of him as תמים דעים, a 'master mind' or 'perfect in knowledge' (37.16). The two expressions are virtually identical and suggest that Elihu is claiming a mind with capacities and insights as perfect as those of his God. Foolish indeed!

Elihu the arbiter, therefore, for all his rhetorical skills and orthodox teachings, is made to look foolish by the style, language, and placement of his speeches. Rather than considering Elihu's speeches the reflection of a mature theology from the pen of the Joban poet, I would interpret them as the articulate and orthodox, but inevitably ludicrous, efforts of a self-taught younger generation which claims to know the ways of God intuitively and presumes to judge traditional beliefs about the heroic ways of the past. The inclusion of these speeches is a significant feature of the legal metaphor developed within the narrative design of the book and a deliberate ironic anticlimax in the plot progression. Through Elihu we are led, as a perceptive audience, to discern the folly of ignoring a mythic answer to the heroic human cry and of reducing God to his predictable orthodox forms of communication and *modus operandi*.

V. *Authenticity and Focus*

The preceding analysis challenges the cogency of many traditional arguments against the authenticity of the Elihu speeches. These

arguments focus on structural, stylistic, linguistic and theological features of the text.[19] Elihu's words are reduced to the inept but orthodox comments of a later interpreter.[20] An extreme position is enunciated by Pfeiffer: 'The author of the speeches of Elihu was so shocked, after reading the Book of Job in its original form, that he felt the urge to write a refutation which he placed in the mouth of a character which he invented, Elihu'.[21] Some critics believe these speeches may have been the work of the author of the poems of Job, but that they are misplaced,[22] or reflect a later stage of the author's thinking.[23] Irwin even finds in chapters 32-33 the author's notes for the original ending of Job.[24] In general, however, the Elihu speeches are belittled because they 'lack the afflatus of poetic inspiration which the author of the dialogue exhibits'.[25]

The structural argument emphasizes the intrusive and inappropriate nature of the Elihu speeches in their present location. They are thought to detract from the *dénouement* of Yahweh's oration from the tempest. However, given the development of the legal metaphor as integral to the literary structure of the book, the Elihu speeches are, as indicated above, effective and significant moments of the work precisely at this juncture. Elihu establishes the appropriate human court to arraign Job in direct response to his oath demanding a formal hearing (ch. 31). The speeches of Yahweh intrude as the unexpected divine answer which raises the dispute between Job and God to a new level of significance. Yahweh's speeches are the ultimate in one-up-manship!

The absence of any reference to Elihu in the prologue or epilogue of the book is also considered a serious problem by some scholars. They argue that Elihu should have been applauded or denounced as the friends were (42.7). But Satan, who from a logical standpoint ought also to have been put in his place, is likewise ignored in the epilogue. It is typical of the Joban narrator that he introduces and discards his characters as appropriate to the plot. In Job 32.1-5, which is also part of the narrative framework of the book, the designer introduces Elihu with the same precision as he did the three friends (2.11-13) and Job himself (1.1-5). By not appearing in the prologue, Elihu, in his role as arbiter, is clearly distinguished from the three earlier companions in their roles as friends.

Arguments about style are notoriously subjective and those adduced against the Elihu speeches are no exception. These speeches are said to lack imagination, rhythm and vividness; they are derided as

monotonous, repetitive and prolix. Even if we recognize that Elihu's speeches do not match the grandeur of Yahweh's address from the whirlwind (chs 38-41), such difference in style does not *per se* imply irrelevance or inauthenticity. If we accept the voice of poet as both creator and critic of Elihu's speeches, their distinctive style is understandable. The role and characterization of Elihu as both a self-appointed legal official and a brash verbose youth justify an appropriate style. Were Elihu to sound as magnificent as Yahweh, their roles would be less clearly differentiated. As it is, Yahweh obviously upstages Elihu.

Other features of Elihu's style are his repeated use of direct or indirect quotations from the preceding dialogue between Job and his friends, and the technique of addressing Job by name. These features, rather than being evidence of secondary authorship, are quite appropriate for one playing the role designated for Elihu. Those arraigned as witnesses or defendants are regularly summoned by name (cf. Mic. 6.1-5). The quotation of speeches by a defendant or a witness is fitting court procedure (cf. Jer. 26.9, 18).

The linguistic evidence regarding the Elihu speeches is hotly disputed and extremely ambiguous. The major arguments, as surveyed by Gordis and Snaith,[26] will not be rehearsed here. To a large extent the use of certain pronouns, terms, or divine names in preference to others is a reflection of a particular style appropriate to a new character. As a representative of the younger generation, Elihu tends to speak with a different 'accent' and use fewer of the 'archaisms' typical of Job and his aged companions. In view of Snaith's study[27] there is no convincing evidence to show that Elihu's speeches are replete with late Aramaisms; most alleged Aramaisms reflect the Northwest Semitic heritage of the materials.

The major objection of scholars to the theological and philosophical content of the Elihu speeches tends to focus on their apparent lack of originality. They are said to offer no new or significant contribution to the problem of suffering raised by Job's condition and cries. But this objection fades once we recognize that the 'answer' of Elihu is not first and foremost theological, but forensic and dramatic. As part of the narrative design, Elihu presents the case of the earthly arbiter, the 'answer' of orthodoxy from a trial context. It is Elihu's role as much as his message that is significant in the plot of Job.

Given this forensic framework of Elihu's speech, the substance of his arguments are far from trite repetitions of ideas presented by the

friends. Each speech is directly related to specific allegations of Job and attempts to provide alternative answers. The following outline summarizes the major themes of Elihu's five speeches in their juridical context:

32 The *apology* of Elihu for intervening as the qualified, impartial arbiter ready to handle Job's case.
33 The *summoning* of Job to a formal hearing and a refutation of Job's charge that El does not answer human claims; an argument presenting the diverse but indirect ways El communicates to redeem people.
34 A *trial speech* addressed to a legal assembly; a refutation of Job's claim that El perverts justice; a verdict is announced for Job.
35 A *defense* of El's transcendence emphasizing that he does not 'answer' human claims in person.
36-37 A *defense* of El's just governance by interpreting how he works through affliction and manipulates the weather to his purposes.

Of special significance is Elihu's continuing theme that El communicates and answers humans indirectly through a diversity of modes, from dreams to thunder and from the cult to the sickbed. Direct revelations of God are neither necessary nor fitting. Furthermore, not only does Elihu emphasize that affliction is educative but also that suffering is itself a trial which Job is experiencing within himself (33.19). Nor does Elihu merely repeat the theme of El's justice; rather, he emphasizes the negative side of the question and focuses on El's guiltlessness, that is, the impossibility of El being guilty before a court of justice, whether human or heavenly (34.10-30). His defense of El's righteous cosmic order answers Job's hymn to the lord of chaos (12.13-25) in a lyric style that overshadows the speeches of the friends, but is itself overshadowed, in turn, by Yahweh's own majestic word from the whirlwind (note especially 36.24–37.18). Kraeling wrote that the 'Elihu speeches would be extremely impressive if it were not for the fact that they collide with the speeches of God'.[28] Elihu's words, he continued, would provide an appropriate termination of the book if there were no intervention of Yahweh. Indirectly, therefore, Kraeling supports the argument of this paper. The Elihu speeches are designed to be a formal orthodox

ending, an ending overridden by an answer from Yahweh that lies beyond the canons of orthodoxy and the strictures of an earthly court.

VI. *Conclusion*

I argue, therefore, that three distinct voices are discernible through a literary and rhetorical analysis of Elihu's speeches: that of Elihu as a speaker in the role of arbiter, that of the creative narrator who designed the present work, and that of the poet as critical theologian. These three voices complement each other in the portrayal and placement of Elihu, and seem to be the work of one imaginative author. In the poet's portrait of Elihu's self-understanding, he is an arbiter who justifies his role, summons Job to a hearing, addresses a legal assembly with appropriate trial speeches and defends El as Lord of justice. As critic, the poet cum theologian offers obvious clues to render his verdict on Elihu's role and reasoning as being that of a brash fool, in spite of his intellect and orthodoxy. These two roles of Elihu as arbiter and fool might appear to be at odds with each other were it not for their strategic place in the design of the Joban narrative structure.

The design of the plot of Job in its present form has Elihu appear at that point where Job has called for a formal public hearing in which God is asked to present his case. The three friends remain silent at that juncture; they have played their roles in the pre-trial precedings. Elihu enters as the arbiter who establishes an appropriate earthly court for hearing and deciding Job's case. After he has concluded his proceedings, God unexpectedly answers from the whirlwind and thereby makes Elihu look insignificant and foolish. He is rendered so insignificant, in fact, that most scholars wish to eliminate him as unworthy of the Joban poet. It is a significant contribution of the book, however, that the formal effort of Elihu to reflect the orthodoxy of a younger generation and to defend God anew *in absentia* is revealed as folly, a judgment which is also reflected in the poet's presentation of Elihu's style and rhetoric. Yahweh's self-manifestation through a voice from the tempest is of a different order than those indirect modes of manifestation which Elihu had cited in God's defense. The ancient heroic style of God is not *passé*. When God reveals himself, he not only challenges his opponents to rethink their charges, but makes his most ardent supporters look foolish. Such is the fate of Elihu, the arbiter.

NOTES

1. R. Gordis, *The Book of Job* (New York: The Jewish Theological Seminary of America, 1978), 358, describes the Elihu speeches as 'the product of the poet's experience during a lifetime'; cf. p. 553.

2. J.F.A. Sawyer, 'The Authorship and Structure of the Book of Job', in *Studia Biblica 1978. I. Papers on Old Testament Themes, Oxford, 3-7 April, 1978*, ed. E.A. Livingstone (JSOTS, 11; Sheffield: JSOT Press, 1978), 253-57; J.W. Whedbee, 'The Comedy of Job', *Semeia* 7 (1977), 18-20; D. Robertson, *The Old Testament and the Literary Critic* (Philadelphia: Fortress Press, 1977), 47-53; J.W. McKay, 'Elihu—A Proto-Charismatic?', *ExpTim* 90 (1979), 167-71; S. Hemraj, 'Elihu's Missionary Role', *Biblebashyam* 6 (1980), 49-80; and H. Beeby, 'Elihu—Job's Mediator', *S.E. Asian Journal of Theology* 7 (1965), 33-54.

3. S.H. Scholnick, 'Lawsuit Drama in the Book of Job' (Ph.D. dissertation, Brandeis University, 1975), 227ff., 28, n. 41.

4. M. Dick, 'The Legal Metaphor in Job 31', *CBQ* 41 (1979), 37-50; J.B. Frye, 'Legal Language in the Book of Job' (Ph.D. dissertation, University of London, 1973); and J.J.M. Roberts, 'Yahweh's Summons to Job: The Exploitation of a Legal Metaphor', *Restoration Quarterly* 16 (1973), 159-65.

5. Dick, 'The Legal Metaphor', 46.

6. On *chiasmus* in Job see M. Dahood, 'Chiasmus in Job: A Text-Critical and Philological Criterion', in *A Light to My Path*, ed. H. Bream, et al. (Philadelphia: Temple University Press, 1974), 119-30.

7. Dick, 'The Legal Metaphor', 47.

8. Frye, 'Legal Language', also recognizes the importance of this dual discourse for interpreting the work.

9. N. Habel, 'Only the Jackal is my Friend: On Friends and Redeemers in Job', *Interp* 31 (1977), 227-36.

10. Dick, 'The Legal Metaphor'.

11. Dick, 'The Legal Metaphor'.

12. Cf. T. Donald, 'The Semantic Field of Folly in Proverbs, Job, Psalms and Ecclesiastes', *VT* 13 (1963), 285-92.

13. Donald, 'The Semantic Field', 287, concurs with this analysis and sees the כסיל as a more sinister figure than the אויל.

14. H. Cazelles, 'אויל', in *TDOT* 1, 137-40.

15. J.A. Wilson, 'Egyptian Inscriptions', in *ANET*, 421-24.

16. W. McKane, *Proverbs* (Philadelphia: Westminster Press, 1970), 107.

17. A.B. Davidson and C. Toy, 'The Book of Job', in *The Voice of the Whirlwind*, ed. R. Hone (San Francisco: Chandler, 1960), 99.

18. Whedbee, 'The Comedy of Job', 19f.

19. Cf. F. Andersen, *Job: An Introduction and Commentary* (London: Intervarsity Press, 1977), 50.

20. M. Pope, *Job* (AB 15; Garden City: Doubleday, 1973), xxviif.; and H.

Nichols, 'The Composition of the Elihu Speeches', *AJSL* 27 (1911), 11ff.

21. R. Pfeiffer, *Introduction to the Old Testament* (London: A. and C. Black, 1948), 673.

22. D.N. Freedman, 'The Elihu Speeches in the Book of Job', *HTR* 61 (1968), 51-59.

23. Gordis, *The Book of Job*.

24. W.A. Irwin, 'The Elihu Speeches in the Criticism of the Book of Job', *JR* 17 (1937), 37-47.

25. E. Kraeling, *The Book of the Ways of God* (London: SPCK, 1938), 139.

26. Gordis, *The Book of Job*, 546-48; and N.H. Snaith, *The Book of Job—Its Origin and Purpose* (London: SCM Press, 1968), 81.

27. Snaith, *The Book of Job*, 104ff.

28. Snaith, *The Book of Job*, 138.

THE REDACTIONAL HISTORY OF ISAIAH 5.1–10.4

Conrad E. L'Heureux

It is well known that the literature collected in the Hebrew Bible has undergone extraordinarily complex editorial procedures. This is especially apparent for the book of Isaiah. A major effort to untangle the redactional history of the Isaiah material is found in the work of J. Vermeylen.[1] In the present article we will summarize Vermeylen's understanding of the growth of Isaiah 5.1–10.4, evaluate the methodology which he employs, and propose some alternatives to the redactional history which he has reconstructed.

Vermeylen's analysis operates in terms of four major blocks of material: the Song of the Vineyard in 5.1-7; a series of woe sayings in 5.8-23 and 10.1-4; a five strophe poem with a repeated refrain in 9.7-20 and 5.24-30; and the Emmanuel Booklet of 6.1–9.6. The last three of these contain redactional elaborations of various lengths coming from different stages in the composition of the final work. We will first review Vermeylen's understanding of each of the four original units and then look at the way he thinks they came to be combined together.

I. *The Four Basic Units*

Vermeylen's most striking departure from conventional scholarship is his rejection of the authenticity of the Song of the Vineyard in 5.1-7. He characterizes the passage as a *rîb* (ריב) emanating from Deuteronomistic sources during the Exile, an origin he also claims for 1.2-20.[2] The oft-noted similarities with the parable of Nathan in 2 Samuel 12.1-12 pose no obstacle to this dating, for the latter passage too is classified as Deuteronomistic.[3] Finally, his study of 19 vocabulary items in the Song of the Vineyard leads him to the conclusion that the closest contacts in lexical stock are with the book of Jeremiah and other texts of the late monarchy and the Exile.[4]

The material in 5.8-23 and 10.1-4 is taken as a very old collection of woe sayings. Passages judged on literary critical grounds to be editorial expansions are eliminated and the saying of 5.8-10 is thought to have been originally positioned between 5.22-23 and 10.1-3. The original sequence, then, consisted of the following (the enumeration is mine):[5]

Section 1	Woe 1	5.11-13
	Woe 2	5.18-19
	Woe 3	5.20
	Woe 4	5.21
Section 2	Woe 5	5.22-23
	Woe 6	5.8-10
	Woe 7	10.1-3

This reconstruction is supported by the symmetry it produces: each of the two sections begins with a saying on drunkenness; the first section, dealing with human self-sufficiency, is arranged in order of decreasing length, whereas the second section, dealing with social injustice, is in order of increasing length. Furthermore, as is explained in greater detail below, the reconstruction of 5.8-10 as Woe 6 in the original series helps Vermeylen to explain how the Emmanuel Booklet got to be inserted between chapters 5 and 10.

In 9.7-10 and 5.24-30, Vermeylen, along with many other authors, finds the separated parts of what was originally a multi-strophe poem having the refrain, 'For all this, his anger has not abated and his hand is still outstretched' (9.11, 16, 20; 5.25).[6] He follows the view of E.J. Kissane that the poem originally was addressed to both the northern and southern kingdoms, but was modified editorially in 9.8 and 9.10 after the fall of Samaria in order to sharpen its focus against the North.[7] Eliminating once again what he takes to be later expansions, he comes up with the following reconstruction:

Strophe 1	9.7-8aα, 8b-11
Strophe 2	9.12-13, 16b
Strophe 3	9.17-20
Strophe 4	5.24a, 25
Strophe 5	5.26-27aα, 27b-29

Vermeylen's discussion of the Emmanuel Booklet (6.1–9.6) is long and detailed.[8] Since we are interested principally in the redactional procedures which led to its combination with other material in chapters 5 and 9–10, we can be fairly brief about the inner structure

of the Emmanuel Booklet itself. Vermeylen assigns the following passages to the original Isaianic document: 6.1-11; 7.3-17*; 8.1-6a, 7-8a; 8.11-14; 8.16-18. His reconstruction is very convincingly supported by a detailed study of the careful structure of the original document.[9] He identifies 7.20 as a very ancient interpretive addition.[10] During the first half of the seventh century, modifications in 7.8b and 8.6b-7a redirected material originally against Judah so that it appeared to be against Samaria. The same editor added glosses in 7.4b, 5b, 17b, 10b and, perhaps, the date in 7.1-2 which is based on 1 Kings 16.1, 5 or its source. This led to the insertion of third person references in 7.3, 10, 13 where Isaiah's autobiographical account originally had the first person. Possibly at the same time, 8.8b-10 and 8.15 were added, viewing the Assyrian invasion from the mythological perspective of the inviolability of Zion. Then 7.18-19 was added and a correction was made in 7.16.[11] A more significant editorial stage is reached with the insertion of the coronation hymn in 9.1-6a coming from the time of Josiah and identifying him as the Emmanuel. The hymn was joined to the preceding material with the help of 8.23aβ-b. The insertion of 7.15 may come from the same time. Then after the fall of Jerusalem, a Deuteronomistic redactor added 6.12-13bα connecting 6.11 with the fall of Judah. At the same time 8.19, 21-22 ascribed the misfortunes of Judah to cultic disorders. It is perhaps at this stage that 7.23-25 originated. Finally, the last modifications were made by the post-Exilic community which identified itself with the Emmanuel in 7.21-22. They believed that the promise was just beginning to be fulfilled and that much still lay in the future (9.6b). The remnant had now been converted (6.10b) and was the 'holy seed' (6.13bβ). Those who follow pagan practices of divination will perish (8.20), but those who are now in the dark will see the light (8.23aα).

II. *Redactional Combination of the Basic Units*

The following summary of the way in which Vermeylen describes the redactional combination of the four units discussed above will be most easily understood in reference to the diagrams of Figure 1. On those diagrams, a solid line indicates the changes which will be effected to produce the next stage of the process. Dotted lines point to transpositions which occurred to produce the given stage. The designation of the three steps as Stages A, B and C is my own way of

summarizing (and simplifying somewhat) the redactional history proposed by Vermeylen.

First, the Outstretched Hand Poem was made to apply against the northern kingdom by adding אפרים ויושב שמרון in 9.8 and רצין in 9.10.[12] This facilitated a rapprochement between this poem and the Emmanuel Booklet to which the former was appended. This procedure, of course, had to be later than the (Josianic) addition of 9.1-6a to the earlier form of the Emmanuel Booklet.[13]

Stage B resulted from the insertion of the combined Emmanuel Booklet and Outstretched Hand Poem into the series of woe sayings which themselves were already connected with the material in 10.5-14*, 27b-32, 33-34. This insertion Vermeylen dates to the time of the Exile.[14] The point at which the insertion was made was determined by the connection between 5.8-10 (originally Woe 6) and the culmination of Isaiah's vision in 6.11 which by now had already been expanded with the Exilic addition of 6.12-13bα.[15] This explains how Woe 7 got to be separated from the other six.

Two major changes led to Stage C. First, an Exilic redactor took Strophes 4 and 5 of the Outstretched Hand Poem and, reading them as references to the Babylonians, placed them as a fitting conclusion to the series of woe sayings.[16] Next, the connection between the Song of the Vineyard and Woe 6 (the key words are 'house[s]' and 'vineyard') led to the placement of this woe at the head of the list so that it would come right after the Song of the Vineyard which was now prefaced to the whole.[17] Finally, since the Outstrectched Hand Poem had been left without an ending when its last two strophes were moved, Woe 7 was converted into a concluding strophe by the addition of 10.4 which includes the refrain.

Other slight modifications (e.g., in 5.15-16 and 5.27) reflect even later post-Exilic reinterpretations.

III. *Critique of Vermeylen*

Vermeylen is especially vulnerable in his handling of the Song of the Vineyard in 5.1-7. The argument that its closest contacts in lexical stock are with texts dating from the late monarchy[18] results in part from the radical nature of his own literary-critical measures which reduce the corpus of Isaianic and other eighth-century prophetic texts to an extreme degree. In particular, his refusal to recognize the existence of the 'vine(yard)' or 'planting' imagery for Israel before the

seventh century[19] is most difficult to sustain. The vine(yard) image appears to be a specific development of the more general metaphor of the nation as Yahweh's planting, found as early as the Song of the Reed Sea in Exodus 15.17.[20] This text combines with Judges 9.7-15, the Jotham Fable, to indicate that the use of agricultural imagery in a political sense is very ancient, perhaps being at home in folk-wisdom contexts. The specific metaphor of the vineyard is found in Hosea 10.1-2, the authenticity of which is generally recognized and the diction of which is, in any case, hardly Deuteronomistic as Vermeylen would have it.[21] Finally, the use of the vineyard metaphor in Isaiah 3.14, a text which Vermeylen himself recognizes as authentic,[22] is conclusive. Granted, in 5.1-7 the vineyard is the whole community, whereas in 3.14-15 it consists only of the poor and so excludes the elders and princes who oppress them. Nonetheless, the fact that even here the vineyard is called 'my people' shows that it is not far from 5.1-7. It is only natural that the leaders are sometimes spoken of as separate from the community they lead while at other times they are treated as part of it. Such shifts in the application of a metaphor are frequent in the Bible as indeed all poetry. In the final balance, then, 3.14 argues *for* rather than *against* the Isaianic authorship of 5.1-7.

It is not only Vermeylen's late dating of the Song of the Vineyard in 5.1-7 which is problematical. His explanation of how it came to be joined to the other material in chapter 5 is also open to criticism. He believes the parable comes from a Deuteronomistic author of the exilic period. It would have been placed as a preface to the series of woes because of similarities of content.[23] Against this view it should be stressed that the contacts between the parable and the woes are many and close.[24] It is unlikely that a parable composed independently would have matched so well with a pre-existent series of woes. Much more likely, this specific set of woe sayings was assembled because they were appropriate as a spelling out of the intention of the Song of the Vineyard. Indeed, the complex consisting of the parable and the woes is a carefully crafted redactional whole which may go back to the prophet himself.

A second major objection to Vermeylen's reconstruction of the redactional history concerns the way in which he believes the Emmanuel Booklet (6.1–9.6*) came to interrupt the Outstretched Hand Poem and the series of woe sayings. First, in the late monarchy, the Outstretched Hand Poem would have been appended to the Emmanuel Booklet because of a common concern (at least in

their redactional form at that time) with Ephraim.[25] There is nothing intrinsically implausible about this, though one wonders how the three units (Emmanuel Booklet, Outstretched Hand Poem and Woe Sayings) could, in spite of their authenticity, have been preserved in separation from one another for approximately a century. What kind of traditioning process would have resulted in the independent handing on of a number of relatively short Isaianic pieces in isolation from the rest of the corpus? Be that as it may, it is the next step in the process which is most interesting.

During the Exile, according to Vermeylen, the combined Emmanuel Booklet and Outstretched Hand Poem was inserted into the pre-existent series of woes between what were originally Woe 6 and Woe 7, the point of insertion being determined by contacts between Woe 6 (now 5.8-10) and 6.11-13 (see above, n. 15). The suggestion is ingenious, but is it plausible? Even the concept of such a large unit as was constituted by the joined Emmanuel Booklet and Outstretched Hand Poem being an 'insertion' is slightly grotesque, especially when the base passage into which it is inserted is itself such a small one.[26] Even if one grants the contacts between 5.8-10 and 6.11-13, the two passages were separated by 10 verses! An 'insertion' after Woe 7 would have preserved the unity of the woes and increased the separation between 5.8-10 and 6.11-13 only negligibly. Finally, it is somewhat disturbing that such a major redactional step would be motivated by nothing more than a rapprochement between three verses of chapter 5 and three verses of chapter 6, without any significant consequences for the understanding of the larger whole which is being manipulated. It would be more convincing if we could find less superficial motivation for such redactional procedures—motivation related to new interpretative frameworks provided for the whole of the material in question rather than for just a few verses.

The next major step reconstructed by Vermeylen was the transposition of original Strophe 4 (5.24a, 25) and Strophe 5 (5.26-29) of the Outstretched Arm Poem to their present position. This was the work of a Deuteronomistic redactor who took these passages as references to the coming of the Babylonians in 587 BC. Introduced by לכן in v. 24, the transposed passaged seemed a fitting conclusion to the legal process initiated in 5.1-7 and elaborated in the woes. Chapter 5 then constituted a cohesive editorial whole. In the meantime, however, the Outstretched Hand Poem was deprived of an appropriate ending. Vermeylen proposes that this lack was made up by the addition of

10.4 to what was originally Woe 7, the new entity then functioning as the concluding strophe of the poem. Here one may object that if the tradents of the Isaiah material were so keenly aware that the Outstretched Hand Poem required a certain kind of ending, it becomes less likely that they would have destroyed its original integrity by dislocating Strophes 4 and 5. Could they not have looked elsewhere for material which would complete the pattern of chapter 5? In fact, Vermeylen has correctly discerned the redactional structure of this chapter, although, in my opinion, he has not grasped the full scope of the procedure which led to the placing of 5.24-29* in their present position.[27]

Finally, there is 5.8-10. Vermeylen had proposed this was orginally Woe 6, a suggestion he advocates because it ostensibly explains the point of insertion of the Emmanuel Booklet complex. The reasons he gives for their transposition to the head of the list of woes (above, n. 17) appear inadequate. When one considers the many contacts between the woes and the Song of the Vineyard (above, n. 24) it is not apparent why this rather than one of the other woes deserves to come closest to the parable. It also appears very unlikely, given the context of 5.8-10, that the word בתים could have been understood by a redactor as a reference to the two dynastic houses of Jerusalem and Samaria. In view of his difficulty in getting 5.8-10 back where it belongs, one might suggest he should have left it there in the first place.

My last criticism of Vermeylen is a more general one. Virtually no attention is given in his work to the poetic structure of larger compositional units. The demonstration that such analysis can produce results which are relevant to uncovering redactional history is the purpose of the next section of this paper, devoted to a study of the Outstretched Hand Poem.

IV. *Poetic Features in 5.25-29; 9.7–10.4*[28]

It has been recognized by a considerable number of commentators that materials now separated by the Emmanuel Booklet, namely 5.24-29 and 9.7–10.4, once constituted a multi-strophe poem with a recurrent refrain, though there has been debate as to whether 5.24 and 10.1-4 should be considered part of that original whole.[29] Vermeylen appears to be on solid ground when he accepts the view of scholars who have compared the basic structure of this poem to

Amos 4.6-12.[30] There we have a series of divine interventions which should have produced conversion, but did not. Each of these interventions is followed by the sentence לא שבתם עדי. At the end of the series is the statement that because of the lack of conversion, a final and definitive disaster is about to come upon Israel. Naturally, this last item does not have the refrain. The parallel with the Amos passage is a valuable guide in reconstructing the original order of strophes in the Outstretched Hand Poem. The stichometric and strophic arrangement of the original text, as I understand it, is incorporated in the Hebrew texts reproduced at the beginning of each of the following six sections. The original sequence is indicated by ordinal numerals (First Strophe, etc.) in order to avoid confusion with the proposal of Vermeylen which uses cardinal numbers (Strophe 1, etc.).

In what follows, each strophe will be discussed in order, pointing out its place in the structure of the overall poem, explaining departures from the Masoretic text and, most important, summarizing poetic devices which are apparent.

First Strophe–5.25

....
....

....
....

....
....

....
....

25aα על כן חרה אף יהוה בעמו
ויט ידו עליו ויכהו

25aβ וירגזו ההרים ותהי נבלתם
כסוחה בקרב חוצות

25b בכל זאת לא שב אפו
ועוד ידו נטויה

This strophe is obviously fragmentary as it is the only one of the six which does not consist of seven bi-cola. The fact that על כן in 25aα comes at precisely the same position in the strophe as the identical expression in the Third Strophe suggests that the first four bi-cola were dropped by the redactor because they did not suit his purposes.

The על כן, on the other hand, provided the logical transition from the woes of chapter 5 to the contents of the First and Fifth Strophes, producing a cohesive redactional whole in 5.1-29 as correctly seen by Vermeylen.[31] The expressions חרה אף יהוה and ויט ידו in 25aα mark the initial kindling of the divine wrath, the continuation of which will be picked up in the refrain לא־שב אפו ועוד ידו נטויה. In addition, ויכהו sets the stage for המכהו in 9.12 (Third Strophe).

The meter of 25aα is either 4 + 4 or 4 + 3. The other two bi-cola are 3 + 3. We have already referred to the *inclusio* formed by the occurrence of the roots אף and נטה + יד in 25aα and 25b. The following repetitions of consonantal sounds occur: in 5.25aα, ו-4x and ע-3x; in 5.25aβ, ר-3x. Also, 25aβ has three long ū sounds and the refrain in 25b has a sequence of six long ō sounds followed by a long ū sound in the penultimate syllable of the bi-colon. This very distinctive vocalic pattern heightens the impact of the bi-colon as a refrain.

Second Strophe–9.7-11

7 דבר שלח אדני ביעקב
ונפל בישראל

8a וידעו העם כלו
אפרים ויושב שמרון

8b ⟨ויאמרו⟩ בגאוה
ובגדל לבב לאמר

9 לבנים נפלו וגזית נבנה
שקמים גדעו וארזים נחליף

10 וישגב יהוה את צריו
עליו את איביו יסכסך

11a ארם מקדם ופלשתים מאחור
ויאכלו את ישראל בכל פה

11b בכל זאת לא שב אפו
ועוד ידו נטויה

Since the identity of first and last strophes is assured, for reasons discussed at the relevant places, the three strophes of 9.7-20 must be in the center of the poem and I presume that their correct order has been preserved. The following textual and grammatical observations may be made. The temptation to replace אדני in v. 7 with יהוה (with the support of 1QIsa[a]) must be resisted. The use of אדני by Isaiah is well illustrated by 6.1, 8, 11. In 8b a verb of speaking must be reconstructed both to fill out the meter and to prepare for the לאמר at the end. The ויאמרו which I have provided is only one of several

possibilities. In 10 I read צריו for צרי רצין and place עליו in the second colon against the position of *atnaḥ* in the MT. The initial ו of ואת I have deleted as a dittography which, in fact, prompted the Masoretic punctuation. Most of the verbs in the strophe are clearly past except for two futures in v. 9. The ו before a perfect in 7 and 8a is not conversive. יסכסך in 10 is explained by Wildberger as an action contemporary with the preceding *wayyiqtōl*.[32]

In meter, 7 and 11a are 4 + 3; 9 is 4 + 4. The other cola are 3 + 3. An *inclusio* is provided by the word ישראל in 7 and 11 and, perhaps, by the word כל in 8a and 11b. There is a lovely chiasm of verb : object :: object : verb in 10. The following consonantal repetitions occur: in 7, ב-3x and ל-3x; in 8a, נ-3x; in 8b, ב-4x and ל-3x; in 9, ל-3x, מ-4x and נ-5x (a very striking concentration of liquids!) in 10, ו-6x and י-4x; in 11a, מ-5x and ל-4x. Furthermore, the ending יו occurs three times in 10. The play upon the roots נפל and לבן as well as בנה and לבן in 9 is especially striking.

Third Strophe–9.12-6

12 והעם לא שב עד המכהו
ואת יהוה צבאות לא דרשו

13 ויכרת יהוה מישראל ראש וזנב
כפה ואגמון יום אחד

14 [זקן ונשוא פנים הוא הראש
ונביא מורה שקר הוא הזנב]

15 ויהי מאשרי העם הזה מתעים
ומאשריו מבלעים

16aα על כן על בחוריו לא ישמח אדני
ואת יתמיו ואת אלמנתיו לא ירחם

16aβ כי כלו חנף ומרע
וכל פה דבר נבלה

16b בכל זאת לא שב אפו
ועוד ידו נטויה

In 13 it is tempting to delete יהוה *metri causa*, especially since it is provided in the immediately preceding colon. Nonetheless, I have left it in the text as reproduced above because of the subjective nature of this kind of emendation. Verse 14 is certainly a later addition to the strophe. The presupposition throughout is that the *whole* of Israel is guilty so that 'head and tail' refer to upper *and* lower classes. Verse 14, however, wants to put special blame on the leadership class. This fact is significant for the redactional history of the poem and will be

discussed below. For now the essential point is that whoever added this bi-colon was careful to preserve the 14-colon structure of the strophe. This means that a bi-colon of the original was dropped to be replaced by what we now have. The wording of 15 is strikingly similar to 3.12b. It is apparently 3.12b which is secondary and dependent upon 9.15. The verbs are all past, the two *yiqtōl* forms in 16a being past durative.

Bi-cola 13, 15 and 16aα are 4 + 3. The rest of the authentic lines are 3 + 3. In 12, המכהו links the Third Strophe with the First Strophe's ויכהו (5.25aα). In the same line, שב echoes the same word in the refrains of the two preceding strophes as well as forming an *inclusio* with 16b. In 13 the phrase ראש וזנב is placed in chiasm with כפה ואגמון. The following examples of alliteration occur: in 13, ה-4x, י-4x and מ-3x; in 15, מ-6x, ו-3x, ע-3x and ה-3x; in 16aα, ל-5x, מ-4x, נ-3x (note the liquids!), ת-4x, י-4x and ה-3x; and in 16aβ we have כ-3x and ל-3x. Also, 16aβ has three *ṣere* sounds plus פה. Note that כל פה echoes the same expression in 11a, at the end of the Second Strophe. Finally, we can point to the effective use of participial forms in 15.

Fourth Strophe–9.17-20

כי בערה כאש רשעה שמיר ושית תאכל	17a
ותצת בסבכי היער ויתאבכו גאות עשן	17b
בעברת יהוה צבאות נעתם ארץ ויהי העם כמאכלת אש	18abα
איש אל אחיו לא יחמלו	18bβ
איש בשר רעו יאכלו	19b
ויגזר על ימין ורעב ויאכל על שמאול ולא שבעו	19a
מנשה את אפרים ואפרים את מנשה יחדו המה על יהודה	20a
בכל זאת לא שב אפו ועוד ידו נטויה	20b

In 18abα the נֶעְתַּם of MT is repointed to *nāᶜatmi*, third person feminine singular from the root נוע (cf. 24.20 and, less directly, 6.4; 7.2) meaning 'to tremble, totter', with enclitic מ. To improve parallelism, 19b has been transposed before 19a. At the same time רעו is read for MT זרעו. Most verbs are obviously past tense. The two *yiqtōl* forms in 18 and 19 are past durative. The form תאכל in 17a is understandable when

the whole colon is taken as an asyndetic relative clause attached to the previous רשעה 'wickedness which (over and over again) consumes the thorns and briars'.

In meter 18abα is 4 + 4 or 4 + 3 while the other lines are 3 + 3. In 20a מנשה : אפרים :: אפרים : מנשה constitutes a chiasm. The cases of alliteration are as follows: in 17a, כ-3x, ר-3x and ש-4x; in 17b, ת-4x and ב-3x; in 18abα, ת-4x, ב-3x, מ-3x, ה-3x, and ע-3x; in 18bβ-19b, ל-4x; in 19a, ו-4x, י-3x, ל-5x, and ע-4x. Play on sound is also found in 17-19 where אש and איש each occurs twice.

Fifth (Final) Strophe–5.26-29

26a ונשא נס לגוי מרחוק
ושרק לו מקצה הארץ

26b והנה מהרה קל יבוא
27a אין עיף ואין כושל בו

27b ולא נפתח אזור חלציו
ולא נתק שרוך נעליו

28a אשר חציו שנונים
וכל קשתתיו דרכות

28b פרסות סוסיו כצר
נחשבו גלגליו כסופה

29a שאגה לו כלביא
ישאג ככפירים

29b וינהם ויאחז טרף
ויפלט ואין מציל

The first four strophes dealt with divine visitations in the past which should have produced conversion but didn't (see 9.12). The last strophe announces that, as a result of this failure, the Lord is sending the agent of final and definitive punishment: the Assyrians. In 26a, the original poem read גוי. The גוים of MT is not a textual error but the result of intentional alteration of the text by a later redactor.[33] I omit לא ינום ולא יישן from 27. The usual explanation of this as a gloss from Ps. 121.4 suffers from the fact that there is no apparent reason for connecting the present passage with that Psalm. The expression was perhaps a stock phrase describing an ever-watchful friend or enemy and entered 5.27 as a gloss, but not from Ps. 121. In 28b נחשבו is placed at the beginning of the second colon, against the accentuation in MT. The initial ו before גלגליו is dropped as dittography which occasioned the Masoretic punctuation. In 29a I

read ישאג with MT *qere*. The two ו + perfect forms in 26a can be read as future or, if the ו is not conversive, present perfect. The *yiqtōl* form in 26b as well as the four *wĕyiqtōl* forms of 29 could be future or present durative.

The meter throughout is 3 + 3, which means assigning two stresses to the word כפירים in 29a. The following examples of alliteration occur: in 26a, ר-3x and ק-3x, with a nice sound play in נשא־נס; in 26b-27a, נ-3x; in 27b, ו-4x, ל-4x, and נ-3x; in 28a, ש-3x, ו-3x and ת-3x; in 28b, ס-4x; in 29a, כ-3x; and in 29b, ו-3x and י-3x. The word אין, which occurs twice in 27a, is echoed in the last colon of the poem.

Supplementary Strophe–10.1-4

1 הוי החקקים חקקי און
ומכתבים עמל כתבו

2a להטות מדין דלים
ולגזל משפט עניי עמי

2b להיות אלמנות שללים
ואת יתומים יבזו

3a ומה תעשו ליום פקדה
ולשואה ממרחק תבוא

3b על מי תנוסו לעזרה
ואנה תעזבו כבודכם

4a בלתי כרע תחת אסיר
ותחת הרוגים יפלו

4b בכל זאת לא שב אפו
ועוד ידו נטויה

This strophe was not part of the original poem but is a secondary creation built upon a woe-saying. Not only would the introductory word הוי be strange in the Outstretched Hand Poem, the analogy with Amos 4.6-12 requires that all the strophes except the last one should deal with events in the *past*. The verbs in 10.3, however, can only be translated as future. Nonetheless, the redactional history of this piece is of importance and its poetic structure needs to be looked at.

The meter is 3 + 3 throughout. An *inclusio* is found in the use of the root נטה in 2a and 4b. There is verb:adverb :: adverb:verb chiasm in 31 as well as the pattern verb:propositional-phrase :: prepositional-phrase:verb. The patterns of alliteration are as follows: in 1, מ-4x and ק-4x; in 2a, ל-4x, מ-4x and נ-2x (liquids!); in 2b, ל-4x, מ-4x and ת-4x; in 3a, מ-4x; in 3b, ע-3x; and in 4a, ת-5x and ר-3x. Assonance is exhibited in 2a with four long ī sounds and in 2b with four long ō

sounds. Word play is also seen in the combination חקקים חקקי and מכתבים . . . כתבו of 10.1 where anomalous grammatical forms are intentionally used to heighten paranomasia. There is another nice sound play in the combination מדין דלים of 2a.

It is especially striking that this strophe, put together by a redactor at a later time, took care to follow the seven bi-colon framework as well as the other typical poetic devices which occur in the original parts of the poem.

Conclusions. The above discussion reveals the Outstretched Hand Poem as a carefully crafted poetic whole. It is has a logical structure from beginning to end and is tied together by the recurring refrain. The meter is predominantly 3 + 3. There is abundant use of alliteration, assonance and other forms of play on sound. Patterns of *inclusio* and chiasm occur well as echoes of earlier strophes occurring later in the poem. Most impressive is the consistent length of the strophes: 7 bi-cola each. This pattern was so strong, that when the intrusive 9.14 entered the text, an original bi-colon was dropped to make up for it. Similarly, the Supplementary Strophe (10.1-4) was so constructed as to preserve the 7 bi-colon pattern as well as to reflect the same kinds of poetic device found in the original part of the poem.

In the light of these conclusions, additional objections can be raised against the position of Vermeylen:

1. His dropping of the words אפרים ויושב שמרון in 9.8 breaks the 7 bi-colon structure and leaves an isolated colon without a parallel.[34] This brings into question his view that the focusing of the poem against the northern kingdom was due to redactional modification.

2. The radical surgery he performs in the Third Strophe (his Strophe 2)[35] leaves the strophe much too short. Specifically, the position of על כן in 9.16 coming at the same position in the strophe as it does in my First Strophe (5.25) argues for the authenticity of 16a.

3. Vermeylen believes that 5.24a and 25 constituted Strophe 4. His explanation of the presence of 5.25 in its present position depends upon its having been moved along with the final strophe which immediately followed it in the original order.[36] However, if the three bi-cola of 5.25 are what remains of the First Strophe, as argued above, then his hypothesis can not explain the presence of that verse in chapter 5 and his whole reconstruction of the redactional history is further weakened.

4. Lack of attention to poetic structures results in failure to observe the important fact that the redactionally constructed strophe of 10.1-

4 deliberately imitates the structure of the original strophes of the Outstretched Hand Poem. The significance of this obsersvation will be discussed in the next section where a new proposal is offered for reconstructing the redactional history of 5.1–10.4.

V. *The Redaction of Isaiah 5.1–10.4 : A New Proposal*

The situation of Isaiah 5–10 may be simply summarized as follows: Two literary units which were originally distinct wholes in their own right, namely the Outstretched Hand Poem and the series of woesayings (which were probably attached already to the Song of the Vineyard), are now broken up so that parts of each come before the Emmanuel Booklet and parts come after it. Instead of thinking in terms of an 'insertion' with additional shifting around of materials, I would like to propose a very simple approach. What we have amounts to the phenomenon of *inclusio*, a literary device which we have seen in the Outstretched Hand Poem and which also occurs over larger redactional units.[37] The 'framing' of the Emmanuel Booklet by this double *inclusio* produces the following concentric structure:

Woe-sayings (5.8-24)
Parts of Outstretched Hand Poem (5.25-29)
Emmanuel Booklet (6.1–9.6)
Parts of Outstretched Hand Poem (9.7-10 plus 10.1-4)
Woe-sayings (10.14 plus 10.5ff.)[38]

The reason for the redactional inclusion of a literary unit in this way can only be to provide a new 'framework' or context for understanding the passage which is so enclosed. The proposal will gain in plausibility if we can ascertain what new interpretational framework is provided for the Emmanuel Booklet by the double *inclusio*. I believe that it is in fact possible to discern the redactor's intention in both cases.

We begin with the complex constituted by the Song of the Vineyard and the woe-sayings. One of the most consistent thematic elements of this complex is that the reason for the destruction of Yahweh's vineyard is *social injustice*.[39] The principal responsibility for the coming disaster lies with the upper classes who oppress the poor. This is in marked contrast to the Emmanuel Booklet where the main reason for the coming of doom (= the Assyrians) is the failure

to *trust* in the promises regarding David and Zion. In this case, the blame falls principally on King Ahaz. The redactor is using the framework of the woe-sayings to insist that the events during the Syro-Ephraimite War which led to Assyrian interference in Judean affairs are due to the corruption of justice in society, even though this is not brought out in the Emmanuel Booklet itself.

The concern with social justice is also apparent in the secondary modifications of the Outstretched Hand Poem. That poem, in its original form, placed the blame for the coming of Assyria upon the *whole people*, without specific condemnation of the wealthy and the powerful class. The transformation of one of the original woes into a Supplementary Strophe of the poem (10.1-4) is not for superficial or merely aesthetic reasons. For the new strophe brings into the Outstretched Hand Poem itself a sharp and vigorous attack against the leadership class which is guilty of oppressing the poor. The same concern is apparent in the Third Strophe of the poem. The original meaning was clearly that the *whole* people, 'head and tail', were guilty and deserving punishment. The intrusive verse 14, however, is meant to insist that special blame lies with the leadership class.[40] The concern with social justice and with assigning blame to the leaders of Judean society, therefore, appears as one of the principal motivating factors in the redaction of Isaiah 5.1–10.4. The clearest indication of this is the 'framing' of the Emmanuel Booklet by the woe-sayings.

The theological intention behind the second *inclusio*, that involving the Outstretched Hand Poem, is convincingly demonstrated by Hermann Barth.[41] In the original poem, the hand of the Lord remained outstretched until the final disaster, which was the sending of Assyria against the northern kingdom of Israel. In the present form of the larger complex, with the final strophe of the original poem transposed, the Lord's hand continues to be outstretched as the theme of Assyria begins to be developed (10.5ff., and already in 5.25-30). It is the punishment called for by Assyria's arrogance that is the reason why the hand continues to be outstretched. This situation is not brought to a conclusion until 14.24-27 where the final 'breaking' of Assyria is announced with the revelation that *this* is the outstretched hand (זאת היד הנטויה). The framing of the Emmanuel Booklet within parts of the Outstretched Hand Poem, therefore, intends to point out that the events unleashed during the Syro-Ephraimite War were only the beginning of a much longer series of events in which the

outstretched hand of Yahweh would first strike Ephraim, then Judah, and finally, Assyria itself.

The evidence suggests that both of the *inclusiones* discussed above are the work of a single redactor. First of all, it is simpler to think of the process that way since the likelihood of a second redactor wrapping a second *inclusio* around material which was already part of a larger literary complex is somewhat difficult to visualize. Secondly, the fact that the structure of 10.1-4 imitates the poetic features of the strophes of the original Outstretched Hand Poem suggests that the person who is interested in the social justice issue is identical with the person for whom the Outstretched Hand Poem was so important. Third, the conception of an overarching plan of Yahweh which is presumed by the redactor who transformed the Outstretched Hand Poem is also reflected in the woe-sayings at 5.12 and 19. Finally, the fact that chapter 5, as it now stands, constitutes a coherent and logical redactional whole while at the same time 5.25-30 bridges over to 9.7–10.4 and further to 14.24-27 bespeaks a single undisturbed redactional plan. The combination of the basic building blocks of 5.1–10.4, therefore, seems to be the work of a single redactor. Provisionally, he may be called the Primary Redactor of this pericope. Of course, there are many smaller and later redactional modifications which were made by others.

There are two possibilities for the dating of the work of the Primary Redactor. A *terminus ad quem* is established by the fact, convincingly argued by Barth, that 5.25-29, 10.5-34*, and 14.24-27 refer to the real historical Assyrian Empire and must be dated before the fall of Assyria towards the end of the reign of King Josiah.[42] The *terminus a quo* depends upon the dating of 9.1-6. It seems quite clear that this passage, celebrating the birth and/or enthronement of a Judean king, was *appended to* the Emmanuel Booklet by someone who identified that king as the child whose birth was announced in 7.14. This procedure is intelligible only if the addition of 9.1-6 came *before* the (expanded) Emmanuel Booklet was framed by the materials in chapter 5 and 9.7ff. If the king in question was Hezekiah,[43] then it is possible that the Primary Redaction also dates to his reign. The view of the Primary Redactor that Yahweh was about to break Assyria would fit with the nationalistic fervor which prompted the reform movement in the time of Hezekiah and transformed the disastrous events of 701 into a legend of miraculous deliverance (2 Kings 18.13, 17f.).

The other possibility is that the Primary Redactor worked during the reign of Josiah. In this case, my Primary Redaction would merge with H. Barth's *Assur-Redaktion*.[44] Even so, the proposal made here adds significantly to Barth's views in several ways: it uses the phenomenon of *inclusio* to explain the *mechanics* of the arrangement of materials in 5.1–10.4; it accounts more adequately than Barth does for the presence of the woe saying in 10.1-4;[45] and it highlights the importance for the redactor of the social justice theme.[46] As such, it advances our understanding of the redactional history of 5.1–10.4.[47]

NOTES

1. J. Vermeylen, *Du prophète Isaïe à l'apocalyptique: Isaïe, I-XXXV, miroir d'un demi-millénaire d'expérience religieuse en Israël*, I (Paris: Gabalda, 1977).
2. Vermeylen, *Du prophète Isaïe*, 166, 65-71.
3. Vermeylen, *Du prophète Isaïe*, 160-61.
4. Vermeylen, *Du prophète Isaïe*, 163-67.
5. Vermeylen, *Du prophète Isaïe*, 169-77, and the summary on 185-86.
6. Vermeylen, *Du prophète Isaïe*, 177-85.
7. Vermeylen, *Du prophète Isaïe*, 178-79.
8. Vermeylen, *Du prophète Isaïe*, 187-249.
9. Vermeylen, *Du prophète Isaïe*, 199-204.
10. Vermeylen summarizes all of the editorial changes reviewed in this paragraph (*Du prophète Isaïe*, 245-49).
11. Vermeylen, *Du prophète Isaïe*, 211-12.
12. My analysis of the three stages is based largely on Vermeylen's summary (*Du prophète Isaïe*, 185-86).
13. Vermeylen, *Du prophète Isaïe*, 241.
14. Vermeylen, *Du prophète Isaïe*, 272.
15. The devastation mentioned in 5.9-10 was linked with that in 6.11-13, both of which passages were connected with the destruction of the kingdom of Judah in 587. Both passages concern the destruction of houses (בתים in 5.9 and 6.11) and the failure of agriculture (cf. שמה in 5.9 and שממה in 6.11). There is mention of one tenth in 6.13 which was reminiscent of 5.10 where ten measures of land are said to produce only one measure of wine. Finally, compare מאין יושב in 5.9 and מאין אדם in 6.11 (Vermeylen, *Du prophète Isaïe*, 170-71).
16. 5.24b would be a Deuteronomistic addition to the original fourth strophe. The לכן at the beginning of v. 24 is intended by the redactor to introduce the whole unit 5.24-29 which would thus culminate the legal procedure initiated in 5.1-7 and continued through the indictments contained

in the woe sayings by pointing to the coming of the Babylonians as the fulfillment of the sentence against guilty Judah (Vermeylen, *Du prophète Isaïe*, 174-76).

17. Vermeylen believes that the use of the word בית meaning 'royal house, dynasty' in 5.7, at the conclusion of the Song of the Vineyard, made possible a rereading of the word בתים in 5.8-10. The 'great houses' which were destroyed were the two kingdoms! (Vermeylen, *Du prophète Isaïe*, 171-72).

18. Vermeylen, *Du prophète Isaïe*, 167.

19. Vermeylen, *Du prophète Isaïe*, 162-63.

20. See F.M. Cross, Jr, *Canaanite Myth and Hebrew Epic* (Cambridge: Harvard University Press, 1973), 112-144, and D.A. Robertson, *Linguistic Evidence in Dating Early Hebrew Poetry* (SBL Dissertation Series, 3; Missoula, MT: Scholars Press, 1972), 155.

21. Vermeylen, *Du prophète Isaïe*, 162.

22. Vermeylen, *Du prophète Isaïe*, 147-50.

23. Vermeylen, *Du prophète Isaïe*, 186.

24. The thematic unity of the woes among themselves and with the Song of the Vineyard is far reaching. The woes all concern, directly or indirectly, the issues of social injustice and are thus aimed at one particular class in society. This is the class which is engaged in the unjust acquisition of property (5.8) through corruption of the legal system (5.23; 10.1-2)—a class notorious for its lavish banquets (5.11-12) and excessive consumption of alcohol (5.22). Their arrogant attitudes blind them them to the signs of the times and the recognition of the demands of justice (5.18-21). These specific details fill out what is only hinted at in the words משפט and צעקה (cry of the plaintiff in a legal dispute) of the Song of the Vineyard. As elsewhere in the Old Testament, the demand for social justice is based on Yahweh's ownership of the land (כרם היה לידידי, 5.1).

There are other specific contacts between the parable and the woes. The subject matter of the song, namely the vineyard, is reflected in the references to wine (5.10, 11, 22) and feasting (5.12, 14!) in the woes. All of this is particularly appropriate if the parable was first delivered in the context of a Sukkoth festival as many commentators believe. The parable is called a 'song' in 5.1 which accords with the musical instruments of 5.12. The theme undergoes a reversal in the hunger and thirst of 5.13 and the idea of Sheol feasting on the feasters in 5.14. More generally, the agricultural ruin in which the parable culminates (5.5-6) is picked up in the woes at 5.9-10, 17, 24a. The statement in the parable that 'I will tell you (אודיעה) what I am about to do (עשה)' is played upon in the woes at 5.12b and 13a where the wine-bibbers are said to be unaware of the work (מעשה) of Yahweh and will go into exile for lack of knowledge (דעת). Similar play on the concepts occurs in 5.19 where they want Yahweh to hasten his work (עשהו) so they will know (ונדעה). Finally, the reversal of values mentioned in 5.20 echoes the reversal which takes place when the meaning of the parable is revealed (5.7) and the

conviction that they are wise in their own eyes (5.21) is an ironic contradiction to their inability to understand until the point of the משל is revealed to them.

The connection between the Song of the Vineyard and the woes is discussed more fully in A. Fitzgerald's 'Isaiah 5', an unpublished paper presented to the Task Force on Hebrew Poetry of the Catholic Biblical Association in August, 1977. I am indebted to Fitzgerald for many of the points made in this footnote.

25. Vermeylen, *Du prophète Isaïe*, 186.

26. The length of the overall structure of which the series of seven woes formed a part of this stage of its transmission is not made clear by Vermeylen. He does note that the material of 10.5-14*, 27b-32, 33-34 was joined to the series of woes before the insertion of the Emmanuel Booklet (*Du prophète Isaïe*, 272).

27. See my own proposal, where, however, 5.24a is treated as an original part of the woe in 5.22-23 and the transposed section of the Outstretched Hand Poem is presumed to begin with v. 25.

28. The material in parts IV and V of this paper is a revision of a paper I presented to the Task Force on Hebrew Poetry of the Catholic Biblical Association in August, 1978. The late Msgr Patrick W. Skehan of Catholic University provided me with a long detailed written critique which has been most helpful in the revision. I am happy to acknowledge my indebtedness to this teacher who was always kind and generous in offering his help.

29. For bibliographical references see Vermeylen, p. 177 and nn. 2-4, as well as H. Barth, *Die Jesaja-Worte in der Josiazeit* (WMANT, 48; Neukirchen: Neukirchener Verlag, 1977), 109-111 and nn. 38-49.

30. Vermeylen, *Du prophète Isaïe*, 177. See also H. Wildberger, *Jesaja 1-12* (BKAT, 10/1; Neukirchen: Neukirchener Verlag, 1972), 203-29.

31. Vermeylen, *Du prophète Isaïe*, 186, and previous discussion in this article.

32. Wildberger, *Jesaja 1-12*, 205.

33. Vermeylen, *Du prophète Isaïe*, 184.

34. Vermeylen, *Du prophète Isaïe*, 178-79.

35. Vermeylen, *Du prophète Isaïe*, 184-86.

36. Vermeylen, *Du prophète Isaïe*, 186.

37. See, for example, Vermeylen, (*Du prophète Isaïe*, 226, 290) where *inclusio* patterns function to identify larger redactional wholes. Also, Barth's treatment of the connection between the refrain of the Outstretched Hand Poem in 5.25 and the passage 14.24-27 amounts to an *inclusio*.

38. The woe-saying which begins in 10.5 was not part of the same series to which the woe-sayings in 5.8-24 and 10.1-4 originally belonged. Nonetheless it *was* part of the larger complex to which what I will call the Primary Redaction of 5.1–10.4 belonged. As such it is relevant to list it here although the present paper is strictly concerned only with 5.1–10.4.

39. Above, n. 24.

40. The identity of intention behind 9.14 and the transformation of the woe-saying into a strophe of the Outstretched Hand Poem (10.1-4) would suggest that both belong to the work of the same redactor. On the other hand, the indications that 9.14 is relatively late (see M. Goshen-Gottstein in *Textus* 8 [1973], 100-106) suggest caution in assigning the verse to the Primary Redactor discussed below where his work is assigned to the monarchichal period.

41. Barth, *Die Jesaja-Worte*, 109-19.

42. Barth, *Die Jesaja-Worte*, 17-76, 103-19, and *passim*.

43. This view has most recently been defended by R.E. Clements, *Isaiah 1-39* (Grand Rapids, MI: Eerdmans, 1980), 103-109.

44. Barth, *Die Jesaja-Worte*, 141-77 and 203-75. Vermeylen, *Du prophète Isaïe*, 232-45, also identifies the king of 9.1-6 with Josiah but with a different understanding of the redactional history of the larger context.

45. Compare Barth, *Die Jesaja-Worte*, 114, nn. 56-57; p. 117, n. 64; and pp. 234 and 266.

46. See, however, Barth, *Die Jesaja-Worte*, p. 268, n. 8.

47. The question of the relationship between other parts of Barth's *Assur-Redaktion* and what I have called the Primary Redaction of 5.1–10.4 remains open to further study.

Figure 1

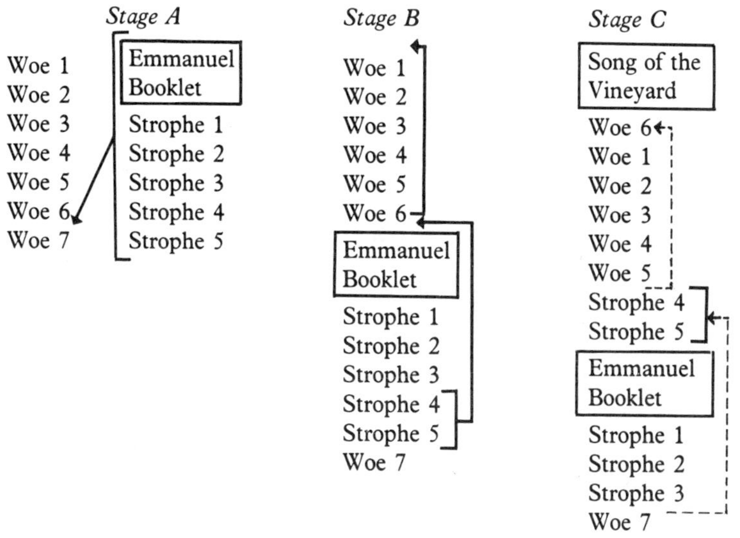

THE SEMANTIC PARALLELISM OF PSALM 89

Dennis Pardee

The present contribution to a volume in honor of G.W. Ahlström[1] should be viewed as a purely experimental attempt at noting the semantic parallelism of an entire work. The procedure was to assign a number to each word of the text, with parallel terms to any one word considered as sub-sets of that word. This corresponds to the old A//A′ in the analysis of a bi-colon and all that I have done is to expand that notation to cover an entire work. I have used numbers instead of letters and roman numerals instead of priming simply because of the high number of constituents involved in an entire work as opposed to a bi-colon. Because of this relatively high number, I have also added another superscript Arabic number which denotes the number of times a given root has occurred so far in the text. $\underset{\text{mšpṭy}}{1\ \mathrm{V}^{2}}$, for example, in v. 31, means that this is the second occurrence of *(m)špṭ* in Psalm 89 and that *(m)špṭ* is here analyzed as the fourth synonym of the first word in the text. After the annotation of the Psalm is found a list of all the words with their synonyms.

This notation is open to innumerable criticisms,[2] but the most serious, in my view, is that this system of notation does not permit (except through assignment to more than one set) the notation of bifurcations in parallelistic usage, i.e., X can appear in parallel with Y in one place, but with Z in another, with X and Z themselves showing little overlap—and Y itself can be used in quite different senses (as in the example of *ymyn* cited below).

A prime example is *zrʿ//ksʾ* in v. 5. Here the close grammatical parallelism of the two terms and the functional parallelism[3] of the two words (both equivalents here of 'dynasty') led me to label them semantic parallels. Moreover, they are repeated in v. 30 (and 37) in the same order and with the same function. But the neatness of the system for Psalm 89 is immediately overthrown by v. 31 and the word *bnyw*, which has already been assigned a slot (#25) with its own

good parallel term (*ʾb*, v. 27) and which is in many ways a much better parallel to *zrʿ* than is *ksʾ*.[4]

Another example: I at first called *ʾšyrh* and *ʾwdyʿ* semantic parallels in v. 1, because of their grammatical and functional parallelism in that verse, then decided that there should be two groups, one stressing proclamation (*šyr* and *hwdh*, #4), the other stressing knowledge and transmission thereof (*ydʿ*, *ʾmr*, *dbr*, #7).

An example of a different phenomenon: *ymyn* has one set of synonyms when a body part (#42 III) and another when a direction (#46 II).

Finally, *mšḥtyw* was not considered parallel to *ʿbdy* in v. 21 because of grammatical discord,[5] but later on the substantive *mšyḥ* appears (vv. 39, 52). In an attempt at noting the semantic parallelism of an entire work, one would certainly like to see that word as somehow parallel to *bḥyr* and *ʿbd* (#15).

Anyone attempting an analysis such as this one is constantly faced with problems such as these of classification and grouping. It is worth doing once, if only to learn first-hand the difficulties involved.

The above-mentioned examples, and many others from the list, point out another major problem: What is repetitive parallelism?[6] I have defined it as root parallelism,[7] but this definition must confront the problem of root recognition in the ancient world, for much of what we regard as root parallelism was for the ancients only paronomasia.[8] On the other hand, even limiting repetitive parallelism to one form of a word will not solve all of our problems, as the example of *ymyn*, just cited, shows.

This paper then, is an attempt to do something that probably cannot adequately be done at all. Its goal is not only to show up the difficulties of devising a notational system for even one aspect of the parallelism of an entire work, but also to show that it is the constantly changing nuances of the poet's vocabulary which make the task of analysis so difficult. What can artificially be noted as 'like' in a few pages would take many pages of prose discussion to describe as 'unlike' or 'different'.

Semantic Parallelism

2) 1 I[1] 2 I[1] 3 I[1] 4 I[1]
ḥsdy yhwh ʿwlm ʾšyrh
5[1] 3 II[1] 6[1] 3 II[2] 7 I[1] 1 II[1] 8[1] 9 I[1]
l- dr w- dr ʾwdyʿ ʾmwntk b- py

[9]The mercies of YHWH forever I will sing,
For all time will I make known your faithfulness by my mouth.

3) 10^{1} $7\,\mathrm{II}^{1}$ $3\,\mathrm{I}^{2}$ $1\,\mathrm{I}^{2}$ $11\,\mathrm{I}^{1}$ ky ’mrty ‘wlm ḥsd ybnh $12\,\mathrm{I}^{1}$ $11\,\mathrm{II}^{1}$ $1\,\mathrm{II}^{2}$ 8^{2} šmym tkn ’mwntk bhm	For, I have said, forever is mercy established. As for the heavens, you will establish your faithfulness there.
4) $13\,\mathrm{I}^{1}$ $14\,\mathrm{I}^{1}$ 5^{2} $15\,\mathrm{I}^{1}$ krty bryt l- bḥyry $13{+}14\,\mathrm{I}^{1}$ 5^{3} 16^{1} $15\,\mathrm{II}^{1}$ nšb‘ty l- dwd ‘bdy	I have made a covenant for my chosen one, I have sworn to David my servant.
5) 17^{1} $3\,\mathrm{I}^{3}$ $11\,\mathrm{II}^{2}$ $18\,\mathrm{I}^{1}$ ‘d ‘wlm ’kyn zr‘k 6^{2} $11\,\mathrm{I}^{2}$ 5^{4} $3\,\mathrm{II}^{3}$ 6^{3} $3\,\mathrm{II}^{4}$ $18\,\mathrm{II}^{1}$ 19^{1} w- bnyty l- dr w- dr ks’k slh	For all time will I establish your progeny, I will build up your throne for all time. Selah.
6) 6^{4} $4\,\mathrm{II}^{1}$ $12\,\mathrm{I}^{2}$ $1\,\mathrm{III}^{1}$ $2\,\mathrm{I}^{2}$ w- ywdw šmym pl’k yhwh 20^{1} $1\,\mathrm{II}^{3}$ 8^{3} $21\,\mathrm{I}^{1}$ $22\,\mathrm{I}^{1}$ ’p ’mwntk b- qhl qdšym	The heavens praise your marvel(ous deeds), O YHWH, Even your faithfulness in the assembly of the holy ones.
7) 10^{2} $23\,\mathrm{I}^{1}$ 8^{4} $12\,\mathrm{II}^{1}$ $24\,\mathrm{I}^{1}$ 5^{5} $2\,\mathrm{I}^{3}$ ky my b- šḥq y‘rk l- yhwh $24\,\mathrm{II}^{1}$ 5^{6} $2\,\mathrm{I}^{4}$ 8^{5} $25\,\mathrm{I}^{1}$ $2\,\mathrm{II}^{1}$ ydmh l- yhwh b- bny ’lym	For who in the clouds can line up with YHWH? (Who) is like YHWH among the sons of the gods?
8) $2\,\mathrm{II}^{2}$ $26\,\mathrm{I}^{1}$ 8^{6} $21\,\mathrm{II}^{1}$ $22\,\mathrm{I}^{2}$ ’l n‘rṣ b- swd qdšym $27\,\mathrm{I}^{1}$ 6^{5} $26\,\mathrm{II}^{1}$ 28^{1} 29^{1} 30^{1} rbh w- nwr’ ‘l kl sbybyw	El is fearful in the assembly of the holy ones, Great and frightful (is he) over all those who surround him.
9) $2\,\mathrm{I}^{5}$ $2\,\mathrm{III}^{1}$ 31^{1} $23\,\mathrm{I}^{2}$ 32^{1} yhwh ’lwhy ṣb’wt my kmwk $27\,\mathrm{II}^{1}$ $2\,\mathrm{IV}^{1}$ 6^{6} $1\,\mathrm{II}^{4}$ 30^{2} ḥsyn yh w- ’mwntk sbybwtyk	O YHWH, God of Hosts, who is like you? Mighty is Yah! Your faithfulness (is) all around you.
10) $33\,\mathrm{I}^{1}$ 34^{1} 8^{7} $35\,\mathrm{I}^{1}$ 36^{1} $37\,\mathrm{I}^{1}$ ’th mwšl b- g’wt h- ym 8^{8} $38\,\mathrm{I}^{1}$ $35\,\mathrm{II}^{1}$ $33\,\mathrm{I}^{2}$ 39^{1} b- św’ glyw ’th tšbḥm	You rule over the pride of the sea, When it lifts its waves you quiet them down.

11) 33 I^3 40 I^1 32^2 41 I^1 37 II^1
'th dk't k- ḥll rhb
8^9 42 I^1 27 III^1 40 II^1 43 I^1
b- zrw' 'zk pzrt 'wybyk

You crush Rahab (till he is) like a casualty of battle,
With your mighty arm you scatter your enemies.

12) 5^7 12 I^3 20^2 5^8 12 III^1
lk šmym 'p lk 'rṣ
12 IV^1 6^7 44^1 33 I^4 45 I^1
tbl w- ml'h 'th ysdtm

The heavens are yours, as is the earth,
You are the one who founded the world and everything in it.

13) 46 I^1 6^8 46 II^1 33 I^5 45 II^1
ṣpwn w- ymyn 'th br'tm
46 III^1 6^9 46 IV^1 8^{10} 47^1 48 I^1
tbwr w- ḥrmwn b- šmk yrnnw

North and South—you created them,
Tabor and Hermon—at your name they rejoice.

14) 5^9 42 I^2 49^1 27 IV^1
lk zrw' 'm gbwrh
27 III^2 42 II^1 38 II^1 42 III^1
t'z ydk trwm ymynk

Yours is the (mighty) arm, along with power,
Strong is your (fore-)arm, high up-lifted is your right (arm).

15) 1 IV^1 6^{10} 1 V^1 11 II^3 18 II^2
ṣdq w- mšpṭ mkwn ks'k
1 I^3 6^{11} 1 II^5 50^1 9 II^1
ḥsd w- 'mt yqdmw pnyk

Right and justice are the foundation of your throne,
Mercy and faithfulness go before you.

16) 51^1 36^2 52^1 7 I^2 48 II^1
'šry h- 'm ywd'y trw'h
2 I^6 8^{11} 53^1 9 II^2 54 I^1
yhwh b- 'wr pnyk yhlkwn

Happy the people who know the festal shout,
O YHWH, (happy are those who) go in the light of your face.

17) 8^{12} 47^2 48 III^1 29^2 36^3 55^1
b- šmk ygylwn kl h- ywm
6^{12} 8^{13} 1 IV^2 38 II^2
w- b- ṣdqtk yrwmw

In your name do they rejoice all the day,
In your righteousness are they uplifted.

18) 10^3 56 I^1 27 III^3 33 I^6
ky tp'rt 'zmw 'th
6^{13} 8^{14} 56 II^1 38 II^3 27 V^1
w- b- rṣnk trym qrnnw

For the glory of their strength are you,
And in your favor do you lift up our horn.

19)	10^{4} 5^{10} $2\,\mathrm{I}^{7}$ 57^{1} ky l- yhwh mgnnw	For our shield is YHWH's,
	6^{14} 5^{11} $2\,\mathrm{V}^{1}(22\,\mathrm{I}^{3})$ 58^{1} 59^{1} w- l- qdwš yśr'l mlknw	Our king belongs to the Holy One of Israel.
20)	60^{1} $7\,\mathrm{III}^{1}$ 8^{15} $61\,\mathrm{I}^{1}$ 'z dbrt b- ḥzwn	Once you did speak in vision,
	5^{12} $1\,\mathrm{I}^{4}$ 6^{15} $7\,\mathrm{II}^{2}$ l- ḥsydyk w- t'mr	Even to your faithful did you say:
	$62\,\mathrm{I}^{1}$ $15\,\mathrm{III}^{1}$ 28^{2} $27\,\mathrm{IV}^{2}$ šwyty ʿzr ʿl gbwr	I have set a young hero over the seasoned warrior,
	$38\,\mathrm{II}^{4}$ $15\,\mathrm{I}^{1}$ 63^{1} 52^{2} hrymwty bḥwr m- ʿm	I have raised my chosen one over the people.
21)	64^{1} 16^{2} $15\,\mathrm{II}^{2}$ mṣ'ty dwd ʿbdy	I have found David my servant,
	8^{16} 65^{1} $22\,\mathrm{I}^{4}$ $66\,\mathrm{I}^{1}$ b- šmn qdšy mšḥtyw	I have anointed him with my holy oil.
22)	67^{1} $42\,\mathrm{II}^{2}$ $11\,\mathrm{II}^{4}$ 49^{2} 'šr ydy tkwn ʿmw	Now my hand is established firmly on his side,
	20^{3} $42\,\mathrm{I}^{3}$ $27\,\mathrm{VI}^{1}$ 'p zrwʿy t'mṣnw	My arm strengthens him.
23)	68^{1} $69\,\mathrm{I}^{1}$ $43\,\mathrm{I}^{2}$ 8^{17} l' yš' 'wyb bw	No enemy will deceive him,
	6^{16} $25\,\mathrm{I}^{2}$ $70\,\mathrm{I}^{1}$ 68^{2} $69\,\mathrm{II}^{1}$ w- bn ʿwlh l' yʿnnw	No iniquitous person will afflict him.
24)	6^{17} $71\,\mathrm{I}^{1}$ 63^{2} $9\,\mathrm{II}^{3}$ $43\,\mathrm{II}^{1}$ w- ktwty m- pnyw ṣryw	I will beat his oppressors back from him,
	6^{18} $43\,\mathrm{III}^{1}$ $71\,\mathrm{II}^{1}$ w- mśn'yw 'gwp	I will smite his hateful (enemies).
25)	6^{19} $1\,\mathrm{II}^{6}$ 6^{20} $1\,\mathrm{I}^{5}$ 49^{3} w- 'mwnty w- ḥsdy ʿmw	My faithfulness and mercy are with him,
	6^{21} 8^{18} 47^{3} $38\,\mathrm{II}^{5}$ $27\,\mathrm{V}^{2}$ w- b- šmy trwm qrnw	His horn will be lifted high by means of my name.
26)	6^{22} $62\,\mathrm{II}^{1}$ 8^{19} $37\,\mathrm{I}^{2}$ $42\,\mathrm{II}^{3}$ w- śmty b- ym ydw	I will set his hand against the Sea,
	6^{23} 8^{20} $37\,\mathrm{III}^{1}$ $42\,\mathrm{III}^{2}$ w- b- nhrwt ymynw	His right hand against the Rivers.

27) 33 II^{1} 72^{1} 25 II^{1} 33 I^{7}	He will call me: My father are you,
hw’ yqr’ny ’by ’th	
2 II^{3} 6^{24} 2 VI^{1} 73 I^{1}	My God and the Rock of my salvation.
’ly w- ṣwr yšw‘ty	
28) 20^{4} 33 III^{1} 74^{1} 62 III^{1}	And I for my part will set him up as a firstborn,
’p ’ny bkwr ’tnhw	
38 III^{1} 5^{13} 59^{2} 12 III^{2}	As one high and lifted up with respect to the kings of the earth.
‘lywn l- mlky ’rṣ	
29) 5^{14} 3 I^{4} 75^{1} 5^{15} 1 I^{6}	Forever will I keep for him my mercy,
l- ‘wlm ‘šmwr lw ḥsdy	
6^{25} 14 I^{2} 1 II^{7} 5^{16}	And my covenant will retain its validity for him.
w- bryty n’mnt lw	
30) 6^{26} 62 II^{2} 5^{17} 3 III^{1} 18 I^{2}	I will establish his progeny for all time,
w- śmty l- ‘d z‘rw	
6^{27} 18 II^{3} 32^{3} 55^{2} 12 I^{4}	And his throne like the days of the heavens.
w- ks’w k- ymy šmym	
31) 76^{1} 77^{1} 25 I^{3} 1 VI^{1}	If his sons abandon my law,
’m y‘zbw bnyw twrty	
6^{28} 8^{21} 1 V^{2} 68^{3} 54 I^{2}	And if they do not walk according to my justice;
w- b- mšpṭy l’ ylkwn	
32) 76^{2} 1 VII^{1} 41 I^{2}	If they profane my statutes,
’m ḥqty yḥllw	
6^{29} 1 VIII^{1} 68^{4} 75^{2}	And do not keep my laws;
w- mṣwty l’ yšmrw	
33) 6^{30} 78^{1} 8^{22} 79^{1} 70 II^{1}	Then I will punish their sin with the rod,
w- pqdty b- šbṭ pš‘m	
6^{31} 8^{23} 71 III^{1} 70 III^{1}	With blows their iniquity.
w- b- ng‘ym ‘wnm	
34) 6^{32} 1 I^{7} 68^{5} 41 II^{1} 63^{3} 49^{4}	But I will not break off my mercy with him,
w- ḥsdy l’ ’pyr m- ‘mw	
6^{33} 68^{6} 41 III^{1} 8^{24} 1 II^{8}	I will not deal falsely with my own faithfulness.
w- l’ ’šqr b- ’mwnty	

35)	68^{7} 41 I^{3} 14 I^{3}	I will not profane my treaty,
	l' 'ḥll bryty	
	6^{34} 54 II^{1} 9 III^{1} 68^{8} 41 IV^{1}	Nor will I change that which
	w- mwṣ' śpty l' 'šnh	I have pronounced.
36)	80^{1} 13+14 I^{2} 8^{25} 22 I^{5}	Once I swore in my
	'ḥt nšb'ty b- qdšy	sanctuary,
	76^{3} 5^{18} 16^{3} 41 V^{1}	Can I (now) play false with
	'm l- dwd 'kzb	David?
37)	18 I^{3} 5^{19} 3 I^{5} 11 III^{1}	His progeny will go on
	zr'w l- 'wlm yhyh	forever,
	6^{35} 18 II^{4} 32^{4} 81 I^{1} 82^{1}	Even his throne like the sun
	w- ks'w k- šmš ngdy	before me.
38)	32^{5} 81 II^{1} 11 II^{5} 3 I^{6}	Like the moon will it stand
	k- yrḥ ykwn 'wlm	firm forever,
	6^{36} 3 III^{2} 8^{26} 12 II^{2} 1 II^{9} 19^{2}	For all time it is established
	w- 'd b- šḥq n'mn slh	in the clouds. Selah.
39)	6^{37} 33 I^{8} 41 VI^{1} 6^{38} 41 VII^{1}	But you, you have rejected,
	w- 'th znḥt w- tm's	have spurned,
	83 I^{1} 49^{5} 66^{2}	Have become infuriated with
	ht'brt 'm mšyḥk	your anointed one.
40)	41 VIII^{1} 14 I^{4} 15 II^{3}	You have rejected the coven-
	n'rth bryt 'bdk	ant of your servant,
	41 I^{4} 5^{20} 12 III^{3} 14 II^{1}	You have profaned to the
	ḥllt l- 'rṣ nzrw	earth his crown.
41)	41 IX^{1} 29^{3} 84 I^{1}	You have broken down all
	prṣt kl gdrtyw	his 'fences',
	62 II^{3} 84 II^{1} 85^{1}	You have turned his
	śmt mbṣryw mḥth	fortresses into ruins.
42)	41 X^{1} 29^{4} 86^{1} 87 I^{1}	Anyone who passes by on
	šshw kl 'bry drk	the road plunders him,
	11 III^{2} 88 I^{1} 5^{21} 89^{1}	He has become a(n object
	hyh ḥrph l- šknyw	of) reproach for his
		neighbors.

43)	38 II^{6} 42 III^{3} 43 II^{2} hrymwt ymyn ṣryw 48 IV^{1} 29^{5} 43 I^{3} hśmḥt kl ’wybyw	You have lifted up the right (arm) of his oppressors, Have allowed all his enemies to rejoice.
44)	20^{5} 54 III^{1} 2 VI^{2} 90 I^{1} ’p tšyb ṣwr ḥrbw 6^{39} 68^{9} 38 IV^{1} 8^{27} 90 II^{1} w- l’ hqymtw b- mlḥmh	Indeed you have caused the Rock (flint ?) of his sword to turn back, And have not kept him/it upright in battle.
45)	41 XI^{1} 63^{4} 22 II^{1} hšbt m- ṭhrw 6^{40} 18 II^{5} 5^{22} 12 III^{4} 41 XII^{1} w- ks’w l- ’rṣ mgrth	You have caused (him) to cease from his purity, You have cast his throne to the earth.
46)	41 XIII^{1} 55^{3} 91^{1} hqṣrt ymy ‘lwmyw 92^{1} 28^{3} 88 II^{1} 19^{3} h‘ṭyt ‘lyw bwšh slh	You have cut short the days of his youth, You have covered him with shame. Selah.
47)	17^{2} 23 II^{1} 2 I^{8} 93^{1} 5^{23} 3 IV^{1} ‘d mh yhwh tstr l- nṣḥ 83 I^{2} 32^{6} 94^{1} 83 II^{1} tb‘r kmw ’š ḥmtk	How long, O YHWH, will you stay so definitively hidden? Will your anger burn like fire?
48)	95^{1} 33 III^{2} 23 II^{2} 3 V^{1} zkr ’ny mh ḥld 28^{4} 23 II^{3} 96^{1} 45 II^{2} 29^{6} 25 I^{4} 97 I^{1} ‘l mh šw’ br’t kl bny ’dm	Remember of what duration I am, How you created all men nothingness.
49)	23 I^{3} 27 IV^{3}/97 II^{1} 98 I^{1} 6^{41} 68^{10} 61 II^{1} 98 II^{1} my gbr yḥyh w- l’ yr’h mwt 73 II^{1} 98 III^{1} 63^{5} 42 II^{4} 98 IV^{1} 19^{4} ymlṭ npšw m- yd š’wl slh	What man will live and not see death? Or will rescue his life from the clutches of Sheol? Selah.
50)	23 III^{1} 1 I^{8} 36^{4} 99^{1} 2 VII^{1} ’yh ḥsdyk h- r’šnym ’dny 13+14 I^{3} 5^{24} 16^{4} 8^{28} 1 II^{10} nšb‘t l- dwd b- ’mwntk	Where are your former mercies, O Lord? (When) you swore an oath to David by your faithfulness.

51) 95^2 $2\ VII^2$ $88\ I^2$ $15\ II^4$
zkr ’dny ḥrpt ‘bdyk
$38\ I^2$ 8^{29} 100^1 29^7 $88\ III^1$ 52^3
ś’ty b- ḥyqy kl (rbym) → dbt ‘mym

Remember, O Lord, the reproach (which is heaped on) your servants,
(How) I have borne in my bosom all the slanders of the peoples;

52) 67^2 $88\ I^3$ $43\ I^4$ $2\ I^9$
’šr ḥrpw ’wybyk yhwh
67^3 $88\ I^4$ $87\ II^1$ 66^3
’šr ḥrpw ‘qbwt mšyḥk

How your enemies reproach, O YHWH,
How they reproach the footsteps of your anointed one.

101^1 $2\ I^{10}$ 5^{25} $3\ I^7$ $1\ II^{11}$ 6^{42} $1\ II^{12}$
brwk yhwh l- ‘wlm ’mn w- ’mn

Blessed be YHWH forever. Amen and Amen

List of Words as Semantic Parallels[10]

1	I HṢD	ḥsdy (2^1, 25^5, 29^6, 34^7)
		ḥsd (3^2, 15^3)
		ḥsydyk (20^4)
		ḥsdyk (50^8)
	II ’MN	’mwntk (2^1, 3^2, 6^3, 9^4, 50^{10})
		’mwnty (25^6, 34^8)
		’mt (15^5)
		n’mnt (29^7)
		n’mn (38^9)
		’mn ($52^{11,12}$)
	III PL’	pl’k (6^1)
	IV ṢDQ	ṣdq (15^1)
		ṣdqtk (17^2)
	V ŠPṬ	mšpṭ (15^1)
		mšpṭy (31^2)
	VI YRH	twrty (31^1)
	VII ḤQQ	ḥqty (32^1)
	VIII ṢWH	mṣwty (32^1)
2	I YHWH	(2^1, 6^2, $7^{3,4}$, 9^5, 16^6, 19^7, 47^8, $52^{9,10}$)
	II ’L	’lym (7^1)
		’l (8^2)
		’ly (27^1)

	III ’LH	’lwhy (9[1])
	IV YH	(9[1])
	V QDŠ	qdwš yśr’l (19[1]) (also listed as ##22, 58)
	VI ṢWR	ṣwr yšw‘ty (27[1], 44[2][?])
	VII ’DN	’dny (50[1], 51[2])
3	I ‘LM	‘wlm (2[1], 3[2], 5[3], 29[4], 37[5], 38[6], 52[7])
	II DWR:	dr (2[1,2], 5[3,4])
	III ‘D:	‘d (30[1], 38[2])
	IV NṢḤ:	nṣḥ (47[1])
	V ḤLD:	ḥld (48[1])
4	I ŠYR:	’šyrh (2[1])
	II YDH:	ywdw (6[1])
5		l (2[1], 4[2,3], 5[4], 7[5,6], 12[7,8], 14[9], 19[10,11], 20[12], 28[13], 29[14,15,16], 30[17], 36[18], 37[19], 40[20], 42[21], 45[22], 47[23], 50[24], 52[25])
6		w (2[1], 5[2,3], 6[4], 8[5], 9[6], 12[7], 13[8,9], 15[10,11], 17[12], 18[13], 19[14], 20[15], 23[16], 24[17,18], 25[19,20,21], 26[22,23], 27[24], 29[25], 30[26,27], 31[28], 32[29], 33[30,31], 34[32,33], 35[34], 37[35], 38[36], 39[37,38], 44[39], 45[40], 49[41], 52[42])
7	I YD‘:	’wdy‘ (1[1])
		ywd‘y (16[2])
	II ’MR:	’mrty (3[1])
		t’mr (20[2])
	III DBR:	dbrt (20[1])
8		b (2[1], 3[2], 6[3], 7[4,5], 8[6], 10[7,8], 11[9], 13[10], 16[11], 17[12,13], 18[14], 20[15], 21[16], 23[17], 25[18], 26[19,20], 31[21], 33[22,23], 34[24], 36[25], 38[26], 44[27], 50[28], 51[29])
9	I PH:	py (2[1])
	II PNH:	pnyk (15[1], 16[2])
		pnyw (24[3])
	III ŚPH:	śpty (35[1])
10		ky (3[1], 7[2], 18[3], 19[4])
11	I BNH:	ybnh (3[1])
		bnyty (5[2])
	II KWN:	tkn (3[1])
		’kyn (5[2])
		mkwn (15[3])
		tkwn (22[4])
		ykwn (38[5])
	III HYH:	yhyh (37[1])
		hyh (42[2])

12	I ŠMYM	(3^{1}, 6^{2}, 12^{3}, 30^{4})
	II ŠḤQ	(7^{1}, 38^{2})
	III ’RṢ	(12^{1}, 28^{2}, 40^{3}, 45^{4})
	IV TBL	(12^{1})
13	I KRT:	krty (4^{1})
13 + 14	I ŠB‘:	nšb‘ty (4^{1}, 36^{2})
		nšb‘t (50^{3})
14	I BRH:	bryt (4^{1}, 40^{4})
		bryty (29^{2}, 35^{3})
	II NZR:	nzrw (40^{1})
15	I BḤR:	bḥyry (4^{1})
		bḥwr (20^{2})
	II ‘BD:	‘bdy (4^{1}, 21^{2})
		‘bdk (40^{3})
		‘bdyk (51^{4})
	[cf. mšyḥk, #66^{2,3}]	
	III ‘ZR	(20^{1})
16	DWD:	(4^{1}, 21^{2}, 36^{3}, 50^{4})
	[note use of *hw’*, #33^{1}, for David]	
17		‘d (5^{1}, 47^{2})
18	I ZR‘:	zr‘k (5^{1})
		zr‘w (30^{2}, 37^{3})
	II KS’:	ks’k (5^{1}, 15^{2})
		ks’w (30^{3}, 37^{4}, 45^{5})
19		slh (5^{1}, 38^{2}, 46^{3}, 49^{4})
20		’p (6^{1}, 12^{2}, 22^{3}, 28^{4}, 44^{5})
21	I QHL	(6^{1})
	[note that *bny ’lym* (v. 7, ##25 I^{1}, 2 II^{1}) functions as the real parallel to *qhl qdšym*]	
	II SWD	(8^{1})
22	I QDŠ:	qdšym (6^{1}, 8^{2})
		qdwš (19^{3} [also 2 V^{1}])
		qdšy (21^{4}, 36^{5})
	II ṬHR:	ṭhrw (45^{1})
23	I	my (7^{1}, 9^{2}, 49^{3})
	II	mh (47^{1}, 48^{2,3})
	III	’yh (50^{1})
24	I ‘RK:	y‘rk (7^{1})
	II DMH:	ydmh (7^{1})
25	I BN:	bny (7^{1}, 48^{4})
		bn (23^{2})
		bnyw (31^{3})
	II ’B:	’by (27^{1})

26	I ‘RṢ:	n‘rṣ (8^{1})
	II YR’:	nwr’ (8^{1})
27	I RBB:	rbh (8^{1})
	II ḤSN:	ḥsyn (9^{1})
	III ‘ZZ:	‘zk (11^{1})
		t‘z (14^{2})
		‘zmw (18^{3})
	IV GBR:	gbwrh (14^{1})
		gbwr (20^{2})
		gbr (49^{3} [also 97 II^{1}])
	V QRN:	qrnnh (18^{1})
		qrnw (25^{2})
	VI ’MṢ:	t’mṣnw (22^{1})
28		‘l (8^{1}, 20^{2}, 46^{3}, 48^{4})
29		kl (8^{1}, 17^{2}, 41^{3}, 42^{4}, 43^{5}, 48^{6}, 51^{7})
30	SBB:	sbybyw (8^{1})
		sbybwtyk (9^{2})
31	ṢB’:	ṣb’wt (9^{1})
32		k(mw) (9^{1}, 11^{2}, 30^{3}, 37^{4}, 38^{5}, 47^{6})
33	I	’th ($10^{1,2}$, 11^{3}, 12^{4}, 13^{5}, 18^{6}, 27^{7}, 39^{8})
	II	hw’ (27^{1})
	III	’ny (28^{1}, 48^{2})
34	MŠL:	mwšl (10^{1})
35	I G’H:	g’wt (10^{1})
	II GLL:	glyw (10^{1})
36		h- (10^{1}, 16^{2}, 17^{3}, 50^{4})
37	I YM	(10^{1}, 26^{2})
	II RHB	(11^{1})
	III NHR:	nhrwt (26^{1})
38	I NŚ’:	św’ (10^{1})
		ś’ty (51^{2})
	II RWM:	trwm (14^{1}, 25^{5})
		yrwmw (17^{2})
		trym (18^{3})
		hrymwty (20^{4})
		hrymwt (43^{6})
	III ‘LH:	‘lywn (28^{1})
	IV QWM:	hqymtw (44^{1})
39	ŠBḤ:	tšbḥm (10^{1})
40	I DK’:	dk’t (11^{1})
	II PZR:	pzrt (11^{1})
41	I ḤLL:	ḥll (11^{1})
		yḥllw (32^{2})

		'ḥll (35^{3})
		ḥllt (40^{4})
	II PR(R):	'pyr (34^{1})
	III ŠQR:	'šqr (34^{1})
	IV ŠNH:	'šnh (35^{1})
	V KZB:	'kzb (36^{1})
	VI ZNḤ:	znḥt (39^{1})
	VII M'S:	tm's (39^{1})
	VIII N'R:	n'rth (40^{1})
	IX PRṢ:	prṣt (41^{1})
	X ŠSS:	šshw (42^{1})
	XI ŠBT:	hšbt (45^{1})
	XII MGR:	mgrth (45^{1})
	XIII QṢR:	hqṣrt (46^{1})
42	I ZR':	zrw' (11^{1}, 14^{2})
		zrw'y (22^{3})
	II YD:	ydk (14^{1})
		ydy (22^{2})
		ydw (26^{3})
		yd (49^{4})
	III YMN:	ymynk (14^{1})
		ymynw (26^{2})
		ymyn (43^{3})
		[also listed as #46 II]
43	I 'YB:	'wybyk (11^{1}, 52^{4})
		'wyb (23^{2})
		'wybyw (43^{3})
	II ṢRR:	ṣryw (24^{1}, 43^{2})
	III ŚN':	mśn'yw (24^{1})
44	ML':	ml'h (12^{1})
45	I YSD:	ysdtm (12^{1})
	II BR':	br'tm (13^{1})
		br't (48^{2})
46	I	ṣpwn (13^{1})
	II	ymyn (13^{1}) [see also #42 III]
	III	tbwr (13^{1})
	IV	ḥrmwn (13^{1})
47	ŠM:	šmk (13^{1}, 17^{2})
		šmy (25^{3})
48	I RNN:	yrnnw (13^{1})
	II RW':	trw'h (16^{1})
	III GYL:	ygylwn (17^{1})
	IV ŚMḤ:	hśmḥt (43^{1})
49		'm (14^{1}, 22^{2}, 25^{3}, 34^{4}, 39^{5})

50	QDM:	yqdmw (15[1])
51		’šry (16[1])
52	‘MM:	‘m (16[1], 20[2])
		‘mym (51[3])
53	’WR	(16[1])
54	I HLK:	yhlkwn (16[1])
		ylkwn (31[2])
	II YṢ’:	mwṣ’ (35[1])
	III ŠWB:	tšyb (44[1])
55	YWM:	ywm (17[1])
		ymy (30[2], 46[3])
56	I P’R:	tp’rt (18[1])
	II RṢH:	rṣnk (18[1])
57	GNN:	mgnnw (19[1])
58		yśr’l (19[1])
59	MLK:	mlknw (19[1])
		mlky (28[2])
60		’z (20[1])
61	I ḤZH:	ḥzwn (20[1])
	II R’H:	yr’h (49[1])
62	I ŠWH:	šwyty (20[1])
	II ŚWM:	śmty (26[1], 30[2])
		śmt (41[3])
	III NTN:	’tnhw (28[1])
63		m(n) (20[1], 24[2], 34[3], 45[4], 49[5])
64	MṢ’:	mṣ’ty (21[1])
65	ŠMN	(21[1])
66	MŠḤ:	mšḥtyw (21[1])
		mšyḥk (39[2], 52[3])
67		’šr (22[1], 52[2,3])
68		l’ (23[1,2], 31[3], 32[4], 34[5,6], 35[7,8], 44[9], 49[10])
69	I NŠ’:	yš’ (23[1])
	II ‘NH:	y‘nnw (23[1])
70	I ‘WL:	‘wlh (23[1])
	II PŠ‘:	pš‘m (33[1])
	III ‘WH:	‘wnm (33[1])
71	I KTT:	ktwty (24[1])
	II NGP:	’gwp (24[1])
	III NG‘:	ng‘ym (33[1])
72	QR’:	yqr’ny (27[1])
73	I YŠ‘:	yšw‘ty (27[1])
	II MLṬ:	ymlṭ (49[1])
74	BKR:	bkwr (28[1])

75	ŠMR:	'šmwr (29[1])
		yšmrw (32[2])
76		'm (31[1], 32[2], 36[3])
77	'ZB:	y'zbw (31[1])
78	PQD:	pqdty (33[1])
79	ŠBṬ:	(33[1])
80	'ḤD:	'ḥt (36[1])
81	I ŠMŠ	(37[1])
	II YRḤ	(38[1])
82		ngd (37[1])
83	I 'BR:	ht'brt (39[1])
		tb'r (47[2])
		[note *'br* 'pass' #86]
	II YḤM:	ḥmtk (47[1])
84	I GDR:	gdrtyw (41[1])
	II BṢR:	mbṣryw (41[1])
85	ḤTT:	mḥth (41[1])
86	'BR:	'bry (42[1] [note *'br* 'burn, be angry' #83 I])
87	I DRK	(42[1])
	II 'QB:	'qbwt (52[1])
88	I ḤRP:	ḥrph (42[1])
		ḥrpt (51[2])
		ḥrpw (52[3,4])
	II BWŠ:	bwšh (46[1])
	III rbym → DBB:	dbt (51[1])
89	ŠKN:	šknyw (42[1])
90	I ḤRB:	ḥrbw (44[1])
	II LḤM:	mlḥmh (44[1])
91	'LM:	'lwmyw (46[1])
92	'ṬH:	h'ṭyt (46[1])
93	STR:	tstr (47[1])
94	'Š	(47[1])
95	ZKR	(48[1], 51[2])
96	ŠW'	(48[1])
97	I 'DM	(48[1])
	II GBR	(49[1] [also 27 IV[3]])
98	I ḤYH:	yḥyh (49[1])
	II MWT	(49[1])
	III NPŠ:	npšw (49[1])
	IV Š'WL	(49[1])
99	R'Š:	r'šnym (50[1])
100	ḤYQ:	ḥyqy (51[1])
101	BRK:	brwk (52[1])

NOTES

1. Psalm 89 was chosen because of Professor Ahlström's identification with this work.

2. The primary general criticism would be that this notation is limited to what is now viewed as old-fashioned semantic criticism and does not take into account recent strictures on that pursuit in general (J.L. Kugel, *The Idea of Biblical Poetry* [New Haven: Yale, 1981]) nor the newer emphasis on grammatical parallelism (T. Collins, *Line-Forms in Hebrew Poetry* [Rome: Biblical Institute, 1978]; S.A. Geller, *Parallelism in Early Biblical Poetry* [Chico: Scholars Press, 1979]; M. O'Connor, *Hebrew Verse Structure* [Winona Lake: Eisenbrauns, 1980]). As will be seen when my paper on 'Parallelism' prepared for the First International Symposium on the Antiquities of Palestine (Aleppo, 1981) appears, I agree fully with the need for a broad approach but offer the present study because of limitations of space and because it does attempt something previously, to my knowledge, unattempted. For this type of analysis within a proper surrounding study of distributions of semantic and other types of parallelism, see my study of *'nt* I and Proverbs 2 (in preparation) which served as the groundwork for the Aleppo Symposium paper mentioned above.

3. By 'functional parallelism' I refer to those parallel pairs which do not belong to the natural world of like objects (sun//moon, father//mother, etc.) but which in a given verse create a statement by their association. For the general concept of creative parallelism, see W.R. Watters, *Formula Criticism and the Poetry of the Old Testament* (Berlin: de Gruyter, 1976), and for a discussion of the example *zr'//ks'*, see B. Halpern, *The Constitution of the Monarchy in Israel* (Chico: Scholars Press, 1981) 283, note 161.

4. 'Near parallelism', parallels between immediately contiguous lines, is discussed in my papers mentioned above in note 2. In those papers I take into account four distributions of parallelism: 'half-line' (within one colon of a line), 'regular' (between members of a line), 'near' (just defined), and 'distant' (between cola separated by at least one complete line). All types of parallelism, semantic, grammatical, and phonetic, can be observed in all distributions and an overall structure for a given work can be observed. It is this study of distributions which has had to be omitted in this paper because of space limitations.

5. *mṣ'ty* and *mšḥty* show grammatical parallelism but, I felt, do not show semantic parallelism and are not so listed below. This is a good illustration of the different directions in which one is led by considering the various types of parallelism. By the variation of types and distributions of parallelism, the poet could create a constantly changing face on the old device of parallelism.

6. O'Connor (*Hebrew Verse Structure*, 109) explicitly excludes *figurae etymologicae* from his 'trope of repetition'. This appears to me too exclusivistic,

but the difficult dividing line between true root recognition and simple paronomasia makes any precise definition difficult.

7. See my papers cited above in note 2.

8. See, for example, J. Barr, *The Semantics of Biblical Language* (London: Oxford University Press, 1961); *id.*, 'Hypostatization of Linguistic Phenomena in Modern Theological Interpretation', *JSS* 7 (1962) 85-94; J.F.A. Sawyer, 'Root-Meanings in Hebrew', *JSS* 12 (1967) 37-50.

9. This is intended to be a fairly literal translation which reflects to some extent the word order and thus the parallelism of the Hebrew.

10. The number in parentheses indicates the verse in which the given form is found, while the superscript number indicates the nth occurrence of the root.

JOSHUA 24 AND THE PROBLEM OF TRADITION IN THE OLD TESTAMENT

John Van Seters

I

In a thoughtful article on 'Oral and Written Transmission', G.W. Ahlström raises an important issue in the discussion of oral tradition, namely, the relationship between oral tradition and the written text.[1] One useful distinction that he makes is between oral tradition as an initial mode of composition and oral transmission or communication which may be based upon a written text.[2] Ahlström's discussion centers primarily upon the question of how the prophetic oracles, undoubtedly composed orally in the pre-exilic period, found their way into written collections and were eventually preserved and transmitted in this form.

This matter of oral and written transmission and communication is quite important when it comes to considering the nature of the Pentateuch or the historical works of the Old Testament. Conclusions have often been drawn that the various narratives they contain reflect an oral mode of composition and transmission in a long history of tradition. This conclusion, based upon the observation that the style of the narrative suggests oral communication, may not be entirely legitimate. Ahlström points out that in the semi-literate societies of the ancient Near East it was often necessary for certain written texts to be communicated orally because only a rather restricted class of learned scribes could read and write. Now while several categories of written documents were intended to be kept merely as records or transmitted as part of a written scribal tradition, others were carefully and deliberately composed for oral delivery.

This phenomenon is, of course, abundantly clear from ancient Greece. Whether in the realm of epic or lyric poetry or in the composition of tragedies, the authors received much of their material and inspiration from oral tradition, and they skillfully composed

their works for oral delivery. Yet on neither account can one categorize all of these works as oral tradition and regard the various poets and tragedians as tradents or members of a circle of tradition. Their works are carefully composed literature, however closely they may stand to oral sources and oral modes of delivery.

The same is true of early Greek historiography, and here we have a body of literature that is close both in time and space to early Hebrew historiography.[3] The early prose historians of Greece certainly depended heavily upon local traditions and popular lore for their historical works, whether they were writing the history of a particular state like Athens or composing history on a grand scale to include many peoples and nations.[4] This does not mean that they simply rendered into prose the fixed traditions of particular places. On the contrary, they were themselves responsible for collecting, selecting, ordering, and even inventing, the materials that filled their accounts. The genre of history that they created was a form of literature that only became identified with specific authors. Out of the oral tradition of their sources these authors created literary traditions and these in turn became sources to be modified, expanded or contradicted by later historians as time went on.[5]

At the same time it should be emphasized that these historians were, for the most part, also public performers.[6] Their works were composed in such a way as to appeal to an audience that heard the histories presented. For precisely this reason they often contained those rhetorical and dramatic features that could hold the attention of such an audience while at the same time entertaining and instructing them. The style of Herodotus, for instance, is not so far removed from that of the oral storyteller, and any particular episode that he relates may or may not have come from a traditional source. His own claim is that virtually all of his material is derived from oral tradition.[7] Nevertheless Herodotus and his contemporary historians were authors who produced works of literature and must be treated as such. One cannot judge the oral character of the whole work on the basis of a particular *logos* within it. The works of the early prose historians from Hecataeus onwards are the products of literacy.

The same holds true for the Old Testament. Unlike their Greek counterparts the Israelite historians are anonymous, yet their relationship to oral tradition and their concern for the oral communication of their works are the same. Furthermore, what was already committed to writing and accepted by the religious community could also be

viewed as 'traditional', however recent or old. Thus Deuteronomy was tradition for the Deuteronomists, the Yahwist for the Priestly Writer and all the earlier histories for the Chronicler. There is no reason to suppose that later historians did not know and make full use of earlier historical works. Yet it is equally true that these historians—the Yahwist, the Priestly Writer, the Deuteronomist—were also intent on constructing for Israel *the* tradition which spelled out Israel's true identity and the legitimation of its beliefs and institutions. This was more than just the random collection of traditions. It was a great intellectual achievement which, by means of his own framework and interpretation, a historian could make out of the variety and disparate pieces of tradition a comprehensive view of the people—a history.

With these preliminary remarks in mind I want to look at the problem of tradition in Joshua 24. Does the substance of the chapter point to oral tradition that can be traced back to early days? Or is it a piece of literature whose form merely suggests oral communication? Are there any literary traditions that are antecedent to the work? And what relationship does it have to a work of history and the time of the historian? These are the questions that will be explored below.

II. *The Tradition-History of Joshua 24*

The basis for the traditio-historical approach of Joshua 24 is to be seen above all in the work of M. Noth.[8] Unlike his treatment of the earlier chapters of Joshua, Noth's assessment of the antiquity of the tradition in this chapter does not arise out of his discussion of form. He denies that there is any evidence of early folklore, such as an etiology or a hero-legend. Instead, his reason for seeing an ancient tradition behind the present text is his hypothesis of an amphictyonic league as a religio-political institution uniting the tribes of Israel in the pre-monarchical period. It is in this chapter that Noth believes he has found a tradition that goes back to the actual event which inaugurated the twelve tribe league and to Joshua as its founder.[9]

In his literary analysis of Joshua 24 Noth finds a number of glosses and Dtr (Deuteronomistic) additions that have been made to the text, including the whole of vv. 19-24. He does not, however, regard the Dtr reworking as having essentially changed the content of the whole. Yet the remainder, after the Dtr material has been removed, cannot be attributed to one source. The shift from Yahweh speaking

in the first person to a reference to Yahweh in the third person as well as the fluctuation between 'you' and 'your fathers' and 'we/us' and 'our fathers' has suggested to some a diversity of sources. Noth denies that a clear source division is possible but asserts instead that the basic tradition has experienced an uneven development.

Noth states that the text is strongly isolated from both its literary and traditio-historical context. He lists a number of points of tension with the earlier conquest account in Joshua 1-12, and he denies that it is possible to associate Joshua 24 with a specific Pentateuchal source, either J or E. Consequently, it is to be rooted in an independent tradition. Here Noth appeals to G. von Rad's theory of a cultically rooted tradition of the proclamation of the events of salvation-history.[10] On this basis Noth can account for the transmission of the tradition at a sanctuary and explain the indirect relationship with the Pentateuchal sources as well. Noth then makes out of this 'assembly of Shechem' a regularly repeated cultic event, conducted at the Shechem sanctuary, through which the Israelites remembered the original commitment and pledged themselves anew to worship Yahweh only.

Just how this pre-monarchical liturgical tradition received its literary form with its supposedly uneven development and finally reached its present literary context at a rather late stage of Dtr revision is not at all clear. Nor does Noth have any interest in an interpretation of the text from the literary perspective of the chapter, i.e., as part of a larger historical work.

E. Nielsen takes up the positions of both Noth and von Rad although he understands the development of the text as the product of a circle of traditionists.[11] In this way he accounts for, and discounts, the Dtr element that it contains. Nielsen takes as clear evidence for a pre-Deuteronomy (pre-Dtn) tradition the reference to Shechem and its sanctuary as well as parallels to parts of the Tetrateuch. He also agrees with Noth that Joshua 24 reflects a particular historical event—the establishment of the house of Joseph[12]—but he places greater emphasis, following von Rad, upon the text as reflecting a liturgical tradition in which a kerygmatic recital of sacred history played a vital role. Nielsen states: 'The kerygma presupposes a congregation, conscious of its own character in contrast to foreign elements'.[13] Nielsen sets the origins of such a kerygma in the period of the Judges. He further conjectures that from this early period down to the end of the Northern Kingdom a special

assembly, a 'thing day', was observed during an annual festival in which both the kerygma and the recital of law played an important part.[14]

Nielsen's modification of Noth's position in terms of an ongoing living tradition within a circle of traditionists seems to overcome the problem of continuity, but only superficially so. Apart from his special interpretation of this and other texts, nothing is known directly about any such festival or 'thing day'. It certainly does not explain why Joshua 24 is a secondary addition after Joshua 23. Nor does it come to terms with the close relationship between this tradition within the supposed Dtn circle of tradition and its many precise connections with the Tetrateuch.

Subsequent to Nielsen's study, support for the antiquity of the tradition in Joshua 24 seemed to come from a new quarter. Following the studies of G. Mendenhall[15] and K. Baltzer[16] the underlying form of the text in Joshua 24 is interpreted as corresponding to the covenant-treaty pattern used in Hittite suzerainty treaties during the latter half of the second millennium BC. The difficulty with this approach has been that the basic features of the treaty form are forced rather roughly onto the material of the text. Some endeavor to make up for missing elements has sometimes been made by combining other texts regardless of the problems of source.[17] In the end it has not greatly clarified the problems of the text's form or of the literary relationship to its context and to any broader historical work.

The quest to find an ancient tradition in Joshua 24 has fallen on hard times. The hypothesis of an Israelite amphictyony in the pre-monarchic period, which is the basis of Noth's interpretation, has been rather severely criticized.[18] Likewise von Rad's interpretation of the 'little credo' in Deuteronomy 26.5ff. as a pre-Dtn liturgy has also been called into question.[19] Finally, D. McCarthy, from his detailed study of Near Eastern treaties, strongly disputes that the form in Joshua 24 corresponds in any meaningful way to the treaty-covenant model.[20]

III. *Joshua 24 as an Independent Literary Work*

A quite different approach, which takes the chapter as a literary work, has been put forward in two recent studies, that of McCarthy and L. Perlitt.[21] While they approach their respective analyses from somewhat different perspectives, they nevertheless have much in

common. Both agree that Joshua 24 is a unified literary work of some sophistication, whatever its use of oral tradition might have been. Both relate it to the broad stream of Dtn theology, although they consider it earlier than the Dtr History in which it is now placed. Both consider the references to the warning against the worship of the gods of Mesopotamia as an important clue to the historical setting for the work. Both date the chapter to the time of the monarchy although their specific identifications of the historical context differ considerably.

While McCarthy declines any attempt at tradition-history he nevertheless uses the earlier discussions to assert that the traditions about Shechem, its sanctuary and sacred stone, and much of the material in the speeches are based upon older traditions. The basic evidence for this assertion is the various parallels that can be cited in the J and E sources of the Pentateuch. But unlike the older literary critics McCarthy leaves entirely vague what the relationship of this unit is to the Pentateuch. The notion that they share common ancient traditions is taken as self-explanatory.

At the same time, McCarthy recognizes language and phraseology throughout the text that are characteristic of the Dtn-Dtr corpus. He is unwilling, however, to view these as later additional glosses since he puts strong emphasis upon the literary unity of the work.[22] Consequently, he construes this language as evidence of a proto-Dtn style, and because the setting is located in Shechem he would place the work in the Northern Kingdom.

McCarthy finds in the admonition against worshipping the gods from Beyond-the-River the means of identifying the historical situation of the text. He identifies these gods as the gods of the Arameans because Arameans inhabited Upper Mesopotamia during the monarchy, and because the time when the Israelites were tempted to worship either the local gods of the Amorites (Canaanite deities) or the gods of Mesopotamia (Aramean deities) was in the reign of Ahab when both Phoenician and Aramean influence was strong in the Israelite court.

A number of objections may be raised against this proposal. First, it seems rather far-fetched to identify the gods of the Arameans of Damascus with the gods from Beyond-the-River. Secondly, while the Biblical traditions strongly suggest Phoenician cultural and religious influence in Israel in the time of Ahab there is no evidence of any kind for Aramean religious influence during this same period.

Thirdly, there are sound historical reasons for doubting the accounts of Aramean political domination or influence during Ahab's time. These stories have been misplaced from a later period.[24] Finally, the use of the term Amorite to characterize the local population of Palestine could not have come into vogue before the political domination of the region by Assyria more than a century later.[25]

Beyond this attempt at identifying the historical context of Joshua 24 McCarthy has not explained the nature of the work. Does he think of it as a religious pamphlet and can one substantiate such a genre? In what circles was it used and how was it transmitted to later times? And how was it that this written piece was incorporated so late into its present literary context?

Perlitt's study, much more than McCarthy's, may be viewed as a radical departure from the earlier traditio-historical approach.[26] Perlitt puts his emphasis upon the literary composition of the chapter and does not attempt a tradition-history because he can find no clear evidence of an ancient Shechem tradition or liturgical form. He insists that one cannot begin with the assumption that Joshua 24 stems from the earliest period of Israel's history. Important in this regard is Perlitt's insistence that vv. 25-27 do not constitute a self-contained narrative tradition but only a brief narrative framework for the speeches that precede. It is in the nature and form of the speeches that the whole is to be understood. Here the form of historical recollection and challenge to obedience and fidelity that is so characteristic of the Dtn preaching tradition comes to the fore. The evidence from language also corroborates this conclusion so that one must see it as a composition made in rather close association with the Dtn style.

This analysis of the text leads Perlitt to a consideration of its historical context. His stress upon the Dtn character of the text limits his dating to the time between Hezekiah and Josiah, i.e., close to Dtn but not yet DtrH. This still leaves him with three possible settings: 1. the Northern Kingdom after it became an Assyrian province; 2. the Southern Kingdom in the time of Manasseh; and 3. the northern region of Samaria in the time of Josiah's reform. The 'gods of Mesopotamia' would either be the gods of peoples from Mesopotamia brought into Samaria by the Assyrians or the gods of the Assyrians to whom Israelites and Judeans might have been forced to offer allegiance during their time of political subservience and whose influence was eradicated only by the Josiah reform. These proposals

suffer from the weakness that there is little evidence of any Mesopotamian religion in Judah or Samaria at this time. The Dtn reform speaks only of purification from the religion of the 'Amorites' and it does so in a much more aggressive manner than the kind of appeal found in Joshua 24.

While Perlitt has given many helpful suggestions about the literary character of this chapter, a number of problems still remain. These have to do with the question of genre and the relationship of this work as an addition to the rest of Joshua. The search for a historical and religious setting and an adequate explanation of its literary character cannot yet be said to have reached a satisfactory conclusion.

IV. *Observations on the Text of Joshua 24*

Most treatments of the text of Joshua 24 consist of finding elements of ancient tradition by referring to parallels in the Tetrateuch and of eliminating late Dtr additions and glosses. However, once one is open to the possibility that the author of Joshua 24 may have had at his disposal written traditions, both historical and prophetical, then an entirely different kind of literary analysis is suggested. In order to test this possibility a few salient aspects of this text will be explored.

Scholars have been quick to note that the convocation in Joshua 24.1 has its parallel in 23.2a. In fact the language of 24.1bα is so close to the other text that most of this statement is regarded as a Dtr gloss.[27] The rest of 24.1, which speaks of an assembly of the tribes at Shechem where 'they took their stand before God', has been accepted as an older source. The statement of convocation is followed by a divine speech, introduced in v. 2 by a formula from prophetic speech: 'Thus says Yahweh, the God of Israel'.[28] This combination of assembly and divine speech has a remarkable parallel in 1 Samuel 10.17ff. Here Samuel summons the people to Yahweh at Mizpah and addresses them with the same formula: 'Thus says Yahweh, the God of Israel'. He then proceeds to recite briefly the saving history of God's rescue of the people from Egypt and their deliverance from their enemies. Following this divine speech, with scarcely any hint of transition, is a rebuke by Samuel (v. 19) that the people have rejected Yahweh, and he then summons them to 'take your stand before Yahweh by your tribes and by your thousands'. While this last item in 1 Samuel 10.19b is not in the same order as in Joshua 24.1, where it comes before the divine speech, yet the number of elements that are the same in both texts cannot be fortuitous.

That the basic pattern in 1 Samuel 10.17ff. is thoroughly Dtr can be seen from Judges 6.8-10. The latter lacks the mention of the assembly but contains the prophetic speech: 'Thus says Yahweh, the God of Israel', followed by a summary of the salvation history and a divine admonition against worshipping the 'gods of the Amorites in whose land you dwell'. In 1 Samuel 12.7ff., where a convocation is presupposed, Samuel summons the people to take their stand before Yahweh and then recounts to them God's acts of deliverance towards them and their forefathers. At the end of this is a warning against disobedience and disloyalty.

Already it is possible to say something about the form of the text. It is modeled directly upon Dtr parenesis. It is not just a question of some vague prophetic influence but the kind of prophetic style that is the hallmark of the Dtr tradition both in DtrH and in the late prophetic works.[29] Another observation that confirms this conclusion is the use, in both the divine speech and the subsequent dialogue, of the terms 'you/your fathers' or 'we, us/our fathers'.[30] This reference back to the fathers, whether in terms of what God has done for them or how they sinned against Yahweh by serving other gods and the consequences for the present generation addressed in the second person by prophet or speaker, is found most frequently in Dtr preaching. One even finds the same shift in the course of the dialogue from the 'fathers' (third person) to 'you' (second person) as in 1 Samuel 12.8ff.[31] This same feature occurs in the Dtr prose sermons in Jeremiah (7.21-26; 11.1-13; 16.10-13).[32] This is not a feature of early prophecy so that one must conclude that it is a special feature of the Dtr tradition.[33]

Joshua 24.2-13 contains a historical summary, and therefore it invites comparison with other similar summaries. Deuteronomy 26.5-9, usually regarded as the classic model for the rest,[34] is a confession to be recited by the people on the occasion of the offering of first fruits. But this is not a public liturgy of covenant renewal any more than it is in the case of Deuteronomy 6.20-25. The content of Deuteronomy 26.5ff. is also quite simple. There is a brief allusion to the patriarchs in the 'fugitive Aramean' who went down to Egypt.[35] The main focus is on the rescue from Egypt with 'signs and wonders' and the gift of the land of Canaan. When such summaries are given in later Dtr texts (Jud. 6.7-9; 10.11-12; 1 Sam. 10.18; 12.8-12) they all start essentially with the exodus event and usually bring the historical sketch down to the time of the speaker.[36] Such free literary

adaptations make any fixed liturgical use unlikely. Furthermore, in all of these cases there has been a shift away from its confessional use to making the summaries the substance of a divine or prophetic speech and the basis for admonition. This pattern also holds true for Jeremiah 2.5ff., the Dtr prose sermons (Jer. 7.21-26; 11.1-13) and Ezekiel 20.

Joshua 24.2-13 likewise shows this shift to making the historical summary into a divine speech. Yet the Dtn version has been retained for the people's confession in vv. 16-18. But Joshua 24.2-13 departs radically from the Dtr tradition when it comes to matters of detail. The patriarchal history is added; the exodus event is filled in with new information; and the Balaam episode from the wilderness period is mentioned. Although the new materials come from the pre-Priestly tradition of the Tetreteuch they do not make this historical summary earlier—as many scholars have argued. On the contrary, one must conclude that such an expansion makes it *later* than all the Dtr examples. This is confirmed by the fact that a similar elaboration of the historical summary is found in the latest example in Nehemiah 9.6ff.

This is not just a case, as one might argue, in which Joshua 24.2-13 is more inclusive of older traditions. There are also some significant differences in those items that are shared with the Dtr summaries. In a recent study, B.S. Childs notes that the Dtn formula that refers to the exodus, 'Yahweh brought you out of the land of Egypt', does not refer specifically to the sea event, nor does the formula of Yahweh performing 'signs and wonders in Egypt' designate the plagues.[37] There are no references to the sea event or the plagues in the Dtn-Dtr tradition, in Jeremiah or Ezekiel. In fact, the first mention of the sea event in prophetic literature is in Second Isaiah.[38]

In the case of Joshua 24.5-7 the mention of the plagues and the sea event is not merely a later addition[39] but a part of the account itself. The details manifest a very close relationship with the Yahwist's version of the sea event. The people depart from Egypt (Ex. 12.37ff.) and they arrive at the sea (Ex. 13.17f.); the Egyptians pursue them (Ex. 14.5ff.); the people cry to God (Ex. 14.10ff.); he puts darkness between the two forces (Ex. 14.19f.); the sea overcomes the Egyptians (Ex. 14.21aβ, 24-25, 27aβb, 30). Since the sea event is construed somewhat differently in various poetic versions of the account and in the Priestly source, this close agreement cannot be based merely on a vague notion of ancient traditions.

The same observation can be made about the author's relationship to the patriarchal traditions of the Yahwist,[40] such as the genealogy of the forefathers, the election of Abraham, his guidance and blessing, and his line down to Jacob. The Balaam episode is also taken from the Yahwist's account. But as soon as the summary touches on matters dealt with in the DtrH, it reverts to a number of Dtr themes and clichés and uses these to bring the whole down to the time of the speaker—Joshua.

From these observations the conclusion seems to me inescapable. The author of Joshua 24.1-27 is none other than the Yahwist of the Pentateuch. However, contrary to the views of earlier literary critics, it was not composed before the DtrH but comes later as an addition, just as the Tetrateuch was also an addition to Dtn and DtrH.

Turning now to the dialogue section, the challenge by Joshua in Joshua 24.14-15 follows the theme of a number of Dtr texts that call upon the people to put away their foreign gods. In most cases this has to do with the 'gods of the Amorites in whose land you dwell' (Jud. 6.10; see also Jud. 2.11–3.6; 10.10-16; 1 Sam. 7.3-4; 12.10; 2 Kings 17.7ff.). In addition to this the Dtr tradition suggests that Israel was also tempted to serve the gods of her neighbors (Jud. 10.6). Joshua 24.14-15, however, goes further to include the worship of the gods of Mesopotamia and Egypt as their forefathers had done.[41] The only parallel to such a perspective is in Ezekiel. In Ezekiel 20.7f. the prophet suggests that already in Egypt the fathers worshipped the idols of Egypt. In Ezekiel 23 the notion of Israel and Judah 'playing the harlot' in Egypt in their youth is extended to include their subsequent practice of adopting the gods of Assyria and Babylonia. The author of Joshua 24 has found an even earlier precedent than Egypt by suggesting that the forefathers worshipped the gods of Mesopotamia before Abraham's migration to Canaan.

As indicated above, the people's response in Joshua 24.16-18 is in language that corresponds rather closely to the Dtn pattern of the recital of history as confessional. On the basis of what God has done for the people in the exodus and the events of the conquest, they promise to serve God faithfully. Yet one must emphasize that this is not a ceremony or liturgy whereby a particular group repudiates its former gods in order to worship a new god. On the contrary, the people's statement simply recognizes the logic of the argument which is so characteristic of the Dtr preaching (see especially 1 Sam. 12.7ff.).

The unit in Joshua 24.19-24 has often been judged a Dtr addition,[42]

but its removal would make the transition from v. 18 to v. 25 too abrupt. It is meant to anticipate the statement of covenant making in v. 25 by suggesting the element of blessing and cursing as well as the witnesses to the covenant, but in a rather unique way. The element of threat in v. 20 has its obvious parallel in the warning of Joshua 23.14-16 where there is the same succession of good followed by evil and divine punishment. In the case of Joshua 24.19-20, however, the warning has become a prediction. The people's inability to serve such a god as Yahweh means that when (כי) they forsake Yahweh they will experience his judgment.[43] Stating that Israel cannot serve Yahweh because he is a holy God and a jealous God implies that the people will prove unholy and unfaithful, and this combination of themes is particularly characteristic of the prophet Ezekiel and his explanation for the people's exile.

When the people insist that they will serve Yahweh then Joshua calls the people as witnesses against themselves (not the gods as in the treaties). This same pattern is evident in Second Isaiah. There too the people are called as God's witnesses to the fact that the events of history leading to the exile were predicted by God in their presence (Is. 43.8ff.).

The interpretation of Joshua 24.25-27 is rather disputed. Much depends upon whether or not one believes that the verses contain remnants of an early tradition. Yet, as Perlitt has pointed out,[44] no elements in the narrative can stand as independent from the previous speech units. If one accepts the late date for the speeches then vv. 25-27 cannot be otherwise. The series of actions undertaken by Joshua are vaguely related to each other but the relationship is not very clear. The covenant that Joshua makes 'for' the people obviously has to do with their solemn commitment to serve Yahweh. A parallel is that of Josiah's covenant in 2 Kings 23.1-3, but there the king himself is the principal party, the one responsible for upholding the covenant while the people are included ('stand') in the covenant with him. The covenant consists of the commandments, testimonies, and statutes that were already contained in the book of the covenant. That, of course, represents the Dtr view of covenant as a solemn commitment to the Dtn law.

The Mosaic covenant of the Yahwist in Exodus represents another parallel. As a prelude to the covenant in Exodus 19.3-8 God recounts his deliverance of Israel from Egypt. He then calls for obedience to his covenant in order that Israel may become God's own people.

Moses then assembles the elders and after they hear the words of Yahweh they declare, 'All that Yahweh has spoken we will do'. This constitutes the prelude and anticipation of the laws and covenant-making which follows. In Exodus 24.3-8 the covenant ceremony itself is set forth. Moses first declares to the people the words and ordinances (המשפטים) and the people answer that they will do what Yahweh has said. So Moses inscribes 'the words of Yahweh' in a book. Then the ceremony with its blood rite follows. In this Moses now reads from the book of the covenant and the people again consent to obey Yahweh. The ceremony of blood is then completed.

A full discussion of this text is not possible here.[45] Our interest is primarily in those elements that correspond with Joshua 24. In Exodus we have the divine speech containing the historical summary and the call to commitment followed by the people's assent. The laws are then given and inscribed in a book after which the covenant is finally completed. On the basis of this parallel it seems reasonable to suggest that the covenant in Joshua 24.25a, which follows on the people's assent, is inclusive of the actions that follow it. The 'statute and ordinance' are promulgated as part of the covenant and are then subsequently inscribed in a book of the law of God. The stone is set up as a memorial witness to the events much like the twelve pillars (מצבות) of Exodus 24.4.

Within this unit of Joshua 24.25-27 two pieces of evidence are most often cited as indications of ancient traditions. The first is the statement in v. 25b, 'He set down for them statute and ordinance in Shechem', which has its closest parallel in Exodus 15.25b, 'There he set down for them statute and ordinance'. The divine exhortation to obedience in v. 26 is regarded as a Dtr expansion because of the parallel to Deuteronomy 7.15.[46] But there is a difference. In Dtn the diseases of Egypt were part of the hardship that Israel experienced there. In Exodus 15.26b God promises: 'I will not put upon you any of the diseases that I put upon the Egyptians'. In agreement with the Yahwist's own account, the diseases have now been interpreted as the plagues, a theme that is not in Dtn/Dtr. This is the same development of tradition that we noted earlier in Joshua 24.5. The final statement, v. 26bβ, 'For I am Yahweh your healer', refers back to the healing of the water in v. 25a. The whole is a unity and a post-Dtr creation. One cannot merely isolate a single phrase and make an ancient tradition out of it.[47]

The second piece of evidence for antiquity in Joshua 24 is the

reference to the setting up of a stone under a sacred tree (vv. 26b, 27). It is true that the Dtr tradition took a dim view of standing stones and sacred trees but it is doubtful that their veneration came to an end immediately with the Dtn reform. The Yahwist associated the oak of Shechem with the patriarchs (Gen. 12.6; 35.4) and thereby historicized it. It appears again in Deuteronomy 11.30 in a secondary addition to the text. Apparently it was still venerated at a rather late date, otherwise that geographic detail would have little meaning. As far as Joshua's setting up a stone is concerned, the tradition has preserved, without protest, many such actions by the patriarchs, by Moses, by Joshua at the Jordan and by Samuel (1 Sam. 7.12—a Dtr text). The use of the stone pillar (מצבה) as witness is also mentioned in Genesis 31.45ff.

Furthermore, the statement that the stone 'has heard all the words of Yahweh that he spoke to us' has been described as a remnant of animism and therefore primitive.[48] But that depends entirely upon the speaker/author and the audience. There are at least two other possibilities. The statement could suggest that the stone was inscribed with the details of the events that had taken place and in that way could function as a witness as well. The other possibility is that the stone serves as a memorial of the event and confirms the written account of Joshua 24.[49]

As in the case of examples in the Pentateuch,[50] I believe that the author intended to give a new meaning to the sacred stone under the oak in the sanctuary at Shechem. The precinct may have survived any Dtn reform which hardly reached as far north as Shechem. It was not unusual in Greek historiography for sacred sites to constantly receive new associations with mythical and legendary times and by this technique the Biblical author could make the event much more concrete than the vaguely placed sermon of Joshua 23.

V. *The Historical Setting for Joshua 24*

As McCarthy and Perlitt have clearly seen, the piece touches on the concerns of the author's own time in the dialogue between Joshua and the people. The nature of the appeal placed in the mouth of Joshua is quite remarkable in that a choice of gods is set before the people with no serious threat or curse invoked, only the example of Joshua himself and his household (vv. 14-15). This election is altogether different from that of Dtn where it is clear that Yahweh

chose Israel as his people through the exodus and the people *as a nation* bound themselves to Yahweh by solemn covenant under Moses. So the choice was already made and any subsequent departure by even a part of the nation—and especially by its political leader, the king—could have dire consequences for the whole. Anyone who violated the covenant-law, whether Israelite or non-Israelite, would have to be eradicated. That, at least in theory, was the Dtn-Josianic reform.

Joshua 24, however, seems to envisage an entirely different situation, and therefore a different conception of covenant. The challenge is made to the people no longer as one nation but as so many individual households who are called to follow Joshua's example.[51] Joshua does not function as the centralized authority to keep the nation pure—as in the story of Achan—but as a religious leader who leads by admonition and example. The same perspective is found in the story of Abraham (Gen. 18.18f.), where God says in a soliloquy, 'Shall I hide from Abraham what I am about to do [his judgment on Sodom and Gomorrah]? . . . No, for I have chosen him that he may charge his children and his household after him to keep the way of Yahweh by doing what is right and just, so that Yahweh may bring to Abraham what he has promised.' Here too Abraham is the prophet of God who receives the message of judgment so that he can admonish his children and intercede for the righteous. But he also represents the father of the people of God, the 'household' of Abraham.

The historical and religious *Sitz im Leben* where the primary role of the prophet was to exhort his fellows to 'keep the faith' and where the households individually commit themselves to a covenant with God is not the period of the monarchy but the exile. To be the people of Yahweh is to make confession of one's faith in Yahweh in terms of the historical credo (vv. 16-18) and to Yahweh exclusively. This commitment is the essence of the covenant, and while the law is still important it is treated almost as an afterthought. The reference to the foreign gods, the gods of Mesopotamia and the gods of Egypt, also becomes quite explicable. The theological crisis of the exile meant that the Jews in these regions of the diaspora were sorely tempted to worship the gods of these regions.[52]

Why was the setting of this speech located in Shechem? Shechem had its traditions associated with the early history of Israel. While Samaria may have been the political capital of Israel, Shechem was its traditional and religious center and remained so down to later times. That was reason enough to choose this setting.

VI. *The Place of Joshua 24 in the Hexateuch*

I have indicated earlier in my analysis that scholars have had difficulty in the past explaining how this chapter came into its present context. If Joshua 24 does not belong to the original Dtr work and was an earlier independent piece why would a later Dtr editor want to reclaim this discard to supersede the existing Dtr conclusion? Especially awkward is the fact that as a self-contained work it would have had to include v. 28, 'So Joshua sent the people away, every man to his inheritance'. But it is equally clear that the larger Dtr work would originally have gone from the convocation in Joshua 23 to its proper conclusion in Judges 2.6ff. which contains exactly the same ending.[53]

There is only one solution to this dilemma and that is that Joshua 24.1-27 was composed as an addition to the Dtr work. It is post-Dtr and was inserted before ch. 23's original ending as a second conclusion to the history of Joshua. All our literary analysis confirms the fact that while Joshua 24 was influenced by the Dtr tradition it was in fact a later development of that tradition in the exilic age and must be viewed as post-Dtr.

One can, I feel, go even further than this. Joshua 24 is not an independent piece that comes out of nowhere and exists for a century or two in limbo. Its connections with the Yahwist are manifest, as I have tried to show. It betrays the same historiographical scope and sophistication as the Yahwistic work. However, the Yahwist's history from creation to the death of Moses was not intended to supersede the DtrH but to provide it with a prologue that would give to it a new perspective and direction. The Yahwist made only a few additions to the early part of the DtrH. Joshua 24 represents such an addition which was at the same time his summing up and conclusion to his own history as he had combined it with DtrH.

What kind of a historian was the Yahwist? Returning to our opening remarks, we may safely assert that the Yahwist used oral tradition through his work. Its form and character still remain close to such sources. But at many points in his work, and at that of Joshua 4 in particular, the Yahwist built upon the existing written traditions of the DtrH and the prophetic works that had taken written form by the time of the exile. To be sure, the Yahwist's work was not written as an archival document but as something intended for public oral delivery, like the sermonic passages of the DtrH. The Yahwist's work was not just a vehicle that contained traditions, it was intended to be

the tradition, the living tradition for the religious community to which it was recited.

It is the Yahwist as historian and theologian[54] who through his work addresses the exilic crisis of faith and in the figure of Joshua calls out to the households of Israel—the children of Abraham—to join in the household of faith.

NOTES

1. G.W. Ahlström, 'Oral and Written Transmission: Some Considerations', *HTR* 59 (1966), 69-81.

2. See also Robert C. Culley, 'An Approach to the Problem of Oral Tradition', *VT* 13 (1963), 113-25.

3. For a more extensive treatment of early Greek historiography see my study, *In Search of History: Historiography in the Ancient World and the Origins of Biblical History* (New Haven: Yale University, 1983), ch. 2.

4. Lionel Pearson, *The Local Historians of Attica* (Philadelphia: American Philological Association, 1942); idem, *Early Ionian Historians* (Oxford: Clarendon, 1939).

5. See A. Momigliano, 'Historiography on Written Tradition and Historiography on Oral Tradition', in *Studies in Historiography* (New York: Harper and Row, 1966), 127-42.

6. B. Gentile and G. Cerri, 'Written and Oral Communication in Greek Historiographical Thought', in *Communication Arts in the Ancient World*, ed. E.A. Havelock and J.P. Heshbell (New York: Hastings House, 1978), 137-55.

7. In a recent study by Detlev Fehling, *Die Quellenangaben bei Herodot: Studien zur Erzählkunst Herodots* (Untersuchungen zur antiken Literatur und Geschichte, 9; Berlin: Walter de Gruyter, 1971), the author argues that a rather large portion of Herodotus' oral traditions were his own invention. While the degree to which Herodotus invented his sources and stories may be debated, the fact that at least some of his stories were invented can scarcely be doubted.

8. Martin Noth, *Das Buch Josua*, 2nd edn (Tübingen: J.C.B. Mohr, 1953), 135-41.

9. See already, M. Noth, *Das System der zwölf Stämme Israels* (Stuttgart: W. Kohlhammer, 1930), 65ff. Other recent studies committed to this approach that might be mentioned here are G. Schmitt, *Der Landtag von Sichem* (Stuttgart: Calwer Verlag, 1964); Hans-Joachim Kraus, *Worship in Israel* (Richmond, Virginia: John Knox, 1965), 136ff.; and J. Alberto Soggin, *Joshua* (Philadelphia: Westminster, 1972), 220ff.

10. Gerhard von Rad, 'The Form-Critical Problem of the Hexateuch

(1938)', in *The Problem of the Hexateuch and Other Essays* (New York: McGraw-Hill, 1965), 1-78.

11. Eduard Nielsen, *Shechem: A Traditio-Historical Investigation* (Copenhagen: G.E.C. Gad, 1955), 86-141.

12. Nielsen, *Shechem*, 352.

13. Nielsen, *Shechem*, 93. The appropriateness of such a description for the exilic period cannot go without notice.

14. The model for this notion is the Islandic assemblies of the Middle Ages. See also Eduard Nielsen, *Oral Tradition* (SBT, 11; Chicago: Allenson, 1954), 47f. The notion is also used in Albrecht Alt and Martin Noth.

15. George Mendenhall, *Law and Covenant in Israel and the Ancient Near East* (Pittsburgh: Biblical Colloquium, 1955).

16. Klaus Baltzer, *Das Bundesformular*, 2nd edn (WMANT, 4; Neukirchen-Vluyn: Neukirchener Verlag, 1964).

17. See also Soggin, *Joshua*, 231f.

18. See most recently, C.H.J. deGeus, *The Tribes of Israel* (Amsterdam: van Gorcum, 1976). See especially pp. 54ff., where he reviews the criticisms to date.

19. See L. Rost, 'Das kleine geschichtliche Credo', in *Das kleine Credo und andere Studien zum Alten Testament* (Heidelberg: Quelle und Meyer, 1965), 11-25; and Brevard S. Childs, 'Deuteronomic Formulae of the Exodus Traditions', *SVT* 16 (1967), 30-39.

20. Dennis J. McCarthy, *Treaty and Covenant*, 2nd edn (AnBib, 21a; Rome: Pontifical Biblical Institute, 1978), 239-84.

21. See the work cited in note 20; also see L. Perlitt, *Bundestheologie im Alten Testament* (WMANT, 36; Neukirchen-Vluyn: Neukirchener Verlag, 1969), 239-84.

22. Here he appeals to the study of C.H. Giblin, 'Structural Patterns in Jos 24,1-25', *CBQ* 26 (1964), 50-69.

23. See C. Brekelmans, 'Das sogenannten deuteronomistischen Elemente in Gen.—Num.: Ein Beitrag zur Vorgeschichte des Deuteronomiums', *SVT* 15 (1966), 90-96. Cf. the new directions in Pentateuchal studies in H.H. Schmid, 'Auf der Suche nach neuen Perspektiven für die Pentateuchforschung', *SVT* 32 (1981), 375-94.

24. See J.M. Miller, 'The Elisha Cycle and the Accounts of the Omride Wars', *JBL* 85 (1966), 441-54; idem, 'The Fall of the House of Ahab', *VT* 17 (1967), 307-24.

25. J. Van Seters, 'The Terms "Amorite" and "Hittite" in the Old Testament', *VT* 22 (1972), 64-81.

26. Since McCarthy's work follows that of Perlitt, it could be viewed as occupying a mediating position between that of the older traditio-historical approach and Perlitt's clear break with it.

27. Noth, *Josua*, 135.

28. Noth (*Josua*, 139) and McCarthy (*Treaty and Covenant*, 225) argue

that the phrase 'Yahweh, the God of Israel' has a very old association with Shechem. However, note parallels in 1 Sam. 10.17 and Jud. 6.8 cited below.

29. One might even argue that Josh. 24.1 is a combination of elements drawn from both Josh. 23.2 and 1 Sam. 10.17, 19.

30. Noth (*Josua*, 137) sees in the fluctuation in terminology between 'you' and 'your fathers' evidence of different stages of development in the text. Nielsen (*Shechem*, 85) takes it as evidence for a liturgical *Sitz im Leben*.

31. See also 2 Kings 17.7-18.

32. For a study of these texts, see Ernest W. Nicholson, *Preaching to the Exiles: A Study of the Prose Tradition in the Book of Jeremiah* (Oxford: Blackwell, 1970).

33. See also Amos 2.4 (late) and Ezek. 20.

34. Based on von Rad's study. See note 10 above.

35. See also 1 Sam. 12.8 where Jacob is named.

36. See also 2 Kings 17.7ff.

37. See note 19 above.

38. An exception to this claim would appear to be Deut. 11.2-7, but as Childs points out ('Deuteronomic Formulae', 35), all the details in vv. 3b-6 have been added as an explanation of the 'signs and deeds'. These include an oblique reference to the plagues, a clear mention of the sea event (very similar to Josh. 24.6-7) and the wilderness experience, including the Dathan and Abiram episode. The text has been expanded on the basis of the Tetrateuch.

39. So Childs, 'Deuteronomic Formulae', 36; but he is merely following Noth's suggestion of various redactional expansions to the text.

40. By Yahwist I mean the whole pre-Priestly corpus of the Tetrateuch including any so-called E material, as I have suggested in *Abraham in History and Tradition* (New Haven: Yale University, 1975). For a similar understanding see H.H. Schmid, *Der sogenannte Jahwist* (Zurich: Theologischer Verlag, 1976).

41. The clues for such worship by the forefathers in J are slight. Note, however, in Gen. 24 that the servant of Abraham is careful, in the company of his Mesopotamian host, always to characterize Yahweh as 'the God of my master Abraham'. In the story of Jacob, Rachel's theft of Laban's gods (תרפים), Gen. 31.30ff., also suggests that the forefathers worshipped other gods in Mesopotamia.

42. Noth, *Josua*, 136; Nielsen, *Shechem*, 107f.

43. It obviously anticipates the time of the Judges and presupposes that literary context. In this respect it parallels the warning in Josh. 23.14-16. The latter text also has the same succession of good followed by evil and divine punishment.

44. Baltzer, *Bundestheologie*, 239-47.

45. The literature is too extensive to list here. However, see Schmid, *Jahwist*, 83-118, and also my own observations, 'Recent Studies on the

Pentateuch: A Crisis in Method', *JAOS* 99 (1979), 669-70.

46. Cf. Brevard S. Childs, *The Book of Exodus* (Philadelphia: Westminster Press, 1974), 266-67.

47. The text may reflect a tradition in Ezek. 20.10f., which states that God brought Israel out of Egypt and into the wilderness, 'and I gave them my statutes [חקותי] and revealed to them my ordinances [משפטי] by which the one who observes them might live'. Since Ezekiel does not mention Sinai, it is possible that the author of Ex. 15.22f. interpreted this statement to mean that at the first stop in the wilderness God gave such statutes and ordinances to Israel.

48. Most recently, see McCarthy, *Treaty and Covenant*, 223.

49. Note the similar language in Mic. 6.1-2; Deut. 31.38; 32.1.

50. J. Van Seters, 'The Religion of the Patriarchs in Genesis', *Biblica* 61 (1980), 230-33.

51. The attempt to interpret Joshua's 'household' as a special tribal confederacy (as Noth) or some other group or community is quite unwarranted; cf. Nielsen, *Shechem*, 106, and Soggin, *Joshua*, 230.

52. Soggin, *Joshua*, 236-37, also sees this significance in the text but regards it as a secondary application by the Dtr.

53. What to do with the rest of the intervening material in Josh. 24.29-33; Jud. 1.1-2.5 cannot be dealt with here. I have addressed this problem in *In Search of History*, ch. 10.

54. Cf. R. Rendtorff, 'Der "Jahwist" als Theologe? Zum Dilemma der Pentateuchkritik', *SVT* 28 (1975), 158-66 = 'The "Yahwist" as Theologian? The Dilemma of Pentateuchal Criticism', *JSOT* 3 (1977), 2-9; idem, *Das überlieferungsgeschichtliche Problem des Pentateuchs* (BZAW, 147; Berlin: Walter de Gruyter, 1976).

THE SHINING OF MOSES' FACE: A CASE STUDY IN BIBLICAL AND ANCIENT NEAR EASTERN ICONOGRAPHY

Menahem Haran

I

Exodus 34.29-35 deals with one of Moses' unique peculiarities, practically unmentioned elsewhere in the Hebrew Bible, though it may be paralleled in ancient Near Eastern iconography. As the narrative has it, when Moses came down from Mount Sinai with the two tablets in his hands, he did not know that while the Lord had been speaking with him, 'the skin of his face shone'. The verb *qāran*, used in this passage, appears in the qal conjugation only here, while in the hiph'il it occurs in Psalm 69.32, referring to the growth of an ox's horns. It was apparently on the basis of the latter verse that Aquila understood that the skin of Moses' face also sprouted horns, an interpretation which was adopted by Jerome in his commentary to Amos 6.13 and serves as the basis of the Vulgate's translation of Exodus 34.29: *quod cornuta esset facies sua*.[1] This translation had its effect, as we know, on portrayals of Moses in Renaissance art works (and some centuries earlier). However, most commentators, both the older and the more contemporary, have already concurred that the verse refers to rays of light radiating from the brilliance of Moses' face, just as in Habakkuk 3.4 it is said of God himself: 'rays of light, *qarnayim* [cognate with *qāran*], flash from his hand' (before which we read that 'his brightness is like the light'). The splendour surrounding the image of God is alluded to in several additional biblical passages: the seventy elders of Israel saw God 'and under his feet there was the likeness of a pavement of sapphire, like the very sky for purity' (Ex. 24.10), Ezekiel saw 'radiance all about him' (Ezek. 1.27-28), while the psalmist describes the Lord as 'wrapped in light as with a garment' (Ps. 104.2; see also below). Something of the divine radiance was imparted, then, to Moses' face, which thereafter also

shone. Later on the passage relates how the people, being repulsed by this radiance, were afraid to get close to Moses, but he dispelled their fears, and after telling them the Lord's message he put a *masweh* over his face. The substantive *masweh*, also mentioned only in this passage, is mostly explained, according to the context, as a veil or scarf hung over the face, though the etymology is uncertain.

The first part of the passage (vv. 29-33) is thus the account of an event which took place when Moses descended from the mountain. The second part describes a recurring situation: whenever Moses spoke with the Lord or communicated the Lord's word to the people, he would remove the veil—at all other times he would walk about with the veil over his face (vv. 34-35). What happened to Moses upon his descent from the mountain is thus but the beginning of a new situation, that is, it constitutes a change in his condition which endured from that moment on.

A full understanding of this passage calls for the elucidation of some basic problems, interconnected with each other: clarification of the textual unity and narrative continuity of this passage must precede any attempt to define the matter related therein, while a correct definition of the reported matter entails the problem of its anthropological pattern and its biblical and extra-biblical parallels.

II

At the acme of biblical literary criticism, scholars sought to discover contradictions, tensions and disharmonies within this passage. After Moses' face shone and caused the people to be afraid of approaching him, he calls to them and speaks to them, communicating the words of the Lord to them (vv. 31-32). After finishing this, however, he puts a veil over his face (v. 33). This gave several scholars cause to wonder, for, if Moses could speak to the people without a veil, why should he put it on after he has already finished speaking? The two halves of v. 34 seemed not to connect with each other, since in the first half it is said that when Moses went in to speak with the Lord he would remove the veil 'until he went out'. But the second half has it that 'he went out and spoke to the people of Israel', that is, without the veil. Again, the first part of the narrative apparently implies that the veil was meant to conceal the shining of Moses' face, except that at first, when Moses did not know as yet what had happened to him, he did not avoid speaking with the people even before putting on the

veil (vv. 30-33). The second part (vv. 34-35), however, clearly imports that even when Moses spoke to the people on subsequent occasions he did not wear the veil.

Due to these difficulties—which are in fact only apparent and derive from a certain preconception imposed on the narrative—a good few scholars have been quick to transpose parts of verses in order to obtain a different 'reading' of the narrative which would fit their general notion. At the same time, many of them tended to detach the two parts of the passage from each other and to regard the second part (vv. 34-35) as an addition, a 'legendary expansion', or as an indication of different layers in the priestly source (to which this passage is mostly attributed), or even as a fragment originating from another source.[2] A sharp and far-reaching expression of these tendencies was given in the opinion of Gressmann, who postulated that the passage consists of two variant forms of the same story. According to one form (vv. 29-33), when Moses came down from Mount Sinai with his face radiant, the people were frightened and drew away from him, but when he put on a veil they returned to him and he then announced the words of God; when he concluded he removed the veil. According to the second form (vv. 34-35), each time Moses would go in before the Lord to speak with him he would remove the veil, and when he went out and announced the words of God to the people he would wear the veil, which was kept on until he went in before the Lord again.[3]

The trouble with all this is that the purported difficulties in the narrative's continuity are in fact negligible, and though the language is slightly jagged and it is quite possible that some mishaps have taken place in the text, there is no difficulty in understanding the intent of the narrative as it is. Instead of claiming that there was a 'deliberate alteration of the text' (*absichtliche Änderung des Textes*), an alteration which, as Gressmann argues, 'sets matters almost on their head' (*stellt die Dinge nahezu auf den Kopf*), it would be much more to the point to assert that what the narrative reports is precisely the opposite of what scholars have tried to discover in it. In v. 34 it is said that whenever Moses went in before the Lord to speak with him, he would take the veil off not 'until his coming out', but 'until his coming out and he came out and spoke to the people of Israel', that is, the preposition *'ad*, 'until', referring up to the end of the verse. Thus, Moses' speaking to the people of Israel that took place immediately after his coming out from before the Lord was also done without the

veil. This very point is explicitly set forth in the narrative's first part as well: when Moses descended from Mount Sinai with his face shining, Aaron and the people were afraid to approach him—and what helped them overcome their fear was not the veil but Moses' calling to them, as a result of which Aaron and the chieftains 'return' to him, followed by all the people of Israel who come near to him and hear 'all that the Lord spoke with him on Mount Sinai'. Only after concluding his words does Moses put a veil over his face (vv. 30-33). The same is said explicitly in the narrative's conclusion as well, that whenever Moses came out from before the Lord and spoke with the people, they would see that 'the skin of Moses' face shone', and only after speaking with the people would he replace the veil over his face (v. 35). The descent from Mount Sinai is thus completely parallel to the comings out from before the Lord: just as the former is accompanied by Moses' face shining and followed by his announcing to Israel the word of the Lord, after which he puts on the veil, so also is the latter. And just as the tent into which Moses enters 'before the Lord to speak with him' is in the nature of a portable reflection of Mount Sinai, so it affects Moses in the same way, and the rules of his behaviour after descending the mountain and after coming out of the tent are the same. The only difference between the descent from Mount Sinai and the comings out from before the Lord is that at first, while coming down from the mountain, 'Moses did not know that the skin of his face shone' (v. 29), which he surely realized pretty soon, whereas afterwards he was already aware of this shining, with which he had to live permanently.

The scholars who exert much effort to shift the meaning of the narrative in question seem to base their reasoning on the assumption that the *masweh*, the veil, is meant to protect the public from the divine radiance emanating from Moses' face. But it is precisely the point, that according to the plain meaning of the text the people are not prevented from seeing this radiance as long as Moses announces to them the word of God. It can be said that the veil is meant to disguise the divine light so that it would not be wasted, but it is not at all impossible for the radiance itself to be seen by the people. On the contrary, it serves as a kind of optical and tangible confirmation of the fact that it is God's word that is being spoken to them when they see the light radiating from Moses' face.[4] The aforementioned scholars seek a *cultic* significance for the use Moses makes of the veil. But according to the narrative's plain import Moses wears the veil

not in the role of a cultic functionary but precisely as a 'private individual', *Privatmann*—not while transmitting the word of God to the people but precisely when he is unoccupied with any activity of this sort. This being the case, it can hardly be contested that it is the light radiating from Moses' face, not the veil, that constitutes the main point of the biblical narrative.

III

Since the main point is the radiance, not the veil that hides it, it is quite inappropriate to draw an analogy between this *masweh* and the scarf which the pre-Islamic Arab *kāhin* used to put over his face when he uttered prophecies, as was suggested by Wellhausen.[5] For according to the biblical narrative and in contradistinction to the practice of the Arab *kāhin*, Moses wears the veil not while he is engaged in divination but only afterwards, when he does not fulfil any function.

Gressmann, for his part, conjectured that in the biblical narrative, the *masweh*, which he also took to be a veil, replaces the mask which priests of various religions would put on their faces during cultic ceremonies. In his view, the mask is the anthropological parallel and the tangible cultic basis for the semi-mythical story of the shining of Moses' face. In its cultic use the mask was conceived of as a portrait of the deity and whoever wore it would be identified with the god. In Gressmann's opinion, ancient Israelite worship was also acquainted with the use of cultic masks, in biblical Hebrew referred to as *terāphîm* and set over the ephod which, according to a view adopted by Gressmann too, was none other than a statue of god. In the narrative's priestly editing, according to which the high priest is prohibited from entering the holy of holies except for one day a year, the use of the mask was made to take place outside the tent. In the conditions of ancient times, however, when anyone who 'sought the Lord' would come to the tent of meeting (Ex. 33.7), Moses had to make the cultic use of the mask only inside the tent. This is the explanation provided by Gressmann for the narrative, or as he would say, for the two narratives, analysing them according to the form-critical method and defining them as etiological sagas, or as burlesques in their literary form.[6] It seems that it is due to the attempt to apply that innovative method, and only because of this, that Gressmann's views on this matter won such considerable echoes, various scholars

having felt obliged to reiterate them.[7] For apart from this merit, namely, the attempt to make use of that particular method, the attempt itself is nothing but a chain of conjectures, rather curious in themselves and quite loosely connected with each other.

For the sake of brevity, let us leave alone the identification of *terāphîm* with a mask, an identification which has nothing in it except the conjecture itself. Let us also forgo discussing the hypothesis that the concept of ephod could possibly switch from 'a statue of deity' to 'a priestly garment'. Let us likewise skip over the confusion of the priestly tabernacle with the non-priestly tent of meeting (Ex. 33.7-11), the former of which is a reflection of a temple, that is, a 'house of God', located in the middle of the camp, whereas the latter is an institution of ecstatic activity 'outside the camp, far off from the camp'.[8] Even disregarding these major stumbling-blocks, it has yet to be explained how the biblical narrative underwent such substantial changes and from where can they be proven: the use of a mask inside the tent moves outside; subsequently, the mask—the *terāphîm*, as it were—becomes a veil; after this, a 'deliberate alteration of the text' still occurs, setting matters 'on their head' and making the cultic-divining use of the mask (now of a veil) into that of a 'private individual'—precisely when he is not engaged in fulfilling his function. Anyone who seeks to prove that these changes did take place in the narrative must not only search for difficulties—real or illusory—in the forms into which the story presumably evolved, but also explain why the story could not be preserved in any one of its preceding crystallizations, which were closer to its authentic form (for most of the changes that Gressmann claims to have taken place, he does not even pose such a question). Thus, for example, it is not clear at all why in this narrative the *terāphîm* had to become a *masweh*, a veil. Why was the mention of *terāphîm* preserved in relatively old narratives (such as Gen. 31; Judg. 17–18; 1 Sam. 19.13-16) as well as in relatively late texts (such as Zech. 10.2; 2 Kgs 23.24; Ezek. 21.26), but it had to disappear from Exodus 34.29-35.

Moreover, even when Gressmann believes he can find one or another difficulty in one of the narrative's forms and it seems to him sufficient proof for a change which the narrative had to undergo, it is mostly far from being a real difficulty. It has already been remarked that Gressmann fails to define correctly even the meaning of the narrative in its 'final' form, since he posits that the veil is meant to protect the people from the light radiating from Moses, whereas in

fact it is meant only to cover the light when Moses is not announcing the word of God. If one is to be cautious in understanding the narrative as it is before us, all the more should one be cautious when departing from the solid textual ground to the reconstruction of the story's previous stages, which exist only hypothetically, while the conjectures accompanying such a departure must be carefully considered and supported.

There is thus no real connection between the use made of the veil in the biblical narrative of the shining of Moses' face and the anthropological pattern of cultic mask. The connection comes about only by flattening the narrative, or rather not the narrative itself but its previous form, which exists only as a feeble conjecture, 'reconstructed' in order to match the pattern. Indeed, some scholars were not allured by the appearance of an innovative method and did not refrain from using sharp words against Gressmann's suppositions on this score.[9] In this respect they were surely in the right.

IV

However, both those who followed Gressmann and those who disagreed with him seem to have overlooked the fact that the shining of Moses' face has an additional mention in the priestly source, and that, in a different manner than in the account of Exodus 34.29-35. Before his death Moses asks the Lord to appoint a person who will lead the people after him. In response, he is commanded to lay his hand upon Joshua, to have him stand before Eleazar the priest and the whole community, to commission him in their sight, and then we read: 'you shall bestow some of your radiance, *wenātattā mēhôdekā*, upon him' (Num. 27.20).[10] The connection between Moses' shining face and his *hôd*, radiance, was already sensed in the Midrash, where the combination *qarnēy hôd*, 'rays of *hôd*' (*qarnēy* being cognate with *qāran* in Ex. 34.29-35), was coined and applied exclusively to Moses, and Jewish medieval commentators followed suit.[11] In P the substantive *hôd* is mentioned only once, but it is quite common in the Hebrew Bible, where it is obviously used as one of Yahweh's attributes: all in all it has 24 occurrences (including one in Zech. 10.3, where *hôdô* is doubtful), at least 12 of which refer explicitly to God. From the divine realm it was transferred to the king, becoming one of his attributes as well, and in the latter use it appears seven additional times (of these once in Hos. 14.7: 'his *hôd* shall be like the

olive', metaphorically referring to Ephraim; the lament in Jer. 22.18: 'Ah, lord! Ah, his *hôd*' also seems to refer to a king). In one of the royal psalms the poet says: 'you have endowed him with *hôd* and majesty' (Ps. 21.6), which implies that *hôd* is one of those qualities that originate with God.[12]

In its primary meaning the concept *hôd* apparently signifies the light radiating from the figure. An indication of this meaning is the depiction of God as one who is 'clothed' with *hôd* (Ps. 104.1; this psalmodic wording reverberating in Job 40.10), after which the text goes on to say that God is 'wrapped in light as a garment'. Another indication of *hôd*'s basic meaning is the fact that in Habakkuk 3.3-4, too, the mention of Yahweh's *hôd* is made in the same breath with *nōgah*, 'brightness', *'ôr*, 'light' and *qarnayim*, 'rays' (probably of light). At the same time, the notion that Yahweh's figure is surrounded with a halo of light has some further expressions in the Bible, in addition to the verses referred to at the beginning of this paper. The statement 'You shall not, *lō' tûkal*, see my face' (Ex. 33.20) surely does not intend only to prohibit seeing Yahweh's face, but also to assert the inability of a mortal to look upon the divine. Any such gazing would be fatal, as the second half of the verse goes on to say: 'for man shall not see me and live', which means not a capital punishment by a court but an incapacity of man to stand the exceeding brilliance radiating from the divine image (*lō' tûkal* implying 'you shall not be able' rather than 'you must not'). Another, somewhat sublimated and refined reference to the same notion is the mode of speech of the priestly blessing, 'Yahweh cause his face to shine upon you' (Num. 6.25; echoed in Ps. 67.2), and also the entreaties recurring in several psalms that Yahweh would cause his face to shine on the worshipper (Ps. 31.17; 80.4, 8, 20; 119.135), as well as the allusions to the light of Yahweh's face (Ps. 4.7; 44.4; 89.16) and the depiction of Yahweh as a source of light (Isa. 2.5; 60.19-20; Ps. 36.10).[13] An additional reference in this vein is the story about angels of the divine retinue that strike all the men surrounding them with *sanwērîm*, that is, with temporary blindness caused by a sudden flash of excessive light (Gen. 19.11). In another story, slightly later and containing signs of inflated ornamentation, the same is done at the prophet's request in his prayer (2 Kgs 6.18).[14] Moreover, Yahweh's rainbow also radiates light (Gen. 9.13-14; cf. Ezek. 1.28) and the arrows he lets off also produce light and sparkle like lightning (2 Sam. 22.15 = Ps. 18.15; Hab. 3.11; Zech. 9.14). We

also find that this light as well, though primarily a divine characteristic, is metaphorically transferred to the king (Prov. 16.15).

In a relatively late combination of construct state we find that the concept of *kābôd*, 'glory', is also mentioned alongside *hôd* (together with *hādār*, the usual complement of *hôd*): *hādār kebôd hôdekā*, 'the splendour of glory of your radiance' (Ps. 145.5). It seems that the concrete, tangible meanings of both these concepts, *hôd* and *kābôd*, evolved into general and descriptive usages, or that their varying meanings had a synchronic existence as different forms of style.[15] However, each of them bears its own primary drift and they should by no means be confused, though moderns occasionally tend to do so. The basic meaning of *hôd* is, as has been said, the halo of light surrounding and radiating from a figure. Yahweh's *kābôd*, as against this, in its concrete and tangible meaning, which is particularly characteristic of the language of P and Ezekiel, signifies the extraordinary, 'thick' covering that envelopes the divine image, concealing it from the outside. In day-time this covering is seen as a cloud, but at night it takes on the appearance of fire (Ex. 40.38; Num. 9.16; etc.).[16] It is the nature of fire, too, to give off light and the cloud, particularly in Ezekiel's descriptions, also possesses a brilliance (Ezek. 1.28; 10.4; 43.2; cf. Isa. 60.1-3). Nevertheless, *hôd* and *kābôd* are not the same, since *hôd* does not conceal the figure it surrounds, whereas *kābôd* functions as a screen, hiding God's image from view. Indeed, there is no prohibition against seeing Yahweh's *kābôd*, and the text says explicitly that it appeared in the sight of all the congregation and was seen by everybody (Ex. 16.10; 24.17; Lev. 9.6, 23; etc.). Moreover, *hôd*, which is basically divine, prevailed upon Moses too, and according to Exodus 34.29-35 the people could not see this light shining whenever Moses announced the word of God. As we have seen, before his death Moses even bestowed some of his *hôd* on Joshua (Num. 27.20)—not all, but only a certain part of it.[17] However, God's *kābôd*, 'glory', is one of those things that cannot possibly be bestowed upon someone else, and it is inconceivable that any mortal should be wrapped in it.

V

The closest ancient Near Eastern anthropological parallel to the shining of Moses' face is the Mesopotamian concept of *melammu*. This substantive basically indicates the brilliant light that radiates

from the gods and seems to be taken as mostly surrounding their heads, as is said of Marduk in the Babylonian Creation Epic: *me-lam-mi ra-šub-ba-ti a-pi-ir ra-šu-uš-šu*, 'with his terrible *melammu* his head was turbaned' (*Enuma eliš*, IV, 58). Moreover, all the weapons of the gods, as well as anything that relates to the gods, also radiate *melammu*. The gods are even able to impart this light to other beings and apparently also to take it from them, as Ea did to Mummu, whom he tricked into falling asleep and then *me-lam-me-šu it-ba-la*, 'removed his *melammu*' (*ibid.*, I, 68).[18] The king, as the representative of the gods, also 'bears *melammu*' (cf. what is said in Zech. 6.13 concerning *hôd*), and when he assumes his throne the gods crown him with *melammu* as a token of their divine authorization of his kingship.[19] Cylinder seals sometimes portray divine figures surrounded with a nimbus of rays (terminating in small balls, symbolizing sparks or stars), which apparently is the graphic representation of *melammu*, though it appears only at the end of the Assyrian period.[20]

At the same time, the semantic range of *melammu* seems to encompass some additional connotations, which may either come close to, or move away from, the primary meaning of 'radiant light', just as the biblical notions of *hôd* and *kābôd* do not stay affixed to their basic meanings only.[21] The later offshoots of the Akkadian *melammu* and biblical *hôd* according to their basic meaning, taking on the form of a halo crowning the heads of Christian saints, are too well known to be treated here.

A real parallel to the shining of Moses' face and the divine *hôd* that is said to have surrounded that face is thus to be found only on the level of ancient Near Eastern mythical and iconographic imagery, not in the cultic practice of the time. This cannot be denied, because there is nothing to prove that the biblical legend itself concerning what happened to Moses on Mount Sinai and his subsequent behaviour has any cultic basis. The biblical narrative has no such basis, because its main focus is the shining of Moses' face, a focus on which the extra biblical parallel also rests—not on the *masweh*, which is not a mask, nor can it serve as a key for comprehending the narrative.

NOTES

1. On Jerome's rendering of the verb *qāran* in Exodus 34.29-35, which differs from all ancient versions including the targums (though Jerome

himself refers at times to the accepted meaning), see now M. Tsevat, 'The Skin of his Face was Radiant', *Eretz-Israel* 16 (1982), 161, 165-66 (Hebr.).

2. A first hint in this direction was apparently made by J. Wellhausen, *Die Composition des Hexateuchs*, 3rd edn (Berlin: Georg Reimer, 1899), 97; cf. the commentaries on Exodus by H. Holzinger (KHC, 1900), B. Baentsch (HKAT, 1900), G. Beer–K. Galling (HAT, 1939) and others, in their remarks *ad loc.*; also B.D. Eerdmans, *Alttestamentliche Studien III: Das Buch Exodus* (Giessen: A. Töpelmann, 1910), 80-81; H. Gressmann, *Mose und seine Zeit* (FRLANT, 18; Göttingen: Vandenhoeck & Ruprecht, 1913), 246-47, n. 7; O. Eissfeldt, *Hexateuch-Synopse* (Leipzig: J.C. Hinrichs, 1922), 56-57; G. von Rad, *Die Priesterschrift im Hexateuch* (BWANT, 13; Stuttgart: W. Kohlhammer, 1934), 78-80; M. Noth, *Überlieferungsgeschichte des Pentateuch* (Stuttgart: W. Kohlhammer, 1948), 33 n. 118.

3. Gressmann, *Mose und seine Zeit*, 246-48.

4. This point was already observed by some medieval commentators. See, e.g., Ibn Ezra, Rashi and Abarbanel, in their comments *ad loc.*

5. See J. Wellhausen, *Reste arabischen Heidentums*, 2nd edn (Berlin/ Leipzig: De Gruyter, 1927), 134-35.

6. Gressmann, *Mose und seine Zeit*, 249-51.

7. See especially the commentaries on Exodus by M. Noth (ATD, 1959) and, more recently, B.S. Childs (OTL, 1974), in their observations *ad loc.*; also some of the publications referred to above, note 2. The impact of Gressmann's method is also recognizable in the curious hypothesis put forward by A. Jirku, 'Die Gesichtsmaske des Mose', *ZDPV* 67 (1945), 43-45, that the mask Moses wore was decorated with horns and that when he spoke to the people he put a veil over the *mask*, so that his audience should not be frightened. Jirku is one of the very few contemporary scholars who attempt to come back to the explanation of *qāran* as 'sprouted horns' (cf. also J.M. Sasson, 'Bovine Symbolism in the Exodus Narrative', *VT* 18 [1968], 385-87); but this is also hardly tenable. What is capable of sprouting horns is the head, not the skin of the face, as is said of Moses. According to Ps. 69.32, too, that which sprouts horns (*qrn* being here used in the hiph'il conjugation) is the bull, not the skin of its face. On the mask itself see also below.

8. Some arguments for the basic unity of the ephod, which in all the sources is considered a garment (not an image of a deity which came to mean garment), and some proofs of the fundamental difference in the comprehension of the nature of the tent of meeting (which in P's view is only a term for the tabernacle, whereas in the non-priestly view is a tent for ecstatic activity taking place outside the camp), will be found in my articles in *Tarbiẓ* 24 (1956), 380-91, and 25 (1957), 11-20, and most recently in my book *Temples and Temple Service in Ancient Israel* (Oxford: Clarendon Press, 1978), 166-68, 260-75.

9. See, e.g., J. Morgenstern, 'Moses with the Shining Face', *HUCA* 2

(1925), 3-4; W. Rudolph, *Der 'Elohist' von Exodus bis Josua* (BZAW, 68; Berlin: A. Töpelmann, 1938), 60; F. Dumermuth, 'Moses strahlendes Gesicht', *ThZ* 17 (1961), 241-43. The reservations these scholars had against Gressmann's method do not vindicate their own solutions (though Morgenstern did make some additional commendable distinctions, his overall conclusions seem quite far-fetched and unwarranted; Dumermuth's view, apart from his criticism of Gressmann's conjectures, is also far from being plausible).

10. The prepositional *m* has here the *partitive* sense, for which cf. Gesenius–Kautsch–Cowley, *Grammar*, §119, *w*, n. 2 (see also below, n. 17).

11. 'From where did Moses gain the rays of *hôd*? Our Rabbis, of blessed memory, said, From the cave, as it is written [Ex. 33.22], "As my glory passes by, I will put you in a cleft of the rock [and shield you with my hand]"; the Holy One, blessed be He, put his hand over him and thence he acquired the rays of *hôd*; thus the text says, "Rays flash from his hand, that is where his power lies hidden" [Hab. 3.4]' (Tanḥuma, *Kî Tiśśā'*, 37); cf. the references in E. Ben-Yehuda, *Thesaurus Totius Hebraitatis* (New York/ London: T. Yoseloff, 1959), 6194. Thus, e.g., Rashi on Num. 27.20: "'you shall bestow some of your *hôd* upon him"—this is the shining of the skin of the face'. The combination 'rays of light' occurring in modern Hebrew, with 'light', *'ôr*, as the *nomen regens*, is attested in neither mishnaic nor biblical Hebrew (and as far as I can see, not even in medieval Hebrew), and is apparently only late. I am doubtful whether any of the moderns saw the connection between the shining of Moses' face and the *hôd* ascribed to him. For the meaning of *hôd*, which according to the Rabbis is the brilliant light emanating from Moses' face, cf. also bḤagigah 16a; Baba Bathra 75a (and below, n. 17).

12. For 'endowed him' the Hebrew text has *tešawweh*, which bears the connotation of 'make equal' (cf. dictionaries). Thus, as far as the qualities of *hôd* and *hādār* ('majesty, splendour') are concerned, qualities which primarily belong to God and imparted by him to the king, the king becomes, as it were, equal to God.

13. Cf. G.B. Gray, *Numbers* (ICC; Edinburgh: T. & T. Clark, 1912), 73. The expression 'Yahweh cause his face to shine upon' is, to be sure, not connected with Exodus 34.29-35, as Gray rightly comments, but the matter is essentially the same.

14. For the supposed derivation of the noun *sanwērîm* which seems to have been borrowed from the Akkadian (Assyrian) **sunwurum* (an adjectival form in the superlative, from the root *nur*), see E.A. Speiser, 'The "Elative" in West-Semitic and Akkadian', *Oriental and Biblical Studies* (ed. by J.J. Finkelstein and M. Greenberg; Philadelphia: University of Pennsylvania, 1967), 486, n. 52; idem, *Genesis* (AB, 1; Garden City: Doubleday, 1964), 139-40.

15. Just as *hôd* is basically a halo of light but is also employed in the

meaning of 'majesty, sublimity', so *kābôd* has its physical-material significance, especially in reference to God, but is also used in the meaning of 'honour, respect' (as well as in the tangible meaning of 'property, possessions'). In its physical-material meaning the Lord's *kābôd* appears in passages the antiquity of which is undoubted (Num. 14.21-22; 1 Sam. 4.21-22; 1 Kgs 8.11; etc.), but it particularly characterizes the language of P and Ezekiel (see further). At times, however, the *kābôd* is identified with God himself, as may be seen from the context. See, e.g., Ex. 33.18, 22 (cf. vv. 20 and 23); possibly also Ezek. 1.28 (cf. vv. 26-27); apparently also such passages as Jer. 2.11; Ps. 106.20 (cf. also Isa. 60.1-2). The reason for this identification is the fact that, as a rule, one can take a look not at the image of God himself, but only at the (cloud of) *kābôd* enveloping it. For the various meanings of the concept *kābôd* see most recently C. Westermann, in *Theologisches Handwörterbuch zum Alten Testament*, I (ed. by E. Jenni and C. Westermann; Munich/Zurich: C. Kaiser, 1971), 802-12; M. Weinfeld, in *Theologisches Wörterbuch zum Alten Testament*, III (ed. by G.J. Botterweck and H. Ringgren; Stuttgart: W. Kohlhammer, 1982), 222-25, 229-32.

16. In Exodus 24.15b-18a the text is either brief or has been slightly contracted, and its purport is: in those six days when the Lord's *kābôd* abode on Mount Sinai, 'the cloud covered' the mountain in the daytime (v. 16), and 'the appearance of the *kābôd* of the Lord was like a devouring fire on the top of the mountain in the sight of the people of Israel' (v. 17) at night. The non-priestly parallel to the Lord's *kābôd* is the pillar of cloud which goes before Israel, and there should be no doubt that, presumably, this cloud also functions as a covering of the image of God (cf. Ex. 14.19 and the references further below). This pillar, too, appears as a cloud in day-time, but obtains the form of fire at night (Ex. 13.21-22; Num. 14.14; Deut. 1.33). However, at the morning watch, a time that is neither day nor night, the Lord looked upon the Egyptian camp 'in a pillar of cloud and fire' (Ex. 14.24). The language of this verse should be closely observed: *be'ammûd 'ēš we'ānān*, 'in a pillar of fire and cloud' (not *be'ammûd 'ēš we'ammûd 'ānān*, 'in a pillar of fire and a pillar of cloud')—in one pillar that is both cloud and fire at one and the same time (not 'between the two pillars', as Ibn Ezra explained). The non-priestly sources also depict Yahweh's descent to the entrance of the tent of meeting as carried out in a pillar of cloud (Ex. 33.9-10; Num. 11.25; 12.5, 10; etc.), and it is quite possible that this pillar does not become fire simply because, in accordance with actual circumstances, the ecstatic activity connected with the tent of meeting is reported only upon the background of the daytime. This may also account for other appearances of the Lord in a cloud, which likewise take place in daytime with no fire being mentioned in those cases (Ex. 19.9, 16; 34.5; etc.). Yet, this does not rule out the possibility that, according to other notions, the Lord's appearance will be concealed by fire even in the daytime (Ex. 3.2; 19.18; Deut. 4.11-12; etc.). Thus, the fire

and the cloud are here conceived of neither as God's messengers nor as members of his retinue, but merely as coverings concealing his image. They therefore can hardly be considered on the same plane as the stars that 'from their courses fought against Sisera' (Judg. 5.20), as does M. Weinfeld, 'They Fought from Heaven', *Eretz-Israel* 14 (1978), 24-28, 30.

17. '"You shall bestow some of your *hôd* upon him"—and not all of your *hôd*; the elders of that generation said: Moses' face is like the face [the appearance] of the sun, Joshua's face is like the face [the appearance] of the moon' (bBaba Batra 75a). Similar to this is the case with the imparting of Moses' spirit to the seventy elders, where the text reads: 'And I will take some of the spirit, *we'āṣaltî min hārûaḥ*, which is on you and put it upon them' (Num. 11.17)—some of Moses' spirit, not all of it; cf. also G.B. Gray, *Numbers*, 110-11. To be sure, here, unlike with the bestowing of *hôd*, it is not Moses but the Lord who imparts the spirit, but it is on Moses' spirit that he draws (A. Ehrlich, however, explained otherwise).

18. However, A. Heidel, *The Babylonian Genesis* (Chicago: University of Chicago, 1951), 20, is of the opinion that the possessive pronominal form for 'his' refers to Apsû, mentioned before (in line 65), not to Mummu, who, being only a vizier and adviser was entitled to wear neither a crown (line 67) nor *melammu* (line 68). According to this explanation, a god was able to take the *melammu* of another god if he managed to subdue him.

19. See on this matter A.L. Oppenheim, 'Akkadian *pul(u)ḫ(t)u* and *melammu*', *JAOS* 63 (1943), 31-32; E. Cassin, *La Splendeur divine* (Civilisations et Sociétés, 8; Paris: Mouton & Co., 1968), 65-82; *CAD*, M/II, 9-12; W. von Soden, *AHW*, 643; also Weinfeld, 'They Fought from Heaven', 25. A concept similar to *melammu*, mentioned frequently alongside it and considered one of its synonyms, is *pulḫu*—yet, they are not exactly identical with each other. *Pulḫu* basically indicates the awe that the god or the king inspires, but it is metaphorically depicted as a garment that clothes the figure. In contrast to *melammu*—which is borne on the head and the verb indicating its use is mostly *našû*, 'to carry' (the same verb that is used in connection with *hôd* in Zech. 6.13)—in *pulḫu* one wraps himself and the verb accompanying it is *labâšu*, 'to wear, to be covered up in'. The *pulḫu* clothing is frequently metaphorized as a covering of fire and, moreover, at times it points to the wearer himself, implying his own personality (Oppenheim, 'Akkadian *pul(u)ḫ(t)u* and *melammu*', 32-33; cf. above, n. 15). It seems therefore that *pulḫu* has in it something analogous to the biblical *kābôd*.

20. See, e.g., G.A. Eisen, *Ancient Oriental Cylinder and other Seals . . . of Mrs. W.H. Moore* (OIP, 47; Chicago: University of Chicago, 1940), Nos. 83-84, 95; A. Moortgat, *Vorderasiatische Rollsiegel* (Berlin: Gebr. Mann, 1940), Nos. 598-599, 601-603; E. Porada, *Corpus of Ancient Near Eastern Seals* (Bollingen Series, 14; New York: Pantheon, 1948), Nos. 679-682, 685, 691, 698, 704-705. Such a nimbus is also portrayed on the relief of Ishtar of

Arbela, on a stela from Til-Barsib (J.B. Pritchard, *ANEP*, No. 522). It should be noted that Tsevat, 'The Skin of his Face', bases his argument not on the concept of *hôd* and *melammu*, as I do, but on the fork of lightning streaks (the bunch of 'whips') which in the ancient Near Eastern representations serves as the symbol of the god of thunder and storm and is held in his hand. It must be admitted that this symbol accords quite well with the text of Hab. 3.4, but it has nothing to do with Ex. 34.29-35. Yet, Tsevat also comes to the same conclusion, that the shining of Moses' face is to be explained by the radiation of bright light (not by sprouting horns on the head).

21. In Oppenheim's view ('Akkadian *pul(u)ḫ(t)u* and *melammu*', 33), *melammu* encompasses the following meanings: terror-inspiring cultic mask, which functionally corresponds to the headgear of *dei superi*, whose sparkling *agu melammu* was spiritualized into the glamour emanating from sacred objects. In his opinion, 'these are three levels of one and the same concept which do not represent stages of a genetic development but coexistent aspects'. But his final suggestion—that the terms *melammu*, *puluḫtu* and others similar to them fundamentally refer to the same concept (corporeal shape, likeness—and mask), and that the differentiation between them is the result of *secondary* literary development (*ibid.*, 34)—seems to me somehow too bold and hardly supported by his own discussion. See, on the other hand, the summing up of Mme Cassin's position on this problem (*La Splendeur divine*, 9-15). Yet, Weinfeld, 'They Fought from Heaven', 29-30 (also in *Tarbiẓ* 37 [1968], 116-18, 131-32) holds a view of his own on this issue: Oppenheim's suggestion that the *primary* meaning of *melammu*, *puluḫtu* and their synonyms was one and the same, serves him as a starting point for fusing together *biblical* terms. At the same time, he identifies *melammu* with *kābôd*—without even distinguishing between the various meanings of the latter—while *hôd* he also identifies with *kābôd*.

THE PROPHETS AND THE COVENANT

Arvid S. Kapelrud

I

The importance of the covenant between YHWH and his people in ancient Israel was demonstrated and emphasized by two great scholars: Johannes Pedersen and Walther Eichrodt.[1] The idea of covenant was a pillar in their conception of Israelite religion, and it was strongly underlined by the Uppsala school. In his most personal work, the 2nd edition of the *Svenskt Bibliskt Uppslagsverk* (SBU), 1962, Ivan Engnell wrote, 'Covenant (Hebr. *berit*) is the most important of all Old Testament notions, of basic importance for the way of thinking in the Old Testament and for its structure, in both private and public connections, in questions about religion, ethics and law'.[2] According to Engnell, the description of the covenant at Sinai (Ex. 19.1ff.; 24.1ff.) was formed against the background of cultic realities, namely the making of covenant at the two principal feasts of the year, the Passover (פסח) and the Succoth (סכת) festivals. The function of these feasts was to confirm again and again the covenant with YHWH as the foundation of the life of the people and the land, as a new creation of the cosmos and thus as the renewal of the fertility and blessing promised by YHWH.

The election and covenant were also foundations for the preaching of the prophets. In their words to the people the idea of covenant serves a negative aim, to illustrate how the people through their constant apostasy had broken the covenant. As an illustration, the prophets beginning with Hosea preferred to use the image of adultery when the people broke from the covenant.

As might be expected, the Uppsala school's view of covenant, which spread among scholars and was widely accepted as a true picture of phenomena in ancient Israel, was also attacked or at least doubted by scholars who had a less holistic view and more of a

critical approach. They did not, however, always apply this critical sense to their own positions.

One of the first scholars to take up the discussion was D.J. McCarthy, in his *Treaty and Covenant*.[3] In this book, McCarthy picked out some special questions connected with the covenant idea, such as the relationship with the Hittite vassal treaties and the question of covenant formula.

A more direct attack was made by L. Perlitt in his *Bundestheologie im Alten Testament*.[4] He maintained that the theological use of the covenant developed late in Israel and that it was actually Deuteronomic. The silence of the earlier prophets on the covenant was simply caused by the fact that they knew nothing of this theology. This must be characterized as a one-sided view which disregards facts in the Old Testament itself, as will be illustrated below. One must agree with James Barr when he says: 'Yet with all the will in the world it is a little hard to believe that the covenant of YHWH with Israel became significant only so late . . . A current of tradition that used *berit* in one kind of linguistic context might use other terminology in another, without this being evidence of a basic theological conflict.'[5]

The lack of self-criticism is also obvious in E. Kutsch, *Verheissung und Gesetz: Untersuchungen zum sogenannten 'Bund' im Alten Testament*.[6] His discussion, where he finds distinctions in the use of the word 'covenant' (ברית) where no distinctions were intended, has been characterized by F.M. Cross thus: 'In some instances, idealistic antinomianism and Christian apologetics combine to furnish the special tendencies of the treatment of covenant and law. See especially the series of studies by E. Kutsch.'[7] Barr's conclusion goes in the same direction: 'The whole discussion seems dominated by a strong sense of the opposition between grace and law, promise and law, which makes the reader uncomfortable'.[8]

In this short paper a discussion in detail of the scholars mentioned above cannot be considered, but a few features may shed some light on the problems. However, a discussion of the different kinds of covenantal relationships, such as the Abrahamic, Davidic and Mosaic covenants, will not be taken up.

II

According to the investigations of James Barr, ברית covers a very wide semantic territory, but syntactically it operates in a very limited

way. Barr emphasizes that 'covenant' includes the establishment of a relationship as well as obligations.[9] If one takes only a superficial look at the covenants connected with Abraham, Moses and David, it is easily seen that they all include both a firm relationship and a series of obligations. This relationship requires a positive attitude between the partners and includes some kind of obligation. These elements may be observed far back in history in the Hittite vassal treaties and in ancient Israelite covenants. In the covenant (ברית) between YHWH and Abraham in Genesis 15, no obligations are mentioned expressly, but it is an underlying basic supposition that both YHWH and Abraham remain faithful to each other and especially that Abraham will go on in his אמונה, his steadfastness and faithfulness. To disregard this fact is to misinterpret Genesis 15. The Davidic covenant must be understood accordingly. The promises to David and his dynasty are based on the supposition that he and his descendants remained 'righteous' (צדיק). They were to adhere to the obligations normally laid upon a צדיק within the ברית between YHWH and his people.

The description in Genesis 15 of the making of the covenant (ברית) between YHWH and Abraham indicates clearly that a special relationship was established. A relationship of this kind, concerning the whole people, the descendants of Abraham, was the responsibility of kings, priests and prophets. In the words of the prophet Hosea: 'Hear this, O priests! Give heed, O house of Israel! Hearken, O house of the king! For judgment pertains to you' (Hos. 5.1a).

To Hosea, however, the dominating conception seems to have been the Mosaic covenant. This may be seen from Hosea 4.2: 'There is swearing, lying, killing, stealing, and committing adultery, they break all bounds and murder follows murder'. That Hosea knew the idea of making a covenant is obvious in Hosea 10.4, 'They utter mere words, with empty oaths they make covenant [כרת ברית] so judgment [משפט] springs up like poisonous weeds in the furrows of the field'.

The prophet knew very well, and said so expressly, that the people had a covenant with their God. This covenant implied a set of obligations, which were mentioned by the prophet in Hosea 4.1f.; 6.6; 10.12; and these obligations were broken by the people: 'But at Adam [ב for Masoretic כ] they transgressed the covenant [ברית], there they dealt faithlessly with me [בגדו בי]' (Hos. 6.7).[10] The attitude of Hosea can also be seen clearly in Hosea 8.1-3, 'Set the trumpet to your lips, for a vulture is over the house of YHWH, because they have

broken my covenant [בריתי] and transgressed my law [תורתי]. To me they cry: My God, we Israel know thee. Israel has spurned the good; the enemy shall pursue him.' Faced with these statements by an early prophet like Hosea, it needs some courage to maintain that the prophets did not mention the covenant because they knew nothing about it.

All quotations given above are taken from the poetic parts of the book of Hosea. They bear no deuteronomistic stamp, and they are integrated parts of the preaching of the prophet. That means that they may be dated to a time between 750 and 730 BCE, a good time before deuteronomistic circles had become dominant.

Hosea did not merely mention the covenant in passing; he describes it as the basic foundation in the people's relationship with their God, a foundation which he considered as self-evident. It was not necessary for him to define ברית expressly; everybody knew what the word meant. Nevertheless, he actually gave a definition of the obligations included in the covenant, as may be seen in Hosea 4.2. The list of sins found there was no accidental enumeration. It was carefully considered, and the intention of the prophet was clearly to confront the people with their breach of the obligations that were well known to them. If that was not so, his reproach would have been without meaning and without any appeal at all. What Hosea wanted to demonstrate was the hard fact that the people, through their apostasy, had broken the covenant with YHWH. If they did not turn back, take up their obligations and obey the commandments of their God, doom and destruction would inevitably follow.

III

The people, however, were of another opinion, and here is to be found the explanation of the fact that the prophets do not say much about the covenant in their preaching. To speak about the covenant to the people was to evoke their ideas of a national God who was going to protect his own people in any danger which might threaten. They expected to be safe because they were living in the covenant, where God's duty was to take care of his people. Their own obligations within the covenant were fulfilled through rich offerings and sacrifices, with which they flooded the temple. In doing so they expected the covenant to function as it had always done. The prophet Micah has given a clear and sharp picture of this situation in 6.6-8:

'With what shall I come before YHWH? . . . He has showed you, O man, what is good, and what does YHWH require of you, but to do justice, and to love kindness, and to walk humbly with your God?' Thousands of rams, calves and rivers of olive oil were rejected, the precise remedies which the people thought were the right ones.

The people's idea of the covenant was a wrong one. That is expressed in a clear and impressive way in the preaching of another early prophet, Isaiah. He called the people's concept a 'covenant with death': 'Because you have said: we have made a covenant with death, and with Sheol we have an agreement, when the overwhelming scourge passes through it will not come to us, for we have made lies our refuge, and in falsehood we have taken shelter' (Is. 28.15). In this, the prophet unveiled what was the real kernel in the people's idea of the covenant. Their illusion that the covenant meant that YHWH would protect them in any case could be appropriately characterized through the term the prophet preferred to apply: בריתכם את־מות, 'your death covenant' (Is. 28.18). A covenant conceived in the way the people did was not a real, life-giving covenant. It was a covenant leading to death. However, this was not going to hold. The people's idea of a covenant was untenable. The words of YHWH left no room for illusions of this kind: 'And I will make justice the line, and righteousness the plummet; and hail will sweep away the refuge of lies, and waters will overwhelm the shelter. Then your covenant with death will be annulled, and your agreement with Sheol will not stand; when the overwhelming scourge passes through you will be beaten down by it' (Is. 2.17-18).

It is important that Isaiah characterized the situation of the people by using the ancient term ברית. That is an all-embracing term for both the promises and the obligations which were of the highest importance in the life of the people. It is obvious that when the prophets judged the people's conception of the covenant in this way, it was not necessary to remind their audiences of the fact that they were living in a covenant that laid certain obligations on them. They just preached the obligations! That was what the people could understand, and so any misunderstanding concerning the covenant was overlooked. Nevertheless, when Isaiah did mention the people's ברית, he chose to call it ברית את־מות, a covenant that carried death in it.

IV

The idea of a binding covenant of a general nature was alive at an early period in Israel, as indicated above. The prophets in the eighth century knew it, and it was the background of their preaching. In addition, passages in the books of the prophets which may be of a later origin speak about covenants of different kinds.

In Amos 1.9, in a passage which may well have its origin in the prophet himself, the threat was directed against Tyre: 'Thus says YHWH: for three transgressions of Tyre, and for four, I will not cause it to return, because they delivered up a whole people to Edom, and did not remember the covenant of brotherhood [ברית אחים]'. The words of doom of the prophet demonstrates that certain obligations were connected with this covenant, as with others. A covenant of brotherhood was a covenant where both parties had obligations to which they had to adhere. The nature of the obligations was not indicated, but it may have been in the line of mutual help, and Tyre did not give this help. The central idea is clear; the covenant between two parties was binding. Thus when Tyre broke the covenant, the city was under divine doom. A covenant was under God's supervision, and, in cases such as that of Tyre, people in Israel and Judah were of the firm conviction that their God was a universal God who took care of all kinds of covenants.

This way of seeing the covenants and the divine authority watching over them may be observed also in the book of Isaiah: 'The earth lies polluted under its inhabitants, for they have transgressed the laws, violated the statutes, broken the everlasting covenant [ברית עולם]. Therefore a curse devours the earth, and its inhabitants suffer for their guilt' (Is. 24.5). Here laws (תורה) and statutes (חק) are closely connected with a binding covenant, which was considered obligatory for all peoples and which was under the supervision of a universal God who would not let transgressions pass unpunished. And this universal God was *Yahweh Seba'ot*, who would reign on Zion and in Jerusalem (Is. 24.23) and who would hear songs of praise from the ends of the earth, from the east and the west and the coastlands (Is. 24.14-16).

The same world of ideas is found in Isaiah 33, where the breaking of the covenant is also mentioned (Is. 33.8). Even when the conception of YHWH as a universal God is dominant, the idea of a covenant between him and his creatures is alive. Its ancient foundations were so deeply rooted that it lived on also under new conditions.

Two of the great prophets, Jeremiah and Ezekiel, lived and preached under the worst possible conditions, when Judah and Jerusalem were ravaged and destroyed; and the word ברית is found spread profusely throughout the books of these two prophets (Jer. 3.16; 11.2ff.; 31.30ff.; 33.20ff.; Ezek. 16.59ff.; 17.13ff.; 34.25ff.; 37.26). The main idea in most of these passages is the importance of the covenant and the bitter fact that the people had broken this covenant and turned their back upon YHWH. The prophets emphasized the necessity of conversion and presaged the coming doom. They lived in a time when an immediate reaction from the people was totally decisive, and the prophets preached accordingly. There was no time to restore the covenant; in the twelfth hour the people had to act immediately. Preaching on the subjet of covenant could thus not be expected and is consequently not found in these prophets.

In the prose texts of the book of Jeremiah the covenant is mentioned in just this way, and there can be no doubt that what is found there are mainly deuteronomistic additions. That explains also why the ideas have an unmistakably deuteronomistic character. As is well known, the Deuteronomists worked out the idea of the covenant in detail and forged it into a penetrating weapon in their instruction of the people. However, it must be emphasized that it was an ancient weapon they polished.

In the book of Ezekiel the case is more complicated. It speaks of a covenant with Israel-Judah (Ezek. 16.59f.), of a peace covenant with David as the leader (Ezek. 34.35), of an eternal covenant (Ezek. 37.26), and of a covenant between rulers, as in ancient times (Ezek. 17.13ff.). The term ברית and the idea itself were used in a broad way, indicating a comprehensive conception of the term, without the special deuteronomistic color.

In his eagerness to awaken the people and give them new courage and hope, Second Isaiah tried to renew ancient ideas and ancient terminology. At the same time he also gave them a new turn, and, though he was in many ways a nationalistic prophet, he expanded his perspective to comprise the whole world. The salvation, which YHWH was to initiate in helping his suffering people and taking them back to their homeland, was going to be extended to the peoples of the larger world (Is. 55.4f.). The words of YHWH were going out to all nations, but first and foremost to his own people: 'Incline your ear, and come to everlasting covenant, my steadfast, sure love for David. Behold, I made him a witness to the people, a leader and a

commander for the peoples' (Is. 55.3f.). The covenant was going to be a constant one, and it is seen as the foundation of all relationships between God and mankind.

Second Isaiah also went back to a covenant with Noah, as depicted by the priestly traditions in Genesis 9.8ff. As I have tried to show elsewhere, Second Isaiah and the Priestly Code were contemporaries, at the end of the Exile, and they may well have drawn upon the same source.[11] The prophet's words about the covenant with Noah is one of the texts that may indicate this: 'For this is like the days of Noah to me, as I swore that the waters of Noah should no more go over the earth, so I have sworn that I will not be angry with you and will not rebuke you. For the mountains may depart and the hills be removed, but my steadfast love shall not depart from you, and my covenant of peace [וברית שלומי] shall not be removed, says YHWH, who has compassion on you' (Is. 54.9f.).

In two, practically identical, cases found in Second Isaiah, the word ברית was used in an unusual connection, ברית עם, 'people-covenant' (Is. 42.6; 49.8). In both instances the word was used in a passage which is a continuation of a Servant text, e.g.: 'I am YHWH, I have called you to righteousness, I have taken you by the hand and kept you, I have given you as a covenant to people, a light to the nations, to open the eyes that are blind' (Is. 42.6). The meaning seems to be that the covenant made with the servant Israel will be extended to reach other peoples, as expressed in Isaiah 55.3f. The question of whether or not the covenant in these texts is connected with Messianic ideas will not be discussed here, but if such were the case, it would emphasize the importance of the covenant in exilic and post-exilic times.

V

The conclusion may be drawn that already among the early prophets there was an awareness of a particular covenant between YHWH and his people in Israel-Judah. This covenant included special obligations on the part of the people; and the early prophets, and most probably the later ones also, took it for granted that the people had known these obligations since ancient times (cf. e.g. Mic. 6.8). This perspective was the foundation for their preaching. They would take their admonitions directly to the people, in order to make them adhere to their obligations. Later, a more definitive understanding of the covenant was developed by the Deuteronomists, but they used

material which was present a long time before they emphasized the importance of the covenant between YHWH and his people.

NOTES

1. Johs. Pedersen, *Israel I-II, III-IV* (Copenhagen: Branner og Korch, 1920-34; English edition, 1926-40); and W. Eichrodt, *Theologie des Alten Testaments*, vol. 1, 8th ed., vol. 2/3, 6th ed. (Göttingen: Vandenhoeck und Ruprecht, 1968, 1974); English edition, *Theology of the Old Testament*, 2 vols, trans. by J.A. Baker [Philadelphia: Westminster Press, 1961, 1967]).

2. Ivan Engnell, *Svenskt Bibliskt Uppslagsverk*, 2nd ed. (Stockholm: Nordiska Uppslagsböcker, 1962-), vol. I, col. 688.

3. D.J. McCarthy, *Treaty and Covenant* (AnBib 21; Rome: Pontifical Biblical Institute, 1965).

4. L. Perlitt, *Bundestheologie im Alten Testament* (WMANT 36; Neukirchen-Vluyn: Neukirchener Verlag, 1969).

5. J. Barr, 'Some Semantic Notes on the Covenant', in *Beiträge zur Alttestamentlichen Theologie: Festschrift für Walter Zimmerli zum 70. Geburtstag* (Göttingen: Vandenhoeck und Ruprecht, 1977), 37.

6. E. Kutsch, *Verheissung und Gesetz: Untersuchungen zum sogenannten 'Bund' in Alten Testament* (BZAW 131; Berlin: Walter de Gruyter, 1972).

7. F.M. Cross, *Canaanite Myth and Hebrew Epic* (Cambridge: Harvard University Press, 1973), 272.

8. Barr, 'Some Semantic Notes on the Covenant', 37.

9. Barr, 'Some Semantic Notes on the Covenant', 34.

10. The verb בגד means to break obligations, to deal with somebody in a way that breaks the rules.

11. A.S. Kapelrud, 'The Date of the Priestly Code (P)', *ASTI* 3 (1973), 58-64.

THE PROPHET ELIJAH'S VISIT TO ZAREPHATH

Magnus Ottosson

The traditions about the prophet Elijah have been subjected to careful analysis from several different perspectives in recent years. O.H. Steck has tried through literary-critical analysis to identify the different sources behind the MT.[1] L. Bronner has attempted a motif analysis (more or less) of the prophet's deeds against a Canaanite background.[2] Of particular interest is a paper by my colleague A. Carlson which drew attention to the frequent repetitive forms of style by which the composer underlined the ideological motifs in the Elijah cycle.[3] Thus, for example, the prophet's visit to Mt Horeb strongly emphasizes the symbolism of the Wilderness wanderings; 'the God of Elijah' (2 Kgs 2.14) was 'the God of the Wilderness'. Among the interesting observations on 1 Kings 17–19 made recently by F.C. Fensham is the view that the visit of Elijah to Zarephath in Phoenicia is described so as to emphasize the power of Yahweh over Baal who is then regarded as dead (the drought) and thus incapable of helping the widow.[4] In what follows I hope to show that Elijah's visit to Zarephath also has symbolic and ideological implications regarding the borders of Yahwistic Canaan and, more interestingly, the borders of the Davidic Kingdom.

It is hard to find any discussion of the motivation for Elijah's trip to Zarephath anywhere in the Judaic Scriptures.[5] The episode is mentioned in Luke 4.25-26 as a scriptural illustration of the saying 'No prophet is acceptable in his own country' (v. 24). This unit of Jesus' words is used to explain why miracles did not happen in Nazareth as the people there had expected: a prophet is sent by God, and human beings cannot exact anything from him. I am reluctant to enter the domain of New Testament scholars, but to my mind Luke 4 is composed as an Elijah typology. Jesus is brought to the other side of the Jordan and the chapter, punctuated by the explicit references to Elijah in vv. 25-27, is built up in accordance with 1 Kings 17 (cf. Matt. 15.6ff.).

Most exegetes agree that the Deuteronomist or the Deuteronomistic School is responsible for the composition of the Elijah traditions as we have them.[6] We naturally can suppose that the Deuteronomist's ideological view of history has coloured those traditions to some degree. The dominant theme is the fight between Yahweh and the Sidonian Baal, Baal Melqart.[7] The principal characters in this fight are Elijah and the North-Israelite royal couple Ahab and Jezebel (1 Kgs 16.31). At the outset Elijah appears to be in hiding (1 Kgs 17.3f.); a malignant atmosphere permeates the account; and we are told of the slaughter of prophets of both Yahweh (1 Kgs 18.4) and Baal (1 Kgs 18.40). The larger ideological background of the fight can be appreciated if we first consider the history of relations between Phoenicia and Israel.

I

When Omri obtained power over the North-Israelite Kingdom around 886 the political situation on the international front was very advantageous. Virtually the same situation had existed in the time of King David. Like David, Omri was interested in obtaining hegemony east of the Jordan in order to control the trade routes running from North Arabia through Gilead and at the same time to provide a buffer against Aramean attempts at further encroachments on his borders.[8] Omri's contemporary, Ittobaal of Tyre (c. 887-856), was fighting to gain hegemony over the area west of the Lebanon mountains; he succeeded in extending his empire as far north as Beirut and also gained some influence in Cyprus. Both would profit more from an alliance than from hostile relations, Ittobaal securing the commercial routes from the east for the importation of goods to Tyre and other cities, and Omri bringing a taste of the Phoenician 'good life' to North-Israel. Omri's *Westpolitik* did bring great prosperity to his country, as is shown from excavations at Samaria, Megiddo, and Hazor. But the Old Testament tells us more about the accompanying Phoenician cultural influence which brought to the country a new type of thinking alien to the Yahwistic faith and personified in the cult of the Tyrian Baal Melqart which acquired a broad popular following. This development was due to Omri's son Ahab and especially the new crown princess Jezebel who fought bitterly to promote her native religion in her adopted country.

The relations between the Kingdom of Tyre and North-Israel could be disturbed only by the Arameans. After their defeat at the hands of David they had directed their attention mainly toward Mesopotamia during the period of Assyrian weakness. Commercial activity in the 10th century had brought them inconceivable wealth.[9] Although Assyrian pressure increased around 880, the Arameans had not yet organized themselves on a large scale in the south (cf. 1 Kgs 19.15). During the reign of Omri and at least the early years of Ahab's reign conditions in Palestine were peaceful. Accordingly, it was a time of political stability in which Elijah was sent to oppose the growing Baal cult in North-Israel.

In the context of this brief historical survey the important question of the border between North-Israel and the Kingdom of Tyre should be addressed. The Old Testament is silent on this question. Some form of Israelite infiltration into the Acco plain between the Ladder of Tyre and Mt Carmel may be reflected in the pronouncement about Zebulun in Genesis 49.13; in the tribal border description in Joshua 19.26 all of the Acco plain is included in the territory of Asher, with Mt Carmel as Asher's southwestern border. According to Judges 1.32, the Canaanites were not driven out of this territory. Any greater activity in this area is not reported. If we suppose that the list of Levitical cities in Joshua 21.30. reflects Davidic times, we have a hint of the border conditions between the Davidic state and Tyre, evidenced in more detail by the choice of roads of the census patrol in 2 Samuel 24. This would mean that Tyre was forced to recognize David's superiority (cf. Amos 1.9).

For Solomon the situation was a bit different. Through King Hiram's shrewd generosity towards Solomon's building projects David's successor found himself forced to deliver the region of Cabul—i.e., a large part of the Acco plain—to Tyre (1 Kgs 9.11). Much evidence points to the fact that hereafter the greater part of this region became Tyrian territory. In the Annals of Sennacherib the cities of Achzib and Acco are mentioned among others as belonging to King Luli of Sidon.[10] If *ba'ali ṛa'si* in the Annals of Shalmaneser III is identical with Mt Carmel, it may have been a border point in the west during the reign of Jehu as is thought to have been the case during the reign of Ahab. We agree with Y. Aharoni that in the period of the Divided Monarchy Mt Carmel was the southern limit of the Acco plain and the town of Cabul, located about 14 km southeast of Acco, was the eastern limit.[11] This means that, in

terms of the actual political situation in Ahab's days, Elijah's trip to Zarephath took him deep into Tyrian territory.

The inhabitants of Tyrian territory, from Mt Carmel in the south northward along the Mediterranean coast, are commonly referred to as Phoenicians. The Old Testament does not know this term, but speaks instead of Sidonians.[12] We do not hear very much about them. Deuteronomy 3.9 states that they had their own name for Mt Hermon, namely Sirion. They were regarded as skilful craftsmen and artisans (1 Kgs 5.20), and on the basis of their renown as shipbuilders and sailors were considered a prideful people and were condemned by the prophets (Is. 23; Jer. 25.22; 27.3; Ezek. 26–29; 32.30). More interesting are references to the Sidonians in what may be called an ideological connection. In Judges 3, an obviously deuteronomistic frame-tradition (*Rahmenerzählung*), we hear of some peoples whom the Israelites could not remove: the Philistines in their five סרנים, and all the Canaanites, Sidonians, and Hivites who live in the area of the Lebanon mountains from Baal-Hermon as far as Lebo-Hamath (cf. Josh. 13). These peoples are said to have been left in the land in order *to tempt* Israel.[13] We may observe that these peoples belong to the border areas of the conquered land. The gods of the surrounding peoples were always a temptation for the Israelites (e.g., Judg. 10.6). The Israelites are said to live among many peoples, but never among the Sidonians (Judg. 3.5). In any event, the Sidonians did exert a strong cultural influence in the north. When the Danite spies visited the area around Laish (Dan) they found the inhabitants living 'according to the manner of the Sidonians' (כמשפט צדנים), although they were 'far from the Sidonians and had no dealings with anyone' (Judg. 18.7).[14]

According to the books of Joshua and Judges the Canaanites and some other peoples were not always wiped out and these circumstances resulted in the widespread worship of gods other than Yahweh. The tradents of the Old Testament do not hide the fact that syncretism flourished among the Israelites, especially in North-Israel. The measures taken by Jeroboam I regarding the worship of the bull-gods in Dan and Bethel were aimed at cutting off his subjects' religious dependence on the temple in Jerusalem. And this development does not seem to have met much opposition in North-Israel itself, suggesting that the people there were living according to the manner of the Canaanites for whom the fertility cult was quite natural.[15] From the deuteronomistic point of view, however, this sin of

Jeroboam I was a catastrophic step, and every North-Israelite king after him was condemned as long as the bulls were worshipped. The religious controversy heated up dramatically in the middle of the ninth century with the growing popularity of the Sidonian Baal Melqart in Syria (Ben Hadad), in North-Israel, and for a time also in Judah (Athaliah). In North-Israel the cult of Baal Melqart, supported by Ahab and Jezebel, became a fighting religion which almost succeeded in suppressing the Yahwistic spirit. To understand the reason for Elijah's appearance it is important to remember the first role of the Sidonians as *tempters*, a role which reached an intolerable culmination under Ahab and Jezebel. From a deuteronomistic perspective, the time for an accounting had come. Ahab was the seventh king of North-Israel to follow Jeroboam's evil example; given the Deuteronomist's use of the number seven as a maximal number, Yahweh's patience had become exhausted.[16] Several prophets had arisen in North-Israel—the man-of-God from Judah (1 Kgs 13), Ahijah of Shiloh (1 Kgs 14.2f.), Jehu ben Hanani (1 Kgs 16.1ff.)—but the ideological dimension of the fight between Yahweh and Baal is first given a striking profile with Elijah.

The Deuteronomist's introduction of Elijah in 1 Kings 17.1 indicates that the North-Israelite apostasy is regarded as very serious; 'dew and rain' (טל ומטר) will cease. This collocation reoccurs only at 2 Samuel 1.21 where it is used as an expression of great catastrophe, the deaths of Saul and Jonathan.[17] The situation which arose through the words of Elijah is in line with Deuteronomy 28.23: 'And the heavens above your head will be like copper and the earth under your feet will be like iron' (cf. Lev. 26.19f.). This verse expresses one of the punishments which will come upon Israel for disobedience to Yahweh.[18] With the expression 'dew and rain' the tradent seems to have used Canaanite vocabulary, for a similar motif is found in the Aqhat legend: 'Thereupon Danel the Rephaite prayed (that) the clouds in the heat of the season, (that) the clouds should rain early rain (and) give plentiful dew in summer for the fruits. Baal failed for seven years, the rider on the clouds for eight (years, leaving the land) without dew, without showers' (III, I i 35ff., Driver's translation). Both Yahweh and Baal could cause dew and rain to cease, but the great difference between these gods is intended to appear through Elijah's deeds. Yahweh will then show that he stands above the forces of nature. And remarkably enough this will happen at two places which at the moment functioned as borderpoints. Mt Carmel

was the actual border in Elijah's time but was ideologically unacceptable, and Zarephath was the ideological border in Elijah's time but should also have been the actual one.

II

Elijah's deeds on Mt Carmel are introduced with Yahweh's command: 'go and show yourself to Ahab, then I want to give rain (מטר) on the earth' (1 Kgs 18.1). One part of the collocation in 1 Kings 17.1 will thereafter be brought to function (1 Kgs 18.41ff.). But what of the 'dew' which is not mentioned further? Does the collocation 'dew and rain' in 1 Kings 17.1 express the idea of fructifying moisture generally, or is it possible that 'dew' has a special meaning? The first point can be accepted without difficulty, but the second is also worth exploring. We know that in Hebrew thought dew is in some way related to the renewing of life and resurrection (cf. Is. 26.19).[19] Elijah's second deed at Zarephath was the revival of the widow's son (1 Kgs 17.24). Can the expression 'then I want to give rain (מטר) on the earth' in 1 Kings 18.1 imply that the 'dew' has fallen with the revival of the widow's son in 1 Kings 17.17-24?

It has been suggested that dew in Canaanite religion was a kind of symbol for the fairly undifferentiated concept of the renewal of life. We know very little about the practice at Zarephath, but there are hints which suggest that the cult there had the same outlines as elsewhere in the ancient Near East. In the Keret legend we find reference to *ilt ṣdynm*, 'the goddess of the Sidonians' (I, IV 35, 38), presumably a form of Anath. Callimachus (c. 280 BC) mentions a local variant of that goddess, namely the Saraptian heifer, a traditional Canaanite guise (Hymns and Epigrams, Lycophon, 1280-1300; cf. Baal IV, III 1). That this type of goddess was popular at Zarephath is proved by the discovery of heifer figurines and also a Tinnith figurine in Iron II levels, just about Elijah's time.[20] With the bull-gods of Jeroboam I in mind, Elijah should not have been unfamiliar with the fertility cult at Zarephath. Anath appears in the shape of a heifer as a partner of Baal. But this goddess has other strings on her lyre, and it is in her role as giver of life that we may find a parallel to Elijah's life-giving deed.

Leah Bronner has linked the contents of the Aqhat legend to Elijah's appearance at Zarephath.[21] Aqhat is promised the life of the

gods by Anath if he would give her his arrows. Aqhat is still alive here and there is no reference to resurrection from the dead. In Aqhat I, I, 15f., however, the situation is different. The assumption here is that Anath has killed Aqhat and then shouts: *emḫ̮ṣh.ʿl.qṣʿth.hwt.l.aḥw* 'I smote him for his arrows, but verily I will surely revive him' (Driver's translation). If this is the correct understanding of the text, it indicates that the Canaanite goddess could revive man. The Aqhat legend also makes the connection between dew and rain and revival in the prayer of Danel, Aqhat's father, quoted above. Danel is asking Baal, the Lord of life, to restore his son by asking for dew and rain. It may be noted that in 2 Samuel 1.21 David asks that dew and rain *not* fall after the deaths of Saul and Jonathan.[22] Aqhat's death was on an impulse by Anath and (perhaps) she also revived him. We have quoted these Ugaritic texts in order to show that some Canaanite gods were able to revive man. Also from Zarephath itself we have now an archaeological find of a Ugaritic inscription which proves a southern spread of the Ugaritic alphabet. Although it does not throw light on our problem, the inscription has many connections with texts in the Old Testament.[23] Further finds in late Iron Age II levels also show that gods of healing were known here and certainly were worshipped. These finds are inscriptions of personal names as Eshmunyaton, 'Eshmun has given', and Germelqart, 'client of Melqart'.[24] Eshmun was a famous Phoenician god of healing. One of his temples has been excavated just to the north of Sidon. In later times Eshmun was identified with Asclepios. There is a close relation between Melqart and Eshmun. I take for granted that here are the gods whom Elijah challenged and also in a spectacular way would defeat at Zarephath and on Mt Carmel. Elijah understands the death of the widow's son as an act by Yahweh (1 Kgs 17.20) and Yahweh also revives him. That would have been a good demonstration of the power of the Israelite god to Sidonian worshippers of Eshmun. We do not know whether the widow herself was a Sidonian. Later tradition (Gemara) makes her an Israelite woman; her attribution of the death of her son to her own sin (1 Kgs 17.18) seems to be an Israelite idea.

With the rain motif stressed in 1 Kings 18, it is not impossible that the revival of the widow's son is connected with the dew, the symbol of resuscitation. If this is the case, of course, we must reject the common idea that 1 Kings 17.17-24 is a secondary insertion based upon the traditions of Elisha.[25]

III

Elijah's visit to Sidonian territory could have been prompted by the alliance between Samaria and Tyre, but why did Zarephath alone receive the prophet's special attention? Zarephath was located 15 km south of the town of Sidon, and, as noted above in our discussion of the border between Tyre and North-Israel, this was deep inside Tyrian territory. Elijah's visit to Zarephath often is regarded as a missionary labour among the Sidonians, but I would rather say that it was for the Israelites.[26] Such a motivation can be seen if we follow Elijah's itinerary. He is ordered by Yahweh to hide himself at the brook of Cherith in Gilead. The region east of the Jordan was during this period a safe place of refuge. But after his stay in Gilead he begins a journey which has an ideological relationship with the borders of the lands of Yahweh's inheritance and also of the Davidic Kingdom. Elijah travels between these points: Gilead, Zarephath, Mt Carmel,[27] and Beer-Sheba.

The Promised Land is often delimited by the general expressions 'from the Great Sea to the River Euphrates' or 'from sea to sea'. This demarcation has no realistic political basis, but reflects instead the idea of Yahweh's universal supremacy.[28] In some prophetic texts specific geographical regions are used to mark the extent of the Promised Land (e.g., Jer. 22.6, 20; Zech. 10.10; 11.1). These texts use Gilead or Bashan or Abarim as the eastern boundary, but the Lebanon mountains for the western or northwestern point. Parts of this range were included in Israelite Canaan. Elsewhere, however, and especially in the *Landnahme* texts, the northwest frontier always is drawn to or from Sidon. In Genesis 10.19 the borders of Israelite Canaan are drawn 'from Sidon in the direction of Gerar as far as Gaza, and in the direction of Sodom, Gomorrah, Admah, and Zeboiim as far as Lasha'. Genesis 49.13 says that Zebulun 'lives at the seaside . . . and his border shall be at Sidon'. According to Joshua 11.8 and 13.6, Joshua pursued his enemies as far as Great Sidon and Misrephoth-maim. In the allotment in Joshua 19.28 Asher received a vast territory to the north 'as far as Sidon the Great' (cf. Jud. 1.31). These texts may reflect the frontiers in different phases of the *Landnahme*-work, but the border point in the northwest seems to be well fixed as Sidon.

The town of Zarephath אשר לצידון, 'belonging to Sidon', is mentioned by name elsewhere in the Old Testament only in Obadiah 20. The

extent of the dwelling-places of the restored Israel envisioned in Obadiah corresponds to the idealized Promised Land. Gilead is included, and the northwestern frontier is said to extend עד צרפת, 'to Zarephath'. It could be that the name צרפת is etymologically related to the place-name משרפות מים in Joshua 11.8 and 13.6.[29] Zarephath is first mentioned in Papyrus Anastasi I (in the time of Rameses II) and reappears as an Assyrian conquest in the eighth century (Luckenbill, II, 205). With its good harbour Zarephath would have been an excellent complement to Sidon. Excavations there thus far indicate that the town enjoyed great prosperity, especially during Iron II.

The political boundary between North-Israel and Tyre in Ahab's time was Mt Carmel–Cabul, and thus Elijah's visit to Zarephath took him far into the Sidonian area. But as the texts cited above indicate, 'Zarephath belonging to Sidon' lay within and marked the northwestern boundary of the Promised Land. With this in mind, Elijah's journey to Zarephath is an ideological confirmation of Yahweh's authority within the Promised Land. That Yahweh was thought of as a god bound to a specific territory in this period, at least in some circles, is evident from 2 Kings 5.17. It is thus conceivable that through the revival of the widow's son in Zarephath Elijah sought to demonstrate Yahweh's power in what was traditionally his own territory. Political realities aside, Zarephath was Israelite and the Sidonian god had no place there.

There is a concrete background to this ideological dimension, for Elijah's destination was the northwestern border of the Promised Land and of the Davidic Kingdom as well.[30] It is instructive to compare Elijah's itinerary with the itinerary of David's census patrol in 2 Samuel 24. The patrol departed from Gilead via Dan, then 'round about to Sidon' (v. 6: סביב אל צידון) and into מבצר צר (v. 7; cf. Josh. 19.28.), and then continued south to Beer-Sheba. The route of the Davidic census-takers delimits the area of Yahweh's inheritance, the same area delimited in the *Landnahme* texts cited above.[31] The route Gilead–Sidon–Beer-Sheba corresponds to Elijah's journey from Gilead to Zarephath to Beer-Sheba. Bearing in mind the motifs of the Wilderness wanderings stressed in the Elijah cycle,[32] we ought not be surprised to find that Elijah, as a traditional forerunner of a Davidic-messianic restoration, follows this pattern. The Kingdom must be founded on the Mosaic law.[33]

Elijah's journey to Zarephath has powerful ideological implications. There he will show that Yahweh can still demonstrate his power in

territory traditionally his own but now ruled by 'other gods'. North-Israel had fallen completely under the sway of the gods of foreigners. But this domination was illegitimate. North-Israel should oust the Sidonian Baal and restore the rule of Yahweh over a united kingdom. These implications are consistent with the rest of the Elijah traditions and are symbolically demonstrated in Elijah's use of twelve stones to build Yahweh's altar on Mt Carmel (1 Kgs 18.31). The Deuteronomist has regarded the prophet as the messianic forerunner.

The malediction which opens the Elijah traditions, 'dew and rain will cease', is in line with the treaty curses in Deuteronomy 28. These curses will strike Israel if they do not obey Yahweh but worship other gods. From the statutes given in the book of Deuteronomy the people will know their conditions in the land. The fulfilment of the Law gives them blessing, victory over their enemies, and an area in which to live. The largest area possible to keep is identical with the Davidic Kingdom.[34] Texts such as Genesis 15.18 picture a land which is related to a complete fulfilment of the Law (Deut. 11.22f.). Elijah's most spectacular act, the revival of the widow's son, takes place in a town situated on the ideal northwestern border. In my opinion, this act dissolves the first part of the curse expressed in 1 Kings 17.1. The act on Mt Carmel dissolves the second.

It may be coincidental but I do not think so. Curses are very often written on *kudurru*-stones which seem to be an original *Sitz im Leben* of maledictions.[35] In Elijah's case we do not hear about any *kudurru*-stones but through his activity, healing and rain-making just on the boundaries, he dissolves the curse and ideologically reestablishes the boundary of the Davidic kingdom. One can also say that Elijah's acts 'surrounded' the Sidonian area which in that way was demonstratively 'incorporated' into Israel. Yahweh had shown that he could defeat the tempters and their gods.

NOTES

1. O.H. Steck, *Überlieferung und Zeitgeschichte in den Elia-Erzählungen* (WMANT, 26; Neukirchen-Vluyn: Neukirchener Verlag, 1968). According to Steck, Ahab alone is found in the oldest stratum; Jezebel has been added after Jehu's revolt, and Israel in its entirety belongs to the Redactor. This trisection of the text has been criticized recently by R. Smend ('Das Wort Jahwes an Elia: Erwägungen zur Komposition von 1 Reg XVII-XIX', *VT* 25 [1975], 525-43) who argues that the author of 1 Kings 17–19 lived in the time

of Jehu (cf. 1 Kgs 19.15–17) and that the scene on Mt Horeb (1 Kgs 19) is the deliberate conclusion of the stories beginning in 1 Kings 17.1.

2. L. Bronner, *The Stories of Elijah and Elisha as Polemics against Baal Worship* (Leiden: E.J. Brill, 1968). According to Bronner, we can use the Ugaritic texts to illuminate 1 Kings 17–19. Although the time-gap between the Ugaritic texts and the Old Testament evidently is very large, it is beyond dispute that the Canaanite culture of the Bronze Age has coloured the Hebrew language and the Israelite way of thinking. This has been the general opinion of many Scandinavian scholars in the exegetical field: e.g., I. Engnell, *Studies in Divine Kingship in the Ancient Near East*[2] (Oxford: Blackwell, 1967); A.S. Kapelrud, *Baal in the Ras Shamra Texts* (Copenhagen: G.E.C. Gad, 1952); G.W. Ahlström, *Psalm 89: Eine Liturgie aus dem Ritual des leidenden Königs* (Lund: Gleerup, 1959); R.A. Carlson, *David, the Chosen King* (Stockholm: Almqvist and Wiksell, 1964); K. Aartun, 'Eine weitere Parallele aus Ugarit zur kultischen Praxis in Israels Religion', *Bibliotheca Orientalis* 33 (1976), 285ff.; H. Ringgren, *Israelitische Religion* (Stuttgart: Kohlhammer, 1981). None of the scholars just mentioned has become a 'Pan-Ugaritist', however.

3. A. Carlson, 'Elie à l'Horeb', *VT* 19 (1969), 416-39.

4. F.C. Fensham, 'A Few Observations on the Polarization between Yahweh and Baal in 1 Kings 17–19', *ZAW* 92 (1980), 227-36.

5. A. Wiener, *The Prophet Elijah in the Development of Judaism: A Depthpsychological Study* (London: Routledge and Kegan Paul, 1978), does not enter into the question.

6. The text material is naturally much older; see the discussion by J. Gray, *I–II Kings: A Commentary* (Philadelphia: Westminster Press, 1964), 13. It is hard to know to what extent the Deuteronomist has changed the composition of the Elijah traditions handed over to him. There is no need to think that the geographical outlines of Elijah's itinerary belong to a Deuteronomistic composition. Ideological geography in terms of the Davidic Kingdom was known long before the Deuteronomistic movement. But we can suppose that the Deuteronomist underscored the idea of the United Kingdom (1 Kgs 18.30.).

7. There has been a long and intensive discussion about the name 'Baal' in the Elijah traditions; Fensham gives a comprehensive survey of the different opinions (Fensham, 'A Few Observations', 228f.). The rain motif must be the main starting-point when judging the character of the god Baal in 1 Kings 18. This motif represents one essential side of Baal Shamen. As Tyrian domination through Jezebel's activity is so striking, it is reasonable to suggest that it was the city-god of Tyre, Baal Melqart, who was Yahweh's adversary on Mt Carmel.

8. On the historical situation, cf. G.W. Ahlström, 'Jehu—A Prophet's Mistake', *Scripture in History and Theology: Essays in Honor of J. Coert*

Rylaarsdam, ed. A.L. Merrill and T.W. Overholt (PTM, 17; Pittsburgh: Pickwick Press, 1977), 47-69.

9. The Aramean-Phonecian relations are proved through the stele dedicated to Melqart by King Barhaddad; see J.B. Pritchard (ed.), *The Ancient Near East in Pictures Relating to the Old Testament* (Princeton: Princeton University, 1954), fig. 499, and R. de Vaux, 'Les prophètes de Baal sur le mont Carmel', *Bible et Orient* (Paris: Editions du Cerf, 1967), 486f.

10. J.B. Pritchard (ed.), *Ancient Near Eastern Texts Relating to the Old Testament* (Princeton: Princeton University, 1950), 287. Luli was then removed and Tuba'lu (Ethbaal) installed in his place. Although Tyre was the dominant Phoenician city in Elijah's time and was later eclipsed by Sidon, the two cities alternately governed the same area, the southern boundary of which reached Mt Carmel.

11. Y. Aharoni, 'Mount Carmel as Border', in *Archäologie und Altes Testament*, ed. A. Kuschke and E. Kutsch (Tübingen: J.C.B. Mohr, 1970), 1-7.

12. The term, also found in Ugaritic and Assyrian texts, is certainly derived from the city-name 'Sidon'. But in the Old Testament it encompasses the population of all of southern Lebanon, including Tyre; the designation 'Sidonians' accentuates their status as border peoples.

13. In the scope of the Land Theology of the Old Testament this statement explains why Yahweh had not conquered the area in the north (Josh. 13.6).

14. This is a difficult passage. The expression 'according to the manner of the Sidonians' is here understood to mean that the people of Laish were influenced by Phoenician culture. This can be demonstrated by a comparison of the Iron Age pottery from Zarephath and Tell Dan.

15. See G.W. Ahlström, *Aspects of Syncretism in Israelite Religion* (Horae Soederblomianae, 5; Lund: Gleerup, 1963).

16. The number 'seven' is used this way in the Deuteronomistic history-work: e.g., the 'total' number of peoples living in the country (Josh. 3.10; etc.); cf. 2 Kings 4.35; 1 Kings 18.43.; etc. In maledictions the number 'seven' occurs quite often: Leviticus 26.18, 21, 24, 28; outside the Old Testament, *inter alia*, the Sefire treaty (cf. M. Weinfeld, *Deuteronomy and the Deuteronomic School* [Oxford: Clarendon Press, 1972], 124f.). The number 'ten' also has the same meaning of totality or maximum (Gen. 15.19-21; 31.7; 41.3; etc.).

17. Some parallels are found in Job 29.19, 23, and 38.28, and figuratively in Deuteronomy 32.2. 2 Samuel 1.21—a curse upon Mt Gilboa—parallels the situation found in 1 Kings 17.1.

18. Deuteronomy 28.23 forms an integral part of a group of curses, vv. 20-25 belonging to the vocabulary of a treaty. As the same malediction occurs in Leviticus 26.19 which has no Assyrian influence, there is a great possibility

that such metaphors have a Canaanite origin. See D.R. Hillers, *Treaty Curses and the Old Testament Prophets* (Rome: Pontifical Biblical Institute, 1964), 30, and Weinfeld, *Deuteronomy*, 116ff.

19. See Ringgren, *Israelitische Religion*, 293f.

20. J.B. Pritchard, *Recovering Sarepta, a Phoenician City* (Princeton: Princeton University Press, 1978), 105ff.

21. Bronner, *The Stories of Elijah*, 116ff.

22. The negations could here express an anti-Canaanite attitude, but it is more probable that David's utterance describes the curse to which Israel is subjected by the deaths of Saul and Jonathan.

23. The inscription consists of two lines: '(This) ewer, the work of my hands, 'Obal made for (the festival of?) the new moon'. The name 'Obal is known from a Ras Shamra text and from the Old Testament (Gen. 10.28; 1 Chron. 1.22). The phrase 'the work of my hands' is found in Isaiah 45.11 (cf. Deut. 33.11), but is thus far not attested in Ugaritic. See J.B. Pritchard, *Sarepta: A Preliminary Report on the Iron Age* (Philadelphia: University of Pennsylvania Press, 1975), 102f., and idem, *Recovering Sarepta*, 108f.

24. See Pritchard, *Sarepta*, 99, and idem, *Recovering Sarepta*, 97ff. Shadrapa, another god of healing, is mentioned on a sherd belonging to the shoulder of a jar. The preposition *l-* precedes the name of the god, indicating that the contents of the jar were offered to Shadrapa. The inscription is dated to the fifth century BC.

25. Cf. Commentaries *ad loc.*, and G. Fohrer, *Elia* (Zürich: Zwingli Verlag, 1957), 34.

26. Since there are strong indications that Sidon/Zarephath could have been a centre for the worship of gods of healing, the revival of the widow's son by one of Yahweh's prophets naturally would have been a clear demonstration of power. Gods of healing certainly were worshipped elsewhere in Phoenicia as well. It is the location of Zarephath at the ideal boundary that makes Elijah's act so important; his demonstration of power will nullify the 'curse' on a *kudurru*-place (see below).

27. The episode on Mt Carmel (1 Kgs 18) is outside the scope of this paper. Elijah's demonstration of Yahweh's superiority over Baal Melqart there has the same ramifications as at Zarephath, Mt Carmel being the actual border in Elijah's day. Cf. A. Alt, 'Das Gottesurteil auf dem Karmel', *Kleine Schriften*, II (München: C.H. Beck, 1953), 135-49; A. Jepsen, 'Elia und das Gottesurteil', *Near Eastern Studies in Honor of W.F. Albright*, ed. by H. Goedicke (Baltimore: Johns Hopkins Press, 1971), 291-306; H. Seebass, 'Elia und Ahab auf dem Karmel', *ZTK* 70 (1973), 121-36; R. Smend, 'Der biblische und der historische Elia', *VT* 28 (1978), 167-84.

28. See recently M. Saebø, 'Vom Grossreich zum Weltreich', *VT* 28 (1978), 251-61.

29. *ṣārap* means 'smelt' (of metals) and *śārap* means 'burn'. The excavations

at Zarephath have found much evidence of such industrial activity as burning pottery and metal. See Pritchard, *Recovering Sarepta*, 78f., 111ff.

30. On this problem see Z. Kallai, 'The United Monarchy of Israel: A Focal Point in Israelite Historiography', *IEJ* 27 (1977), 103-109.

31. A careful study of the book of Joshua shows how important it was for the composer, the Deuteronomistic redactor (*Dtr*), to include the land of Gilead in the widest sense in his composition of the Conquest. Though the historical events behind the Conquest are difficult to trace, the geography of both it and the division of the land which follows is a detailed map of the united Israelite kingdom. The book of Joshua is, in my opinion, *Dtr*'s programme for the re-establishment of the Davidic Kingdom. See my paper on 'Josuaboken: En deuteronomistisk Programskrift', *Religion och Bibel* 40 (1981), 3-13, and a forthcoming study of the book of Joshua.

32. Cf. K. Seybold, 'Elia am Gottesberg', *Evangelische Theologie* 33 (1973) 3-18; R.P. Carroll, 'The Elijah-Elisha Sagas: Some Remarks on Prophetic Succession in Ancient Israel', *VT* 19 (1969), 400-415; Carlson, 'Elie à l'Horeb'. See also A. Schmitt, 'Die Totenerweckung in 1 Kön XVII 17-24: Eine form- und gattungskritische Untersuchung', *VT* 27 (1977), 454-74, who has seen a structural relationship with some texts in the Moses tradition; Elijah is thus regarded as the new Moses.

33. This pattern is underscored in the book of Joshua where Joshua is described as the ideal 'king' always keeping the Law of Moses (Josh. 1.7ff.). Sometimes the tradent depicts him as a 'copy' of Moses (Josh. 5.15; 8.18; etc.).

34. This can be understood according to the composition of the book of Joshua. The book opens with a description of the land, the boundaries of which run as far east as the river Euphrates, although the Israelites at the moment are on the east side of the river Jordan. But the area described in Joshua 1.3. is linked to the strict observance of the Mosaic Law (Josh. 1.7ff.). The incidents at Ai (Josh. 7) and Gibeon (Josh. 9) are clear crimes against the Law, and these circumstances cause a diminution of the land which then becomes identical with the Davidic Kingdom (cf. Josh. 1–13; 14–24).

35. Weinfeld, *Deuteronomy*, 120.

HEAVENLY VISIONS IN EARLY JUDAISM: ORIGIN AND FUNCTION

Benedikt Otzen

A few years ago Gösta Ahlström published an article about the temples at Hazor and Arad.[1] Concentrating on the Late Bronze II temple in Area C of Hazor Ahlström adduces many good arguments for the idea that the statue and the stelae found in the holy of holies in this temple represent deities from the Canaanite pantheon. This implies that the holy of holies was considered to be 'the place where the gods "live" and where they meet the worshippers, represented by the priests'[2]—in short: the temple was conceived of as heaven on earth.

Further, according to Ahlström, the same idea is reflected in the Arad temple, in the stone slabs or stelae, presumably מצבת, which were placed in the cult niche or holy of holies. These stelae may have represented Yahweh and Baal, thus establishing an interesting connecting line between Canaanite and Israelite religion and at the same time furnishing additional archaeological evidence for the idea of the temple as heaven on earth.

In the introduction to his article Ahlström has collected material from various religions shedding light upon the conception of the temple as 'heaven on earth'. Both in ancient Egypt and in the Mesopotamian cultures there was a close connection between the temple and the heavenly world: the temple was of heavenly origin; it was the spot where heaven and earth were united; the gates of the temple were the gates of heaven; and the *adyton* of a Sumerian temple could be called 'a corner of heaven, a corner of earth'.[3]

That the same basic idea of the temple is also found in Israelite religion is pointed out by Ahlström with a reference to Psalm 11.4: 'Yahweh is in his holy temple, his throne is in heaven'.[4] I should like to make Old Testament passages of this kind my point of departure for the following reflections upon the heavenly visions found in Early Judaistic texts. For we certainly must go back to the Old Testament

if we want to understand Early Judaistic descriptions of heavenly visions. Therefore, before we look at the reports on heavenly visions as we find them in the Book of Daniel and in the Pseudepigrapha, we will turn to a few groups of narratives in the Old Testament that have a similar character. If we can say something about the origin and function of these Old Testament narratives, we may also be able to throw some light on the later Jewish visions. We may be able to see whether there is a connection between temple ideology, divine epiphany and heavenly vision. And we may be able to say something about the 'Sitz im Leben' of the visions and about the circles in Israelite and Jewish society that handed down the visionary traditions to later times.

II

A conspicuous literary genre in the Old Testament is the so-called sanctuary legend or cult legend telling how a temple or a sanctuary achieved its character of holiness in days of old. From a form-critical point of view these tales are in many cases uniform in structure: the foundation of a sanctuary or a temple is based upon an event that is characterized by three elements: a divine epiphany, the divine word, and the erection of an altar by the cult hero.[5] We find this structure in the tale about Abraham at Shechem (Gen. 12.6-7), in the account of Jacob's dream at Bethel (Gen. 28.10-22), and in the parallel account of Jacob's return to Bethel (Gen. 35.9-15). Outside of Genesis a similar structure is found in the narrative about Gideon in Ophrah (Judg. 6.11-24), and it certainly also underlies the famous story about the sacrifice of Isaac in the Land of Moriah (Gen. 22). This scheme is present in other cult legends in more or less dissolved form (Ex. 3; 2 Sam. 24; Judg. 2.1-5; etc.).[6]

These various narratives encompass the *hieroi logoi* of the respective sanctuaries to which they are attached. In most cases the sanctuary legend consists of several elements and has had a complicated history of transmission until achieving its final shape. If, for instance, we take the story of Jacob at Bethel, which is one of the most typical examples of Patriarchal sanctuary legends, we can easily discern several layers in the tale as we have it now. These layers denote steps in the development of the story: an ancient narrative about the cult hero of Bethel and the founding of the sanctuary (probably a Canaanite legend), a younger elaboration from the Jacob cycle about

Jacob's flight, and a still younger presentation within the framework of the Patriarchal Narratives, with their typical blessings and promises. I cannot go into particulars about these problems but will have to refer the reader to modern treatments of Genesis 28.[7]

What is important in our connection is the close relationship between divine epiphany and holy place. And we feel, based on this story in Genesis 28, that the ancient Israelites also regarded the holy place as the domicile of their deity: 'How dreadful is this place! This is none other but the house of God, and this is the gate of heaven' (Gen. 28.17). Not least Houtman in his recent article about Genesis 28 emphasizes that 'Jacob is in the gate of heaven, at the place which gives entry to heaven, at the place where the abode, the house of God is . . . At this place heaven and earth cannot be distinguished.'[8]

The origin of this legend presumably is lost in distant Canaanite mythology. But if we inquire as to the 'Sitz im Leben' of the sanctuary legend in Genesis 28, we can hardly doubt that the tale was transmitted and reworked in priestly circles attached to the later important sanctuary at Bethel—as will have been the case with other legends concerning the founding of various sanctuaries.[9] It is a reasonable assumption that the priests at the Bethel sanctuary must have adopted and transmitted to posterity the ancient story about the cult hero of Bethel, harmonizing it with Israelite traditions. It is also likely that the narrative had, in one shape or other, some function in the cult of the temple at Bethel—just as it is probable that cult legends from other sanctuaries had a cultic function where they belonged. A good example is Psalm 132, in which the legend of the ark—one of the *hieroi logoi* of Jerusalem—is presented in a cultic form which will have played a central role in the priestly cult at Zion.

Thus we can assume that the sanctuary legends represent priestly traditions and have had a cultic function. A story about the meeting in ancient times between the divinity of the sanctuary and the cult hero, the founder of the sanctuary, has been carefully preserved by the priests and used in the cult as a tradition intended to strengthen the authority and the sanctity of the shrine in the eyes of the worshippers. Again, we are best informed about conditions in Jerusalem; quite a lot of psalms bear witness to the development of an ideology that accords to Jerusalem a position of eminence which has persisted to the present. And this ideology is saturated with conceptions originating in the ancient legends that clustered round the earliest times of the sanctuary 'when Yahweh chose Zion for his

abode on earth'. The theophanic element is very strong in these psalms and the above-mentioned verse from Psalm 11 is only one of many examples of Zion conceived of as the place where Yahweh appeared at the beginning of time and where he will remain as long as he is the God of Israel.[10]

We have in the sanctuary legends observed a strong priestly tradition in ancient Israel encompassing reports of theophanies on the spot where in later times a temple was to be erected. The theophany seems to be a *conditio sine qua non* for the temple; through the theophany the sanctuary obtains its holiness and becomes 'heaven on earth'.

In order to follow the line of development from these conceptions to the heavenly visions in later Jewish literature we must turn to another kind of characteristic story in the Old Testament that has quite a lot in common with the sanctuary legend: the call narrative. Indeed, some of the sanctuary legends have been combined with call narratives, or are, so to speak, at once both sanctuary legends and call narratives. This is evident as far as Judges 6 is concerned, where the call of Gideon is combined with the cult legend of Ophrah. But also in Genesis 28 the words to Jacob in vv. 13-15 may easily be viewed as a kind of call or consecration of Jacob to his future position as the father of the twelve tribes. And in Exodus 3 some scholars find both the narrative about the call of Moses and the sanctuary legend of Sinai/Horeb.[11]

In 1965 N. Habel published an excellent analysis of the various call narratives in the Old Testament and found a common structure behind them.[12] He also tried to trace their origin: 'the *Gattung* for the call of a divine representative was taken over from the practice reflected in Gen. 24.34-48 according to which ambassadors or messengers on a special mission presented their credentials in a specific order and manner'.[13] In 1962, however, Walter Zimmerli had published his treatment of Ezekiel's inaugural vision. In this context he offered a broad analysis of the other call narratives and went a step further than Habel was to do a few years later. He distinguished between two main types of call narrative: one in which the divine word to the person called is central; to this group belong Exodus 3; Judges 6 and Jeremiah 1. The other type has its centre in the vision of Yahweh on his throne surrounded by his heavenly court, and the message to the person called is subordinate to the vision; to this group belong 1 Kings 22; Isaiah 6 and Ezekiel 1–3.[14]

Just as the theophany played a dominant role in the sanctuary legends treated above, the vision of the enthroned deity—a special kind of theophany—is the most conspicuous trait in this second group of call narratives. And the connection with the sanctuary legends is even closer! This connection is unambiguously seen in Isaiah 6. Confronted with this vision one inevitably poses the following questions: does Isaiah see Yahweh on his throne in the Jerusalem temple, or, does Isaiah in the temple have a vision of Yahweh on his throne in heaven, or, finally, does he simply have a vision of Yahweh on his heavenly throne without any connection whatever with the terrestrial temple? The question is put by most scholars commenting upon Isaiah 6, and their answers are fairly equally distributed among the three possibilities.[15]

Several modern scholars, however, think this way of presenting the problem is wrong. It is not a question of either-or. Knierim, for instance, says as follows: 'the temple on Mount Zion is the place on earth where Yahweh rests his foot. It still belongs to the heavenly space, and Yahweh can be regarded as experienced sitting upon his throne in heaven as well as in the temple.'[16] It is easily seen that we are back where we started: Isaiah 6 also bears witness to the idea of the identity of temple and heaven. And it is not accidental that Isaiah's vision has this close connection with the temple. As we learned from the sanctuary legends the temple is *the* place where theophanies are experienced. These temple traditions are so strong that they also influence the prophetic traditions about Isaiah meeting his God. Moreover, not only the theophany proper has its origin in traditions attached to the sanctuary, but the whole narrative of the call of Isaiah is saturated with elements stemming from the cult of the Jerusalem temple.[17]

The same holds true for the vision in Ezekiel 1–3, for Ezekiel also has a vision of Yahweh on his throne, and the connection between the vision and the temple of Jerusalem is evident, not least in ch. 8 and ch. 10 where the 'glory of Yahweh', as the vision is called, leaves the temple which ought to be the proper abode for Yahweh. The development of these chapters is very complicated,[18] but at least in its final shape the text makes it clear that Ezekiel's vision is borne by ideas that originate in the temple cult. That cultic and priestly theophany traditions should be found behind the Ezekiel vision is not difficult to understand. Ezekiel is a priest himself and his message is to a large extent determined by his background in the Jerusalem

temple. In the words of von Rad: 'Ezekiel has his roots in the priestly-sacral traditions'.[19]

The function of the theophany at the call of both Isaiah and Ezekiel is obvious: the authority of both prophets is confirmed by the reference to an inaugural experience; they have received their message in a direct confrontation with Yahweh. And this confrontation took place in the holy sphere of the Jerusalem temple; the descriptions of the call events are in both cases marked by material that we also met with in the sanctuary legends—above all the theophany motif—and which can be traced back to priestly traditions about the divine presence in the temple.

III

In the literature of Early Judaism, especially in the Pseudepigrapha, descriptions of heavenly visions play a dominant role. Such visions belong, so to speak, to the fixtures of apocalyptic writings. Often the visions have the shape of a description of a journey through the heavenly world undertaken by the hero of the apocalyptic narrative in question, such as Enoch or Baruch. In other cases a hero—like Daniel or Levi—has a vision more or less in the Old Testament style. In any case, the heavenly vision or the heavenly journey is a conspicuous genre in Early Judaistic apocalyptic—so conspicuous that when the American scholar John Collins attempts a survey of the different apocalypses in Early Judaism, he divides them into two main sections: those describing a heavenly journey and those without such a description.[20] We have apocalyptic writings with fragments of descriptions of heavenly journeys or visions, and others that have very full descriptions. We can only take a look at a few of them.

Daniel 7 forms the connecting link between the heavenly visions in the Old Testament that we have treated already and the heavenly visions in apocalyptic materials. In the first three scenes of the chapter (7.1-6), Daniel sees three animals coming out of the sea: the lion representing the Babylonian world power; the bear representing the Median world power; and the panther representing the Persians. In the fourth scene of the chapter (vv. 7-12) Daniel sees the fourth animal representing the Greek world power being taken before the throne of the Ancient of Days and condemned to destruction. After this, in the fifth scene (vv. 13-14), power is given to 'the one like a man' representing the eternal Kingdom of God as opposed to the worldly powers.[21]

The relationship between the central vision in Daniel 7—the 'Ancient of Days' on his throne—and the two throne visions, Isaiah 6 and Ezekiel 1–3, treated above, is unmistakable, and we cannot doubt that the scene in Daniel 7 is depicted under the influence of the prophetic call narratives, as seen by most commentators on the Book of Daniel. In all three visions God is seen as a king on his throne; fire and smoke accompany the theophany in all three visions; celestial beings serve the kingly god; and—not least—all three visions have the same aim: to describe God as judge. In the two prophetic visions he is to judge his chosen people, Israel, and in the Daniel vision he will judge the heathen powers of this world.

Thus the connecting line from Daniel 7 back to the call narratives is clear. The epiphany of the enthroned God is in the centre. It is more difficult to see the connecting line to the sanctuary legends where we observed, as an important element, the close relationship between the theophany and the holy place, the temple. This idea was also present in the call narratives, but in Daniel it is hardly discernible, and only the connection to Isaiah 6 and Ezekiel 1–3 is an indirect evidence.

However, the relations between heaven, theophany and temple are evident if we turn to another heavenly vision in apocalyptic. In the Testaments of the Twelve Patriarchs we are confronted with Levi on his deathbed. Just before dying he reports on a vision he had in his youth. The account of the vision is found in T.Levi 2–5, and text-critically and traditio-historically the section is most complicated.[22] In its final shape T.Levi certainly reveals an idea of seven heavens. After an introduction which mentions only three heavens (2.6-12),[23] ch. 3 allows Levi to pass through: the first heaven which is gloomy because of the sin of man (3.1); the second heaven containing fire, snow and ice, and the spirits of retribution for the Day of Judgment (3.2); the third heaven containing armies to punish Beliar and his spirits (3.3a); the fourth heaven containing holy ones and thrones and dominions offering praise to God (3.3b + 3.8); the fifth heaven containing angels bearing answers to the archangels (3.7); the sixth heaven containing the archangels and the angels of the presence of the Lord, offering sacrifice to propitiate sins (3.5); and he ends up in the seventh heaven where 'dwelleth the Great Glory, in the holy of holies, far above all holiness' (3.4), and where, further, Levi 'saw the holy temple, and upon a throne of glory the Most High' (5.1).[24]

Quite a number of interesting questions arise from these chapters.

First, do these ideas about multiple heavens have their origin in the Old Testament, or have they come into apocalyptic from elsewhere? And secondly, where in Early Jewish society did these descriptions of the heavens originate, or, we could ask, what function do these descriptions have?

The very idea of multiple heavens could have arisen from Old Testament expressions like 'the heaven and heaven of heavens' (Deut. 10.14 or 1 Kings 8.27). The rabbis discussed whether such expressions implied two or three heavens.[25] When, however, it comes to the conception of a certain, fixed number of heavens (3, 5, 7 or 10), it becomes more difficult, and we have to seek the origin of such numbers outside Israel. The Egyptians and the Babylonians had different systems,[26] but if we stick to the predominant number, 7, it is certainly derived from Babylonian astronomical speculations, specifically Babylonian knowledge of the planets (they knew five planets + sun and moon). The planets represented gods, and their seven orbits formed the basis for the idea of heaven divided into seven spheres, an idea that was taken over by the Jews, the rabbis, the Gnostics and the Christians.[27]

Of course it is interesting to trace such conceptions back to their origin. On the other hand, the astronomical insights that seem to have started speculations about the number of heavens with the Babylonians will hardly have played a great role with the Jews. We have, indeed, in Jewish apocalyptic literature quite a lot of astronomical speculations about the orbits of the celestial bodies. But these speculations have a special function: they demonstrate the well-ordered world created by Israel's God. And the descriptions of the orbits of the celestial bodies do not form the basis of the description of the seven heavens; they are, so to speak, subordinated to the heavenly system, as the angels responsible for the different orbits are placed in special departments in one or more of the heavens (so for instance in the Slavonic Enoch). We tarry in the outworks of the problem if we occupy ourselves too much with the question of the origin of these ideas.

Our interest in this context is the question of the 'Sitz im Leben', and of the function of such heavenly visions in Early Jewish society. In addition, there is the question of a possible connection between this and similar heavenly visions in Early Judaistic literature on one hand and the sanctuary legends and the call narratives in the Old Testament on the other.

If we are to determine the function of the heavenly visions in Early Judaism, we must first try to understand the frame of reference, or the horizon of perception, within which the Jew finds himself when he ventures into speculations about the organization of the heavenly world. A way of understanding this is found in the thinking which is reflected by the conceptual pair macrocosm and microcosm, 'the great world' and 'the small world'. The idea behind these conceptions—which can be found in much ancient mythology[28]—is that conditions on earth have their counterparts in corresponding conditions in heaven. Or, expressed the other way round, the heavenly macrocosm is reflected in the earthly microcosm. Further possible variations are expressed in the following examples: that the created world is a microcosm in relation to the heavenly macrocosm; or that man is a microcosm in relation to the macrocosm of the created world; or—and of great interest to us here—that the temple is a microcosm in relation to the heavenly macrocosm. The temple is at once an *imago mundi*, 'image of the world', reflecting the cosmos, and is *imago coeli*, 'image of heaven', reflecting the heavenly world. The temple is where heaven and earth meet; indeed, the temple *is* heaven on earth.

And this brings us once more back to where we began! The idea of the close relationship between heaven and temple that in ancient times was reflected in the sanctuary legends and to a certain degree also in the call narratives, crops up in Early Judaism and is now intimately connected with the temple in Jerusalem. This development is easy to understand, if one considers the changes in religious life from classical Israelite times down to the period of Early Judaism. It is only natural that the Zion temple should have acquired a special position in apocalyptic thought and that the idea of the 'Heavenly Jerusalem' is found in various apocalyptic writings more or less directly dependent upon Ezekiel's vision of the new temple (Ezek. 40–48) and upon late priestly traditions in the Old Testament.[29]

We return to the heavenly vision in the Testament of Levi. How does this text fit in here? As a matter of fact Levi's vision furnishes an excellent example of the close connection between the Jerusalem temple and heavenly vision, and further, it illustrates perfectly the idea of the temple as an image of heaven. Modern man, of course, can only understand matters the other way round and must maintain that the Jew, when he had to describe heaven, used the temple for his pattern!

This is exactly the case in T.Levi 3–5. The seventh heaven, we

saw, is simply termed τὸ ἅγιον ἁγίων, the Holy of Holies, the name of the דביר, the *adyton* of the Jerusalem temple, and here Levi sees 'the Great Glory', ἡ μεγάλη δόξα (T.Levi 3.4). In 5.1 the same heaven is called ὁ ναὸς ὁ ἅγιος, the holy temple, and here Levi sees the Most High upon the throne of glory. Just beneath, in the sixth heaven, propitiatory sacrifices are presented (T.Levi 3.5), precisely as such sacrifices are associated with the incense altar in 'the Holy Place', the היכל of the Jerusalem temple. Beneath this we find the fifth heaven with ordinary angels bringing 'answers' to the archangels (T.Levi 3.7); they could correspond to the priests in 'the forecourt of the priests' just in front of the temple proper, establishing the connection between man and the heavenly world. The singing 'holy ones' in the fourth heaven (T.Levi 3.3b + 3.8) could correspond to the congregation in the great forecourt, 'the court of the Israelites'.

It is uncertain, of course, how far we may legitimately pursue such parallels, but the correspondence in general is clear enough. In the temple area one proceeds through sections of increasing holiness until one arrives at the Holy of Holies. And similarly, from the lower heavens one ascends through spheres of increasing holiness until one achieves the highest of heavens, before the throne of God. The temple is microcosm, while heaven is macrocosm.

It is important to bear this relationship in mind when we turn to our next question: what is the function of these visions? How are they used in their literary and traditional contexts? As far as the throne visions in Isaiah, Ezekiel and Daniel were concerned, we saw that the dominating conception was judgment; the enthroned God was going to judge his people Israel or the godless world empires. The notion of judgment is also to be found in the context of the heavenly vision in T.Levi 2-5. But here it is not dominant; it is rather a subplot, perhaps of a secondary character.

The function of Levi's vision is to be sought elsewhere. As a matter of fact, Levi himself puts a question in this direction to the angel. When he has seen the third heaven, he asks a little naïvely: διατί οὕτως, 'why is it so?' (T.Levi 2.9). But the angel rejects the question and tells him instead, *why* he is allowed to see the secrets of heaven. Indeed, the angel answers *our* question about the function of the vision! He says: you, Levi, shall be allowed to see all seven heavens, for 'thou shalt stand near the Lord, and shalt be his minister, and his mysteries shalt thou declare to men' (T.Levi 2.10). And at the end of the vision the Lord, talking to Levi from his throne in the seventh

heaven, says: 'Levi, I have given thee the blessings of the priesthood until I come and sojourn in the midst of Israel' (T.Levi 5.2). All this fits very well with the fact that the centre and climax of the Testament of Levi is to be found in ch. 8, where the seven archangels consecrate Levi as a priest.

Thus the function of the heavenly vision in the Testament of Levi has something to do with the priesthood. It tries to say that it is the privilege of the priests, like their primordial father Levi, to obtain insight into the heavenly secrets, so that they can 'declare his mysteries to man'. The priests are admitted to the temple in Jerusalem and know its 'secrets'. Correspondingly they obtain the right to know the secrets of the heavenly world, the prototype of the temple. And precisely the fact that there is this clear connection between temple and heaven in T.Levi makes it likely that in T.Levi we have a special priestly tradition. In priestly circles this special presentation of the heavenly vision is used for legitimizing the claim of the priests to be the only ones having the privilege of knowing the heavenly secrets.[30]

We could proceed to other heavenly visions in Early Judaistic literature. The Slavonic Enoch, which dates from the first century AD and is certainly dependent upon Ethiopic Enoch, is mainly one great heavenly vision. Enoch's heavenly journey gives him insight into the creation and the Lord's greatness as creator of the well-ordered world. In all this there is presumably an influence from Wisdom which on the whole is an important element in apocalyptic.[31] The centre of gravity in the demonstration of the order of creation lies in the astronomical field; in the different heavens one finds angels responsible for various astronomical phenomena. In the first heaven (chs. 3–6)[32] live the angels who take care of the orbits of the stars and who guard the storehouses containing snow, rain and so forth. In the fourth heaven (chs. 11–17) live the angels who have reponsibility for the orbits of the sun and the moon and for the calendar. In the sixth heaven (ch. 19) dwell the seven archangels who establish world-order and who are above the angels that 'are appointed over seasons and years', and so on. And in the seventh heaven (ch. 20) Enoch sees the Lord on his throne.

Even if the idea of world-order and the wise Creator is central here, we are able to discern also in this vision the 'Sitz im Leben' of the vision. For who was in ancient Jewish society responsible for the calendar if not the priests? They ensured that the feasts of the temple

were celebrated at the right time, and precisely for this reason the astronomical calculations and the calendrical reckonings were of the utmost importance. So we may surmise that we find priestly traditions behind this heavenly vision as well.[33] And this presumption is strengthened by another consideration:[34] at the end of Slavonic Enoch, as a kind of appendix,[35] one finds the report of Enoch's son, Methusalem, his son Nir and his grandson, Melchizedek, being consecrated as priests. These priestly traditions make it likely that the whole Book of Enoch was transmitted in priestly circles.[36]

IV

We have inquired as to the origin and function of the heavenly visions in Early Judaism. As far as their origins are concerned the connection with various kinds of theophanies in the Old Testament—as represented both in the sanctuary legends and in the call narratives—is obvious and has of course been noticed before, as we mentioned in our treatment of Daniel 7.[37] This holds true even if we may also observe some foreign influence in the development of the idea of multiple heavens. But we have tried to go a step further in fixing our attention on a theme which runs throughout our materials: the temple seems to play a certain role in most kinds of heavenly visions, and we assume that this fact may shed some light upon the question of the 'Sitz im Leben' or social function of these visions. They appear to have been transmitted and 'used' within priestly circles both in ancient and later times.

Before leaving our topic, I should like to touch upon a further consequence of the observations made in this article. It is well known that the question of the origin of apocalyptic as such has been debated in recent years. We have mentioned the discussion between Gerhard von Rad and Peter von der Osten-Sacken—von Rad advocating an origin in wisdom teaching, and von der Osten-Sacken adhering to the usual view that the origin is to be sought in the prophetic tradition. As is often the case, the truth may be found somewhere in between. At least in some cases it seems legitimate to understand an apocalyptic text as representing a prophetic tradition re-interpreted in the light of wisdom teaching.[38] To a certain degree this is what we find in those heavenly visions in Early Judaism which emphasize creation and world order. The prophetic theophany motif is here transformed, and the centre of gravity lies in what could be

called a favourite theme of wisdom teaching. This is only one example, and certainly there is quite a lot of work to be done before the problem of wisdom influence upon apocalyptic is solved.[39]

Another way of coming to terms with the question of the relations between wisdom and apocalyptic has appeared in recent attempts to differentiate the concept of wisdom. Above all, H.-P. Müller has shown that the kind of wisdom one finds in apocalyptic is of a special character and differs from the wisdom found in Proverbs and Job. He introduces the concept of 'mantic wisdom' (*mantische Weisheit*) encompassing such phenomena as divination and the interpretation of dreams; Daniel is a typical representative of this kind of wisdom.[40] John J. Collins moves along the same line, when he tries to distinguish between 'proverbial wisdom' and 'mantic wisdom, as practised by Joseph and Daniel, which includes the interpretation of dreams, signs, and visions'.[41] These ideas are most fruitful for the continued efforts to understand apocalyptic.

But we cannot help posing a final question: can we say anything about the 'Sitz im Leben' of mantic wisdom? In which circles was it found? Müller is reluctant to answer. He does not think that mantic wisdom can be localized to a single institution but talks more vaguely about its being an undercurrent in the religious life from the second century BC on.[42] Collins has developed a fascinating idea according to which mantic wisdom was imported by the wise men (משכילים) from the diaspora.[43] I should prefer another direction: it was mentioned above (note 29 and text relating to it) that Hamerton-Kelly found priestly traditions (especially Ezek. 40–48 and the source P) behind the idea of the Heavenly Jerusalem or the heavenly temple. At the end of his article he suggests that not only did apocalyptic originate in prophetic traditions and in wisdom traditions, but that 'the priestly tradition, as interpreted by Ezekiel, also played a dominant role'.[44] He is certainly right, but he makes a mistake in keeping wisdom tradition and priestly tradition apart, as parallel or, indeed, separate elements in apocalyptic. The question is whether these two entities do not meet precisely in the concept of mantic wisdom? It was further mentioned above (see note 33 and text relating to it) that J.C.H. Lebram finds priestly features in the apocalyptic interest in astronomy, calendars, temple, cult, etc. He talks about 'priestly wisdom' (*priesterliche Weisheit*) and thinks that 'the apocalyptic method above all has been developed in priestly circles'.[45] The distance between mantic wisdom and priestly wisdom

is certainly not great, and with the help of parallels from Mesopotamian divinatory practice it will certainly be possible to throw more light upon mantic and priestly wisdom in Israel and upon the origin of Jewish apocalyptic.[46]

NOTES

1. G.W. Ahlström, 'Heaven on Earth—at Hazor and Arad', *Religious Syncretism in Antiquity: Essays in Conversation with Geo Widengren*, ed. Birger A. Pearson (Missoula, Montana: Scholars Press, 1975), 67-83.
2. Ahlström, 'Heaven on Earth', 79.
3. Ahlström, 'Heaven on Earth', 67-69.
4. Ahlström, 'Heaven on Earth', 69.
5. C.A. Keller, 'Über einige alttestamentliche Heiligtumslegenden I', *ZAW* 67 (1955), 141-68, esp. pp. 151f.
6. See Keller, 'Heiligtumslegenden I', *ZAW* 67 (1955), 141-68; *id.*, 'Heiligtumslegenden II', *ZAW* 68 (1956), 85-97; and J. Lindblom, 'Theophanies in Holy Places in Hebrew Religion', *HUCA* 32 (1961), 91-106.
7. E. Otto, 'Jakob in Bethel. Ein Beitrag zur Geschichte der Jakobüberlieferung', *ZAW* 88 (1976), 165-90; C. Houtman, 'What did Jacob see in his Dream at Bethel? Some Remarks on Genesis xxviii 10-22', *VT* 27 (1977), 337-51; and C. Westermann, *Genesis 2: Gen 12-36* (BKAT, I/2; Neukirchen-Vluyn: Neukirchener Verlag, 1981), 548-61 (with further literature).
8. Houtman, 'Jacob at Bethel', 344.
9. Westermann, *Genesis 2*, 552; V. Maag, 'Zum Hieros Logos von Beth-El', *Asiatische Studien* 5 (1951), 122-33, esp. p. 131 (both about Gen. 28); and H.-J. Kraus, 'Gilgal. Ein Beitrag zur Kultusgeschichte Israels', *VT* 1 (1951), 181-99, esp. p. 184 (about Gilgal).
10. See for instance B.S. Childs, *Myth and Reality in the Old Testament* (SBT, 27; London: SCM, 1968), 85-89; R.E. Clements, *God and Temple* (Oxford: Blackwell, 1965), 63-78; and T.N.D. Mettinger, *The Dethronement of Sabaoth. Studies in the Shem and Kabod Theologies* (CBOTS, 18; Lund: Gleerup, 1982), 24-36.
11. E. Kutsch, 'Gideons Berufung und Altarbau Jdc 6,11-24', *TLZ* 81 (1956), 75-84 and H.W. Hertzberg, *Die Bücher Josua, Richter, Ruth*[2] (ATD, 9; Göttingen: Vandenhoeck & Ruprecht, 1959), 192 (both about Judg. 6); G. von Rad, *Das erste Buch Mose. Genesis* (ATD, 2-4; Göttingen: Vandenhoeck & Ruprecht, 1956), 249 (about Gen. 28); and W. Zimmerli, *Ezechiel* (BKAT, XIII/1; Neukirchen-Vluyn: Neukirchener Verlag, 1969), 17 (about Exod. 3).
12. N. Habel, 'The Form and Significance of the Call Narratives', *ZAW* 77 (1965), 297-323.
13. Habel, 'Call Narratives', 322.
14. Zimmerli, *Ezechiel*, 16-21.

15. R. Knierim ('The Vocation of Isaiah', *VT* 18 [1968], 47-68) gives on pp. 50. a survey of opinions.

16. Knierim, 'Vocation of Isaiah', 52. Cf. I. Engnell, *The Call of Isaiah* (UUÅ 1949:4; Uppsala: A.-B. Lundequist, 1949), 27f.; M. Metzger, 'Himmlische und irdische Wohnstatt Jahwes', *UF* 2 (1970), 139-58, esp. pp. 144.; H. Wildberger, *Jesaja 1: Jes 1-12* (BKAT, X/1; Neukirchen-Vluyn: Neukirchener Verlag, 1972), 246.

17. See Engnell, *Call of Isaiah*, 25-53; H. Cazelles, 'Jesajas kallelse och kungaritualet', *SEÅ* 39 (1974), 38-58.

18. See Zimmerli, *Ezechiel*, 21-37.

19. G. von Rad, *Theologie des Alten Testaments* (München: Chr. Kaiser Verlag, 1960), II, 238; cf. Zimmerli, *Ezechiel*, 81^{+}, 51.

20. J.J. Collins, 'The Jewish Apocalypses', *Semeia* 14 (1979), 21-59, esp. p. 22.

21. See H.S. Kvanvig, 'Struktur und Geschichte in Dan. 7,1-14', *StTh* 32 (1978), 95-117. Esp. on pp. 103-10 Kvanvig argues for the division of the chapter followed here. Cf., by the way, H.S. Kvanvig, 'An Akkadian Vision as Background for Dan 7?', *StTh* 35 (1981), 85-89; very interesting material from the seventh century BC shedding light upon the imagery of Dan. 7 is here adduced.

22. The most recent treatment: M. de Jonge, 'Notes on Testament of Levi II—VII', *Studies on the Testaments of the Twelve Patriarchs. Text and Interpretation*, ed. M. de Jonge (Leiden: Brill, 1975), 247-60. Quotations from The Testaments of the Twelve Patriarchs in the following are taken from *APOT* (Engl. translation) and from *PVTG* I/2 (Greek text).

23. A tradition about three heavens seems to have been fused with a tradition about seven heavens; therefore one group of manuscripts mentions three heavens only. On these confusing problems see: R.H. Charles, *The Greek Versions of the Testaments of the Twelve Patriarchs* (Oxford: Clarendon Press, 1908), 29-35, and *PVTG* I/2, 26-29. Different assessments of the development of the traditions: R. Eppel, *Le piétisme juif dans Les Testaments des douze Patriarches* (Paris: Félix Alcan, 1930), 59-67; J. Becker, *Untersuchungen zur Entstehungsgeschichte der Testamente der zwölf Patriarchen* (AGJU, 8; Leiden: Brill, 1970), 257-69; de Jonge, 'Notes on Testament of Levi II–VII', 247-60.

24. The strange order of the seven heavens in the text is due to the problems mentioned in note 23.

25. G.F. Moore, *Judaism in the First Centuries of the Christian Era* (Cambridge, Mass.: Harvard University Press, 1927-30), I, 368.

26. See H. Bietenhard, *Die himmlische Welt im Urchristentum und Spätjudentum* (WUNT, 2; Tübingen: Mohr–Siebeck, 1951), 11-18.

27. Bietenhard, *Himmlische Welt*, 15-18.

28. See for instance: G. Lanczkowski, 'Makrokosmos und Mikrokosmos', *RGG* 4 (3. Aufl.; Tübingen: Mohr-Siebeck, 1960), 624.; Bietenhard,

Himmlische Welt, 13. J. Barr ('The Meaning of "Mythology" in Relation to the Old Testament', *VT* 9 [1959] 1-10, esp. pp. 5-7) adduces the concept in his attempt to understand the essence of mythology, and B. Otzen ('Die neugefundenen hebräischen Sektenschriften und die Testamente der zwölf Patriarchen', *StTh* 7 [1953], 125-57, esp. pp. 135-42) in his attempt to understand dualism in Early Judaism. Cf. Childs, *Myth and Reality*, 84-94, and Clements, *God and Temple*, 67-69. Both find the idea of correspondence behind the Old Testament concepts about temple and heaven that we have touched on above. R.G. Hamerton-Kelly ('The Temple and the Origins of Jewish Apocalyptic', *VT* 20 [1970], 1-15, esp. pp. 5f.) draws attention to the heavenly model (*tabnit*) for Moses' description of the tabernacle (Ex. 25).

29. Hamerton-Kelly, 'The Temple', 1-11.

30. Seen by P.D. Hanson ('Apocalypse. Genre', *IDBSup*, 28): 'a visionary rapture is described which serves to legitimate the Hasmonean royal priesthood'.

31. See von Rad, *Theologie*, II (5. Aufl., 1968), 316-23. Criticism of von Rad's position in for instance P. von der Osten-Sacken, *Die Apokalyptik in ihrem Verhältnis zu Prophetie und Weisheit* (Theologische Existenz heute, 157; München: Chr. Kaiser, 1969), and K. Koch, *Ratlos vor der Apokalyptik* (Gütersloh: Gerd Mohn, 1970), 40-46.

32. The numbering of chapters is according to Forbes and Charles in *APOT*. The division of chapters in Vaillant (*Le livre des secrets d'Hénoch* [Paris: Institut d'études slaves, 1952]) is different, and the seven heavens are found in chs. 3–9.

33. J.C.H. Lebram ('Apokalyptik und Hellenismus im Buche Daniel', *VT* 20 [1970], 503-24, esp. pp. 523.) adduces the same argument in his attempt to determine the priestly origin of apocalyptic as such (see below, note 45).

34. Part of these reflections on the heavenly visions were presented as a lecture at the Swedish Theological Institute in Jerusalem, and on that occasion Professor David Flusser drew my attention to the following observation.

35. It is not included in the translation in *APOT* but is found in the Danish translation by A. Bugge and E. Hammershaimb (*De gammeltestamentlige Pseudepigrafer* [Copenhagen: Gad, 1953-76], 819-26).

36. Further heavenly visions are found in Ethiopic Enoch 17-36, Greek Baruch, Testament of Abraham, etc. See Collins, 'The Jewish Apocalypses', 36-43.

37. Cf. also C. Rowland ('The Visions of God in Apocalyptic Literature', *JJS* 10 [1979], 137-54) who concentrates on the importance of Ezek. 1–3 for Ethiopic Enoch, Rev. 4 and Medieval Jewish *merkabah*-literature.

38. Cf. Lebram, 'Apokalyptik und Hellenismus', 521.

39. Various aspects of this relationship have been treated in recent years; see for instance B. Otzen, 'Old Testament Wisdom Literature and Dualistic Thinking in Late Judaism', *SVT* 28 (1975), 146-57; J.G. Gammie, 'Spatial

and Ethical Dualism in Jewish Wisdom and Apocalyptic Literature', *JBL* 93 (1974), 356-85; and the last two articles in the Terrien Festschrift *Israelite Wisdom. Theological and Literary Essays in Honor of Samuel Terrien*, ed. J.G. Gammie, *et al.* (Missoula, Montana: Scholars Press, 1978).

40. H.-P. Müller, 'Magisch-mantische Weisheit und die Gestalt Daniels', *UF* 1 (1969), 79-94; *id.*, 'Mantische Weisheit und Apokalyptik', *SVT* 22 (1972), 268-93; *id.*, '*ḥākam*', *TWAT* 2 (1977), 933-37.

41. J.J. Collins, 'The Court-Tales in Daniel and the Development of Apocalyptic', *JBL* 94 (1975), 218-34, esp. p. 232.

42. Müller, 'Mantische Weisheit', 290, and 'Magisch-mantische Weisheit', 85.

43. Collins, 'Court-Tales', 232.

44. Hamerton-Kelly, 'The Temple', 15.

45. Lebram, 'Apokalyptik und Hellenismus', 524.

46. I hope in the not too distant future in collaboration with Frederick H. Cryer to return to these problems.

EVE AND THE CHAMELEON

Åke W. Sjöberg

I

It gives me very great pleasure to dedicate the following notes and thoughts to my dear old friend Gösta on the occasion of his 65th birthday. We have known each other since the end of the 1940s from Uppsala. We spent many years together studying the Old Testament with the enthusiastic Ivan Engnell, trembling in the shadow of the Professor of Semitic Languages H.S. Nyberg, and enjoying the learned Professor Geo Widengren. We were steeped in the tradition of the Scandinavian 'Uppsala School'.

Myths in the Old Testament, the recent work by fellow Scandinavians Benedikt Otzen, Hans Gottlieb, and Knud Jeppesen,[1] provided the impulse to write these short notes. I have read their articles with the eyes of an Assyriologist (with some background as a student of the Old Testament). As Gösta will see, I have in some cases parted from the 'Uppsala School' where, we have to admit, a strong stress was placed on Mesopotamian influences on Old Testament concepts. I will begin with the Babylonian epic of creation, *Enūma Eliš*, and agree with Professor W.G. Lambert that there was hardly any influence from that Babylonian text on the Old Testament creation accounts. Next I venture to fell the Tree of Life in Mesopotamia. Then I will try to revive the chameleon, accusing that animal of having seduced Eve ('Moder för oss alla'), and in conclusion will suggest that Adam himself was a good old Palestinian.

II

Since the Babylonian epic of creation, *Enūma Eliš* ('When above'), became known, it has been assumed that the accounts of creation in Genesis were (at least partially) dependent on this Babylonian mythological text. It is a well-known fact that the major item in

Enūma Eliš, the battle between Marduk and Tiamat (in Genesis *t^e^hōm*), is missing in Genesis. The poetic books of the Old Testament often allude to a battle between Yahweh and the sea, and these allusions have been taken as the missing link between *Enūma Eliš* and the Genesis accounts. It goes without saying that the discovery of the Ugaritic mythological texts has changed this picture. The battle between Yahweh and the sea is probably derived from those Ugaritic texts that allude to battles between a deity and the sea and sea monsters. According to T. Jacobsen,[2] the battle between a deity and the sea originated on the Mediterranean coast and wandered eastward from there to Mesopotamia. The story may have been brought in by the Akkadians from an earlier western home, or it may have entered later during the time Old Akkadian was spoken (i.e., down to the beginning of the Isin/Larsa period); but Jacobsen's personal view is that the motif came to Babylon late, with the Amorites. He dates *Enūma Eliš* to around the middle of the Second Millennium BC, i.e., to the same period when the texts from Ugarit were written down. Some scholars have argued for an earlier date (Landsberger: Old Babylonian period). Lambert is of a different opinion: 'It [i.e., *Enūma Eliš*] is a sectarian and aberrant combination of mythological threads woven together into an unparalleled compositum. In my opinion *it is not earlier than* 1100 B.C.'[3] Lambert thus excludes the possibility that the Old Testament creation accounts have borrowed concepts from the Babylonian epic of creation. Both the Babylonian text and the account in Genesis 1 have a watery beginning, but this fact is in itself no evidence of Mesopotamian influence.[4] Likewise, the etymological equivalence *tiāmat*/*t^e^hōm* is of no consequence since the poetic allusions to the battles in the Old Testament use *yām* and *t^e^hōm* indiscriminately.[5]

It is no longer scientifically sound to assume that all ideas originated in Mesopotamia and moved westward. It is amazing that there is still a tendency among theologians to carry around a lot of pan-Babylonianism in their scientific luggage. Many Assyriologists, on the contrary, stress that we have to be extremely careful when dealing with influences from Mesopotamia on the mythological and religious concepts of the peoples living along the Mediterranean coast, and see instead a strong influence from that region on Mesopotamia.

III

In commentaries on Genesis, in books on comparative religion, and in publications of Mesopotamian seals we meet again and again with the Tree of Life in Mesopotamian myth and religion. Several trees (the date-palm, the tamarisk, the cedar, the *kiškanû*-tree) have been supposed to represent this Tree of Life. But was there really such a thing in Mesopotamia? 'Tree of Life' would be in Sumerian *g̃iš-nam-ti-la*, in Akkadian *iṣ balāṭi*, corresponding to Hebr. *'ēṣ haḥayyîm*. I have not been able to find references for *g̃iš-nam-ti-la* in Sumerian texts. A search of the entry *balāṭu* (s.), 'life, vigor, good health', in *CAD* (B, pp. 46-52) fails to turn up the expression *iṣ balāṭi*. *g̃iš-ti* in Gudea Cylinder A 25.7 has been interpreted as a Tree of Life.[6] The entire passage reads (Cylinder A 25.7-8): *g̃iš-ti* ka_2*-e* us_2*-sa-bi nir-an-na an-*ne_2 us_2*-sa-*am_3; 'its (of the shrine) . . . which is standing close to the gate is a . . . reaching up to the sky'. A translation of *g̃iš-ti* as 'life-giving tree' (*g̃iš*, 'tree'; *ti*, Akk. *balāṭu*, *bulluṭu*, 'to live, to be in good health, to keep alive') is highly uncertain. *g̃iš-ti* means 'arrow',[7] but in Gudea Cylinder A it might be an architectural term (see context, A 24.26–25.12).

Another candidate for the Tree of Life is the *kiškanû*-tree, put forward especially by Widengren in *The King and the Tree of Life in Ancient Near Eastern Religion*.[8] After stating that 'it is a well known fact that the Tree of Life plays an important role in ancient Mesopotamian myth and ritual',[9] he quotes a bilingual text which mentions the *kiškanû*-tree growing in Eridu, the city of Enki, the god of wisdom (CT 16 pl. 46.183ff. and dupls.):[10]

> In Eridu there is a black *kiškanû*-tree,
> growing up from a pure place,
> Its appearance is lapis lazuli,
> stretching forth in the *Abzu*,
> The way of Enki-Ea is full of abundance,
> His dwelling is the place of the netherworld,
> In the cella of his bed
> In a holy temple in the forest,
> the shade of which is cast where no one can enter,
> In the midst (of the temple are) Šamaš and Tammuz . . .

From this passage Widengren concludes: 'That the *kiškanû*-tree, in the Sumerian text *g̃iš-kin*, is identical with the Tree of Life is perfectly clear'. This passage (the beginning of *Utukku lemnūtu*,

Tabl. xii) has a forerunner in an Old Akkadian incantation text from Susa (MDP, 14, no. 91 obv. 2f.):[11]

> The [lord] has grown in a pure place like the *g̃iškin*-tree (*g̃iš-kin*$_2$-*gin*$_7$),
> Enki has grown in a pure place like the *g̃iškin*-tree,
> His flood fills the earth with abundance,
> His place of walking is its shade which
> like the appearance of lapis lazuli,
> stretches across the midst of the sea.
> Like the lord grown in a pure place like the *g̃iškin*-tree,
> Like Enki grown in a pure place like the *g̃iškin*-tree.

g̃iš-kin$_2$ is Akk. *kiškanû*. Under *kiškanû* (a tree) in *CAD* (K, p. 453) we find this tree in lexical texts (also 'white *k.*', 'black *k.*', 'red *k.*', 'multicolored *k.*', 'green *k.*'); three different objects are said to be made from the *k.*-tree; there are a few references to the tree in medical and magic texts (not significant for our purposes); the *k.*-tree is taboo to a certain deity (one reference). Besides the bilingual passage quoted above there is one reference in an unpublished incantation. The identification of the *k.*-tree remains uncertain.[12] What do the texts written in Sumerian tell us about this tree? The name of the tree in Sumerian texts is written *g̃iš-kin*$_2$ and *g̃iš-gana*. *g̃iš-kin*$_2$ is attested already in the lexical texts from Uruk (c. 3000 BC, soon to be published by Dr M. Green), and mention has been made of *g̃iš-kin*$_2$ in an Old Akkadian text from Susa. In Gudea Cylinder A 21.22 we read: *g̃iš-gana*$_2$*-abzu-gin*$_7$ *kur-kur-ra sag̃ ba-ni-ib*$_2$*-ili*$_2$*-ne*, 'they had (the temple) raise the head over all lands like the *g̃išgana*-tree of the *Abzu*'. The connection between the tree and the *Abzu* ('deep waters'), the abode of the god Enki, should be noted. In a Sumerian literary composition called 'Enki and Ninḫursaga'[13] we are told (lines 220ff.) that the gods want to bring back the goddess Ninḫursaga to the ailing Enki: 'The *Anunna*-gods sat in the dust, (when) up speaks the fox to Enlil: "If I bring Ninḫursaga before you, what shall be my reward?" Enlil answers the fox: "If you bring Ninḫursaga before me, in my city (Nippur) I will plant a *g̃išgana*-tree for you, verily your name will be uttered"' (Sum.: *uru-ga*$_2$*-a g̃iš-gana*$_2$ *ga-re-du*$_3$ *mu-zu ḫe*$_2$*-pa*$_3$*-de*$_2$).[14] R. Largement argues that *g̃iš-gana*$_2$ in this text is identical with 'the *g̃išgana*-tree of the *Abzu*' in Gudea Cylinder A 21.22, being 'l'arbre de vie par son lieu d'origine'.[15] In 'Nanna's Journey to Nippur'[16] we find the *g̃iškin* (*g̃iš-kin*$_2$)-tree again (*lines 28-29): [nibru.ki-m]u g̃iš-kin*$_2$ *g̃iš-gi*$_6$ *ki-du*$_{10}$*-ge mu*$_2$*-a [eš*$_3$ *nibru.ki-m]u g̃iš-kin*$_2$ *g̃iš-babbar ki-sikil-e mu*$_2$*-a*; 'my (city) Nippur

(has) a *ĝiškin*-tree, a black tree, growing at a good place, my shrine (of) Nippur (has) a *ĝiškin*-tree, a white tree, growing at a pure place'. This passage shows, if the restorations are accurate, that the *ĝiškin*-tree was not exclusively connected with the god Enki at Eridu.[17]

Let us now consider the date-palm, another tree which is thought to represent the Tree of Life. The famous 'Adam and Eve' seal has been republished most recently by D. Collon[18] who describes it as follows: 'A female figure with her hair in a bun holds out her left hand and sits facing a god who holds out his right hand. Both wear plain robes. Between them stands a date-palm. Terminal, an undulating serpent rises vertically.' In comparison I must quote Fr. Delitzsch's description of the same seal in his famous *Wo lag das Paradies?*:[19]

> Die Situation, die er [the seal] darstellt, ist klar—es ist der Sündenfall: an einem in der Mitte stehenden Baum sitzen einander gegenüber zwei menschliche Figuren, vor allem durch die verschiedene Kopfbedeckung als Mann und Frau leicht erkennbar unterschieden; wie in Gen cap. 3 ist es auch hier das schwächere Weib, an welches die Verführung sich wendet und welches dem sinnlichen Reiz unterliegt, denn hinter dem Weib steht aufrecht die Schlange, die Verführerin ... Ein Baum mit seinen Früchten ist hier wie dort der Anlass zum Sündenfall.

Delitzsch was somewhat indignant that Baudissin had suggested that the seal also could represent 'noch vieles andere als gerade den Sündenfall'.[20] Note that there is a god (and probably a goddess) on the seal and that it certainly has nothing to do with the fall of man. There is no reason to assume that the date-palm between the two figures represents the Tree of Life.

In short, there is no evidence that there was a Tree of Life in Mesopotamian myth and cult. The identification of different trees on Mesopotamian seals as a Tree of Life is a pure hypothesis, a product of pan-Babylonianism which wished to trace all Old Testament religious and mythological concepts back to Mesopotamia. As already noted, there is no Sumerian or Akkadian expression 'Tree of Life'.

IV

Let us now consider a well-known episode from the Babylonian Epic of Gilgameš: Tabl. xi 283ff. On his way back to Uruk, Gilgameš sees a well in which he bathes, leaving on the shore the magical plant which

he had found in the deep. A snake (Bab. *ṣēru*) sniffs the fragrance of the plant, snatches it, and sloughs its skin. Gilgameš sits down and weeps, for he has lost the possibility of keeping his youth, of remaining young; he says (lines 295-296): *ul aškun dumqa ana ramāniia* UR.MAḪ *ša qaqqari dumqa ētepuš*; 'I have not made myself a favor (but) for the "earth-lion" I have done a favor'. Let me quote Otzen:[21]

> There are . . . some characteristics in the biblical story [of the fall of man] that point to an external tradition. Should we initially enquire why it is the serpent that plays such a nefarious part in the story, we are struck by the fact that in the epic of Gilgamesh it is a serpent that steals the magical herb which enables the one who eats it to live for ever, and which is called 'Man Becomes Young in Old Age'.

In my opinion, it is highly uncertain whether there is any significant connection between this episode and the Tree of Life which gives eternal life to the one who eats its fruits in Genesis.

But was it really a serpent that ate the magical plant in the Gilgameš epic? As seen in Tabl. xi 296, the animal that steals the plant is called *nēšu* (logogram UR.MAḪ) *ša qaqqari*, 'the lion of the earth/soil, the earth-lion'. The same expression is found in a commentary:[22] UR.MAḪ *qaq-qa-ri* (i.e., *nēš qaqqari*) = *ḫu-la-m[e-su/šu]*, 'chameleon'. It should be noted that the Greek word χαμαιλέων literally means 'earth-lion' (χαμαί, 'on the ground'). Being a reptile, the chameleon sloughs its skin. One difficulty remains: Bab. *ṣēru*, according to the dictionaries, means 'snake, serpent'. Either 'earth-lion' (*nēšu sa qaqqari*) was interpreted as an epithet of the snake or *ṣēru* might have the more general meaning 'reptile'. The 'earth-lion' also occurs in lexical texts from Ebla, although its exact identification there is unclear.[23]

There just might be a remote connection between this episode in the Gilgameš epic and the story of the fall of man in Genesis 3 after all. The *nāḥāš* in Genesis 3 has been understood as a 'snake, serpent', on the basis of the verb *nāḥaš*, 'to hiss, to whisper'. Since almost all reptiles 'hiss', however, *nāḥāš* might here have the meaning 'reptile'. The curse of the *nāḥāš* in Genesis 3.14-15 makes it clear that the animal originally had four legs. If Bab. *ṣēru* and Hebr. *nāḥāš* do have the more general meaning 'reptile', used in the Gilgameš epic in reference to a chameleon, we might suggest that it was a chameleon

that seduced Eve to eat the apple and thereby deprived her and her husband Adam of a pleasant, eternal life in the Garden of Eden!

In this connection, I should like to make an observation about the name of Adam (*'ādām*). It is a well-known fact that the 'etymological' connection between *'ādām* and *ᵃdāmā(h)*, 'arable land', is a pun, a play on words. Lambert suggests that Hebr. *ᵃdāmā(h)* might be related to Bab. *ammatu*, 'earth', a rare word attested at the beginning of *Enūma Elīš* (line 2) as the opposite of *šamāmū*, 'heavens'.[24] However, *'admat- > ammat-* is difficult to explain. On the other hand, Landersdorfer suggested that *'ādām* might be a cognate of Sumerian a_2*-dam* which corresponds to Bab. *nammaššû*, 'herds of (wild) animals, people, settlement'.[25] As far as I know, Sum. a_2*-dam* refers exclusively to people, never to herds of animals. However, a_2*-dam* has no 'Sumerian' etymology (a_2, 'arm, side'; *dam*, 'spouse'). I venture to suggest that a_2*-dam* is a 'Canaanite', West-Semitic loanword in Sumerian.[26]

NOTES

1. London: SCM, 1980 (original Danish edition: *Myter i Det gamle Testamente*, 2nd edn [Copenhagen: G.E.C. Gad, 1976]).

2. 'The Battle between Marduk and Tiamat', *Essays in Memory of E.A. Speiser* (= *JAOS* 88 [1968]), 104ff.

3. W.G. Lambert, 'A New Look at the Babylonian Background of Genesis', *JTS* 16 (1965), 291 (emphasis supplied). The dating of *Enūma Elīš* is to be connected to Marduk's ascent to power. While the orthodox opinion has been that he was exalted to supremacy when Hammurabi made Babylon the capital of southern Mesopotamia, Lambert (in 'The Reign of Nebuchadnezzar I: A Turning Point in the History of Ancient Mesopotamian Religion', *The Seed of Wisdom: Essays in Honour of T.J. Meek*, ed. W.S. McCullough [Toronto: University of Toronto, 1964], 3ff.) dates his ascent to the reign of Nebuchadnezzar I (1125-1104 BC).

4. See Lambert, 'A New Look', 293.

5. On *tᵉhōm* see C. Westermann, *Genesis*, I (BKAT; Neukirchen-Vluyn: Neukirchener Verlag, 1976), 145-47. His attempt to differentiate *tᵉhōm* and *tiāmat* is praiseworthy.

6. See H. Bergema, *De Boom des Levens in Schrift en Historie* (Hilversum: J. Schipper, Jr, 1938), index.

7. *g̃iš-ti* = *ūṣu*, *uṣṣu*, 'arrow'.

8. *King and Saviour*, IV (UUÅ, 1951:4; Uppsala: Lundeqvist, 1951).

9. Widengren, *The King and the Tree of Life*, 5, with reference in n. 1 to

S.H. Langdon, *Semitic [Mythology]* (The Mythology of All Races, 5; Boston Archaeological Institute of America, 1931), 152, 179, 184, 226.

10. See now Geller, 'A Middle Assyrian Tablet of UTUKKŪ Lemnūtu, Tablet 12', *Iraq* 42 (1980), 28.2'ff.

11. See Geller, *Iraq* 42 (1980), 24.

12. Cf. B. Meissner, *Beiträge zum assyrischen Wörterbuch* (AS, 4; Chicago: University of Chicago, 1931), 41f.

13. S.N. Kramer, *Enki and Ninhursag: A Sumerian 'Paradise' Myth* (BASOR Supplements, 1; New Haven: American Schools of Oriental Research, 1945); translation also in *ANET*, 37ff.

14. Kramer: 'I will *plant trees (and) fields* for thee' (*g̃iš*, 'tree'; *gana*$_2$, 'field').

15. 'L'arbre de vie dans la religion sumérienne', *Akten der 24. Internationalen Orientalisten-Kongresse München . . . 1957*, ed. H. Franke (Wiesbaden: Franz Steiner, 1959), 188.

16. A.J. Ferrara, *Nanna-Suen's Journey to Nippur* (Studia Pohl: Series Maior, 2; Rome: Biblical Institute, 1973).

17. *g̃iš-gana*$_2$ in Kärki, *Die Sprache der sumerischen Königschriften der frühaltbabylonischen Zeit* (Studia Orientalia, 35; Helsinki: Societas Orientalis Fennica, 1967), 123.80 (Nūradad Inscription) remains uncertain. *g̃iš-kin*$_2$-*babbar*, 'white *g̃*.-tree', and *g̃iš-kin*$_2$-*gi*$_6$, 'black *g̃*.-tree', are attested in YBC (Yale Collection) 8640.10 and dupl. (unpublished) (Kusu hymn). CT 36 pl. 3.14-15 (see Kärki, 50 [Nūradad Inscription 1.14-15]) should be read *g̃iš-ḫur-ul-li*$_2$-*a-ka-ni ki-bi mu-na-gi*$_4$, 'he (the king) restored for him (the god Enki) his old "order"', rather than *g̃iš-kin*$_2$, 'his ancient *kiškanu*-tree' (Widengren, *The King and the Tree of Life*, 9 and n. 3).

18. D. Collon, *Cylinder Seals II: Akkadian, Post-Akkadian, Ur III Periods* (Catalogue of the Western Asiatic Seals in the British Museum; London: British Museum, 1982), 124, no. 302, photo pl. XL.

19. Leipzig: J.C. Hinrichs, 1881, 90.

20. W.W.F. Baudissin, *Studien zur semitischen Religionsgeschichte*, I (Leipzig: F.W. Grunow, 1876), 260.

21. *Myths*, 46.

22. B. Landsberger, *Die Fauna des Alten Mesopotamien* (Leipzig: S. Hirzel, 1934), 43, B.4. This reference is quoted in *CAD* (Ḫ, p. 227, s.v. *ḫulamēsu*) and in *AHw* (p. 253, s.v. *ḫulamīšu*, 'Chamäleon (?)' [the question-mark is not necessary]). *nēšu ša qaqqari* in Gilgameš Epic xi 296 is quoted in *AHw* (p. 783, s.v. *nēšu* I 3) with reference to *ḫulamīšu*. In *CAD* (N/2, pp. 193ff., s.v. *nēšu*, 'lion') *nēšu ša qaqqari* in Gilgameš Epic xi 296 is missing! It might be possible to connect Eblaite *na'iš* with Hebr. *nḥš*; if this proves correct, *na'iš gargarim* does not equal Akk. *nēš qaqqari* (*nēšu ša qaqqari*).

23. MEE 4, 386 v 4: *na-iš gar*$_3$-*ga-ri*$_2$-*im* (*na'iš gargarim* = Akk. *neš qaqqarim*). See further MEE 4, 368.0294 (bilingual lexical text): *nin-ki* = *na-iš [gar*$_3$*]-[ga-ri*$_2$*-im]* (restoration by M. Civil). Sum. *nin-ki* is literally 'the

lady of the earth'. It is uncertain whether *nin-ki* = *na'iš gargarim* denotes the chameleon.

24. W.G. Lambert, *Babylonian Wisdom Literature* (Oxford: Clarendon, 1960), 305.

25. W.K. Landersdorfer, *Sumerisches Sprachgut im Alten Testament* (BWAT, 21; Leipzig: J.C. Hinrichs, 1916), 59f. See *CAD* (N/1, pp. 233ff.).

26. The oldest reference to a_2-*dam* in a text written in Sumerian is found in Gudea Cylinder A 14.11. The word is common in Old Babylonian texts (year dates, literary texts); see *ZA* 48 (1948), 98, and 49 (1949), 146, and A. Falkenstein, *Sumerische Götterlieder*, 1 (Heidelberg: C. Winter, 1959), 40f.

YAHWEH'S GATHERING OF THE DISPERSED

Geo Widengren

I

There is an old problem in Israelite prophetic literature: Do the prophecies, oracles, and proclamations of salvation coupled with corresponding prophetical sayings about an inevitable disaster in the near future, as they are now found in the books of some pre-exilic prophets, belong to the authentic sayings of these prophets, or are they entirely later additions belonging to the exilic and post-exilic periods? This problem was treated in an epoch-making work by Hugo Gressmann at the beginning of our century.[1] No universal agreement has been reached since then, although opinion today seems more inclined to favor authenticity than was the case before Gressmann.[2]

It is my intention in this article[3] to discuss a theme which often recurs in these prophecies of salvation: the Gathering of the Dispersed. This theme appears in various genres of Old Testament literature; this fact may explain why it has received no adequate treatment, for it is obvious that Old Testament research in our time is so preoccupied with form criticism and literary genres that what is expressed in these literary genres is in danger of being neglected. I shall also discuss the original setting in life of this theme as it is found already in ancient Mesopotamia, and in so doing also try to ascertain the date of this theme in prophetic literature.

II

Turning now to the passages in which this theme occurs, we find to our surprise that what seems to be the oldest occurrence is in Deuteronomy, in a context that literary criticism considers a late addition to the law code.[4] It is Moses who is speaking to the people:

Then Yahweh, thy Lord, will again restore thy restoration
and have compassion upon thee,
and he will again gather thee from all the peoples,
among whom Yahweh, thy God, hath scattered thee.
(Deut. 30.3)

This passage corresponds to another prophecy in Deuteronomy in which disaster is proclaimed:

And Yahweh will scatter thee among the peoples
and ye will be left (as a remnant) among the nations
to whom Yahweh will lead thee away. (Deut. 4.27)

This prophecy of disaster is found in a second passage:

And Yahweh will scatter thee among the peoples
from one end of the earth to the other end of the earth.
(Deut. 28.64)

The prophecy in Deuteronomy 30.3 takes up and alludes to both 4.27 and 28.64, but changes these two prophecies of disaster by adding a promise of salvation: the scattered Israel, left few in number, will be gathered from among all the peoples to whom it has been led away as prisoners. In all three passages עמים, 'people', and הֵפִיץ (פוץ in hiph.), 'scatter', are used. For 'gather' in 30.3 the term is קבץ.

Is it possible to suggest a date for these passages in Deuteronomy and do 4.27 and 28.64 antedate 30.3? In 4.27 we meet the expression ונשארתם, 'ye will be left (as a remnant)'. This would seem to be an allusion to the idea of the 'remnant', שארית or שאר,[5] well known in pre-exilic as well as exilic and post-exilic prophets. In Amos 5.15 we meet the term שארית, while שאר occurs in Isaiah.[6] Accordingly, the use of the expression נשארתם links up with an idea found in pre-exilic prophetical literature, and for this reason Deuteronomy 4.27 may be assigned to pre-exilic times. Another link between Deuteronomy and early prophetic literature is the expression שוב שבות in Deuteronomy 30.3.[7] In this case too we first meet the expression in the book of Amos, 9.14. The authenticity of both Amos 5.15 and 9.14 is much disputed, a problem to be discussed below.

The verb הפיץ, 'scatter', is used in the prophecy of disaster in the book of Jeremiah:

I will scatter them among the nations. (Jer. 9.15)

Similar expressions are found in the book of Ezekiel:

They will know that I am Yahweh
when I scatter them among the nations. (Ezek. 12.15)

Yet I lifted up my hand against them in the wilderness
that I would scatter them among the nations
and disperse them in the countries. (Ezek. 20.23)

I will scatter thee among the nations
and disperse thee in the countries. (Ezek. 22.15)

Another passage in Ezekiel mentions the scattering of Israel as a past action:

I scattered them among the nations
and they were dispersed in the countries. (Ezek. 36.19)

Thus we find traces of a fixed formula in Jeremiah, but only Ezekiel has employed the formula in full: 'I will scatter thee/them among the nations, and disperse thee/them in the countries'.

The word for 'nations' is גוים in both Jeremiah and Ezekiel, contrasting with עמים, 'peoples', used in Deuteronomy. It should be observed, however, that עמים and גוים are used synonymously in Deuteronomy 4.27. There is a certain parallelism of 'peoples' and 'nations' also in Ezekiel 39.27, a passage to which we shall return. Isaiah 11.12, another passage to be treated below, uses the word גוים in a context of great importance for our subject. Equally important is Ezekiel 11.17—'I will gather you from the peoples'—which shows that Ezekiel could also use the term עמים in this context. The conclusion must be that the variation between עמים and גוים is only a stylistic one and gives no evidence as to the date of the prophetical sayings.

Let us return to the central theme of Deuteronomy 30.3: the gathering of the scattered people of Israel. The question is, of course, whether this theme occurs already in pre-exilic times. This, in turn, is related to the more general problem of the pre-exilic date of the prophecies of salvation. We mentioned above the fact that the two passages in Amos indicating a restoration of a remnant of Israel are of disputed authenticity. In Isaiah, however, the prophet's hope for a return of a remnant cannot be doubted.[9] The symbolical name of the prophet's son, שאר ישוב, sufficiently demonstrates his hope.[10] This hope finds very explicit expression in a famous passage concerning Yahweh's future activity:

And he shall set up a banner for the nations
and shall assemble the dispersed of Israel,
and gather the scattered women of Judah
from the four corners of the earth. (Isa. 11.12)

This oracle of promise for the people of Israel—the dispersed of Israel and the scattered women of Judah—contains four key words: 'assemble', 'gather', 'scattered', 'dispersed'. This passage too, like Amos 5.15 and 9.14 and Deuteronomy 30.3, has been judged to be of more than doubtful authenticity.[11] It must be said, however, that many of the arguments adduced against their authenticity are based upon preconceived ideas. The majority of the scholars of an older generation were unwilling *a priori* to admit the existence of an eschatology of happiness in pre-exilic times and insisted instead that the prophetic message was one of unconditional doom.[12]

In the book of Micah, the contemporary of Isaiah,[13] our theme occurs in two passages, both of disputed authenticity. In one oracle of promise it is said:

I shall assemble all of thee, Jacob,
gather the remnant of Israel. (Micah 2.12)

Here we have the verbs אסף, 'assemble' and קבץ, 'gather', and the subst. שארית, 'remnant'.[14] The second passage runs as follows:[15]

On that day—saying of Yahweh—I shall assemble the limping
and gather the dispersed
and what I have exposed to evil. (Micah 4.6)

The verbs אסף and קבץ recur, and the subst. הַנִּדָּחָה (properly a niph. ptcp.), 'the dispersed ones' (as a collective), is used.

Literary criticism is not inclined to accept as authentic a passage in Jeremiah that speaks of Israel settling anew in the land of Canaan:[16]

I will bring back Israel to his pastures,
and he will feed on Carmel and in Bashan,
and his soul shall be satisfied upon Mount Ephraim and in Gilead.
(Jer. 50.19)

Israel is likened to a grazing herd. The key words 'gather' and 'assemble', found in Isaiah 11.12 and in Micah 2.12 and 4.6, are lacking, but the central theme is there: the return of Israel to Canaan after the fall of Babylon (cf. vv. 15-16). A second passage in Jeremiah takes up the idea of the remnant:

I will gather the remnant of my sheep
from all the lands where I have driven them
and will bring them back to their pastures. (Jer. 23.3)

Here we find the verbs קִבֵּץ, 'gather', and הִדִּיחַ (נדח in hiph.), 'drive away', the same verb used in the expression נִדְחֵי יִשְׂרָאֵל, 'the dispersed of Israel', and the subst. נִדָּחוֹת, 'the dispersed ones'. הֵשִׁיב (שוב in hiph.), 'bring back', links up with the notion of שוב שבות. A third passage contains the following oracle:

Indeed I am with thee—oracle of Yahweh—to save thee,
for I will carry out an annihilation among all the nations
where I have scattered thee. (Jer. 30.11)

The authenticity of both passages is much disputed, but a discussion of the pros and cons cannot be given here. We are chiefly interested in the wording of the formulas in which our theme is expressed. In that connection, we note the occurrence of the term גוים, 'nations', and the verb הפיץ, 'scattered', well known from other passages in prophetic literature already mentioned.

Reminiscent of the wording of the formula found in Jeremiah 23.3 is one of the last sayings in the book of Zephaniah:

I will gather the dispersed. (Zeph. 3.19)

Here again we meet the familiar terms קבץ and נדחה.

Continuing down in time we come to Ezekiel. He too speaks of the hope that the exiled and dispersed people will return to its home in Canaan:

When I restore them from the peoples
and gather them from the lands of their enemies,
I will show myself holy among them
in the eyes of many nations. (Ezek. 39.27)

Observations on the Text: Many commentators propose to delete the word רבים after הגוים. A reading based upon this deletion is supported by most LXX Mss. Another possibility indicated by commentators is to delete the article before גוים. It is true, of course, that the omission of the article before רבים is quite against the rules of Hebrew grammar. But on the other hand, numerous irregularities and deviations from the rule in question are attested.[17] For this reason the possibility cannot be excluded that the MT is correct, a possibility confirmed by Cod. Alex. LXX and Pesh. which has *'ammē saggî'ē*.[18]

In this passage the speaker is Yahweh who personally will gather the dispersed people from the lands of their enemies. We do not hear that this task is delegated to the Messiah, in spite of the fact that Ezekiel reckons with a descendant of David as the head of a restored and united Israel (34.23f.; 37.15-24). But in our passage, and in others where the prophet speaks of the return (e.g. 22.18-22), he does not mention a king as the leader of the returning people.

Another passage in Ezekiel calls for notice:

> Therefore say: So saith the Lord Yahweh:
> I will gather you from the peoples
> and assemble you from the lands
> among which you have been scattered,
> and I will give you the earth of Israel. (Ezek. 11.17)

> *Observations on the Text*: I cannot see any reason to delete as an unnecessary repetition (cf. v. 16), against the text of both MT and LXX, the introductory formula. Nor do I understand why we should read להם instead of אתכם in conformity with LXX, as, e.g., does Fohrer who changes the 2nd pers. pl. into the 3rd pers. pl. throughout and for that reason also reads נְפֻצֹתִים (an emendation which I previously wrongly accepted) instead of נְפֹצוֹתֶם. That there is a direct address to the people in this saying should cause no difficulty. Yahweh's words in v. 16 describe his former dealings with Israel; he now gives a message directly to the people, expressing the old formula of the gathering of the scattered people.[19]

We go down in time to the prophecies assigned to Deutero-Isaiah. It is remarkable that this great prophet, who more than any other prophet in the name of Yahweh promised the return of the exiled Israel in his prophecies of salvation, does not use our fixed formula at all. This prophet expresses Yahweh's promise in quite another way, giving it a clear universalistic accent.[20] The difference between the salvation of the remnant found in the passages we have examined and the salvation spoken of by Deutero-Isaiah is well illustrated in the following prophecy:

> And now saith Yahweh, my fashioner from the womb, to be a servant to him, to bring Jacob back to him and that Israel may be assembled to him . . .

> And He said:
> It is too small for thee to be a servant to me,

to raise up the tribes of Jacob,
and to restore the preserved of Israel.
I will set thee as a light of the nations,
to be my salvation to the end of the earth. (Isa. 49.5-6)

Observations on the Text: The content of this passage obviously demands that in v. 5 we should read לו (with several Mss., with the *qᵉrē*, and with Targ. and Aq.) instead of לא. It is in no way possible to take מהיותך לי עבד as a gloss, since MT is supported by both LXX and Pesh. The LXX text shows some deviations from MT, but MT is obviously the more reliable.[21] Quite impossible is Duhm's proposal to read the *kᵉtîb* לא יאסף and to translate יֵאָסֵף with 'hinraffen', for that verb never means anything but 'assemble'.

We underline the fact that the Servant of Yahweh is commissioned to carry out the 'assembling of Israel'; we may suppose that 'Jacob' and 'Israel' signify the entire Jewish people in its exile. The expressions employed by the prophet in this passage deviate in a remarkable way from the fixed formulas used by Ezekiel. We find 'assemble', not 'gather', the 'preserved of Israel', not the 'remnant', and the nations mentioned only in connection with the idea of Israel set up as 'a light of the nations'. New ideas demand a new language, but it is striking that the traditional idea of the gathering of the dispersed is expressed in such a new way.

We pass to Trito-Isaiah and there meet again the traditional formula:

Oracle of the Lord Yahweh, the gatherer of the dispersed of Israel:
Still more will I gather to him besides his gathered ones. (Isa. 56.8)

The text of the LXX is impossible to follow here, for it spoils the coherence.[22] Again we find the key expressions קבץ, 'gather', and נדחי ישראל. The difference between Deutero-Isaiah and Trito-Isaiah is significant.

Looking back at the linguistic usage, we find that Ezekiel is the prophet who most frequently employs the traditional formula. It occurs not only in his prophecies of salvation, but also in his oracles of doom. As illustrations of the latter the following passages may be cited: 11.16; 12.15; 20.23; 22.15; 29.12 (Egypt); 30.23, 26 (Egypt); 36.19. The two characteristic verbs are the familiar הפיץ and זרה (in niph. and pi.). It should be noted that despite the prophet's predilection for the term גוים in his prophecies and proclamations of disaster, the prophecies of salvation in 11.17 and 39.27 use the word עמים,

'peoples'. I conclude, therefore, that the formula was already fixed in its wording. Furthermore, it is characteristic of Ezekiel that the idea of a 'remnant' of Israel to be brought back is lacking; the terms שארית and שאר are not found in his vocabulary in the usual technical meaning. It is obvious that the notion of שוב שבות also is lacking, for 29.14 is directed to Egypt. This difference in language between Ezekiel and Amos, Isaiah, and Micah is striking.

III

In one of the Assyrian royal inscriptions, a building inscription of Esarhaddon, the king makes the following proclamation concerning his many charitable deeds towards the Babylonians:[23]

For the citizens of Babylon, the oppressed,
I reestablished anew as privileged their freedom,
under the protection of Anu and Enlil.
They who were bought and brought to slavery,
who had been put into chains and fetters,
I gathered and counted as Babylonians.

Their plundered property I restored.
The destitute I clothed in clothes
and caused their feet to take the way to Babylon.
To settle down in the city, to build temples,
to plant orchards, to dig canals
I gave them confidence.

Their privileged status, made vain, which had disappeared,
I restored to its place.
The tablets of their freedom from taxes I wrote anew.
Into the four winds I opened their way,
in order that they might direct their intention
to have intercourse with the totality of countries.

Observations on the Text: For the expression *ṣābē kidinni*, 'people under protection', cf. *CAD*, vol. 8, p. 343b s.v. *kidinnu*; this word has the general meaning of 'protection' and for that reason *ṣābē kidinni* means people who are protected. Babylon is *āl kidinni*.[24] The word *anduraru* has the general meaning of 'freedom' and the special sense of 'manumission'; cf. *CAD*, vol. 2, s.v. *anduraru*, where are quoted relevant passages in which the Assyrian ruler claims to have compensated for the damage suffered by all peoples under his protection.[25]

It is obvious that we have here a traditional theme in the royal ideology of ancient Mesopotamia. The same idea is found in an inscription of Assurbanipal, the son of Esarhaddon. The king says of his own actions towards Babylon:[26]

nišašu saphāti upahhirama	Its scattered people I gathered
utēr ašrušin	and then restored to their place.

In this passage we meet again the two essential verbs found in the building inscription of Esarhaddon: *sapāhu*, 'scatter', and especially the participle *saphu* in the expression *nišī saphāti*, and its correlate *puhhuru* (*pahāru* in II 1), 'to gather'. A third expression occurring in both inscriptions is *turru ašrišu*, 'to restore to its place', II 1 of the verb *tāru*, 'return'.

That our theme goes back to a very remote age in Mesopotamian history is evident from the prologue of Codex Hammurabi where the great Babylonian ruler calls himself *mupahhir nišī saphāti ša Isin*[ki], 'the gatherer of the scattered people of Isin' (II 49f.). This terminology, as we see, agrees perfectly with the phraseology used by the Assyrian kings of the 7th century BC. This fact demonstrates the continuity of royal ideology in Mesopotamia as well as the importance of our motif.[27]

It is not surprising to find this same motif in the 'negative confession' pronounced by the king on the occasion of the New Year Festival at Babylon. In the ritual the ruler solemnly proclaims:[28]

ul uhalliq Bābila[ki]	I have not destroyed Babylon,
ul aqtabī sapāhšu	not commanded its scattering.

It is true that only one of the key words of our theme, *sapāhu*, 'to scatter', occurs here, but as the ruler confesses to have *not* scattered Babylon he cannot possibly mention the ingathering of its dispersed people. This confession sounds somewhat peculiar in the mouth of a Babylonian ruler; it would seem more relevant if uttered by an Assyrian king. What concerns us here, however, is the occurrence of this theme in Mesopotamia from the time of Hammurabi to the period from which the ritual of the New Year Festival dates.[29] It is quite obvious that this theme, the gathering of the dispersed, played a significant role as part of royal ideology in Mesopotamia from very remote times to the days of the last Babylonian kingdom.

The theme survived the fall of the Neo-Babylonian kingdom. In the Cyrus Chronicle we read (32-34):[30]

All their inhabitants I gathered and then restored to their habitation. Furthermore, I resettled upon the command of Marduk, the great lord, all the gods of Sumer and Akkad, whom Nabuna'id had brought into Babylon to the anger of the lord of the gods, unharmed, in the chapels, the place of the gladness of heart.

Observations on the Text: The expression *utēr dadmišunu* corresponds to *ana ašrišunu utērma* (line 32), a variation of *utēr ašrušin* found in the Assurbanipal inscription quoted above. In the Esarhaddon inscription we find *ana ašriša utēr* (lines 34f.). The language is quite fixed. As for the translation, another possibility would be to follow Weissbach and translate 'restored their habitations', taking *dadmišunu* as a pl. The expression *ina salimti*, 'unharmed', could be translated 'in peace', of course, but I have followed Weissbach and Oppenheim. I have translated *ṭūb libbi* according to its literal meaning, following Weissbach.

What is interesting in this passage is the fact that not only were the inhabitants returned to their lands, but also their gods were brought back to their sanctuaries. To translate the word *ilāni*, 'gods, deities', by 'images' (so Oppenheim) obscures its real meaning, even if the gods in question were actually represented symbolically by their cult-images.[31] It is worth noting that the word *ṣalmu*, 'image', is *not* used here (cf. the expression *ṣalam ilāni rabūti* in the Esarhaddon inscriptions).[32] The decisive phrase for our purposes is *kullat nišīšunu upaḫḫirama utēr dadmišun*. Clearly we are dealing with the same motif as before: it is the king who acts as the gatherer of the dispersed.

Turning to the psalms of lamentation, we find that deities fulfill this same royal function. We read, e.g., in King No. 6.53:[33]

ša sapḫi t[upaḫḫara gā]nūnšu	The house of the scattered thou gatherest.

Observations on the Text: Thanks to VAT 13681 it has been possible to restore a gap in King's publication.[34] But the term *ganūnu* in this context causes some difficulty since the general meaning of the word refers to part of a palace or a temple. Ebeling translates it 'Familie' with a question mark;[35] the meaning 'family' is given in *CAD*, vol. 5, p. 43a s.v. *ganūnu*, but no other references are cited.

This passage receives some elucidation from King No. 32:[36]

[illat] nišī^{meš} *sapiḫti tuštēšeri ḫarrāna*
For the scattered clan of the people thou guidest (its) way.

Observations on the Text: Ebeling leaves a gap without restoration, but Weir restores *ḫarrāna* with a question mark.[37] It perhaps would be possible to take the III 2 form of *wšr* in its usual sense of making the march direct and quick. The scattering of the clan is mentioned in two other passages in the psalms, one of them associated with the prayer to the deity to gather the scattered clan.[38] Accordingly, the restoration *illat* has much to recommend it.

The action of the deity glorified or requested in the psalms—the gathering of the scattered—is both a past action as in the royal inscriptions and a future action to be undertaken by the deity. A future action is probably indicated in a series of so-called 'apocalyptic' prophecies where one reads the following prophecy of salvation (CT XIII 50.7-9):[39]

mi-šá-ru iš-šak-kan	An act of justice will be promulgated,
e-šá-tu uš-te-še-ra	the confusion will be set aright,
dal-ḫa-a-tum i-zak-ka-a	the troubles will clear up,
sa-a[p-ḫu-tum i-paḫ-ḫu-ra]	those who have been scat[tered will be gathered],
na-as-ḫu-tum KI.MIN	those who have been uprooted DITTO,
ki-na-a-tum uk-tan-na-ma	the righteous will be re-established.

To judge from the entire context, there can be little doubt about the restoration of the small gap in the fourth line quoted.[40] The gathering of the dispersed here alludes not to a people, but only to a clan or a family, since the context is concerned with groups within a people. The promises clearly contain the aspect of futurity, and I am definitely of the opinion that our theme has been used 'eschatologically' in Mesopotamia.[41] It cannot be denied, however, that these 'prophecies' also have the character of *vaticinia ex eventu* when looked upon as a combination of various oracles.

IV

The preceding discussion has shown that the idea of a gathering of a scattered people (or clan) exists in both Israel and Mesopotamia. In both regions this idea is expressed in a strictly fixed language with special formulas and recurs in different literary genres.

As to the terminology, in Akkadian we find *sapāḫu*, 'scatter', and *puḫḫuru*, 'gather', as well as *turru ašrišu* (or equivalent expressions),

'restore to its place' (i.e., restore the scattered people, or sometimes the clan or family, to its original habitation). The king is *mupaḫḫir nišī sapḫāti*, 'he who gathers the scattered people', or *mutēr ašrišu*, 'he who restores (the scattered people) to its place'. In the corresponding passages in Hebrew we find, above all, the following fixed expressions: קבץ, 'gather', אסף, 'assemble', נדחי ישראל, 'the dispersed of Israel', and other forms of the verb נדח (i.e., hiph. הִדִּיחַ, niph. fem. part. נִדָּחָה). We also encounter the verbs פוץ, 'to scatter' (hiph. הֵפִיץ, niph. fem. pl. part. נְפֻצוֹת [Isa. 11.12], niph. 2nd pl. perf. נְפֹצוֹתֶם [Ezek. 11.17, see above]) and שוב שבות, 'restore', and pil. act. שׁוֹבֵב, 'restore' [Isa. 49.5]).

It is obvious that there existed in the Ancient Near East a general idea that the deity was ready to gather and restore the dispersed people (or clan or family) to its place. In Mesopotamia this general idea found a prominent place in royal ideology as part of the king's religio-social duties. In this connection the theme was applied by individual rulers in their treatment of certain special cities. Of particular interest is the treatment of the dispersed inhabitants of Babylon, having great political importance in late Assyrian times (e.g., the reign of Esarhaddon, as shown above) and still more so after the downfall of the Neo-Babylonian empire when Cyrus the Great emerged as a representative of this same ideological motif. This part of royal ideology evidently was used by Cyrus as *a general political principle* of his government with regard to peoples placed under his own rule.[42] But at the same time it is clear from the wording of his Cylinder Inscription that this theme also still retained its religious value.

As a setting in life of such royal proclamations it would seem appropriate to suggest the promulgation of an act of justice, a *mīšaru*-act, a legislative act existing already in Old Babylonian times.[43] The ruler promulgated such an act in order to restore a disturbed order, to re-establish *mīšaru*, 'justice', in society and in the world. That certainly would be a fitting occasion for him to proclaim that he re-established the deported inhabitants of a city or country, that he was the gatherer of the scattered people. He, as representative of the deity, would have carried out the gathering of the dispersed.

In Israel the starting point was of the same sort, but here from the outset it was Yahweh, God of Israel, who would act as the ingatherer of the dispersed members of the people. With Deutero-Isaiah we find the anointed ruler, the Messiah, also performing this function.

Because of the historical situation emphasis is placed on future events. Both God and his Anointed will carry out their actions in a near future which, however, tends to be postponed into an eschatological future (Isa. 56.8). The prophetic oracles predict what will take place in future times when Yahweh will restore the people. We have found a corresponding conception in Mesopotamia (if the restoration of the gap in the oracle quoted above is correct—which presumably it is). For the most part, however, the motif in Akkadian literature occurs in contexts describing what has already taken place. But in the psalms the deity is glorified as the gatherer of the scattered clan, showing not only past but also present and future time aspects. This speaks strongly in favor of the 'eschatological' dimension of the theme, found in the Mesopotamian oracles.

There is, on the whole, an astonishing agreement between Akkadian and Hebrew use of our theme. We note, however, that it found no place in the Hebrew psalmist's glorification of his national deity, this in contrast to Akkadian psalms. Another point to be noted is its absence—as far as I know—in Ugaritic and Canaanite literature. Not even are the verbs פוץ and קבץ found in Ugaritic or in the entire West Semitic corpus. It would seem, therefore, as if the occurrence of this theme in the Old Testament is due to the direct influence of Mesopotamian civilization. This, of course, is only an hypothesis; the theme may turn up in some West Semitic text, and as long as so comparatively little West Semitic literature is known today conclusions *ex silentio* are hardly absolute. What we are entitled to say is only that the available evidence suggests that the theme of gathering and scattering ultimately comes from Mesopotamia.

What are we entitled to say about the crucial question of its occurrence in Israelite religious thought, above all among the pre-exilic prophets? H.H. Rowley rightly observed that there is an allusion to the idea of a remnant of faithful believers already in 1 Kings 19.18, a passage belonging to the prophet legends, where Yahweh says:[44]

> Yet will I leave (as a remnant) seven thousand in Israel, all the knees that have not bowed unto the Baʿal, and every mouth that hath not kissed him.

This oracle communicated to Elijah brings us to the time of Jehu, as is shown by v. 17. This implies that our theme was known in Israel at least before 800 BC. Amos was preaching his message in Northern

Israel in the reign of Jeroboam II (782-753). Taking 814 as Jehu's last regnal year, there is a gap of roughly fifty years between the careers of Elijah and of Amos. The factuality of 1 Kings 19.18 may be questioned, of course. The essential fact, however, is that these prophet legends were written down at least before 722 and most probably before the downfall of Jehu's dynasty, as Hölscher contends.[45] It could always be argued that 1 Kings 19.18 is a later addition, but we have no evidence to favor such an hypothesis; not even Steuernagel thinks of a later addition here.[46] This fact makes it clear that in the time when these legends were transmitted orally and then later written down the idea of a remnant was found. And this circumstance, in turn, strengthens the probability that Amos too had taken over this theme; 1 Kings 19.18 confirms the authenticity of Amos 5.15. 1 Kings 19.18 and Deuteronomy 30.3 are mutually supportive as well, not surprising since Deuteronomy rests 'on the teachings of the eighth-century prophets'.[47] We may conclude from this that the disputed passages in Micah and Jeremiah also are authentic.

V

To sum up: We have found the theme of the gathering of the dispersed to have its origin in Mesopotamia. It occurs in Northern Israel, in both historical and prophetical literature, from at least the time of Jehu; it is used later also by prophets active in Judah. Its authenticity among post-exilic prophets has not been questioned.

The formality of this theme of scattering and gathering (the remnant) of the Israelite-Judaean people is remarkable. First of all we have two word-pairs in apposition: הפיץ, 'scatter', and קבץ, 'gather'; הדיח, 'disperse', and אסף, 'collect'. Secondly, we have two synonymous expressions: עמים, 'peoples', and גוים, 'nations'. A third synonymous expression is 'remnant', rendered by both שארית and שאר without any apparent variation of meaning. The idea of 'remnant' also is expressed by the niph. 2nd pers. pl. נִשְׁאַרְתֶּם, 'you will be left as a remnant', either among the 'peoples' (עמים) or among the 'nations' (גוים), supplemented by the qualification 'where you have been scattered'. The promise also may be expressed in the following way: 'I will gather the remnant of my sheep from all the lands where I have driven them', or 'from all the lands of their enemies', or even 'from the four corners of the earth'. Smaller variations of this scheme, of course, are many. The scattered peoples are called נדחי ישראל, 'the

dispersed of Israel', or simply הנדחת, 'the dispersed'. Our theme is associated with the motif שוב שבות, 'the restoration', originally an independent idea.

Our formula in its variations presumably was transmitted in prophetic circles from generation to generation. It is a characteristic element in prophetic oracles and sayings from the eighth century on. It is so well attested in an early period that no decisive arguments speak against its authenticity among pre-exilic prophets.

NOTES

1. Cf. H. Gressmann, *Der Ursprung der israelitisch-jüdischen Eschatologie* (FRLANT, 6; Göttingen: Vandenhoeck & Ruprecht, 1905). A revised and enlarged edition appeared after his death as *Der Messias* (Göttingen: Vandenhoeck & Ruprecht, 1929).

2. Cf. H. Ringgren, *Israelitische Religion* (Stuttgart: W. Kohlhammer, 1963), 235ff., where the question is left open and a case-by-case approach to its resolution is advocated.

3. An earlier version of this study appeared in *SEÅ*, 41-42 (1976-77), 224-34.

4. Cf. C. Steuernagel, *Lehrbuch der Einleitung in das Alte Testament* (Tübingen: J.C.B. Mohr, 1912), 183 §43 13a, 197 §46 5c, 245 §56 3c; O. Eissfeldt, *Einleitung in das Alte Testament*, 3rd edn (Tübingen: J.C.B. Mohr, 1964), 307f.; G. von Rad, *Das fünfte Buch Mose: Deuteronomium* (ATD, 8; Göttingen: Vandenhoeck & Ruprecht, 1964), 131.

5. The meaning of this passage clearly is that only a residue of the people will be left, scattered among the other peoples. Accordingly, the verb שאר in niph. corresponds to the subst. שְׁאָר or שְׁאֵרִית. Cf. 1 Kings 19.18 where the hiph. of the same verb is used with an obvious allusion to a residuum of the population of Northern Israel; this is a passage to which we shall return.

6. For the idea of a remnant cf. the old work of J. Meinhold, *Der heilige Rest* (Studien zur israelitischen Religionsgeschichte, 1.1; Bonn: A. Marcus & E. Weber, 1903), and the more recent work of W.E.L. Müller, *Die Vorstellung vom Rest im Alten Testament* (Leipzig/Borsdorf: W. Hoppe, 1939). A rather full bibliography is given by H.H. Rowley, *The Faith of Israel* (London: SCM, 1956), 103 n. 3.

7. For the idea of *šûb š^{e}bût* cf. E.L. Dietrich, *Šûb Šebût: Die endzeitliche Wiederherstellung bei den Propheten* (BZAW, 40; Giessen: A. Töpelmann, 1925); E. Baumann, '*Šûb Šebût*', *ZAW* 47 (1929), 17ff.

8. Cf. E. Hammershaimb, *Amos*, 2nd edn (Copenhagen: Nyt Nordisk Forlag, 1958), 81 (on 5.15), 138 (on 9.14); he is positive about their authenticity. A. Kapelrud accepts 5.15 as authentic but is rather negative concerning 9.14 (cf. *Central Ideas in Amos* [Oslo: H. Aschehoug, 1956], 58,

65, 67, 80); after a careful examination of the pros and cons he concludes that 'it is likely that also 9.13-15 were added to the oracles of doom' (p. 58).

9. Cf. G. Hölscher, *Die Propheten* (Leipzig: J.C. Hinrichs, 1914), 226, 251f.; A. Lods, *Les prophètes d'Israël et les débuts du Judaïsme* (Paris: La Renaissance du Livre, 1935), 116f.; Ringgren, *Israelitische Religion*, 251. It should be noted that Rowley has pointed to the fact that in Isa. 6.13 'there is to be found the germ of Isaiah's teaching on the Remnant' (*Men of God* [London/Edinburgh: Nelson, 1963], 96 n. 4).

10. The name שאר ישוב (Isa. 7.3) corresponds to the prophetic saying שאר ישוב שאר יעקב אל־אל גבור in Isa. 10.21. This passage, like so many others, is considered unauthentic by B. Duhm (*Das Buch Jesaia*, 2nd edn [HAT, 3.1; Göttingen: Vandenhoeck & Ruprecht, 1902], 75), but his argumentation is extremely forced. Rowley seems to regard it and other passages rejected by Duhm as authentic (*Faith of Israel*, 117). I cannot take up this question here.

11. Cf. Duhm, *Jesaia*, 82, where he says that this passage may be from the time of Alexander Jannai (sic). Cf. further H. Wildberger, *Jesaja* (BKAT, 10.1; Neukirchen-Vluyn: Neukirchener Verlag, 1972), 466f.; Hölscher, *Propheten*, 316; Eissfeldt, *Einleitung*, 426.

12. For the problem in general cf. Ringgren, *Israelitische Religion*, 235, where the complexity of the problem is underscored. It is difficult to say whether we are entitled to speak of an eschatology, in a traditional sense, among pre-exilic prophets. For this general problem cf. J. Lindblom, 'Gibt es eine Eschatologie bei den alttestamentlichen Prophetie?', *Studia Theologica* 6 (1952), 79ff. In his great works on prophecy Lindblom is quite negative to the opinion that pre-exilic prophets, with the exception of Isaiah, proclaimed promises of salvation (cf. *Profetismen i Israel* [Stockholm: Svenska Kyrkans Diakonistyrelses Bokförlag, 1934], 503 [Amos had no idea of a remnant], 518ff.; *Prophecy in Ancient Israel* [London: Blackwell, 1962], 360ff.). Another typical representative of the older generation is Lods, *Prophètes*, 97. Among scholars of a somewhat younger generation, both specialists on Amos, as pointed out above (n. 8), Hammershaimb is quite positive whereas Kapelrud is decidedly skeptical.

13. Cf. W. Beyerlin, *Die Kulttraditionen Israels in der Verkündigung des Propheten Micha* (FRLANT, 72; Göttingen: Vandenhoeck & Ruprecht, 1959).

14. For this passage cf. Steuernagel, *Lehrbuch*, 629 §132 6b; Eissfeldt, *Einleitung*, 522ff.; W. Rudolph, *Micha-Nahum-Habakkuk-Zephanja* (KAT, 13.3; Gütersloh: Gerd Mohn, 1975), 63f.

15. For this passage cf. Steuernagel, *Lehrbuch*, 629 §132 6b; Eissfeldt, *Einleitung*, 522ff.; Rudolph, *Micha*, 83 (authentic).

16. For this passage cf. W. Rudolph, *Jeremia*, 2nd edn (HAT, 12; Tübingen: J.C.B. Mohr, 1958), 274f.; Steuernagel, *Lehrbuch*, 563 §11b (regarded as neither authentic nor unauthentic); Eissfeldt, *Einleitung*, 488f.

17. Cf. Gesenius' *Hebrew Grammar*, ed. E. Kautzsch and A.E. Cowley,

2nd edn (Oxford: Clarendon, 1910), 409 y-z (although this passage is not listed).

18. For a discussion of this passage cf. G. Fohrer, *Ezechiel* (HAT, 13; Tübingen: J.C.B. Mohr, 1955), 196, 211. In this commentary, which otherwise has some good qualities, the treatment of the Hebrew text is methodologically unsound and contrary to all acceptable philological principles, for the author constantly rewrites the MT in a way one would have thought belonged to the past. For this passage we may also refer to W. Zimmerli, *Ezechiel* (BKAT, 13.2; Neukirchen-Vluyn: Neukirchener Verlag, 1969), 695f.

19. Cf. Fohrer, *Ezechiel*, 61 (a rather typical treatment). Against his views, my interpretation implies that Yahweh in the latter part of the oracle turns directly to the people of Israel after having described the present situation. Such shiftings of address are not uncommon in prophetic literature; from Amos the following passages, introduced by the so-called messenger formula, can be cited: 2.7-8 in contrast to 2.10-12; 5.10 in contrast to 5.11.

20. It is, of course, not a totally uniform universalism; it is limited insofar as Israel will retain its leading position among the nations. Cf. Ringgren, *Israelitische Religion*, 268.

21. Cf. Duhm, *Jesaia*, 333; P. Volz, *Jesaia II* (KAT, 9; Leipzig: A. Deichert, 1932), 159; C. Westermann, *Das Buch Jesaja: Kap. 40-66* (ATD, 19; Göttingen: Vandenhoeck & Ruprecht, 1966), 170-72.

22. This fact was seen already by Duhm, *Jesaia*, 384.

23. B. Meissner and P. Rost, 'Die Bauinschriften Asarhaddons', *Beiträge zur Assyriologie und semitischen Sprachwissenschaft* 3 (1895-8), 252.12-41; R. Borger, *Die Inschriften Asarhaddons Könige von Assyrien* (Archiv für Orientforschung Beiheft, 9; Graz: E. Weidner, 1956), 25 VII 12ff.

24. Cf. Borger, *Inschriften Asarhaddons*, 21 Ep. 23.18.

25. Cf. H. Winckler, *Die Keilschrifttexte Sargons* (Leipzig: E. Pfeiffer, 1889), No. 63.7.

26. S. Langdon, *Die neubabylonischen Königsinschriften* (VaB, 4; Leipzig: J.C. Hinrichs, 1912), 174.31f.

27. This has been somewhat obscured by the fact that the theme did not find expression in divine or royal epithets.

28. F. Thureau-Dangin, *Rituels Accadiens* (Paris: E. Leroux, 1921), 144.424.

29. According to Thureau-Dangin (*Rituels Accadiens*, I), the extant copies of the relevant ritual at the New Year Festival cannot be dated before the conquest of Alexander the Great; it stands to reason that the original tablets are of much older date, although, as Thureau-Dangin states, how much older is impossible to say.

30. H. Weissbach, *Die Keilinschriften der Achämeniden*(VaB, 3; Leipzig: J.C. Hinrichs, 1911), 6f. For a somewhat different translation cf. Oppenheim in *ANET*, 316.

31. 'Images' is not a *translation* but an *interpretation*—and, as often in such cases, a wrong one—of *ilāni*. The translation given in my contribution, 'The Persian Period', in *Israelite and Judaean History* (ed. J.H. Hayes and J.M. Miller [London: SCM, 1977], 519) was taken mechanically from *ANET*; I ought to have added a note there concerning the inexact rendering of *ilāni).*

32. Cf. Borger, *Inschriften Asarhaddons*, 23 Ep. 32b.39, and other references in *CAD*, vol. 16, p. 79 s.v. *ṣalmu*.

33. E. Ebeling, *Die akkadische Gebetsserie 'Handerhebung'* (Literarische Keilschrifttexte aus Assur; Berlin: Akademie-Verlag, 1953), 44.53.

34. For a wrong restoration cf. C.J.M. Weir, *A Lexicon of Accadian Prayers in the Rituals of Expiation* (London: Oxford University, 1934), 296 s.v. *sapḫu*.

35. Ebeling, *'Handerhebung'*, 45 and n. 2.

36. Ebeling, *'Handerhebung'*, 122.12.

37. Weir, *Lexicon*, 296 s.v. *sapḫu*.

38. Cf. Weir, *Lexicon*, 116 s.v. *illatu*: *sapiḫtu illati lipḫur*.

39. R.D. Biggs, 'More Babylonian "Prophecies"', *Iraq* 29 (1967), 121. The literary form has been investigated by J.G. Heintz, 'Note sur les origines de l'apocalyptique judaïque à la lumière des prophéties akkadiennes', *L'Apocalyptique*, ed. F. Raphaël (Etudes d'Histoire des Religions, 3; Paris: P. Guethner, 1977), 71-87. Several duplicates were added by A.H. Grayson and W.G. Lambert ('Akkadian Prophecies', *JCS* 18 [1964], 7-30) who greatly facilitated the comprehension of this text.

40. I now think that I was far too skeptical in *SEÅ* 41-42 (1976-77), 234, Additional Note.

41. It is, of course, extremely difficult to say whether we are entitled to speak of a real eschatology—this is also a question of definition. Most probably, however, we meet here only a hope for a better future such as is so often found in texts of this literary genre. There is, nevertheless, a slight touch of eschatology here, given the fact that the theme of happiness described here recurs later as a characteristic feature in apocalyptic literature. This topic cannot be further developed here.

42. Cf. Widengren, 'The Persian Period', 496, 519.

43. Cf. *CAD*, vol. 10, pp. 117f. s.v. *mīšaru*.

44. Cf. J.A. Montgomery, *A Critical and Exegetical Commentary on the Books of Kings*, ed. H.S. Gehman (ICC, 10; Edinburgh: T. & T. Clark, 1951), 315. For the bending of knees before Baal as a ritual cf. Rowley, *Men of God*, 50, with a reference to an observation by de Vaux.

45. Hölscher, *Propheten*, 175 n. 1.

46. Steuernagel, *Lehrbuch*, 371 §80 3c.

47. Rowley, *Men of God*, 163. Comparing 1 Kgs 19.18 and Deut. 30.3 with the disputed passages in the pre-exilic prophets makes it possible to assign a pre-exilic date to the ideas of the remnant and the gathering of the

dispersed. One would think that such a self-evident methodological approach to the problem of authenticity would have been tried before. I have not been able to find it indicated in the commentaries, although the time at my disposal has not permitted a more thorough investigation of the relevant literature.

THE BIBLICAL INTERPRETATION OF THE REIGNS OF AHAZ AND HEZEKIAH

Peter R. Ackroyd

I. *The Available Biblical Material*

Narrative and archival information concerning Ahaz occupies the whole of 2 Kings 16; some small part of this appears also in Isaiah 7, where verse 1 is close to 2 Kings 16.5; Ahaz is mentioned also in verses 3, 10 and 12 in material not paralleled in 2 Kings. The death of Ahaz is recorded in Isaiah 14.28 though arguments have been adduced for removing his name by emending the text.[1] A very markedly divergent account of Ahaz appears in 2 Chronicles 28, and 29.19 refers to Hezekiah's reversal of Ahaz's action in respect of sacred vessels. In addition, note may be taken of the reference in Isaiah 38.8 to the מעלות אחז paralleled in 2 Kings 20.11 where it is, however, lacking in LXX*,[2] which may suggest that it is intrusive there in the MT. 2 Kings 23.12 refers to the עלית אחז, clearly in reference to an idolatrous practice. In Isaiah 38.8, 1QIs[a] has במעלות עלות אחז את השמש. These last allusions, their meaning and interrelationship, are problematic.[3]

Narrative and archival material concerning Hezekiah appears in 2 Kings 18-20, the main part of which is found also, in a partially deviant text, in Isaiah 36-39. 2 Chronicles 29-32 has a sharply divergent account of Hezekiah, in which only chapter 32 covers, in substantially abbreviated form, the material found in the Kings and Isaiah texts.

The following discussion does not attempt to deal with all the many problems of content and structure, of viewpoint and shift, revealed by these texts. Nor will many of the details be considered except where they appear relevant to the main issues of interpretation with which this study is concerned. The intention here is simply to look critically at the interpretations offered by the biblical narrators and commentators with a view to some elucidation of the material.

II. *The Assessments*

Ahaz in 2 Kings is given a negative comment, similar to that passed on numerous kings of Judah: 'he did not do that which was right in the sight of Yahweh his God as David his father had done' (16.2). The account which follows exemplifies certain aspects of his conduct. In the Chronicles account there has been a noticeable shift so that in effect he has become the worst king of Judah, thus taking the place of Manasseh in the Kings presentation since Manasseh in Chronicles has become an evil king repentant and hence a reformer. The assessment of Ahaz in Isaiah 7 is also negative, in part directly, though largely by implication. In particular the negative shift in this material in comparison with 2 Kings 16 may be noted. This is especially clear in Isaiah 7.2, 4 which so presents the attitude of king and royal house as to suggest a state of totally unnecessary panic.[4]

Hezekiah in the narrative in Kings is approved, and indeed the style of the approval finds its counterpart only in the Josiah narrative (see 2 Kings 22.2). In fact, the Hezekiah statement goes further. In addition to the generally favourable mention of 18.3, comparing Hezekiah to David, we are further told in 18.5 that 'after him there was none like him among all the kings of Judah', together with a rather loosely added final phrase 'and who were before him', often regarded as a gloss.[5] While this may be a correct view of the final phrase, it is nevertheless itself a further indication of a process by which the stature of Hezekiah has reached ever higher levels.[6] The two approving statements in 18.3 and 5 enclose a note on the so-called 'reform of Hezekiah' in 18.4, which not only records the more conventional removal of high places, pillars and asherah, but specifically the destruction of the 'bronze snake which Moses had made'. The second approving statement in 18.5 is part of a larger unit which records Hezekiah's trust in Yahweh (5a), his total adherence to Yahweh (6a) and his obedience to the commands given to Moses (6b). Hence Yahweh was with him, so that he was successful in all that he undertook: he rebelled against the king of Assyria and did not serve him (7); and he conquered the Philistines and their territory (8). Apart from this last item, we may perhaps best see these statements as a kind of anticipatory summary of what follows in the succeeding chapters. These contain a rich assemblage of material, which in effect serves to show the deliverance of Hezekiah from the Assyrians (chs 18-19) and from death (20.1-11); and prophetically reveals the coming Babylonian conquest and exile (20.12-19).[7] The

final summary of 20.20 adds a reference to his action in regard to the water supply for Jerusalem, an item which is not in any way directly integrated into the assessment of Hezekiah. The recording of this may be neutral, a piece of archival information. It very naturally suggests the action of a good ruler who provides for the needs of his capital by bringing the water supply into the city (העירה). We may perhaps suppose it to have military significance, because we may readily link it with the siege of the city by the Assyrians; but that is not stated in the text, and it is equally possible to regard it as expressing a general rather than a specific benevolent intention. In the context of the whole presentation of Hezekiah, it provides one further element suggestive of the approval of him as ruler.

The contrast between Ahaz in Kings and in Chronicles is matched by the converse for Hezekiah. What in 2 Kings 18.4 is a minimal reference to a 'reform' has as its counterpart the very substantial reform narrative which extends through 2 Chronicles 29–31. The idealization of Hezekiah is continued in the presentation in 2 Chronicles 32 of various elements of the Hezekiah story, at some points so abbreviated that it is clear that it is assumed that the Kings narrative or something like it is familiar to the reader. It underlines divine protection, has a slight warning note in 32.25, but ends with overwhelming approval of the king.[8] It is in various ways clear that already in 2 Kings and still more clearly in 2 Chronicles, we are moving towards that glorification of Hezekiah as 'messiah' which appears in Jewish writings.[9]

III. *The Historical Context*

2 Kings 16.7-9 provides a not entirely lucid statement of the political situation in the reign of Ahaz. It records that he sent messengers to Assyria, using a formula of subservience 'your servant and your son' (עבדך ובנך).[10] The appeal was for deliverance from Aram and Israel. Ahaz sent silver and gold from the temple and from the royal treasury as a present to Assyria.[11] Assyria captured Damascus and 'exiled it to Qir',[12] and Rezin, king of Aram, was put to death. However, the status of Ahaz remains unclear in this narrative. Does his submission formula imply that he was already a vassal of the Assyrians, in the position of a subordinate ruler as 'servant and son'? Or should we suppose that this was his initial act of subservience and that rule by Assyria over Judah existed from this date?[13]

Some clarity on these questions may be provided by examining the rebellion of Hezekiah which is noted in 2 Kings 18.7 and reiterated by implication in 18.13-16. It is significant that 18.14 uses the verb חטא to indicate infringement of the vassal status. Furthermore, an indemnity is required by Sennacherib and set at three hundred talents of silver and thirty talents of gold. Finally, 18.15f. shows Hezekiah obtaining part or all of this indemnity by using materials from the temple and royal treasury. We may note that the same phrases are used of Ahaz in 2 Kings 16.8.

The background to this information is often filled in so as to offer a full and coherent picture, but the reconstruction is inevitably uncertain. 2 Kings 16 contains no comment on Ahaz's appeal to Assyria; any negative view of it depends rather on the broader context in which Ahaz is condemned. Equally, and more significantly, no comment is made on this issue in Isaiah 7. What we find here is an oracle against fear and a message of doom to Aram and Israel (7.4-9). No reference is made to Assyria in this passage. What is evident is that the opening of Isaiah 7 and the following oracle imply rather clearly that the panic of the Davidic house was unwarranted. It is often stated, as if it were self-evident, that Isaiah warned Ahaz against appealing to Assyria for help, but this is not in the text. If it is proper to regard it as a logical position for the prophet to hold—comparison may be made with the warnings of reliance on Egypt in Isaiah 29 and 31 and such a position would place him in the succession of Hosea with his warnings against political intrigue (e.g. Hos. 7.11)—we must still ask why the text does not make the point explicit. In the passages which follow (the end of Isaiah 7 and on into chapter 8), the 'king of Assyria' glosses in 7.17, 20 and the fuller Assyrian references in 8.4 and 7 draw out the theme of doom for Judah at the hands of Assyria. The implication of wrongful trust is present in 8.6 and 7, but again the text does not explicitly condemn political appeal to Assyria. The Isaiah text as it stands appears rather to emphasize that because of divine protection Ahaz and his court had no need to fear Aram and Israel. It also emphasizes that a king who lacks faith in Yahweh must expect doom at the hands of Assyria. But the two elements are left in suspense. Assessment is made problematic by the very evident glossing of the text and the difficulty of deciding to what context that glossing belongs.

The overall picture of Ahaz suggests that a particular politico-religious view, namely that appeal for help to an alien power was to

be regarded as bad theologically, has contributed to the negative assessment of that particular king in the context of the more evidently religious condemnations which are offered of him. To those we must return.

On the other hand, the portrayal of Hezekiah in 2 Kings 18–20 shows him as desirably, by implication, rebelling against Assyria (18.7), submitting to Assyria and paying an indemnity (18.14-16). The relationship between these and other elements in the narrative has been an area of long debate.[14] A markedly contrasting narrative, or more probably double narrative, in 18.13, 18.17–19.37, shows the total inability of the Assyrians to bring about the capture of Jerusalem, and the total defeat of the army and the death of Sennacherib. The various elements of this complex section all contribute to the overall picture of disaster for Assyria and deliverance for Judah. In the context of information from Assyrian sources, it is clear that the overrunning of Judah which Sennacherib claimed, and which is implied in 18.13, did not include the capture of Jerusalem itself. It is clear that there was a major political and military crisis for Judah. It is clear also that if the Assyrians had captured Jerusalem, the narratives could not have been so conceived. The effect is to produce a political judgment which is also a religious judgment. Jerusalem was not captured by the Assyrians, and Hezekiah was the agent of that deliverance, which is clearly described as effected by direct divine intervention against all the political and military odds. Therefore, Hezekiah delivered Judah from the Assyrian yoke, and the implication is that his rebellion against Assyria was linked to this deliverance. This perspective is further underlined in the course of the illness narrative of 20.1-11 (especially v. 6).

Thus we may see that the narratives offer a political assessment in which Ahaz is adjudged to be a bad king and Hezekiah a good king. For good measure 2 Kings 16.6 adds the loss of Eilat, so placed as to indicate an additional item of judgment to the Aram and Israel reference of 16.5.[15] Again this theme is extended in the Chronicler's presentation.[16]

IV. *Religious Assessment*

The treatment of Ahaz begins in 2 Kings 16.2b with a general and conventional condemnation. This is followed in 16.3-4 by three elements: a reference to his conforming to the practices of the kings of Israel (cf. 2 Kings 8.18, 27); a statement that he passed his son

through the fire in accordance with the abominations of the dispossessed nations of Canaan; and a reference to worship on the במות and גבעות and 'under every green tree' (cf., e.g., 1 Kings 14.23). Of these, only the second is distinctive, but even so the condemnation is generalized and not entirely exceptional.[17] The theme of religious impropriety is by implication continued in 16.8 which refers to his taking silver and gold from the temple and the palace treasury for the payment of the שחד (bribe).[18] If, in context, this may be intended to suggest religious impropriety, this is not explicitly stated. As already noted, a similar point is made about Hezekiah (2 Kings 18.14-16).[19]

Much more specific detail appears in 16.10-18.[20] Here Ahaz is presented as travelling to appear before Tiglath-Pileser in Damascus, and as seeing there an altar of which he sent full details to Uriah the priest.[21] While it has often been assumed that this altar was of Assyrian design, and it is associated therefore with the political relationship between Judah and Assyria, it would appear much more probable that it was in fact Aramaean and belonged to the Damascus temple.[22] The sequel tells of the construction of the altar by Uriah according to the plan sent; the emphasis on the precise following out of the instructions suggests an ironic use of a formula frequently to be found in the descriptions of the tabernacle and other matters in the Pentateuch (cf., e.g., Exod. 39.32). This formal connection would appear to be an important element in the derogatory treatment of Ahaz; though at another level it could be read as indicating the degree to which exact divine instructions, as they might be understood, were executed. In 16.12f. Ahaz returns to Jerusalem, and sees the altar—a phrase which implies his approval and acceptance of it;[23] and he offers sacrifice on it, of which the details are supplied. A resulting rearrangement of cult furniture is described in 16.14f., showing that the bronze altar before Yahweh was moved, brought from in front of the temple, that is, between the altar (it is not clear which) and the temple, and placed to the north side of the altar (again it is not clear which). The text is by no means clear and is possibly overloaded. But the nub of the matter appears when it is stated that the new altar is to be for all major and royal and national sacrifices, while the bronze altar, in its new position, is for the king's own inquiries (בקר) of the deity. The section concludes with a repetition of the obedience formula (as in v. 11, see above), again suggestively ironic, but also potentially indicating the carrying through of instructions which are purportedly divinely given.

16.17-18 list some further alterations in the shrine. Ahaz 'cuts off' (קצץ), a term evidently intended to be derogatory. The details are not entirely clear, for the terms are uncertain, but a reference appears to the bronze oxen under the sea and their replacement by a stone support. The text clearly implies the removal of the bronze, perhaps also its cutting up. Is this robbing the temple for a bribe (cf. 16.7)? Is it taking the bronze for some other purpose? Or is it a replacement of worn, damaged, broken temple equipment by new? Can we assume that replacement of bronze by stone, which would be much stronger for holding what may have been a weighty object, was necessarily a nefarious procedure? We are also told of the removal of מוּסַךְ (Q) or מֵיסַךְ (K) (?cover) of הַשַּׁבָּת (?sabbath).[24] The text continues: 'which had been built in the temple and the outer entrance for the king he turned round the temple of Yahweh'. The meaning is very unclear.

At the end of verse 18, there is a statement which appears to refer back to everything that precedes. It was done מפני מלך אשור ('before the king of Assyria'), which appears to imply that all the alterations depicted were due to Assyrian requirements or to meet the Assyrian ruler's demands.

Some further indications of Ahaz's improper religious activity are implied in the reference to the מעלות אחז in Isaiah 38.8 (cf. 2 Kings 20.11, though the text there is less sure), and to the עלית אחז in 2 Kings 23.12, where altars are built on the roof of the עלית. Uncertainties about what is referred to make it difficult to know just what is meant, but it is a fair assumption that these were viewed as undesirable objects or constructions.

2 Chronicles 28.16-21 provides a fuller portrayal of disaster, beginning with an appeal to the 'kings' (plural) of Assyria. Reference is made to what appears to be the tribute Ahaz paid from temple and palace, with the sardonic comment that it did him no good (20-21); Ahaz engaged in idolatrous practice, worshipping the gods of Aram (22-23), which might be an interpretation of the altar theme of 2 Kings; he engaged in wrong cultic acts and such evils as the destruction of holy vessels and the shutting of the temple doors (24a); and he built a multiplicity of altars in Jerusalem (24b-25). The description provides a further though in some respects more generalized statement of Ahaz's irreligion, paving the way for a direct reversal of his actions by Hezekiah in 2 Chronicles 29.19.

It is clear that Ahaz is depicted as an evil king from the religious point of view, and this is pressed even further in the Chronicles

material than in Kings. But is this the only possible interpretation of what we may detect in the Kings narrative? We may note that the items are capable of being viewed rather differently if we start from a neutral view of Ahaz.

(1) The tribute/bribe theme, as we have seen, has its counterpart in the Hezekiah material in 2 Kings 18.14-16; in that context it does not carry any obvious overtones. Hezekiah used the temple treasures; he removed gold with which he had adorned the temple. It is, however, significant that this element of the Hezekiah material is absent in the more idealized presentation in Isaiah 36-39.[25]

(2) The building of a new altar and the revision of religious practice does not in fact at any point directly imply idolatrous practice in the Kings narrative. In fact there is stress on the carrying out of all the normal rites, and no suggestion in the Kings text that Ahaz was worshipping any other deity.[26] How far should we regard the building of a new-style altar as alien in intent? Or should we view it as an updating and improvement of the facilities for worship in the Jerusalem shrine? After all, the fact that the pattern of the Solomonic temple belongs in the general near eastern context and was built by Phoenician craftsmen according to familiar patterns is normally accepted as no indication in itself of alien practice. We may observe that a number of the cult installations of that shrine can be regarded as having parallels to cult objects elsewhere, and some of them, for example the two pillars Jachin and Boaz, are of doubtful interpretation, suggesting survivals of older ritual practice. The further note that the existing bronze altar was now to be used for the king's own inquiring of the deity could be held to imply a more specific piety, though more probably it provides an elusive clue to some aspect of royal worship.[27]

(3) The statement that these actions were performed 'before the king of Assyria' (מפני מלך אשור) has been thought to indicate religious subservience to the Assyrians. As the text stands there is a strong implication of this in that the appeal to Assyria opens the section at 16.7 and the reference to Assyria concludes it at verse 18; thus the whole passage is implicitly related to the one theme. But it appears to be very clear that the Assyrians did not require religious conformity from vassal states; practices such as those of Manasseh's reign, often regarded as due to the Assyrian demands, are only doubtfully if at all associated with Assyrian religion.[28] The text could just as well suggest that it was because of Assyrian tribute demands that certain

political actions were taken, but without any necessary religious implications.

(4) The problems of detail in the text leave many uncertainties, especially in 16.18. The MT שְׁבָת does not seem to make sense and is more probably a deliberate change from שֶׁבֶת to imply that Ahaz disregarded or repudiated some sabbath object or rite. If the שֶׁבֶת refers to a throne of the king in the shrine, perhaps in some way linked to the royal cult,[29] then could not Ahaz just as well be removing a cult object which, by its particular religious associations, could be regarded as improper in the eyes of a reformer? If, as seems possible, the text also alludes to some special entrance for the king—though the wording is obscure—could it originally have suggested that he removed from the house of Yahweh (הֵסִר מִבֵּית יהוה; MT הֵסֵב בֵּית) some privileged entrance for the king thought, again by a reformer, to be improper?

Of course, such comments as these can be no more than tentative, but what they might suggest is that if we start from an unprejudiced position with no prior assumption that Ahaz was a bad king religiously, these actions could be seen as acts of religious reform. Had he been viewed favourably, would they have been acceptable? Is he a bad king religiously because he is regarded as a failed king politically? A similar comment may be made on some aspects at least of the Saul tradition.

On the other hand, Hezekiah is a religious reformer and viewed favourably. A general statement of approval in 18.3 is followed by the conventional removal of במות, breaking of מצבת, cutting down of אשרה in 18.4a. In 18.4b he is credited with the smashing of the נחש הנחשת made by Moses, with the comment that the Israelites had been sacrificing to it and that it was called נחשתן. In 2 Chronicles 29-31 the reform theme is expanded to enormous proportions, but the detail does not here concern us; it is one element in the progressive idealization of Hezekiah.[30] What comment should be made on Hezekiah's actions?

(1) 2 Kings 18.22 records a comment attributed to the Rabshakeh: Hezekiah has removed high places and altars and has commanded that worship should be offered in Jerusalem alone. While too much weight should not be given to the imaginative construction of the Rabshakeh's speech in which we may find a number of examples of Deuteronomic theology turned upside down (especially 18.29-32), such a statement could represent a reflection of actual adverse

comment on Hezekiah's actions by opponents. It is more probably a reflection of later attitudes, for centralization of worship is not alluded to in the reform statement of 18.3-4; hence it looks more like a reading back from Josiah and related to the Chronicler's elaboration. We may perhaps better see in this passage an ironic comment, not unrelated to the Ahaz material: Ahaz and his priest ironically carry out all that is ordered, simply compounding disaster; Hezekiah is ironically described as the king who has offended God by misplaced religious changes, though clearly, in the view of the narrator, the very opposite is true.

(2) A much clearer point is to be seen in the removal of a cult object traditionally associated with Moses, and the explanation of this with a palpably contrived comment on its being treated as an idol.[31] Here we may legitimately ask whether, had Hezekiah been politically adjudged to be a bad king, this piece of religious 'reform' might have been seen as a sacrilegious action and hence disastrous?

V. *Hypothesis*

The degree of hypothetical suggestion in what precedes will be apparent, but since we have progressed so far along such a line, may we not build a final construction, an overall hypothesis of a different possible view of these two rulers?

(1) Could we not argue that Ahaz by submission to Assyria assured Judah of surviving the disaster which overtook the northern kingdom at that very period? Since we have no completely clear notion of where Isaiah stood, and the text does not tell us that he counselled against appeal and hence submission to Assyria, we cannot be sure whether he preferred a quietist policy, nor whether, had such a policy been adopted, the Assyrians would have been satisfied with an absence of clear indication of allegiance. What we do know is that in a very delicate political situation, and a real threat to his throne, since the nominee ben Tabeal[32] of Isaiah 7.6 must have been a viable candidate to take his place, Ahaz managed, contrived perhaps, to keep his throne and his kingdom intact. To survive may have been more important than to make futile gestures of independence.

(2) Could we argue—and see here the evidence of Isaiah 20 and the Assyrian material which points to Hezekiah's involvement in rebellion in 713-711[33]—that Hezekiah by rebelling, more than once, seriously risked total disaster to Judah? If the Assyrians had not withdrawn

from the siege of Jerusalem, which they were perfectly capable of capturing as they captured Lachish, and Judah had fallen totally in 701, not losing just the 46 cities claimed by Sennacherib, what would have been the verdict on Hezekiah? We know that Judah remained in fact subservient to Assyria for the next three quarters of a century. The text, both in Isaiah and in 2 Kings, clearly implies a quite opposite and historically inaccurate view, namely that Judah was totally delivered from Assyrian power. Hezekiah seems to have had a better press than he deserved.[34]

(3) One wider consideration could be a further factor. We may ask whether it is right to detect in the royal narratives of the last century and a half of Judah's history an artificial alternating pattern which has imposed itself on the rulers. A later and more complex interwoven structure is to be found in 2 Chronicles; Ezekiel 18, with its alternating figures, provides another example of a pattern. Ahaz bad, Hezekiah good, Manasseh bad, Josiah good, Jehoiakim bad (omitting the insignificant Amon and Shallum): it is a pattern which makes for good preaching, but is it not just a little too good to be true?

VI. *Conclusion*

This study is not written with a view to reaching firm historical conclusions. It is an attempt at looking beneath the surface of existing narratives and assessments to see how valid they are in the way in which they are designed to be read; to ask whether, if we stand at another angle to them, they may not look rather different. It would be just as unsatisfactory merely to reverse the conventional assessments. Kings, as politicians, are likely to be a mixture of good and bad; their religious policy, if we may judge by analogy, may combine genuine religious concern with political judgment. What does not seem entirely realistic is the oversimple black and white assessment. And the fact that the Chronicler could take the Kings' judgments a stage further in the case of Ahaz and Hezekiah, while effecting a substantial reversal in the case of Manasseh and Josiah, suggests that the motives of the presentation could be more important to consider before we accept the portrayals as given.

Gösta Ahlström in his writings has more than once shown himself to be a skilful iconoclast. This particular piece of turning upside down is offered as a tribute to that independence of judgment and

critical acumen which mark his scholarship and which put all of us in his debt.

NOTES

1. So BHS. See also A.K. Jenkins, 'Hezekiah's Fourteenth Year: A New Interpretation of 2 Kings xviii 13–xix 37', *VT* 26 (1976), 289-94.

2. See again, BHS.

3. Y. Yadin, 'מעלות אחז', *Eretz Israel* 5 (1958), 91-96, 88*. However, Yadin's arguments do not really resolve the problems.

4. For some details of this, see P.R. Ackroyd, 'Isaiah 36-39; Structure and Function', in *Von Kanaan bis Kerala, Festschrift für Prof. Mag. Dr. Dr. J.P.M. van der Ploeg, O.P. zur Vollendung des siebzigsten Lebensjahres am 4. Juli 1979*, ed. J.R. Nelis, J.R.T.M. Peters, et al. (AOAT, 211; Neukirchen-Vluyn: Neukirchener Verlag; Kevelaer: Butzon und Bercker, 1982), 3-21.

5. See BHS.

6. For some discussion of this issue, see P.R. Ackroyd, 'An Interpretation of the Babylonian Exile: A Study of 2 Kings 20, Isaiah 38–39', *ScotJTh* 27 (1974), 329-52.

7. For a discussion of the last two elements, see Ackroyd, 'An Interpretation'.

8. See P.R. Ackroyd, 'The Death of Hezekiah—a pointer to the future?', in *De la Torah au Messie. Mélanges Henri Cazelles. Etudes d'exégèse et d'herméneutique bibliques offertes à Henri Cazelles pour ses 25 années d'enseignement à l'Institut Catholique de Paris, Octobre 1979*, ed. M. Carrez, J. Doré, P. Grelot, et al. (Paris: Desclée, 1981), 219-25.

9. See Ackroyd, 'An Interpretation', and references there.

10. See H. Tadmor and M. Cogan, 'Ahaz and Tiglath-Pileser in the Book of Kings: Historiographic Considerations', *Biblica* 60 (1979), 504.

11. The term שחד may be an appropriate technical term for such support of an appeal. To translate it as 'bribe' introduces a derogatory note, though this may have been intended by the narrator. On שחד see Tadmor and Cogan, 'Ahaz', 500-503, though their arguments do not appear to be conclusive.

12. So the MT, which would seem to mean 'took the people of Damascus into exile to Qir', but since קיר (קירה) means 'city' it is possible that this is really to be regarded as the object of the verb, as is implied in some Greek texts, suggesting the total removal of the city as a political entity.

13. Tadmor and Cogan, 'Ahaz', 505.

14. B.S. Childs, *Isaiah and the Assyrian Crisis* (SBT, 2/3; London: SCM Press; Naperville, Illinois: Allenson Press, 1967).

15. The text of 16.6 is problematical.

16. See 2 Chron. 28.17 for Edom and 28.18 for Philistia.

17. For this element, compare 1 Kings 14.24 and precisely, though in an extended form, 2 Kings 21.6.

18. See note 11.

19. See comments below.

20. For a discussion of this passage, see J.W. McKay, *Religion in Judah under the Assyrians* (SBT 2/26; London: SCM Press; Naperville, Illinois: Allenson Press, 1973), 5-12.

21. The account here includes the two technical terms דמות and תבנית, perhaps indicating a design drawing and a description.

22. M. Cogan, *Imperialism and Religion* (SBLMS, 19; Missoula, Montana: Scholars Press, 1974), 74; and Tadmor and Cogan, 'Ahaz', 506. See also McKay, *Religion in Judah*, 7f.

23. D. Daube, *Studies in Biblical Law* (Cambridge: University Press, 1947), 24-39. See Ackroyd, 'An Interpretation', 340f., for comments.

24. LXX has 'the foundation of the throne' (θεμέλιον τῆς καθέδρας) which suggests a Hebrew מוּסַד הַשֶּׁבֶת.

25. See Ackroyd, 'Isaiah 36-39'.

26. 2 Chron. 28 clearly offers a different view.

27. See Cogan, *Imperialism and Religion*, 73-75, for a fuller discussion.

28. See M. Cogan, 'The Ahaz Altar', in *The Proceedings of the Sixth World Congress of Jewish Studies* (Jerusalem: World Union of Jewish Studies, 1977); and McKay, *Religion in Judah*. It has not been possible in this study to take account of H. Spieckermann, *Juda unter Assur in der Sargonidenzeit* (FRLANT, 129; Göttingen: Vandenhoeck und Ruprecht, 1982), see especially pp. 307-72, who presents a close analysis of Assyrian texts and comes to different conclusions. If these conclusions are accepted, some modification of details in the present discussion would follow: the main argument, however, stands. In particular, Spieckermann's discussion of Ahaz (pp. 362-9) recognizes the king's political sagacity, though he offers a different explanation of 2 Kings 16.15b from that given here.

29. See the עמוד for the king in 2 Kings 11.14; 23.3. It is perhaps a pillar but more probably a 'standing place', a 'station' for the king, the position occupied by him in the ritual.

30. Ackroyd, 'An Interpretation'; and idem, 'Isaiah 36-39'.

31. See the similar assessment of Gideon's ephod in Judges 8.27.

32. Perhaps it should be 'Tabeel'? Who he actually was is of no immediate consequence here.

33. For a view of this see Jenkins, 'Hezekiah's Fourteenth Year'.

34. For some relevant comments on the whole problem area, see R.E. Clements, *Isaiah and the Deliverance of Jerusalem* (JSOTS, 13; Sheffield: JSOT Press, 1980).

KING DAVID'S STATE*

Siegfried Herrmann

Gösta Ahlström's widespread interests span both literary and historical problems. The 'Nordic' or 'Scandinavian' school of thought has tended to give the 'history of the tradition' precedence over 'history'. The problem of the relationship between 'tradition' and 'history' continues to dominate scholarly research in a variety of ways. The following short essay focuses on the development and make-up of the Davidic state, not as a discussion of the history of this period but rather as a critique of the state of research on this, by all appearances, well-documented era.[1]

I

An uneasiness over the amount of material published on the books of Samuel in the last decade and over the differences in the findings—depending on the author's chosen point of view—provided a stimulus for the following thoughts. In spite of the manifest industriousness of the authors, one faces (at least in the case of several of them) what might be termed a pile of sherds, a shattered tradition that seemingly no longer permits writing about David *sine ira et studio* or judging satisfactorily what was possible in his time and what he actually accomplished. The uneasiness increases when one realizes that many of the investigations in question are relatively one-sided. They either present a literary analysis or adopt historico-sociological theories that are difficult to substantiate and pose more questions than they answer. It would require too much space here to name all the works that have appeared recently. One can build a representative sample simply by going through the years and finding that a rather lengthy work, to say nothing of articles and shorter commentaries,[2] has appeared in each year:

1968 R.N. Whybray, *The Succession Narrative* (SBT, 2/9; London: SCM Press)

1969 H.J. Boecker, *Die Beurteilung der Anfänge des Königtums in den deuteronomistischen Abschnitten des 1. Samuelisbuches* (WMANT, 31; Neukirchen: Neukirchener Verlag)

1970 L. Schmidt, *Menschlicher Erfolg und Jahwes Initiative* (WMANT, 38; Neukirchen: Neukirchener Verlag)

1971 J.H. Grønbaek, *Die Geschichte von Aufstieg Davids (1. Sam. 15–2. Sam. 5). Tradition und Komposition* (Copenhagen: Munksgaard)

1972 W. Dietrich, *Prophetie und Geschichte. Eine religionsgeschichtliche Untersuchung zum deuteronomistischen Geschichtswerk* (Göttingen: Vandenhoeck und Ruprecht)

1973 H.J. Stoebe, *Das erste Buch Samuelis* (KAT, 8/1; Gütersloh: Gütersloh Verlagshaus)

1974 E. Würthwein, *Die Erzählung von der Thronfolge Davids—theologische oder politische Geschichtsschreibung?* (Zürich: Theologischer Verlag)

1975 T. Veijola, *Die ewige Dynastie. David und die Entstehung seiner Dynastie nach der deuteronomistischen Darstellung* (Helsinki: Suomalainen Tiedeakatemie)

1976 T.N.D. Mettinger, *King and Messiah. The Civil and Sacral Legitimation of the Israelite Kings* (CBOTS, 8; Lund: Gleerup)

B.C. Birch, *The Rise of the Israelite Monarchy. The Growth and Development of 1 Samuel 7–15* (SBLDS, 27; Missoula, Montana: Scholars Press)

1977 J.H. Hayes and J.M. Miller (eds.), *Israelite and Judaean History* (Philadelphia: Westminster Press)

P.R. Ackroyd, *The Second Book of Samuel* (Cambridge: Cambridge University Press)

1978 F. Crüsemann, *Der Widerstand gegen das Königtum* (WMANT, 49; Neukirchen: Neukirchener Verlag)

D.M. Gunn, *The Story of King David. Genre and Interpretation* (JSOTS, 6; Sheffield: JSOT Press)

1979 A. Malamat (ed.), *The Age of the Monarchies* (The World History of the Jewish People IV/1, 2; Jerusalem: Masada Press)

L.J. Wood, *Israel's United Monarchy* (Grand Rapids, Michigan: Baker Book House)

1980 J.O. Lewis, *1 and 2 Samuel, 1 Chronicles* (Layman's Bible Commentary, 5; Nashville: Broadman Press)
H. Seebass, *David, Saul und das Wesen des biblischen Glaubens* (Neukirchen: Neukirchener Verlag)
1981 J.P. Fokkelman, *King David: Narrative Art and Poetry in the Books of Samuel*, vol. 1 (Studia Semitica Neerlandica 20; Assen: Van Gorcum)
B. Halpern, *The Constitution of the Monarchy in Israel* (Harvard Semitic Monographs, 25; Chico, California: Scholars Press)
1982 T. Ishida (ed.), *Studies in the Period of David and Solomon and Other Essays*, Papers read at the International Symposium for Biblical Studies, Tokyo, December 5-7, 1979 (Winona Lake, Indiana: Eisenbrauns). See especially A. Malamat, 'A Political Look at the Kingdom of David and Solomon and its Relations with Egypt' (pp. 189-204).
1983 A. Malamat, *Das davidische und das solomonische Königreich und seine Beziehungen zu Ägypten und Syrien. Zur Entstehung eines Grossreichs* (Sitzungberichte der Österreichischen Akademie der Wissenschaften, Phil.-hist. Kl., Bd 407; Wien)

Even a quick glance at the titles can have both a paralyzing and irritating effect. Most of the works accept the distinction, made by Wellhausen and Rost, between an *Aufstiegsgeschichte* and a *Thronnachfolgegeschichte*.[3] English-speaking critics have taken up both concepts; Mettinger has even gone so far as to assign them acronyms: HDR ('History of David's Rise to Power') and SN ('Succession Narrative'). It is surprising to find modern authors creating the impression that biblical authors wrote these 'works' as two separate and closed literary unities and, one could almost say, had these titles in mind. Apparently the fact that the established sequence of chapters and their nomenclature are modern and somewhat artificial products has almost been forgotten.

To evaluate each of the works mentioned above is impossible here. Nevertheless, it bears mentioning that many of them reflect the critical and ultimately unprovable tendency to look for various polemical motives behind the wording of the biblical texts. The texts are found to be not only composed of different literary strata but also the result of highly complex mechanisms for judgment and legitimation of historical events. Admittedly, the texts themselves do permit such

esoteric speculation, but in no way should they be considered as works of deliberate propaganda; if that assessment were correct, their propagandistic character would certainly be more pronounced. Even so, several researchers have succeeded in finding within the literary composition of the texts layers of revision apparently based on different perspectives of the events being described. Veijola, for example, proceeds in this manner in his book on *Die ewige Dynastie* (1975). He assumes three strata of deuteronomistic revisions, develops from these three images of David, and in the end even finds treated in the text the three main elements of Old Testament testimony (i.e., history, prophecy, and law) which evolve in the course of the David tradition into a 'total image with considerable nuances'.[4] Proceeding in such a manner undoubtedly produces valuable observations. But one cannot help suspecting that such analyses are sometimes carried too far and their findings exaggerated so that a preconceived theory comes to dominate and ultimately to reduce the historical credibility of what is reported.

To what extent can such literary analyses really be called 'historical research'? Mettinger, who in his book *King and Messiah* (1976) experimented with the texts more intensively than Veijola, defines the maxims that he follows: 'From the methodological point of view, the task of the historian is not to illuminate with the help of the sources a historical past, the main features of which are already taken for granted, but rather the reverse—to reconstruct a past that explains as many features and peculiarities of the source as possible. This is what I have tried to do here.'[5] This is the historian Ranke turned upside down! The goal of historical research should not be to track down what actually happened—Ranke's 'wie es eigentlich gewesen'—but, according to Mettinger, to reconstruct a past that can be justified in one way or another from the sources. Indeed, one is less surprised at such principles if one bears in mind the words of Novalis that Mettinger uses as a motto for his book: 'Hypotheses are nets; only he who casts them will catch'. A kernel of truth in such a procedure is unmistakable; but, just as in criminal investigation, one mustn't stretch the evidence too far. Faced with possible complications, both the detective and the historian, whose common task it is 'to reconstruct a past', must use the standard of what is probable and verifiable.

To take one example from Mettinger's book. For him נגיד ('leader') was originally a secular concept; it was not allied to the ritual of

anointing. Only later did a 'theologization' of the נגיד concept occur, a process that must be seen as secondary. Consequently, all those passages that could or do interpret נגיד in a theological sense before the time of Solomon must be considered secondary, and thus historically inferior, layers of revision. They are the work of a single later author, the author of the 'History of David's Rise to Power' (HDR), who wished to secure—after the fact—the divine designation for Saul, David and Solomon in succession. Mettinger's entire 'reconstruction' assumes one unproved hypothesis: נגיד was originally a secular concept. In this context one could even argue about the definition of 'secular'. Whoever treats the texts in such a manner has a difficult time with history. Mettinger finds a formula for this: 'The reign of David is a blank'.[6] And this in the face of the tradition of two highly complex biblical books! There is one other consequence: what Mettinger terms 'High Messianism' cannot be traced to any genuinely Davidic tradition.

Whereas the studies by Veijola and Mettinger are limited to the literary field, Crüsemann tries to bring sociological speculation to bear in his analysis. The right of kings is in question. By making adept use of both those passages always recognized as critical of royalty and certain attitudes found in wisdom literature, Crüsemann paints a picture that attempts to do justice to modern social criticism. Crüsemann is of the opinion that there existed not only a critical populace but also critical court circles 'that, combining early wisdom and ancient Israelite historical thought into a unique synthesis, confidently opposed the kings and their supporters'.[7] Without doubt Crüsemann's book contains a number of notable observations demonstrating that criticism of the king was possible in Israel. But what kind of society was it that permitted the exercise of such criticism? This is a sociological question and, since Israel's changing ways of life and circumstances give sociologists trouble, Crüsemann (following Sigrist) tries to apply the concept of 'segmented society' to Israel. It must be asked whether these 'segmented societies' arise and develop out of a historical process that is even remotely comparable to Israel's. It is significant that these sociological considerations, for which the 'segmented society' is the key phrase, form a completely independent part of Crüsemann's book and ultimately serve to question the legitimacy of rule, not to bring to light a sociological structure. The specific problem of the development of the Israelite kingdom thereby runs the risk of falling prey to a theory whose

principles are not founded upon the text of the Old Testament itself.

The question still remains as to the beginnings, growth, and governmental organization of the power structure that we call 'King David's state', a structure which, moreover, developed the strength to expand to an 'empire'.[8] Did this state exist or did it not? Have we or have we not been steered onto the wrong path by a piece of Old Testament 'Tendenzliteratur', by later efforts to legitimize a Davidic power apparatus that either no longer existed at that time or had never existed in the form as we know it? Can one legitimately approach this question in terms of a 'sociology of the early Monarchy'? To do so actually requires one to have in hand a convincing opinion about both the pre-state era and the constitution of Israel.

In 1967 Buccellati published his book *Cities and Nations of Ancient Syria*, with the subtitle 'An Essay on Political Institutions with Special Reference to the Israelite Kingdoms'.[9] Beginning with the situation in Syria, he distinguished the city-state as part of a territorial state (e.g., Syria) from the nation-state based on the formation of groups in which genealogical thinking predominated and which found themselves in the end capable of banding together to form a 'tribal league'. Thanks to blood ties and common fates, a 'national history' independent of territory grew within the tribal league. In its final stage, the tribal league led to the formation of a state whose own legitimacy was rooted in the tribal league itself. In Buccellati's words: 'The kingdoms were only the second step in the political history of the same people'.[10] In such a way he argues for an uninterrupted, continuous, indeed almost automatic development of the state from the blood-related groups in the pre-state era.

Whereas Buccellati considers an organic development on the road 'from tribe to state' to have been possible, a completely different point of view was forcefully advanced a short time later. Following Mendenhall's lead, yet differing from him in individual aspects, de Geus and Gottwald in particular questioned the existence of an early nomadic period for Israel and thus contradicted almost entirely the biblical picture of early Israel. For de Geus the road to statehood emanated from the city, not the tribe.[11] The Israelites appear to him to be elements of the population with an Amorite past, found in vaguely defined territories in the period of the Judges. He sees regional organizations of clans that are united ethnically but are independent in all other ways. Banding together more cohesively in

an urban context prompted the growth toward statehood. Gottwald describes the transition to a state in a more complex way.[12] The 'tribes of Yahweh', by inhabiting the eastern side of the less densely populated Ephraimite highland, were placed in a position to gain the upper hand over the city dwellers.[13]

There may be another theory behind Gottwald's ideas: the assumption, of a 'dimorphic society', defended especially by Rowton, and about which W. Dever has written extensively.[14] This concept has helped to understand correctly some Mari texts that deal with the coexistence of native ruling populations and intruding nomadic groups which at first did not change their life styles. It is certainly tempting to see a similar situation in Syria and Canaan and to compare the at least temporary influx of Aramaean and Israelite tribes into the regions of established culture with the conditions in Mesopotamia during the Mari Age. One would have in Israel, at least during the period of the Judges, a 'dimorphic society' that, according to Gottwald, would have changed to benefit the 'tribes of Yahweh' when the inhabitants surrounding the cities became the leading power.

But how can such sweeping sociological theories be reconciled with Old Testament traditions? It is apparent that the interpretations presented here are hypotheses that themselves presume other general developmental trends. One establishes these trends by combining, more or less eclectically, individual facts gleaned from the Old Testament texts. The right to proceed in such manner should not be disputed in principle, but one must remember that Old Testament tradition proceeds differently and that the concrete facts transmitted must yield a complete picture, no matter how theoretical it may be.

Old Testament tradition does not give us social structures but rather individual personalities who had power because they were recognized as power-bearers or commanders. 'Men make history', a phrase still not without a kernel of truth despite frequent criticism, does not apply to structural investigations, which, by their nature, stress the role of the larger social environment and depreciate the role of the individual. Admittedly men exist in social structures and are even borne by them, but one must not forget that men can burst through those structures to reach new shores. One should not merely affirm that certain personalities were magnified in the course of time as the gradual growth of the tradition shaped the literature; it is just as important to find out where and how the tradition began—in

short, who the men were who are talked about in the texts. In the end, this biblical tradition preserves more historical reality than its critics would care to admit. The role of the personality and its charisma appears to be a legitimate source for explanations in those cases of upheaval that did not end in catastrophe but instead brought forth new and constructive developments. Old Testament tradition is clear enough to allow such different personalities as Saul and David—and to a lesser degree Solomon—to emerge even with individual character traits. If they were magnified or changed for literary reasons, these transformations did not contradict their actual nature. Thus, in answer to the question posed above, the thesis is here put forth that the Davidic state was in fact *David's* state and that it would not have been possible without his personality. The next question is obviously what this state looked like and what potential it had. What follows addresses itself to this question.

II

Leonhard Rost gave some important definitions in his essay 'Die Bezeichnungen für Land und Volk im Alten Testament', which appeared already in 1934 in the Procksch Festschrift. According to him, 'a *goy* exists where a group of men has unified on the basis of heritage, language, land, law, the military, and religion, and has become inaccessible to outsiders'.[15] He adds, in clearer and briefer fashion: '*goy* defines the entire population of a territory', while *'amm* defines the men of a people as the collection of married, property-owning full citizens who have the right to serve in the military, to take part in the administration of justice, and to practice the cult'.[16] The term *'amm* is thus restricted to the male portion of the *goy* that is vested with the obligation and authority to guarantee the cohesion of the people and to ensure its existence against outsiders. This, of course, does not take place in thin air but rather on solid ground, a fact addressed in Rost's discussion of ארץ and אדמה. Establishing precise definitions is no easy task given the broad range of meanings of these words. He concludes his discussion with the statement: 'Both Hebrew and German are lacking a work like the Latin "territorium" that clearly defines the area ruled by a state. But in one of its meanings the word *'ereṣ* fills this void and should be understood as "territorium" when used with peoples' names, with suffixes, and also when it is defined more precisely through relative clauses.'[17]

For example, ארץ כנען certainly refers to the area ruled and inhabited by the Canaanites. Similarly, ארץ ישראל refers to the area ruled and inhabited by the Israelites, but with even greater precision. In the few passages where this phrase occurs, the reference is to the territory of the Northern Kingdom and not to the monarchical state (cf. Ezek. 27.17; 47.18; 2 Chron. 30.25; 34.7). Rost concludes in his summary: 'As an apolitical concept in all instances, ארמה can be excluded from this observation. In contrast, ארץ was formulated as the territorial basis for a state, which allows a people (גוי) to achieve independence as a state through its עם, the privileged male class of full citizens.'[18]

These definitions have the advantage of being based entirely on Hebraic concepts, which they thus define more closely, without any immediate connection to an external sociological theory. At the same time it should not be overlooked that Hebrew does not have a clear and solid concept that could be immediately translated by the word 'state'. This is certainly not coincidence and must correspond to the complexity of the historical phenomena and developments in early Israel. Some further investigation confirms this argument.

In 2 Samuel 1.12 there is mourning for Saul and Jonathan, 'and for the people of the Lord and for the house of Israel' (ועל עם יהוה ועל בית ישראל). עם יהוה refers to the tribal levies, but בית ישראל refers to the totality represented by the 'people of the Lord', or, in other words, to the 'state' of Israel. One justifiably hesitates to translate in this manner, however, because the Israel that at the same time existed as groups of clans and tribes does not exactly correspond to the modern concept of a state.

The precise use of language in 2 Samuel 18.7 confirms that the terminology used here is not coincidental but follows a clearly defined pattern. In this passage, recording the decisive battle against Absalom in the woods of Ephraim, the two parties that do battle are described thus: the עבדי דוד, that is, David's mercenaries, and the עם ישראל, evidently again the levies from the northern tribes. In the passage describing the overtaking of David near Gilgal (2 Sam. 19.41), a different expression appears: כל עם יהוה, that is, the privileged group of Judaean men obliged to do military service. However, in the argument that then breaks out over who has the greater rights to the king, significantly it is not the two עמים, Israel and Judah, that struggle with one another, but rather כל איש יהודה fight with the איש ישראל (19.43, 33). If this is not simply a stylistic variation, the אנשים of the two 'states' Israel and Judah appears to be a collective or more

general term for the inhabitants of both parts of the country with full legal responsibilities.

More remarkable is 2 Samuel 6.21. Here it is stated that David, not Saul and his house, had been chosen by Yahweh to be נגיד על עם יהוה על ישראל. The unconnected juxtaposition of the concepts has its own significance here. The reference is not to the בית ישראל which also would make sense; on the contrary, the calling to be נגיד involves first and foremost the full citizens able to do battle, who can be considered the representative members of the 'state' of Israel, the union once led by Saul as king and corresponding to the later so-called 'Northern Kingdom'.

The terminology used is in any case consistent and justifiable. A look at the historical situation will substantiate the applicability of the terms, for Israel and Judah, these two 'states' with their kings, were just beginning to develop but could nonetheless be identified in such convincing terminology. At the same time it is evident that neither new nor abstract legal concepts were chosen, but rather the most concrete older concepts tied to clan thinking, albeit now applied in a modified sense. From this one can deduce at least that Israel and Judah still considered themselves basically outgrowths of tribal and clan, even family units, and that this consciousness persisted through the stages of settling in the land. Only when faced with threats and dangers from neighbouring peoples did these already settled groups find it necessary, first occasionally (judges), then permanently (kings), to subjugate themselves to—even to follow with great enthusiasm—a locally active leader and later one common to and demanding allegiance from them all. This does not mean, however, that the institutions were created first. These leaders were individuals, well-suited to authority and leadership, who either arose from the midst of the particular groups or believed themselves to be specially chosen. They come across as charismatic figures—they are not in the end holding an 'office', but following a calling.[19] Both Saul and David are such 'chosen ones' over the עם יהוה, to be sure over בית יהודה or בית ישראל. Saul does not make the least effort to justify or secure his position in any 'constitutional' way. David acquires his authority through recognized military superiority, and Jerusalem remains for the time being *his* city. The tribes—or perhaps stated more correctly, the אנשי יהודה or זקני ישראל—that had anointed David (2 Sam. 2.4; 5.3) endured and even encouraged this development, for it served the best interest of the defence of their land; on the other hand, they

contributed nothing of their own to the creation of 'offices', or to put it in other terms, to the creation of a 'royal ideology'. The dynastic monarchy itself developed this ideology, based on foreign examples.[20] Formulations like מלך ארץ יהודה and מלך שבטי ישראל are not attested. David is anointed to be מלך על בית יהודה and to be מלך על בית ישראל. The connection with the עם יהודה and the עם ישראל, represented by the אנשי יהודה and אנשי ישראל respectively, is still recognizable in these phrases. The 'state' that emerged from the transition to a centralized power later led to the fixed concepts מלך יהודה and מלך ישראל. Yet this kingdom was supported just as before by the men of the עם. They retained their functions and own importance as independent bodies. One need only mention here the authoritative role of the Judaean עם הארץ in relationship to the Davidic kingdom.[21]

In light of such a development, it becomes obvious that in Israel and Judah one did not think primarily about the kingdom as an institution; one thought instead about persons and their behaviour, about the respective 'office holders' whose function was to direct the tribes without subjecting them to absolutist powers. The traditional material focuses—in much the same way as a family history—on the personalities of these kings and their fates (cf. the concept 'House of David'), and this is done with a critical distance, not from the institution, but from the individual holders of the 'royal office'. The question as to when the office itself was critically examined and asked to justify its existence is a different question that cannot be addressed here. In any case, this would hardly have happened in Samuel's time and hence not in 1 Samuel 8!

'King David's State' was indeed the state of David, and the words 'personal union' in fact mean much more than the mere governing by a single man of the two territories Judah and Israel. The 'personal union' includes *all* the tribal groups who were willing, to a greater or lesser degree, to recognize a 'monarchical' (in its true sense) head, yet otherwise continued their existence in the smaller group of family, clan and tribe.

Solomon failed in his attempt to promote a centrally-oriented, administratively-unified 'state' by introducing to the court a staff of civil servants to provide certain services. According to 1 Kings 12, it was exactly these services from which the Israelites in the northern section of the state wished to be exempted. This failure of 'national' unity only confirms the peculiarity of the relationships involving Israel and Judah.

Finally, one also realizes that, in the course of technical administrative streamlining (not only for religious reasons concerning the just division of the Promised Land), a clear delineation of the tribal territories seemed desirable even during the Monarchy. In this context one might attribute to the lists in the book of Joshua an independent administrative value. One can only regret that the fall of the Northern Kingdom and its aftermath no longer permit us to follow further the development of this Israelite administrative organization. Foreign—namely Assyrian, Babylonian and Persian—administrative structures spread across a landscape that had changed even in its population.

In focusing on this highly complex and (to our way of thinking) complicated internal organization of Israel and Judah during the Monarchy, one should be careful not to spread hasty theories and hypotheses that might seem better suited to explain the early phases of that period than the biblical material itself. The terminological correctness of the biblical reports is not due to a late harmonization, but rather to a great extent reflects actual processes Israel/Judah experienced and survived on the way toward statehood. Thus, one should not try to attribute the so-called 'resistance to the kingdom' to intrinsic structural limitations on the exercise of dominion. The specific reason for such resistance, wherever it broke out, much more probably lies in the independent nature and religiously secure self-identity among the old family and clan unions, a consciousness that had bound together their land, their territory, their נחלה, but did not grow to form a national unity in a modern political sense.

In many respects Israel remains an oddity. Its sense of unity was not tied to particular forms of national institutions. Nor did it develop any city-states and thus become splintered administratively, as happened in Syria. Israel continued to function as a tribal unity and did not consider itself tied together by what we call a 'state constitution', a concept that seems indispensable to us. Any form of government in ancient Israel remained basically relative. As far as we can determine, the strongest unifying element lay in fact in the common god—and that is indeed more than a religious-historical footnote. This element actually constituted Israel, a fact that no political or sociological theory includes. If one does not take this into consideration, one fails to treat the central problem of Israel, regardless of the theory one chooses.

May the scholar honoured by these pages accept the above

remarks amicably and find himself in agreement with the author that Israel does not lose its suggestive power even when in individual instances it evades our scholarly research and knowledge. May it thus remain, for him as well as for all of us, a 'source of life-giving water' *ad multos annos*.

NOTES

*Translated and edited by Richard Weber, Instructor of German, Ohio Northern University.

1. A paper given at a workshop of the 'Biblischer Kommentar. Altes Testament' in Neukirchen on April 11, 1979, formed the basis for this article.

2. From the list of essays and short works that have appeared in the last few years I would note the following: S.W. Baron, 'The Israelite Population under the Kings', in *Ancient and Medieval Jewish History*, ed. L.A. Feldman (New Brunswick, N.J.: Rutgers University Press, 1972), 23-73, 380-99; A.E. Cundall, 'The United Monarchy (of David & Solomon): Fact or Fiction?', *Vox Evangelica* 8 (1973), 33-40; A.S. Rose, 'The "Principles" of Divine Election: Wisdom in 1 Sam. 16', *Pittsburgh Theological Monographs*, 1 (Pittsburgh: Pickwick Publications, 1974), 43-67; G.E. Wright, 'Die Welt Davids und Salomos', in *Alltagsleben in biblischer Zeit* (Luzern/Frankfurt, 1974), 207-55; R. Hallevy, 'To David's Life Story', *Beth Mikra* 21 (1974), 154-57 (Hebrew); A. Caquot, 'L'Histoire de David dans les livres de Samuel (1 Sam. 19–20)', *Annuaire du Collège de France* 75 (1974), 423-26; M. Bič, 'Davids Kriegsführung und Salomos Bautätigkeit', in *Travels in the World of the Old Testament*, M.A. Beek Festschrift, ed. M. Heerma van Voss *et al.* (Assen: Van Gorcum, 1974), 1-11; W. Vogels, 'David's Greatness in his Sin and Repentance (A Commentary on 2 Sam. 11.2-12, 25)', *Way* 15 (1975), 243-54; J. Kegler, *Politisches Geschehen und theologisches Verstehen: Zum Geschichtsverständnis in der frühen israelitischen Königszeit* (dissertation, University of Heidelberg, 1975); M. Garsiel, *The Kingdom of David: Studies in History and Inquiries in Historiography* (Tel Aviv: Don Press, 1975) (Hebrew); J. van Seters, 'Problems in the Literary Analysis of the Court History of David (1 Sam. 26.6-25)', *JSOT* 1 (1976), 22-29; M. Razin, *Census Lists and Genealogies and their Historical Implications for the Times of David and Saul* (Tel Aviv: Pualim, 1976) (Hebrew); T.N.D. Mettinger, 'The Last Words of David: A Study of Structure and Meaning in 2 Sam. 23.1-7', *SEÅ* 41 (1976), 147-56; M. Garsiel, 'David and Bathsheba', *Dor le Dor* 5 (1976), 24-28, 85-90, 134-37; C. Coccioli, *Davide* (Milan: Rusconi, 1976); E. Benedek, *Die Kriegführung und die Organisation des Heeres Davids* (dissertation, University of Wien, 1976); H.J. Stoebe, 'David und der Ammoniterkrieg (2 Sam. 10.11; 12.26-31)', *ZDPV* 93 (1977), 236-46; Z. Kallai, 'Organizational and Administrative Frameworks in the Kingdom of David and Solomon', in

Proceedings of the Sixth World Congress of Jewish Studies, vol. 1 (Jerusalem: World Congress of Jewish Studies, 1977), 213-20; W. Dietrich, 'David in Überlieferung und Geschichte', *Verkündigung und Forschung* 22 (1977), 44-64; K.R.R. Gros Louis, 'The Difficulty of Ruling Well: King David of Israel', *Semeia* 8 (1977), 15-33; E. Ball, 'The Co-Regency of David and Solomon (I Kgs. i)', *VT* 27 (1977), 268-79; S. Abramsky, '2 Sam. 5: (Erzählungs)technik und Historiographie in der Erzählung von Königtum Davids', *Beth Mikra* 22 (1977), 453-72 (Hebrew); T. Veijola, 'David und Meribaal', *RB* 85 (1978), 338-61; J.D. Levenson, '1 Sam. 25 as Literature and as History', *CBQ* 40 (1978), 11-28; R.O. Corvin, *David and His Mighty Men* (Ann Arbor: University Microfilms, 1978); D. Barthélemy, 'Les problèmes de 2 Sam. 11.2–1 Kgs. 2.11 reconsidérés à la lumière de certaines critiques des "Devanciers d'Aquila"', *Orbis Biblicus et Orientalis* 21 (1978), 218-54; T. Polk, 'The Levites in the Davidic-Solomonic Empire', *Studia Biblica et Theologica* 9 (1979), 3-22; J.D. Levenson, 'The Davidic Covenant and its Modern Interpreters', *CBQ* 41 (1979), 205-19; H. Jason, 'The Story of David and Goliath: A Folk Epic?', *Biblica* 60 (1979), 36-70; G. Garbini, '"Narrativa della successione" o "storia dei re"?', *Henoch* 1 (1979), 19-41; J.W. Flanagan, 'The Relocation of the Davidic Capital', *JAAR* 47 (1979), 223-44; Z. Ben-Barak, 'The Legal Background of the Restoration of Michal to David', *SVT* 30 (1980), 15-29; G. Brunet, 'David et le Sinnor', *SVT* 30 (1980), 73-86; *id.*, 'Les aveugles et boiteux Jébusites', *SVT* 30 (1980), 65-72; R. Bickert, 'Die List Joabs und der Sinneswandel Davids: Eine deuteronomistisch bearbeitete Einschaltung in die Thronfolgeerzählung (2 Sam. 14.2-22)', *SVT* 30 (1980), 30-51; N.L. Tidwell, 'The Philistine Incursions into the Valley of Rephaim (2 Sam. 5.17ff.)', *SVT* 30 (1980), 190-212; T. Veijola, 'Salomo—Der Erstgeborene Bathsebas', *SVT* 30 (1980), 230-50; J.A. Wharton, 'A Plausible Tale: Story and Theology in II Samuel 9–20, I Kings 1–2', *Interp* 35 (1981), 341-54; P.K. McCarter, Jr, '"Plots, True or False": The Succession Narrative as Court Apologetic', *Interp* 35 (1981), 355-67; G.W. Coats, 'Parable, Fable, and Anecdote: Storytelling in the Succession Narrative', *Interp* 35 (1981), 368-82; and P.R. Ackroyd, 'The Succession Narrative (So-Called)', *Interp* 35 (1981), 383-96.

3. As a rule the history of David's rise includes 1 Sam. 16–2 Sam. 5(6) and the history of the succession 2 Sam. 7–20 and 1 Kings 1.1–2.11. Cf. principally L. Rost, *Die Überlieferung von der Thronnachfolge Davids* (Stuttgart: W. Kohlhammer, 1926), reprinted in *Das kleine Credo und andere Studien zum Alten Testament* (Heidelberg: Quelle und Meyer, 1965), 119-253.

4. Veijola, *Die ewige Dynastie*, 142.

5. Mettinger, *King and Messiah*, 165.

6. Mettinger, *King and Messiah*, 295.

7. Crüsemann, *Der Widerstand gegen das Königtum*, 192.

8. The concept of an 'empire' as applied here to the area ruled by David has found increasing acceptance, thanks especially to the work of A. Alt, and has recently been taken up again by A. Malamat.

9. G. Buccellati, *Cities and Nations of Ancient Syria* (Studi Semitici, 26; Rome: Istituto di Studi del Vicino Oriente, Università di Roma, 1967).

10. Buccellati, *Cities and Nations*, 125.

11. C.H.J. de Geus, *The Tribes of Israel: An Investigation into some of the Presuppositions of Martin Noth's Amphictyony Hypothesis* (Assen: Van Gorcum, 1976).

12. N.K. Gottwald, *The Tribes of Yahweh: A Sociology of the Religion of Liberated Israel, 1250–1050 B.C.E.* (Maryknoll, N.Y.: Orbis, 1979).

13. Alt and Noth also saw in the same area essentially good conditions for the settlement of the central tribal groups, normally identified with the so-called Rachel tribes.

14. In *Israelite and Judaean History*, ed. by J.H. Hayes and J.M. Miller (Philadelphia: Westminster Press, 1977), 102-20.

15. L. Rost, in *Festschrift O. Procksch* (Leipzig: A. Deichert, 1934), 125-48, reprinted in *Das kleine Credo*, 76-101. (The page numbers cited here refer to the reprint.)

16. Rost, *Das kleine Credo*, 92.

17. Rost, *Das kleine Credo*, 84.

18. Rost, *Das kleine Credo*, 92.

19. On M. Weber's conception of charismatic personalities specifically as related to the Judges, see most recently A. Malamat, 'Charismatische Führung im Buch der Richter', in *Max Webers Studie über das antike Judentum: Interpretation und Kritik*, ed. W. Schluchter (Frankfurt a.M.: Suhrkamp, 1981), 110-33.

20. Many references have been made to the patterning of the Judaean royal ritual after Egyptian models. Cf. now the extensive examination by M. Görg, *Gott-König-Reden in Israel und Ägypten* (BWANT, 6,5; Stuttgart: W. Kohlhammer, 1975).

21. Cf. especially 2 Kings 11.21, 24.

A RECONSTRUCTION OF THE SOCIAL WELFARE SYSTEMS OF ANCIENT ISRAEL*

Stephen A. Kaufman

The importance of oral transmission in the development of the Pentateuchal traditions is probably the major motif of Scandinavian biblical scholarship. This motif has been a primary contributor to the formation of the current mini-consensus among biblicists that regards the strict application of the Documentary Hypothesis to narrative materials as highly tenuous at best and the assignment of literary relationships between prescriptive ('legal') texts and purely narrative pericopes as fruitless speculation.

As regards the prescriptive texts themselves, however, the situation is somewhat different. Although the pedigree of some chapters of Exodus and Numbers can rightfully be questioned, the division of the remaining material into three major, independent compilations can hardly be doubted. Granted the existence, then, of the compilations generally referred to as the Covenant, Holiness, and Deuteronomic Codes, the examination of the relationships among those 'codes' in whole and in part, is a legitimate endeavor, albeit one that, it must be remembered, is not necessarily of any consequence whatsoever in the elucidation of the chronological or literary hierarchy of narrative passages. Moreover, the determination of a specific order of chronological or institutional precedence as regards two subsections of these prescriptive compilations does not necessarily imply the existence of an identical matrix of relationships for the compilations as a whole: for that each 'code' is the product of a substantial period of development (though in this case oral transmission is probably of little importance) can hardly be doubted. Equally to be avoided, however, is the belief so prevalent in European circles, that such texts can be excavated like a Near Eastern tell, so that the various layers of accretion stand revealed to one and all. In the following essay, then, such statements as 'D expands upon C' or 'P presupposes

D's expansion' are to be understood in light of the middle road (a 'golden mean'?) indicated by the above remarks.

Since the existence of a 'mini-consensus' is probably all that one can ever hope to achieve in the area of biblical studies, it is hardly surprising that a topic as textually and historically complex as the history of the social welfare 'legislation' and institutions of Ancient Israel has remained a source of profound confusion for many students of the Bible. Proper elucidation of the subject demands not only a clear conception of possible inter-relationships of the biblical sources themselves but also a working familiarity with parallel material from the ancient Near East and other cultures. It also demands the adduction of consistent theories of ancient Israelite economic and social structure, theories that for all practical purposes have yet to see the light of day. So the confusion is to some extent excusable. Indeed, it is a confusion whose roots may be traced to the biblical and early post-biblical Jewish sources themselves. It remains somewhat disconcerting, however, to see that scholars who should know better regularly confound the fallow year with the sabbatical year and think of the Jubilee (יובל) as a year-long period instead of a point in time. But even those students of the matter who have managed to keep their facts straight have generally failed to combine those facts into a coherent picture conforming to both the biblical and extra biblical evidence.

Thus mindful of the failures of our predecessors, our goal is to trace the history of certain social welfare institutions of Ancient Israel, and the real and would-be legislation concerning them, from pre-Settlement to post-Exilic times. Taken in isolation, few of our observations are original. Taken as a whole, it all is. That our reconstruction overlaps in many particulars that of Julius Wellhausen speaks well, we think, of both.

The institutions involved are those concerning the fallow year, the release of debt slaves, the annulment of debts, and the return of alienated land, institutions treated rather differently in each of the three major biblical legal compilations. The difficulties inherent in this material stem not only from the uncertain history of the biblical sources themselves and as yet unanswered questions posed by the related extra-biblical evidence, but also from the fact that several different theoretically possible histories must be tested for each institution: e.g., a given institution could be an ancient Israelite tradition preserved and continuously practiced or one fallen into

disuse and only subsequently revived. The institution in question could be ancient but borrowed from another culture; or it could have been borrowed at a much more recent date. And in each case we could be dealing with long-term actual practice, temporarily effective reform or even purely utopian dream.

In spite of these complexities, using a consistent literary-critical approach to the biblical sources and accurate adduction of cognate and/or functionally parallel ancient Near Eastern institutions, it should be possible to choose from among these numerous permutations of institutions and institutional histories a reconstruction that best fits the evidence and to thereby unravel the welfare system complex of Ancient Israel.[1] This essay is an attempt to indicate directions for such a reconstruction.

It is not our intention to review again parallel ancient Near Eastern material in depth, inasmuch as this has been done repeatedly in recent years[2] and should, by now, be relatively well known. Some summarizing and clarifying comments are warranted, however. Much of the relevant cuneiform evidence was actually known for many years, through scattered references in year formulae and fragmentary Old Babylonian edict texts; but it was only with F.R. Kraus's publication of the Ammi-Ṣaduqa edict that the interest of both cuneiformists and biblicists was focused on the important extra-biblical parallels to the biblical social welfare institutions.[3]

We know now that in the Old Babylonian period there were periodic royal decrees (*ṣimdat šarrim*)—decrees of 'justice' (*mēšarum*), whose function was to 'establish emancipation' (*andurāram šakānum*). This 'emancipation' or 'amnesty' consisted of the annulment of certain, specified classes of debts, debt servitude contracts and property transferals.[4] Although there is no evidence for any fixed periodicity of these proclamations,[5] there is every reason to assume that they were a regular feature of most ancient oriental monarchies, just as many oriental regimes are still regularly inaugurated with political amnesties.[6] The etymology of *andurārum* remains in dispute, but it is patently the etymon, both linguistic and institutional, of Hebrew *dĕrōr* (דרור).[7] On the other hand, Hebrew *mēšārîm* (משרים), 'justice', and Akkadian *mēšarum* are undoubtedly cognate, yet whether the Hebrew term ever had the technical sense of the Old Babylonian one is uncertain.

Outside of the Bible, the only substantial evidence for similar institutions in the West-Semitic realm comes from Ugarit where

certain property transactions are characterized as *ṣamit*, 'irrevocably transferred'.[8] Only real-estate at the ultimate disposal of the crown seems to be at issue in these cases. Combined with the evidence presented by the use of the term *ṣĕmitut* (צמתת) in Leviticus 25.23, the implication is clear that normal real-estate transactions were subject to royal annulment unless specifically declared to be צמת, a practice prohibited by Leviticus.

Reactions by biblicists to this interesting cuneiform material has been totally predictable. The largest group of scholars (among them North, Neufeld, Gordon, Sarna, Weinfeld and Loewenstamm) feels that these parallels prove that all or most of the biblical institutions are ancient and native. For others, the extra-biblical evidence only confirms that all or most of the biblical institutions are recent and borrowed.

Since the truth undoubtedly lies somewhere between these two extremes, the hypothetical reconstruction that follows adheres, not surprisingly, to the middle of the road.

In pre-monarchic, pre-urban Israel, land was held in common by tribal and sub-tribal units and regularly apportioned and reapportioned to tribal members, no doubt by some system of lots, to take into account intervening changes of tribal demography. Such a system of land tenure is hardly unique. In fact it is widespread among tribal cultures, and on a village-wide rather than tribe-wide basis persisted into modern times among Palestinian Arabs.[9] In Israel, as we learn from the appendix to the story of the daughters of Zelophehad (Num. 36.1-12),[10] this periodic reapportionment was called היבל.[11]

Agricultural science of these early times prescribed a system of crop management wherein various fields and vineyards were left fallow on a rotating cycle. The practices of crop rotation and periodic fallowing are nearly universal among horticultural societies. Indeed, for most crops they are essential, absent of modern fertilizing techniques. But a fallow period as infrequent as one year out of every seven, as prescribed in the Covenant Code (Ex. 23.10-11), is, to my knowledge, unattested in actual practice. So this is almost certainly just the bare minimum prescribed by a religious law that bore little relationship to agricultural reality. Most farmers undoubtedly allowed their fields to lie fallow much more frequently.

While we need not deny the institution of lending to such a society, be it of seed or of capital, in the close-knit tribal society of Ancient

Israel there was probably little need for a procedure of general debt annulment. Fathers regularly sold their daughters to others in times of economic hardship, as recounted in Exodus 21.7-11, but whether the ancient law regulating the period of service of a male 'Hebrew slave' was practiced we cannot say. It is noteworthy that the six-year period of service described in Exodus 21.2-6 is twice as long as the limit of three years (for men and women of the *awīlum* class) prescribed by paragraph 117 of Hammurapi's Law. Of course, as everywhere in the ancient world, indentured citizens could always be redeemed from their servitude prior to the end of the period if the wherewithal could be found.

With the gradual defeat of the Canaanite city-states, concomitant urbanization, the development of the political and economic authority of the monarchy, and the coincident weakening of tribal authority, much of this structure had to change. Family ties to the land replaced tribal ones, while, through taxes, donations, and confiscations, the temple and the palace became the greatest landholders of all. In short, Israel became a typical, centralized Near Eastern society.

The new kings of Ancient Israel, with their royal Near Eastern predecessors as role models, maintained the age-old practice of issuing proclamations of דרור, 'freedom', at or near the start of their reigns.[12] Such proclamations annulled outstanding debts, manumitted debt slaves, and restored to the crown lands that had been earlier granted to loyal subjects (provided, of course, that such lands had not been sold or transferred לצמתת, i.e., permanently alienated, as we learned from the use of the term *ṣamit* in the Ras Shamra texts). Heads of families held land, bequeathed it to their heirs, sold it, and redeemed it for themselves and their families whenever possible, but there is little reason to think that such lands were ever subject to a system of automatic return to the 'original' owner, an idea that can only be a late reinterpretation of the concept of יובל after its original function had fallen into disuse. Indeed, as others have noted, the invectives of the eighth-century Judean prophets against land accumulators give evidence that no such procedure was practiced or known at that time.[13]

In addition to the periodic edicts, the 'law' of the early monarchy (some of which is undoubtedly preserved in the Covenant Code) demanded, in theory, the release of all debt-slaves after a fixed term, just as in Hammurapi's Law (par. 117). Economic realities, however, forced many such slaves, whose families could not acquire the

wherewithal to redeem them prior to the end of their term, or to support them after its expiration, to become perpetual slaves; and the religious law offered a way to sanctify that procedure (Ex. 21.5-6).[14] That same Covenant Code converted the rotating system of fallow fields into an institution of purely humanitarian concern—a welfare system for the poor (Ex. 23.10-11). The Covenant Code's system may well have been workable at one time, but over the years, as the centralized bureaucracy grew, that system may well have been gradually replaced by more cumbersome and ineffective procedures of which we have neither knowledge nor direct evidence. The fact that Deuteronomy sees fit to augment the agricultural support of the indigent by the assignment of the triennial tithe to the destitute and the Levites (Deut. 14.28-29) suggests that at best those fields left fallow no longer provided for the poor.[15]

Deuteronomy, for reasons upon which we may only speculate (but we suspect that the long reign of Manasseh had something to do with it!), removed the proclamation of דרור from the realm of royal whim and regularized it in the form of the septennial institution of שמטה, borrowing the terminology and the periodicity of its new institution from the fallow year of the Covenant Code (Deut. 15.1ff.). That the Deuteronomer is using the term שמטה in a new way is self-evident from the biblical text.[16] At the same time Deuteronomy attempted to reform the procedures governing the release of slaves (still limited to a maximum period of service of six years), by including women within the scope of the release provision and by providing for an endowment from the slave's former master. Not all students of these texts have realized that this latter element of the Deuteronomic legislation implies that alienated lands were not returned to their former owners at the septennial release, else why the need for an endowment? Thus we must reject the position of many modern scholars who have argued that the land release provisions of the Jubilee law of Leviticus 25, like the slave release provisions, must once have been septennial.[17]

There is every reason to believe that these reforms, along with most of the others in Deuteronomy, were actually put into practice in Josianic Judah. There is equal reason to assume that many of them were discarded in the power struggle that followed that king's untimely death.

All of these institutions undergo a complex integration and reworking in Leviticus 25. We need not argue, as did Wellhausen and

others,[18] that the fixed, universal periodicity of the fallow year in Leviticus (where it is now called the Sabbatical year) is dependent on the prior development of the idea of universal periodicity in Deuteronomy. They could well be parallel, independent developments. The primacy of the concept of Sabbath in this material and the theological speculation in Leviticus 26 connecting the exile with failure to observe the sabbatical year are evidence enough that the text of Leviticus is late and that the law of Leviticus was never observed in pre-exilic Judah. Of course, except for the sabbatical year, it was never observed in post-exilic Judah either, according to the rabbinic sources,[19] but we are not prepared to go as far as those who claim to find in Nehemiah 5.1-13 evidence that the law of Leviticus was still unknown in his time.[20] Silence does not necessarily imply ignorance, especially in light of the self-aggrandizing nature of Nehemiah's memoirs.

For Leviticus, the fallow year becomes the universal sabbatical year; the tradition of the old tribal יובל is joined with the monarchic דרור proclamation into a new fiftieth-year proclamation of Jubilee, a proclamation marking the sabbath of sabbatical years. Israelite debt slaves are to be released not after six years of service or at the proclamation of a שמטה every seven years, but only at the Jubilee. Of course, cautions Leviticus 25.35-36, they are not really to be treated as slaves at all, but rather as household retainers. Finally, Leviticus makes no provision at all for the annulment of debts.[21]

With the somewhat unlikely exception of the fallow (sabbatical) year, which was actually observed during Second Temple times, the innovations of Leviticus were even less effective than those of Deuteronomy, but they really were much more practical. Deuteronomy, the earliest known manifesto of human rights, demanded that the individual give willingly of his own for the good of society; dreamed (as we still are wont to do) that people acting altruistically together can create a fair and just society. The Levitical author, though, knew more about human nature—saw that slaves were not ever permanently released and that loans would not be made when lenders knew an annulment was near. Where the Levitical writer put his trust was not in human altruism but in God's ability to provide a double yield in the sixth year, just as, legend had it, he had provided a double yield of manna on the sixth day in the wilderness.

Deuteronomy and Leviticus are thus mutually incompatible systems, a fact that prohibited the practical acceptance of either

when the Pentateuch was adopted as the *torah* of Judaism. If we are to believe the witness of Nehemiah, in the Persian era things were still much as they had been in pre-Deuteronomic times, the Persian governor now taking the role of the earlier king. Nehemiah's supposed debate with the leading citizens of Judea culminating in the return of pledges and the annulment of debts (Neh. 5.1-13) was certainly nothing more than a continuation of the ancient practice of *mēšarum* edicts at the beginning of a reign. In Nehemiah's recurrent prayer, 'Remember for my good, O my God, all that I have done for my people', the echoes of such predecessors as Lipit Ishtar and Hammurapi still ring clear.

NOTES

*This paper is largely based on one presented orally before the American Oriental Society meeting in Toronto, April, 1978.

1. A little knowledge of arithmetic would help! The amount of scholarly red ink devoted to the elucidation of the non-problem of how the Jubilee 'year' can be both forty-ninth and fiftieth is quite beyond belief. (See N.P. Lemche, 'The Manumission of Slaves—the Fallow Year—the Sabbatical Year—the Jobel Year', *VT* 26 [1976], 46f.) There can be no doubt that the year during which the Jubilee was proclaimed was also a sabbatical year (cf. Lev. 25.11-12). But this does not mean that there were two fallow years in a row. (Vv. 20-22, usually misinterpreted to imply this, clearly state that planting was forbidden for one year only.) So how can the יובל (*Yōbēl*) be both fiftieth year and seventh seventh (forty-ninth)? If we keep in mind that the יובל is not really a year but only a proclamation at the beginning of a year, then the solution is clear. The first year of the next יובל cycle is the year at the start of which the יובל itself was proclaimed. Thus the next sabbatical year will be the eighth from the יובל, and at the start of the seventh sabbatical year, the fiftieth from the beginning of the current יובל cycle, the next יובל is to be proclaimed.

2. See especially Lemche, 'Manumission', 38-59; and idem, '*Andurārum* and *Mīšarum*: Comments on the Problem of Social Edicts and their Application in the Ancient Near East', *JNES* 38 (1979), 11-22, and the references given there.

3. F.R. Kraus, *Ein Edikt des Königs Ammi-Ṣaduqa von Babylon* (Studia et Documenta ad Iure Orientis Antiqui Pertinentia 5; Leiden: E.J. Brill, 1958).

4. The evidence for the relevance of the *mēsharum* for property transactions is only indirect, as noted by J.J. Finkelstein in 'Some New *Mīsharum* Material and its Implications', *Assyriological Studies* 16 (1965), 242. Since

there exist Old Babylonian contracts stating that a given transaction has taken place after a *mēsharum* act (or other equivalent term), there is hardly reason to doubt that certain (probably debt related) land transactions were subject to royal release. But we hardly need claim, as did Finkelstein, that 'at the promulgation of the *mīsharum* formal commissions were established to review real estate sales ...'

5. Finkelstein's half-hearted attempt, apparently prompted by B. Landsberger, to suggest a septennial periodicity for such edicts in Old Babylonian times must be deemed a failure. Assyriologists who wish to venture into the realm of biblical parallels ought to pay a little more attention to inner-biblical problems before taking off down blind alleys!

6. Others have surmised, correctly it seems to me, that the biblical motif of the hoped-for arrival of a new king is at least partly related to the expected amnesty that that enthronement would entail. See Lemche, 'Manumission', 40.

7. The shift of long *ā* in *(an)durārum* to *ō* in *dĕrōr* suggests that the borrowing of the term occurred in second-millennium Canaanite where it was subsequently subject to the Canaanite vowel shift. Those, like Lemche ('Manumission', 57), who would argue for a borrowing in Neo-Assyrian times have the burden of linguistic evidence against them.

8. See *CAD* Ṣ, s.v. *ṣamātu*.

9. Cf. Henry Schaeffer, *Hebrew Tribal Economy and the Jubilee as Illustrated in Semitic and Indo-European Village Communities* (Leipzig: J.C. Hinrichs, 1922), passim.

10. It is patently impossible for the יובל of the Numbers story to be the same יובל prescribed in Lev. 25. If the function of the יובל from its inception was to return property to its original owner, then at the יובל the property of the daughters of Zelophehad could not possibly end up in the hands of a new tribe. It is clear, rather, that at the time of this יובל, lands currently allotted to members of the tribe (apparently, no matter how they acquired them) became property of the tribe as a whole and subject to reapportionment by lot (גורל).

11. The etymology of the term יובל remains uncertain. For a summary of the various views, see R. North, *Sociology of the Biblical Jubilee* (AnBib 4; Rome: Pontifical Biblical Institute, 1954), 96-108. I. Shifman's contention that the term can be found at Ugarit ('The Ugaritic Jubilee', *Vestnik Drevnei Istorii* 132 [1965], 94-99 [in Russian]) has been refuted convincingly by L. Milano, 'Sul presunto giubileo a Ugarit (PRU V 9)', *Orientis Antiqui Collectio* 16 (1977), 23-33.

An awareness of the connection between the Jubilee and tribal society may be preserved in the early Rabbinic midrash that tells us that the Jubilee was never observed after the destruction of Samaria and the ensuing dissolution of the twelve tribes (Sifra, BeHar, 2:3).

12. There is some slight evidence that the entire procedure may have

preserved the more general Akkadian name *mēšarum* in the Hebraized version *mēšārîm*. See Moshe Weinfeld, *Deuteronomy and the Deuteronomic School* (Oxford: Clarendon Press, 1972), 152f.

13. Cf. Henry Schaeffer, *The Social Legislation of the Primitive Semites* (New Haven: Yale University, 1915), 177.

14. Jeremiah 34.12f. gives evidence that in his time the prescribed six-year term was regularly ignored in any case.

15. Of course, having disenfranchised the local Levites, Deuteronomy had more poor people for which to provide!

16. Cf. Deut. 15.2, וזה דבר השמטה. There should be no need to define a term referring to a well-known institution.

17. Many have connected the practice of land distribution (i.e., יובל) with the fallow year cycle (cf. Ephraim Neufeld, 'Socio-economic Background of *Yōbēl* and *Šemiṭṭā*', *Revista Studia Orientalia* 33 [1958], 69-72), thus providing an outstanding example of the utter confusion prevalent in this field.

18. Julius Wellhausen, *Prolegomena to the History of Ancient Israel* (New York: Meridian Books, 1957), 116ff.

19. Cf. S. Safrai, 'Jubilee in the Second Temple Period', *Encyclopaedia Judaica* (1971), vol. 14, pp. 578f.

20. Cf. Lemche, 'Manumission', 53.

21. Annulments would have been rather disastrous for the priestly class if, as elsewhere in the Near East, the Temple was a major source of capital.

THOUGHTS ON THE USE OF 'CHARISMA' IN OLD TESTAMENT STUDIES

Thomas W. Overholt

I

In a 1968 article on King Solomon[1] Professor Ahlström took exception to Alt's hypothesis that the monarchy in Israel is to be distinguished from that in Judah by virtue of the fact that it was established on a charismatic rather than a dynastic principle. In doing so he pointed out that charisma, which he defined as 'a gift of favor', may have two aspects. There is 'human charisma', the result of a king's having been chosen by the people or by his father, and 'religious charisma', the result of his having been chosen by the deity. The latter may be expressed in any one of a number of ways, for example, through a prophetic oracle or formulae incorporated in the liturgy. In general he agreed with the main lines of T. Thornton's earlier criticism of Alt, namely that kings in Judah and elsewhere in the Near East claimed divine backing and election (cf. Pss 2, 110), that the so-called charismatic kings of Israel were all succeeded by at least one son and therefore were the founders of dynasties, and that there is no evidence that the Israelite kings themselves or Northern prophets like Hosea recognized any special notion of charismatic leadership.[2]

In Ahlström's opinion, to say that only Israel had divine charismatic kingship is to say that the chaos of dynastic change had Yahweh's blessing, but 'charismatic kingship willed by the deity would best be expressed in political stability'.[3] He then went on to argue that Solomon himself had claim to charismatic gifts, and that it is therefore wrong to view his ascension to the throne as simply the result of palace intrigue. 'Charismatic' kingship must ultimately be seen as associated with the election and appointment of monarchs in both Israel and Judah. Quoting Donner to the effect that charisma does not really concern the individual king so much as the dynasty itself, Ahlström suggested that the reverse is also true: 'It is the

individual king who is the bearer of the reality inherent within the dynasty'.[4]

This raises a problem, however. As usually employed, the term 'charisma' refers to an individual with special gifts. How, then, can we apply it to a king as representative of the institution of the monarchy, especially to Solomon, the archetypal bureaucrat? The term 'charisma', as everyone is aware, enters OT scholarship by way of Max Weber, who clearly applied it to gifted individuals. The charismatic leader, Weber said, was one who knew only 'inner determination . . . and restraint'.[5] Charisma itself is 'a certain quality of an individual personality' not attainable by ordinary men and setting apart its bearer from them. It is regarded by members of the society 'as of divine origin or as exemplary', and forms the 'basis' for treating an individual as a leader.[6] Thus Weber could define a prophet as 'a purely individual bearer of charisma, who by virtue of his mission proclaims a religious doctrine or divine commandment'.[7]

The conception of charisma which centers on the individual bearer of it has been used rather successfully in descriptions of the early Israelite judges. A. Malamat, for example, explicitly adopts Weber's notion that there are three categories of authority: traditional, legal-rational, and charismatic. The first two of these types share a desire for stability and permanence, while the third is personal, sporadic, unstable, and independent of hierarchic structure. Though the three types tend to mix and overlap, the charismatic agent is still identifiable because of his extraordinary qualities and gifts which mark him as a divine agent. Malamat also points out, as did Weber, that a prerequisite for the appearance of such an agent is 'a society willing to recognize this type of authority', since 'without such recognition, charisma lacks all substantiality and remains meaningless'.[8] After describing the historical situation of Israel in the period of the judges, he enumerates the components in the judge's personality and charismatic rule. Among the latter are the fact that authority was bestowed on the charismatic leader spontaneously; that such leadership was not dependent upon class, status, age, or sex; and that the relationship between the leader and the people rested on emotion, not on formal rules, administration, or coercion. Abimelech (Judg. 9) is seen as the opposite of such leaders in these and other respects, and it is noted that Israelites themselves are pictured as desiring to give charismatic leadership a fixed and stable form, a phenomenon Weber referred to as 'routinization' (Judg. 8.22).

To give a further example, Z. Weisman accepts the consensus that the judges represent a type of leadership defined by Weber as 'charismatic', but warns that this term should not be applied 'to a political regime or to any consecutive historical system of leadership', but 'only to individual leaders as such'. In general he expresses reservations about theories which relate 'charismatic saviors to an old religio-political ideology' of the period of the judges in which Yahweh was thought to be the only king of Israel.[9] The charismatic leaders of the period of the judges were, according to him, neither typical leaders of the era nor ideal leaders created by the Deuteronomists. Each was unique, and his activity spontaneous. The 'origin of their charisma' was the individual qualities which motivated them to arise and fight oppression and the readiness of the people to submit voluntarily to their command.[10]

With the judges, then, we appear to have charismatic leaders functioning as individuals without permanent institutional connections. Ahlström's position, on the other hand, is tantamount to conceiving of charisma as embedded in an institution. Given the usual individualistic conception of charisma, this may seem surprising. In what follows, however, I want to suggest that Weber himself hints that such a conception is possible and that sociologists and anthropologists are now using the term in ways that undermine a rigid distinction between individual and institutional authority. I will also suggest that this broader conception of charisma fits well an understanding of prophecy that emphasizes the social location of the Israelite prophets.

Before turning to those tasks, however, some remarks seem in order on the appropriateness of using Weber in the interpretation of the OT. I do not intend here a comprehensive analysis of Weber's method and results, a task of some enormity, but rather an assessment of such an analysis made by J. Holstein.[11] The gist of Holstein's argument is that many biblical scholars have come under the influence of Weber, with the following unfortunate results: often they have misunderstood what Weber meant, and worse, many have accepted Weber's ideas about proper historical method.

Holstein uses the notion of charisma to illustrate what he takes to be a common misunderstanding of Weber:

> ... the very scholars who praise Weber for having introduced this concept into biblical studies do not appear to understand how Weber himself used it. According to Weber, the term charismatic

> was purely descriptive and in no sense explanatory. If an individual succeeded outside the bounds of institutional authority, he had charisma. If he failed, he did not. Since no intrinsic qualities set the category of charisma apart, the term can be applied only after the fact. Accordingly, Weber usually did not use the term to explain why or how an individual prevailed, but simply to separate those who did prevail from those who did not. However, in biblical studies the notion of charisma oftentimes is employed as if it had intrinsic properties which thereby explain success.[12]

This claim, however, is not altogether accurate. Weber himself speaks of charisma as a 'certain quality of an individual personality'.[13] What needs to be noticed is that he conceives of charisma as part of a social process in which both the charismatic qualities of the leader and society's response to them play a crucial role. The leader's claim, Weber says, breaks down unless he is 'recognized by those to whom he feels . . . sent'. Such recognition 'is decisive for the validity of charisma', and is experienced by followers as a 'duty'. Furthermore, continued lack of success will likely bring about the disappearance of charismatic authority because such recognition will be withdrawn.[14] Holstein's failure to take this into account is perhaps explained by his views about Weber's method.

Holstein seems to have two reasons for objecting to Weber's use of 'ideal types' as aids in historical explanation and to the 'controlling methodological principle' of Weber's exegesis, namely 'that different sociological factors produce different world views', or, otherwise put, 'that sociological conditions determine the form and content of an individual's acts and thought'.[15] In the first place different investigators adopting Weber's premise and viewing the same data often come up with quite different results.[16] The method is thus inherently dangerous and subject to bias. As Holstein says with respect to one example,

> Scholars who cannot reach even the most elemental agreement in regard, e.g., to the Levites, aver in unison that the first step in understanding the Hebrew Bible is in becoming familiar with the environmental conditions in which the various sources were created and redacted. Since, as noted previously, the text does not provide this information, modern biblical scholarship is replete with examples of using only those texts which support a given reconstruction or interpretation.[17]

Secondly, the method is itself culturally conditioned and depends upon a notion of the analytic superiority of 20th century Western thought.[18]

Holstein appears to believe that we can achieve an objective account of historical facts and that the conscious adoption of a methodological stance is tantamount to pre-judging all data. He says of Weber that 'he sought corroborative data to justify his ideal types because, in effect, he already knew the essential qualities of biblical thought *before* he consulted the text'.[19] But certainly that is too simple-minded a view. Weber did not pick the 'ideal types' (e.g., charisma) for the study of Ancient Judaism *before* he had *any* familiarity with the texts. C. Rodd says of him that 'that unwillingness to accept secondary evidence which led him to learn Hebrew when he was sent to confirmation classes, so that he could read the Old Testament in the original language, drove him to master the main works in the Old Testament scholarship of his day'.[20] There is always a dialectical relationship between theory and data, and no theory in the social sciences is likely to 'save' all the data. But this ought not to lead to a simple rejection of Weber's exegesis as circular (as Holstein puts it, 'he knew what he knew because he knew it').[21]

Finally, the conclusion Holstein draws from his assessment seems vastly over-stated. He says,

> If a biblical scholar subscribes to Weber's notion of the unavoidable correspondence between thought and environment, then he should provide his reader with information about the environmental dynamics which shaped his *own* thought. He should indicate clearly that his reader is to pay more attention to the *how* and the *why* of his argumentation than to its substance. That is, he should be prepared to be read as he himself reads; he should be prepared not to be taken seriously.[22]

With the first of these assertions who would argue? But the logic of the second eludes me. It is as if Holstein believes it impossible to attempt at the same time to set a document from the past in its social and historical context and be interested in it for its own sake, valuing the intentions and capabilities of the ancient authors and redactors. Attempting to see artifacts from the past in their proper context hardly seems to me the simple equivalent of not taking them seriously.

C. Rodd has also criticized the Weberian approach to biblical studies, contending that the texts are essentially resistant to sociological

analysis. At one point he seems to acknowledge the usefulness of attempting 'to discover general patterns of social relationships', only objecting to the use of some potentially confusing ideal types in the analysis (e.g., 'peasants').[23] But his final assessment is negative:

> This leads me to ask whether the past is ever amenable to sociological analysis, since Weber's attempt to conduct such an analysis of an ancient civilisation set the problem in high relief. The difficulty is not simply a matter of the paucity of data, although for more distant periods this will almost always be a factor. The basic problem lies in the fact that the evidence has a 'set' and cannot be forced by the researcher to reveal a choice between two or more options. The sociologist can neither decide what set of empirical facts he will collect nor posit and test hypotheses, both of which operations are central to scientific sociology, if the study of man in society can every be truly 'scientific'.[24]

This point is emphasized in a recent review of works by J. Gager and R. Carroll in which Rodd criticizes the acceptance by biblical scholars of sociological theories (the validity of which is debated among sociologists themselves), which are then used to organize and interpret evidence. In such an undertaking the chances of error are great, both because the biblical materials are not primarily historical and because one is 'involved in transferring theories derived from evidence in one kind of society to a very different society'. Rodd contends that 'the liability to error is increased when theories that operate at a high level of abstraction [e.g., "ideal types", "millenarian cult", "charismatic personality"] are applied directly and in their totality to a narrow and highly specific situation', and he is critical of any attempt 'to posit parts of [a theoretical] model for which evidence is missing, on the grounds that the absence of such evidence is accidental and the entire model was a reality' in the period of biblical history being studied.[25]

In my opinion this is unnecessarily restrictive. The underlying issue here is Rodd's insistence upon experimentation and participant observation as the means by which sociological theories and models are to be tested, possibilities for which are precluded in exercises in 'historical' sociology. It would seem reasonable to suppose, however, that theories about basic social phenomena widely 'tested' in more contemporary cultures would be found to have some degree of applicability to biblical times as well. One must of course be aware of

the assumptions one brings to the material under study and be cautious in their application, but precisely because the biblical texts are, as Rodd says, primarily theological rather than historical in character one needs help in trying to uncover the social-historical processes and events which lie behind them. To the extent that basic patterns can be observed for, say, charismatic leadership or prophetic intermediation in a wide variety of cultures and periods of time, it would seem reasonable to hope that such patterns might aid us in understanding aspects of life in biblical times which the authors had no interest in discussing directly. One might cite in this connection Gottwald's work on the period of the judges and Wilson's on the prophets.[26] This is a point of general interest for what follows.

II

We have already seen that Weber himself speaks of charisma in terms that transcend the merely individual and idiosyncratic, and subsequent discussion has elaborated upon this point. We need now to sketch the general outlines of this development of Weber's view.

In Weber the whole discussion of charisma arises in the context of an analysis of the three ways of legitimizing claims of authority within a society. Such claims may be based on traditional grounds, in which case one encounters belief in the 'sanctity of immemorial traditions' and personal loyalty to a chief or other leader occupying a traditionally sanctioned position of authority.[27] They may in the second place be based on rational grounds, in which case there will be a belief in the legality of normative rules and the right of those in authority to issue commands. Finally, they may be based on charismatic grounds, 'resting on devotion to the specific exceptional sanctity, heroism or exemplary character of an individual person, and of the normative patterns or order revealed or ordained by him'.[28] Weber noted, however, that there were no historical cases of pure forms of these ideal types.[29] Furthermore, the social dimensions of the operation of charismatic authority are clear in the dependence of the leader upon society's response, as we have already seen.

Weber observes that 'in its pure form charismatic authority has a character specifically foreign to every-day routine structures. The social relationships directly involved are strictly personal, based on the validity and practice of charismatic personal qualities.' It is therefore evident that if such authority is to be anything but transitory, it will have 'to become radically changed. Indeed, in its

pure form charismatic authority may be said to exist only in the process of originating.' It must, in a word, become routinized, and the interest of the followers in establishing a mode of succession for the continuance of leadership and of administrative staff and disciples in appropriating 'powers of control' and 'economic advantages' are strong motivators of the process of routinization.[30]

On the basis of this notion of routinization it is easy to get the impression that after the departure of the individual charismatic figure charisma dies or is lost in the institution. E. Shils, as a matter of fact, criticizes Weber for drawing too sharp a distinction between charisma and rational-legal legitimizations of power. It is rather the case that 'an attentuated, mediated, institutionalized charismatic propensity is present in the routine functioning of society'. The 'charismatic quality of an individual', whether perceived by others or by the individual himself, must therefore be more broadly conceived as having its base in a perceived connection between him and 'some very central feature of man's existence'.[31] In this manner Shils attempts, as Eisenstadt puts it, to bridge the 'gap' between charisma as an 'extraordinary event or quality and as a constituent element in any orderly social life'.[32] The distinction between the charismatic and the routine cannot be complete or extreme, since the charismatic leader or his followers must take some steps to assure the continuation of his/their influence. Though this is 'the first step in the routinization of charisma', it does not necessarily imply the loss of vision and flattening of the initial impetus. Weber in fact used the term 'charisma of office' (and Shils, 'contact charisma') to denote 'the process through which the charismatic characteristics are transferred from the unique personality or the unstructured group to orderly institutional reality' by infusing into it some of the charismatic vision. The dichotomy between charismatic and routine thereby becomes blurred, to be 'revived again only in situations of extreme and intensive social disorganization and change'.[33]

Another way to put the matter is in terms of society's need for order. According to Shils, 'there is a central zone in the structure of every society'. This center is not as such spatially located, but rather is constituted by the symbols, the ultimate and irreducible values and beliefs, which 'govern the society'. But in addition to being a 'phenomenon of the realm of values and beliefs' it is 'also a phenomenon of the realm of action, . . . a structure of activities, of roles and persons, within the framework of institutions. It is in these

roles that the values and beliefs which are central are embodied and propounded'.[34] Now because of the critical nature of society's need for order, that which generates it 'arouses the charismatic responsiveness', and those in contact with the center 'become the objects of the attribution of charisma'. In this sense 'all effective rulers . . . have charismatic qualities attributed to them'. The fundamental laws of a country, says Shils, arouse a sense of *mysterium tremendum*. Therefore, even in a rational-legal bureaucracy charisma will be present, though it may be dispersed among roles rather than attributed to separate individuals. In such cases the persons occupying these roles are understood to manifest a 'larger center of tremendous power'.[35]

The interplay between the charismatic and his society is a constant theme in studies based on actual manifestations of charismatic leadership. W. Friedland, for example, studied native political and union leaders in Tanganyika, and noted that one of the common features of the activities of such persons was that they expressed 'sentiments which had been inchoate in the society but which had been brought to consciousness recently by a handful of people'. This led him to propose that 'it is only when the message conveyed by charismatics to social groups is relevant and meaningful within the social context that authority emerges'.[36] Similarly, T. Oommen's study of Bhoodan Gramdan, a land reform movement in modern India, led him to the conclusion that a charismatic will be accepted as leader when the content of his message 'is appropriate to the social climate'. But he also noted that leaders in modern secular contexts have frequently been labeled charismatic (his examples include Hitler, Nasser, Nkrumah, Kennedy, Krushchev, and Nehru). Now these men were holders of high public office, and therefore 'much of their authority' was rational-legal, that is, came by virtue of their office. This suggests that 'political equilibrium' aparently cannot be maintained by a charismatic leader who does not occupy a high government position.[37] David Aberle states the case from the other side: 'By definition, charisma is associated with any office not wholly bound by rules, and no office can be wholly bound by rules.'[38]

Or consider the case of a small and heterogeneous group of Indians living on the coastal plain in northwest Mexico. These people, who had shown a definite disinclination to follow any leader, were for a brief period in the late 1940s organized into a cohesive unit by a *curandero* named Giobila for the purpose of repulsing outside encroachment into their territory. In considering this series of events

C. Erasmus pondered the question of the extent to which an individual can influence his culture or must be seen as 'simply a tool of tradition'. He concluded that a leader or innovator 'must be intelligible to the group and must appeal to the group through its focus of interests'. This means that 'genius' will 'always be limited by the factors of group interest and understanding. To be achieved, "genius" must also be ascribed'.[39] Somewhat more generally, A. and D. Willner argued that the charismatic leader has a two-fold mission: 'the destruction of the old order' and 'political development' (i.e., 'the building of the promised new and better order'). In the context of new countries this implies the double goal of 'achieving and maintaining' an autonomous and viable state or political community' and 'gaining and maintaining central government capacity to manage technological modernization and cope with its socioeconomic concomitants'. Such an undertaking is necessarily beset by dilemmas and conflicts in the face of which the charismatic leader must function as a unifying symbol 'in a society fissioned by parochial identifications and particularistic goals' and in addition maintain 'internal cohesion' by mounting attacks against outside leaders and countries.[40]

As a final example, we turn to T. Beidelman's study of priests and prophets among the Nuer of Nilotic Africa. One might expect that these two types of religious functionaries would be rather clearly divided with respect to the possession of charisma, the latter manifesting it, the former not, but Beidelman found this not to be the case. To be sure, the priests were born into lineages, held narrowly-defined, life-long authority, and spoke for men to god. But they also sometimes tried 'to augment their power and influence through charisma' both by means of 'political manipulation' (spokesmanship, leadership in raids, and the like) and 'claims to more diffuse supernatural powers'. In the prophets, of course, the charismatic was a primary characteristic. Since 'all adult Nuer men have some contact with Spirit', they were those persons 'who have succeeded in securing wider social endorsement of their peculiar status as mediators'. And 'unlike priests', they had to 'manifest anomalous, extraordinary attributes to demonstrate the validity of their claims to a new and unusual authority'. Yet sometimes these prophets sought 'to routinize their charismatic power by converting this power into corporate, more stable authority'. From this evidence Beidelman concluded that Weber's analytical category of charismatic leadership

must be divided into two sub-categories: revolutionaries who are outside of and opposed to the social system, and persons institutionalized within the system who appear regularly or periodically to effect temporary configurations and provide means by which impediments between social ends and social means are ironed out.[41]

By way of conclusion, then, it seems accurate to say that, while individuals are bearers of charisma, it makes no sense to talk about the manifestation of charisma apart from a social context. Nor is society to be conceived of as simply a passive recipient, since its recognition (authorization) is a necessary part of the coming into being and continued operation of a charismatic leader. This recognition is possible because the charismatic figure's message relates to an existing or emerging center of value and order, and because he or she operates within the bounds of the society's expectations and toleration.[42] And when the charismatic figure is gone, the charisma may remain, embodied in the relationship of rationally-legally authorized leaders to the central powers of the society.

Thus Ahlström, though he cites none of the literature discussing Weber, has correctly seen that the case for a 'charismatic kingship' in ancient Israel is wrongly argued and easily refuted if one focuses on the individualistic side of the phenomenon, while in the broader view one can discern a charismatic element in the monarchies of both Israel and Judah. Solomon, that archetypal Judean bureaucrat, is as much a bearer of royal charisma as Jeroboam I or one of the other Northern kings designated by a prophet, and this in a double sense: he was, according to the ideology of kingship, chosen by Yahweh, and he was, by virtue of his role, the one who stood in the closest relationship to the nation's center of order and value, the religio-political establishment of cultus and court.

III

Of the three groups of individuals in the OT with whom the term charisma is frequently associated, we have already mentioned two, the judges and the kings. The third is the prophets, and when the concept is employed to interpret their activity, it seems only natural to focus attention on the qualities and conditions which set these individuals off from the rest of society and its institutions.[43]

P. Berger's article on 'Charisma and Religious Innovation: The Social Location of Israelite Prophecy' was an attempt to move the discussion in a different direction. After reviewing some of the

'classic Protestant interpretation(s) of the canonical prophets' as 'brave individualists', Berger went on to cite what he considered a more recent scholarly consensus linking them with the cultus. From this he concluded that charisma can 'originate within the traditionally established institutions—and, even there, be sufficiently powerful to effectively change these institutions'. It is therefore not necessary for charisma to orginate 'in social marginality' and individuality. As a result, Weber's notion of 'the innovating power of charisma' is strengthened by allowing us to see it also as a possible trait of individuals located at the center of the institutional fabric in question, a power of "radicalization" from within rather than of challenge from without'.[44] Although Berger has been taken to task for assuming too uncritically the cultic location of Israelite prophecy,[45] he did call attention to a typical over-emphasis on the prophets' individuality and suggest a way of speaking about them as charismatics compatible with their functioning within a social context.

There are two qualities by means of which such prophets can be recognized. The first of these is their actions. Sometimes these are merely unusual or striking, like Hosea's marriages, Isaiah's walking naked and barefoot through the streets for three years, and Jeremiah's wearing a yoke or breaking a pot. Such actions both set the prophet off from his fellows and call attention to his divinely inspired message.[46] On other occasions they have more the nature of miracles, like Elijah's calling down fire from heaven and Elijah's and Elisha's wondrously multiplying food and bringing the dead to life. I believe that such stories give us a glimpse of the social process by which prophets were authorized, as I have elsewhere attempted to show.[47] The second is their words, and indeed such 'words' constitute the bulk of what we have reported about the OT prophets. What can we say about them? I think both that they stand in some relationship to divine revelation and that they were spoken to people upon whose response the fate of the prophet in large part depended. I have previously tried to describe what I take to the nature of this 'prophetic process'.[48]

As to how these prophets stand with respect to the social order, there are two broad possibilities: they may have been 'central intermediaries', who were closely related to the central power structure of their society and served as its official links with the divine, or 'peripheral intermediaries', who were outside of and often antagonistic to this central structure.[49] It is tempting to see only the

latter type as charismatic, but this hardly seems correct. The presence of charisma is at least as apparent in the central prophet Zedekiah b. Chenaanah acting out his vision (1 Kings 22.11) as it is in Micaiah, a peripheral prophet, telling his (vv. 19-23). In Jeremiah 27-28 it is the peripheral prophet who acts (27.2) and the central prophet who speaks (28.2-4), and as the story develops, initial action is accompanied by words (27.3ff.) and initial words by action (28.10). On the exterior there seems little to distinguish these prophets from one another, and each appears to stand in a definable relationship to what he and some group of Israelites or Judeans considered the society's center of value and power. This illustrates again the importance of an amplified definition of 'charisma'. The marks of charisma are real enough, but seem never to be so self-validating (so obviously attributable to divine power and intention) as to be utterly unambiguous, and the OT gives no indication that the problem of distinguishing between 'true' and 'false' prophecy was ever satisfactorily resolved. The later reader, given the advantages of hindsight, may overlook the dilemma of those who originally heard the prophets, and may therefore need to be reminded that in no case is what the prophet does or says intelligible apart from the social context of his performance.[50]

Finally, one of the things that has emerged from social-scientific studies of charisma is that its manifestations can be seen to conform to societal stereotypes. Indeed, C. Keyes has described charismatic individuals as persons who are 'deemed by their fellow men to have an especially close relationship with the sacred because they have assimilated some of their actions . . . to models that are recognized as sacred signs'.[51] This being the case, one sometimes suspects that resistance to using this concept in the interpretation of biblical materials stems at least in part from a theological bias on the part of the interpreter, viz. that the actions of God cannot be limited by such stereotypes.

In my opinion Weber's ideal type 'charisma' has been a productive concept in critical biblical studies, one which has by no means outlived its usefulness.[52] As developed by subsequent discussion the concept has become richer and more analytically powerful, and my own feeling is that in the future the insights it suggests will have less to do with the personal qualities of the charismatic individual than with the nature of the relationship between such individuals and various groups within their societies at large. Since every

religious reality is simultaneously a social reality, how could it be otherwise?[53]

NOTES

1. G.W. Ahlström, 'Solomon, the Chosen One', *HR* 8 (1968-69), 93-110.
2. T.C.G. Thornton, 'Charismatic Kingship in Israel and Judah', *JTS* n.s. 14 (1963), 1-11.
3. Ahlström, 'Solomon', 97.
4. Ahlström, 'Solomon', 110.
5. S.N. Eisenstadt, ed., *Max Weber on Charisma and Institution Building* (Chicago: University of Chicago Press, 1968), 20.
6. Eisenstadt, *Max Weber on Charisma*, 48.
7. Eisenstadt, *Max Weber on Charisma*, 253.
8. Abraham Malamat, 'Charismatic Leadership in the Book of Judges', *Magnalia Dei: The Mighty Acts of God*, ed. F. Cross, W. Lemke, and P. Miller (Garden City: Doubleday, 1976), 159.
9. Ze'ev Weisman, 'Charismatic Leaders in the Era of the Judges', *ZAW* 89 (1977), 401, 410.
10. Weisman, 'Charismatic Leaders', 411.
11. J.A. Holstein, 'Max Weber and Biblical Scholarship', *HUCA* 46 (1975), 159-79.
12. Holstein, 'Max Weber and Biblical Scholarship', 159-60.
13. Eisenstadt, *Max Weber on Charisma*, 48; on prophecy, cf. 253-61. Robert C. Tucker has attempted to specify these qualities for two types of charismatic figures, the prophet and the activist. Cf. 'The Theory of Charismatic Leadership', *Philosophers and Kings: Studies in Leadership*, ed. D. Rustow (New York: Braziller, 1970), 86-89.
14. Eisenstadt, *Max Weber on Charisma*, 20, 49f.; cf. 254. Bryan R. Wilson places a great deal of emphasis on the relationship between the leader and his followers, which he takes to be based on 'faith'. Cf. *The Noble Savages: The Primitive Origins of Charisma and Its Contemporary Survival* (Berkeley: University of California Press, 1975), 5-7, 93-95. Weston La Barre provides a very forcefully stated description of charismatic qualities and relationships from a psychological point of view. Cf. *The Ghost Dance* (New York: Delta, 1970), 44, 48, 357-85.
15. Holstein, 'Max Weber and Biblical Scholarship', 164, 167.
16. Holstein, 'Max Weber and Biblical Scholarship', 165-67.
17. Holstein, 'Max Weber and Biblical Scholarship', 174.
18. Holstein, 'Max Weber and Biblical Scholarship', 169, 175.
19. Holstein, 'Max Weber and Biblical Scholarship', 169.
20. Cyril S. Rodd, 'Max Weber and Ancient Judaism', *SJTh* 32 (1979), 457.

21. Holstein, 'Max Weber and Biblical Scholarship', 173.

22. Holstein, 'Max Weber and Biblical Scholarship', 179 23. Rodd, 'Max Weber and Ancient Judaism', 467.

24. Rodd, 'Max Weber and Ancient Judaism', 469.

25. Cyril S. Rodd, 'On Applying Sociological Theory to Biblical Studies', *JSOT* 19 (1981), 103-105.

26. Norman K. Gottwald, *The Tribes of Yahweh* (Maryknoll, N.Y.: Orbis, 1979); Robert R. Wilson, *Prophecy and Society in Ancient Israel* (Philadelphia: Fortress, 1980).

27. Eisenstadt, *Max Weber on Charisma*, 46.

28. Eisenstadt, *Max Weber on Charisma*, 46.

29. Eisenstadt, *Max Weber on Charisma*, 47.

30. Eisenstadt, *Max Weber on Charisma*, 54, 58; cf. 39-42, 54-61.

31. Edward Shils, 'Charisma, Order and Status', *American Sociological Review* 30 (1965), 200.

32. Eisenstadt, *Max Weber on Charisma*, xxvi.

33. Eisenstadt, *Max Weber on Charisma*, xx-xxii.

34. Edward Shils, 'Center and Periphery', *The Logic of Personal Knowledge: Essays Presented to Michael Polanyi* (London: Routledge and Kegan Paul, 1961); quoted by Eisenstadt, *Max Weber on Charisma*, xxx.

35. Shils, 'Charisma, Order and Status', 203-206; cf. Eisenstadt, *Max Weber on Charisma*, xxix-xxxii. For an application of these insights to early Christianity cf. John H. Schütz, 'Charisma and Social Reality in Primitive Christianity', *Journal of Religion* 54 (1974), 51-70. On the other hand, Bryan R. Wilson would like to limit the use of the term 'charisma' to its 'strong sense', which he equates with Weber's notion of the 'charisma of the prophet', and is critical of Shils and others for debasing the term. Cf. *The Noble Savages*, 1-36.

36. William H. Friedland, 'For a Sociological Concept of Charisma', *Social Forces* 43 (1963), 23, 21.

37. T.K. Oommen, 'Charisma, Social Structure, and Social Change', *Comparative Studies in Society and History* 10 (1967-68), 85, 96.

38. David F. Aberle, 'Religico-Magical Phenomena and Power, Prediction, and Control', *Southwestern Journal of Anthopology* 22 (1966), 227.

39. C. Erasmus, 'The Leader vs. Tradition: A Case Study', *American Anthropologist* 54 (1952), 175f.

40. Ann Ruth Willner and Dorothy Willner, 'The Rise and Role of Charismatic Leaders', *Annals of the American Academy of Political and Social Science* no. 348 (1965), 84-88.

41. T.O. Beidelman, 'Nuer Priests and Prophets: Charisma, Authority and Power Among the Nuer', *The Translation of Culture*, ed. T.O. Beidelman (London: Tavistock, 1971), 381-99, 406. For a view of 'charismatic processes' as involving complex interactions of the leader, his or her movement, and the rest of society and taking place on both the psychological and

organizational levels, cf. J. Fabian, 'Führer und Führung in den prophetisch-messianischen Bewegungen der (ehemaligen) Kolonialvölker', *Anthropos* 58 (1963), 773-809.

42. On the latter point cf. Wilson, *Prophecy and Society*, 51-62, 66-68, and the literature cited there.

43. To cite but one example, G. von Rad makes repeated reference to 'charisma', which appeared in many forms in ancient Israel, including the prophets, and was 'an absolutely constitutive factor in Jahwism'. In these discussions the emphasis is always on divine inspiration of individuals, though such inspiration may result in a social product like 'poems and the Psalter'. Cf. *Old Testament Theology* (New York: Harper and Row, 1962, 1965), vol. I, 93-102, vol. II, 50-69, and *passim*.

44. Peter L. Berger, 'Charisma and Religious Innovation: The Social Location of Israelite Prophecy', *American Sociological Review* 28 (1963), 950.

45. James G. Williams, 'The Social Location of Israelite Prophecy', *JAAR* 37 (1969), 153-65; Wilson, *Prophecy and Society*, 10.

46. Cf. G. Fohrer, *Die symbolischen Handlungen der Propheten*, 2nd edn (Zurich: Zwingli Verlag, 1968).

47. T.W. Overholt, 'Seeing is Believing: The Social Setting of Prophetic Acts of Power', *JSOT* 23 (1982), 3-31. As the studies cited above suggest, one of the most common things said about charismatic authority is that social recognition is, as Weber puts it, 'decisive for the validity of charisma'. Eisenstadt, *Max Weber on Charisma*, 49.

48. Cf. T.W. Overholt, 'The Ghost Dance of 1890 and the Nature of the Prophetic Process', *Ethnohistory* 21 (1974), 37-63; 'Jeremiah and the Nature of the Prophetic Process', *Scripture in History and Theology*, ed. A. Merrill and T. Overholt (Pittsburgh: Pickwick, 1977), 129-50; 'Prophecy: The Problem of Cross-Cultural Comparison', *Semeia* 21 (1981), 55-78.

49. For a discussion of this distinction cf. Wilson, *Prophecy and Society*, 37-41, 69-86. Wilson has been influenced in his use of these terms by I.M. Lewis, *Ecstatic Religion* (Baltimore: Penguin, 1971).

50. Cf. Burke O. Long, 'Social Diemensions of Prophetic Conflict', *Semeia* 21 (1981), 31-53.

51. 'Charisma: From Social Life to Sacred Biography', *Charisma and Sacred Biography*, ed. M. Williams (Chico, CA: Scholars Press, 1982), 1. In the same volume see also Pamela T. Amoss, 'Resurrection, Healing and "The Shake": The Story of John and Mary Slocum', 97-98.

52. Bengt Holmberg's *Paul and Power* (Philadelphia: Fortress, 1980) is an example of a very careful and productive interpretation of NT materials in light of the phenomenon of 'charismatic authority'.

53. David L. Petersen's *The Roles of Israel's Prophets* (JSOTS 17; Sheffield: JSOT, 1981) came into my hands after the completion of this study. While I am inclined to attribute more usefulness to 'charisma' as an

analytical concept than he, I very much agree both that this concept alone is an insufficient basis for an interpretation of prophecy and that the often-assumed opposition between charisma and office only confuses the issue (cf. especially 9-15).

THE BIOGRAPHIC MODE IN HEBREW HISTORIOGRAPHY

Jack M. Sasson

I

Inordinately fond of apothegmatic, Carlyle once wrote that 'History is the essence of innumerable biographies'. Biblical scholarship of the 19th century—not to insist in tracing this perspective within the commentaries of medieval Judaism and Christendom—has frequently recognized that the biblical text—and I am now quoting Skinner—'[treated] the heroes of [legends] as personifications or eponymous ancestors of tribes or peoples, whose history and mutual relations are exhibited under the guise of personal biography'.[1] This scholarship defined its task largely as one which, by fragmenting individual biographies into manageable episodes and by subjecting each of them to rigorous historical analysis, would recover trustworthy evidence in order either to construct a realistic history of Israel or to assess its various institutions. That task, in its manifold permutations and contrasting conclusions, will always remain central to biblical research.

It may be worth our while, however, to supplement these undertakings by delving into the literary processes which convey the past in such a starkly restrictive fashion. While such an inquiry will eventually need to turn to an agenda not too dissimilar from that currently obtaining in historical research, in its initial phases, however, this approach will permit the researcher to shelve judgments regarding the veracity of the Hebrew's facts and to proceed with analysis without confronting extra-biblical accounts. Thus, it will not be the task of this enterprise to gauge the distance which separates biographies from reality nor to speculate on their totemic or euhemeristic potential. The Hebrew text, in the format that is now before us, becomes the focus of attention; the art of historiographer, the object of our observations; and the structure of biographies, the subject in hand.

Despite the variety of its manifestations, the biographical mode of conveying Old Testament history can be allocated *ex hypothesi* to two forms. At the outset it should be made clear, however, that the Old Testament biographies *gravitate* toward one form or the other, with no example fulfilling wholly the requirements of either. Borrowing for the time being the vocabulary of the drama,[2] I label these the melodramatic and the cumulative. A more elegant term, the episodic, could also be attached to the second mode. The melodramatic biography tends to occupy larger space and is infinitely more complex than the episodic. Indeed, in some cases shorter examples of the episodic can be framed within a longer melodrama. Although the language used within both differ—with, for example, the episodic resorting less frequently than the melodramatic to visual paronomasia and semantic leitmotif—I cannot claim any earlier antiquity for one form or the other. The fact that appreciably similar literary categories obtain in Ancient Near Eastern, Greek, Roman, Medieval and Renaissance literature should suggest that these two patterns in biographical presentation were probably always coeval, each fulfilling its own purpose even as it addresses the same audience.

II

THE EPISODIC BIOGRAPHY is structured integrally—that is, each tableau contains a narrative which is complete in itself. This does not necessarily mean that a beginning, middle, and end are fully developed in each scene, but it does imply that no information from one episode is crucial to appreciating the dénouement of another. More importantly, the episodic biography is structured disjunctively; that is, the full account is discordant in the sequence of scenes which alternate between tension and relaxation, merriment and pathos, piety and religious obstinancy, etc. Furthermore, this sequencing is artificially chronological, with the possibility of shifting, shuffling, and even skipping scenes without incurring serious damage to the final portrait. Linkage among and between scenes, when it does occur, tends to be rudimentary, and upon closer inspection, sometimes vestigial, satisfying requirements other than those essential to the biography. Cause and effect can rarely be traced among the various tableaux.

The subject of the episodic biography, the one whose *bios*, that is, whose 'mode of living' or 'conduct of life' is to be captured, remains monochromatic within each of his appearances, since complexity and

diversity can only confuse the audience, hindering its capacity to understand the nature of the character within each scene. The emotional range of the hero is, therefore, sharply circumscribed, with introspection and inner enlightenment rarely in evidence. Each scene, however, will deliver a different manifestation of that character, so that, when the series of tableaux about one individual is complete, the hero's portrait will emerge as the sum total of his virtues and failings.

The episodic is filled with secondary characters. Major ones, generally immediate kin to the hero, are sometimes granted their own limelight; but they only supplement the portrait of the main subject by sharpening certain elements of his character. Other actors move in and out of the narrative as needed, without personal past or future. Opposition to the subject is temporary and hardly menacing. However, a major character in the Hebrew *episode* narrative is God. Unlike the melodrama, where his appearance is largely as a *deus ex machina*—providentially resolving or redirecting events from on high—God in the episodic is invariably personally touched by the encounter with the hero. It is not surprising, therefore, that the anthropomorphic passages in the Old Testament tend to be found in episodic narratives.

By way of rudimentary illustration, let me turn to the surface of narratives regarding Abraham. This particular series of scenes is complicated by the fact that the collection is, for theological reasons, allocated to materials concerning Abram and to those concerning Abraham. Because he is bound by the conventions of the episodic, however, the biographer could underscore the major change in his subject mainly by *repeating*, with some variations, the paradigmatic characterizations within three of his selections. Thus, the hero as cunning but eventually successful is developed in the famous wife-sister scenes of chapters 12 and 20; as trusting his wife to make short range decisions about his progeny in 16 and 18; as magnanimous towards Lot in 13 and 18. Other scenes, spread out over the entire portraiture, offer us differing characterizations: warlike and politically shrewd in chapter 14; spiritual if not mystical in chapter 15; obedient in chapter 17; gambling in 22; duped in 23; and decisive in the early verses of 24.

As a literary achievement, the episodic biography has its drawbacks. Because the character of the hero can be captured best only at his maturity, the biographer pays little attention either to the birth of his

hero or, for that matter, to his death. Thus Abra(ha)m's childhood and death are superficially broached, and even when noted, they serve mostly to link various biographies into a chronological sequence or to provide information about burial places. This can be disconcerting, for the hero appears on stage practically unannounced, and leaves it either awkwardly or unobtrusively. Furthermore, because each scene is relatively self-contained, the passage of time is not stressed, and the setting remains purely ornamental. Paradoxically, perhaps, these conditions endow the complete portrait with a timelessness which allows episodes to belong to each and every period in which it is recalled.

But the episodic biography possesses powerful attributes. It forces sharper focus on each scene and thus conveys more immediately a prominent characteristic of the hero. Because the mood alternates as the scene changes, the episodic effortlessly retains the audience's attention. More importantly, however, those who wish to decode the significance of the heroic act must contribute their own interpretation. With its tendency to pare individual acts into instances of exemplary behavior, the episodic biography permits the audience to locate within it embodiments of the national character. Moreover, the paradigmatic behavior within each scene, and the temporal ambiguity it fosters, allow the audience to break from its concern for a specific historical past and to interpret this past as but adumbrative of the present, if not the future. I now find it obvious that when, in his *Mimesis*, Auerbach wished to highlight the spatial and temporal freedom of biblical prose, he selected the most starkly etched tableau, the *Akedah*, from within Abraham's episodic life story. He might not have fared as well had he chosen from melodramatic portraiture.

III

THE MELODRAMATIC BIOGRAPHY is likewise based on the sequencing of scenes of surface depth, that is, ones whose outlines can be grasped through initial familiarity. However, unlike the episodic in which the activities of the subject may easily duplicate idealized behavior, the melodrama explores the hero's inner world. A full portrait of the subject is not realized by conjoining a series of integral attributes, but by pursuing the character of the hero, progressively and deliberately, over a span of time and space. Thus, by the end of any melodramatic biography, the hero acquires a personality which is unique and

untransferable. The biographer employs a number of devices by which to craft his final portrait. In this presentation, I mention four devices, and will refer to the Jacob saga for illustrations.

1. *Delayed-action plotting*. This is the most obvious tactic which develops a narrative about an individual hero. Only if oracular prognostications occur (e.g. at 25.23) does the biographer describe the birth and youth. At any rate, he moves quickly to establish goals for the hero. In the case of Jacob, the famous trickery scenes in which he obtains the *bekorah* (25.19-24) and in which his mother delivers him the *berakah* (ch. 27) will generate interest in the manner in which Jacob will begin to enjoy their rewards. As a structuring device, trickery also becomes a thematic leitmotif binding sundry other narratives located within the Jacob biography. Thus, trickery, successfully negotiated but ultimately corroding to its practitioners, allows the biographers to accommodate sagas regarding Simeon and Levi at Shechem (ch. 34) and ones regarding Judah and Tamar near Timnah (ch. 38). Most brilliantly, the biographer manages to set the well-realized, essentially episodic biography of Joseph within Jacob's life by returning to the theme of trickery, by Jacob's son (ch. 37) as well as by Joseph (chs 43-44). (It is perhaps worth underscoring the fact that from a biographical perspective Genesis 38 does not intrude into the Joseph story, but both are neatly spliced within that of Jacob.) Such long-range plotting, moreover, generates a diversity of perspectives, thus multiplying the levels of irony afforded by the individual's situation.

2. *Bi-partite allocation of biographic materials*. Under this heading I deal with an unusual characteristic of the Hebrew biographical style. Upon taking the audience on a journey, in which the hero survives all odds and succeeds in fulfilling the goals as established in early moments of the narrative, the biographer rather suddenly relinquishes constant attention from his protagonist. Jacob's life story, which properly begins when his mother, like his grandfather, is elected and called to leave familiar surroundings (ch. 24), will not end until the last verses of Genesis (50.13). It is blocked out, slightly indented along its outer edges, by narratives which feature dim-eyed patriarchs bestowing birthrights, blessings, and parting kisses to the younger of two brothers (at chs 27; 48). Within these outer limits are located blocs of narratives. One, framed by otherwordly encounters at, respectively, Bethel (28.10-22) and Yabbok (32.25-33), is single-minded in its interest in Jacob's personal development and prosperity.

The other, switching its focus from one son of Jacob to another, is framed rather artificially by appeal to a 17-year span in which Joseph lived in the promised land and an equal period in which Jacob finished his life in Egypt. In this second section Jacob is but a presence, resignedly witnessing the fragmentation of his own hopes and aspirations. But, even as he loses his power to control his immediate destiny, he grows in omniscience and in his ability to shape the distant future. Thus, one purpose that the second part of a hero's life fills admirably is to define what could be a stunning conclusion to a patriarch's life: death in exile and dependence on the bounties of a foreign ruler and on the mediation of an expatriate son. I can speculate endlessly on this observation, but will only note that death, whenever called upon to fill a melodramatic canvas, is invariably an occasion for the biographer to make his own comments about the tragic dimensions of the heroic life.

3. *Heightening the emotional range of the characters*. This is done with a variety of means. By exaggerating and by repeatedly calling upon an idiosyncrasy of the hero (in this case Jacob's trickery), the biographer succeeds in raising the stakes by which success can be measured. By endowing the hero with primary emotions—love, hate, revulsion, fear, etc.—and by extending them to the characters closest to him, the biographer entangles the hero's feelings and tests his sensibilities. Consequently, the audience must also make an emotional investment in the hero's life story. Finally, by intensifying the eeriness of particular settings—dreams, visions, meetings with strangers, etc.—the biographer expands the consciousness of his hero and endows his activities with psychological dimensions.

4. *Introduction of opponent*. The biographer most commonly explores the hero's inner world by inserting a force of evil or instability into the narrative. This role can be allocated, *seriatim*, to a number of personalities, thus permitting control of the intensity with which the hero is threatened. Curiously enough, the opponent in the Hebrew biography tends to make his debut before the hero. Laban, for example, already appears in the scene where Rebekah is wooed (24.29). The opponent's role is hardly ever depicted monochromatically, but is often shaped to be opposite the hero's various posturings. Thus, by the time that the series of confrontations, on the one hand between Jacob and Esau and between Jacob and Laban on the other, are complete, the biographer has explored the hero's responses to explosive situations. We might note, however, that as

the Hebrew melodramatic biography enters its second phase, when the hero's disintegrating life is mirrored mostly by the activities of his sons and kinfolk, the opponent's role fades into insignificance.

Here I can hardly speak to the melodrama's many virtues as an artistic creation. While it does lack the episodic versatility, transferability and open-endedness—qualities which can readily leaven theological speculations—the melodrama is the stuff by which we measure the passion of the human mind. Sharply edged and untransferable, the portrait drawn in melodrama intrigues us not merely because of its antiquity or venerability, but because of the uncanny familiarity of its experiences. We therefore repeatedly turn back to it in order to better understand ourselves.

IV

The above remarks have centered mostly on the surface structuring of the Hebrew biography. I have rather unsystematically alluded to some of the techniques that entered in the crafting of two identifiable forms. I have not broached the problem of language and the consequences of using Hebrew in biographical literature; I have not touched upon the reasons which compelled a biographer to allocate some traditions regarding a particular ancestor to the episodic, and others to the melodramatic; nor have I described the sequencing of a series of life-stories. I have not delved into the realities—political, theological, and ethnic—which may have guided the biographer's pen, I have not clarified the links between biography and historiography, and I have not even admitted to the presence of non-biographical material in the Hebrew's accounts. This negative confession needs to be uttered, for it should underscore the complexity of the task at hand.[3]

NOTES

1. J. Skinner, *Genesis*, 2nd ed. (ICC; Edinburgh: T. & T. Clark, 1930), xxix. The topic has not attracted much attention ever since it became unfashionable to view the patriarchal stories as respresenting the personification of actual tribal history. Recently, however, J. Blenkinsopp, *JSOT* 20 (1981), 27-46, addresses the 'Biographical Patterns in Biblical Narrative'. The essay, rambling in its format, is really more concerned with suggesting a morphology for biography, and it imposes Proppian functions to analyze what are deemed to be central moments in Jacob's story. I have briefly overviewed the

structure of biblical biography in 'Love's Roots: On the Redaction of Genesis 30:14-24', a paper scheduled to appear in *Love and Death in the Ancient Near East* (Pope Festschrift).

2. I have adapted vocabulary used in the drama, but I have been most influenced by the analyses of plays which have been especially prepared for musical settings. Opera aficionados may recognize that the modes to be presently discussed obtain, to some degree, in respectively the baroque and the romantic operas; see Patrick J. Smith, *The Tenth Muse: A Historical Study of the Opera Libretto* (New York: Schirmer, 1970).

3. It may be noted here that the Old Testament contains only three bona fide dramatic biographies, those of Jacob, Moses and David. A particular niche can be allocated to the Samson story. The Joseph narrative is, at best, but a torso of a dramatic biography.

TABLE OF CONTRIBUTORS

PETER R. ACKROYD holds MA and PhD degrees from Cambridge University and a DD degree from the University of London. He is Professor Emeritus (Samuel Davidson Chair of Old Testament Studies), King's College, the University of London.

W. BOYD BARRICK received his PhD in Old Testament Studies from the University of Chicago in 1977. He has taught at Case Western Reserve University and Ohio Northern University (Ada).

P.A.H. de BOER was Professor of Old Testament at the University of Leiden from 1938 to 1978. His publications include *Second Isaiah's Message* (1956), *Gedenken und Gedächtnis in der Welt des Alten Testaments* (1962), *Fatherhood and Motherhood in Israelite and Judean Piety* (1974), and text-editions of the books of Samuel in *Biblia Hebraica Stuttgartensia* (1976) and *Vetus Testamentum Syriace* (1978).

BETH GLAZIER-McDONALD received her PhD in Old Testament Studies from the University of Chicago in 1983. She is currently Assistant Professor of Religious Studies at The Pennsylvania State University.

NORMAN C. HABEL was Associate Professor of Old Testament at Concordia Theological Seminary (St Louis) from 1960 to 1973. In 1974 he established the first program in religious studies in his native Australia; he is currently Dean of the Faculty of Humanities at the South Australian College of Advanced Education (Adelaide). A major commentary on the book of Job is in preparation.

MENAHEM HARAN holds MA and PhD degrees from the Hebrew University of Jerusalem. Since 1968 he has been the Yehezkel Kaufmann Professor of Biblical Studies at the Hebrew University. His publications include *Temples and Temple Service in Ancient Israel* (1978).

SIEGFRIED HERRMANN holds doctorates in Egyptology and theology (Dr habil.) from the University of Leipzig. Since 1966 he has been Professor of Old Testament Studies in the Department of Theology at the University of Bochum. His publications include *Geschichte Israels in alttestamentlicher Zeit* (2nd edn, 1980; ET, 1980) and *Zeit und Geschichte* (1977; ET, 1981).

ARVID S. KAPELRUD (teol. kan., Oslo; teol dr, Uppsala) was Professor of Old Testament Exegesis at the University of Oslo from 1954 to 1982; he is now Professor Emeritus. His publications include *Joel Studies* (1948), *Baal in the Ras Shamra Texts* (1952), and *God and his Friends in the Old Testament* (1979).

STEPHEN A. KAUFMAN holds a PhD degree from Yale University. He has taught at the Oriental Institute of the University of Chicago (1971-1976) and the University of Haifa (1974-1976). He is currently Professor of Bible and Cognate Literature at the Hebrew Union College–Jewish Institute of Religion (Cincinnati).

CONRAD E. L'HEUREUX holds a PhD degree in Near Eastern Languages and Literatures from Harvard University. He is Professor of Old Testament and Ancient History at the University of Dayton. His publications include *Rank among the Canaanite Gods* (1979) and *In and Out of Paradise* (1983).

ARTHUR L. MERRILL holds a PhD in Old Testament Studies from the University of Chicago. He is Professor of Old Testament Theology at the United Theological Seminary of the Twin Cities (New Brighton, Minnesota).

MAGNUS OTTOSSON (teol. dr, Uppsala) is currently Professor of Old Testament Exegesis at the University of Oslo. He has recently been appointed Professor of Old Testament at the University of Uppsala. His publications include *Gilead: Tradition and History* (1969) and *Temples and Cult Places in Palestine* (1980). A study of the book of Joshua is in preparation.

BENEDIKT OTZEN holds a doctorate in theology from the University of Aarhus where since 1964 he has been Professor of Old Testament Exegesis. His published works include *Studien über*

Deuterosacharja (1964), *De 12 Patriarkers Testamenter* (1974), *Israeliterne i Palestina* (1977), and contributions to *Myths in the Old Testament* (1980).

THOMAS W. OVERHOLT holds a PhD in Old Testament Studies from the University of Chicago. He is Professor of Philosophy and Coordinator of the Program in Religious Studies at the University of Wisconsin (Steven's Point). His research and publications have focused on prophecy, especially in the Old Testament and among American Indians.

DENNIS PARDEE holds a PhD degree in Northwest Semitic Philology from the University of Chicago. Since 1972 he has taught in the Department of Near Eastern Languages and Civilizations of the University of Chicago where he is currently Associate Professor. His publications include 'The Preposition in Ugaritic' (in *Ugarit-Forschungen* 7 (1975), 329-78; 8 (1976), 215-322; 9 (1977), 205-31) and *Handbook of Ancient Hebrew Letters* (1982).

JACK M. SASSON holds MA and PhD degrees in Mediterranean Studies from Brandeis University. He is Professor of Religion at the University of North Carolina (Chapel Hill). His publications include *The Military Establishment at Mari* (1969), *Ruth: A New Translation* (1979), and *Datable Texts from Mari* (1981).

AKE W. SJÖBERG (fil. dr, Uppsala) taught at the Oriental Institute of the University of Chicago (1963-1966) before coming to the University of Pennsylvania where since 1968 he has been Clark Research Professor of Assyriology and Curator of the Tablet Collections. He is Chief Investigator and Editor-in-Charge of the Pennsylvania Sumerian Dictionary Project.

JOHN R. SPENCER received his PhD in Old Testament Studies from the University of Chicago in 1980. He is currently Associate Professor of Religion at John Carroll University (Cleveland) and on the staff of the Tell el-Hesi archaeological expedition.

JOHN VAN SETERS has taught at Wilfred Laurier University (1965-1967), Andover Newton Theological School (1967-1970), and the University of Toronto (1970-1977). He is currently the James A.

Gray Professor of Biblical Literature and chairman of the Department of Religion at the University of North Carolina (Chapel Hill). Among his publications are *Abraham in History and Tradition* (1975) and *In Search of History* (1983).

GEO WIDENGREN (fil. lic., Stockholm; teol. dr, Uppsala) was Professor of the History and Psychology of Religions at the University of Uppsala from 1940 to 1973; he is now Professor Emeritus. Among his publications are *The Akkadian and Hebrew Psalms of Lamentation as Religious Documents* (1937), *Literary and Psychological Aspects of the Hebrew Prophets* (1948), *King and Savior* I-V (1945-1955), *Sakrales Königtum im Alten Testament und im Judentum* (1955), and *Religionens Värld* (3rd edn, 1971).

INDEXES

INDEX OF AUTHORS

INDEX OF BIBLICAL REFERENCES